City Building in the New South

Technology and Urban Growth

A SERIES EDITED BY

BLAINE A. BROWNELL   MARK ROSE
MARK S. FOSTER   HOWARD J. SUMKA
ZANE L. MILLER

City Building in the New South

The Growth of Public Services in Houston, Texas, 1830–1910

Harold L. Platt

Temple University Press
Philadelphia

Temple University Press, Philadelphia 19122
© 1983 by Temple University. All rights reserved
Published 1983
Printed in the United States of America

Library of Congress Cataloging in Publication Data

Platt, Harold L.
  City building in the new South.
  (Technology and urban growth)
  Includes bibliographical references and index.
  1. Houston (Tex.)—City planning—History. 2. City
planning—Texas—History. 3. Urbanization—Texas—
Case studies. 4. Municipal services—Texas—Houston—
History. I. Title. II. Series.
HT168.H67P58 1982   363'.09764'1411   82-10411
ISBN 0-87722-281-9

To my parents,

SIDNEY AND GLADYS PLATT

Contents

Illustrations

Tables, Charts, and Maps

Tables

Charts

Maps

Series Preface

During the last half of the nineteenth century, American urban residents spent huge sums of money and exerted immense effort to construct modern service technologies. With the development of these technologies came urban sprawl and an inventiveness in the shaping of urban government. By the late nineteenth century, every substantial municipality had franchised its trolley, gas, and electric services, and had commenced the tasks of paving, lighting, and cleaning streets, and of providing clean water and sewage facilities to a widely dispersed urban population. And between 1890 and 1920, an urge to buffer the administration of city services from ward-based politicians and neighborhood interests resulted in attempts to establish citywide bosses or strong mayors, and often in attempts to substitute for both city commissions or city managers. During the early twentieth century, in short, many cities converged toward a predictable and standard array of service technologies, a similar and distended form, and a hierarchical polity.

This apparent similarity in the timing and consequences of the late-nineteenth century revolution in urban technology has encouraged historians to frame their research about cities and technologies along common lines and to concentrate on the late-nineteenth and twentieth centuries. To what degree did the street railway, trolley and later the automobile and highway complexes facilitate the deconcentration of residence and businesses? To what extent did gas and electric service and sanitary sewerage contribute to the creation of self-contained households around the urban periphery? Underlying each of these questions, though, rests the assumption of a dependent, nearly neutral technological system that served as directed by politicians, residents, and business leaders.

Yet another question, indeed a series of questions, might be asked about technologies and their urban and political relationships. To what extent did urbanites and their governments adapt themselves to the rhythms of the technology? In what fashion did urban government take the responsibility for the diffusion of technological knowledge and the protection of young technologies? As much, in other words, as we need to understand the role of technology in shaping the contemporary city, so, indeed, might we seek to analyze the role of urbanistic factors in shaping technological systems and in facilitating their adaptation to the city-building process.

Harold L. Platt's study of the city-building process in Houston asks these and other kinds of questions as well. His central concern is a century of striving by Houston boosters to outstrip Galveston and "bootstrap" their city into a position of regional dominance in the Southwest. The central focus is the use of service technologies in those efforts. The story falls into two parts, the first dominated by "amateurs" and the second by "experts." During part of the first period, Platt argues, Houston's boosters relied almost exclusively on forging inter-city and inter-regional transportation linkages. By 1890, they had begun to articulate an ideal of municipal responsibility for the public welfare that suggested an internal strategy of service development to foster the growth of a central business district tied closely to wharves, railway terminals, and manufacturing sites, and to spread housing over larger areas. Implementing this new ideal proved complicated, frustrating, and expensive, sparked a taxpayers' revolt, implicated state and federal courts in Houston's city government, and brought national utility firms and novel utility technologies to Houston.

During the second period (1890–1910), Platt contends, the development of service technologies and city government came to revolve around two points of view, both rooted in the idea of municipal responsibility for the public welfare. Many endorsed the notion that paved streets and electric lighting, for example, should serve first the needs of residents in all the city's neighborhoods, and that such a program would make Houston attractive to newcomers and investments. Business, political, and labor leaders who identified closely with the local and neigborhood scenes placed the highest priority on this prospect. It was the task of city government to insure service delivery at cheap prices, or so ran the reasoning, even if it meant regulated competition and/or municipal ownership of utilities. Yet businessmen and politicians imbued with a more urgent vision of Houston as the economic metropolis of the Southwest preferred to emphasize the service technologies as vehicles leading to investments and economic prowess, even if it meant denying the distribution of the full range of older and newer service technologies at cheap prices to each of the city's neighborhoods.

Accommodating these competing visions consumed much of the time and creativity of Houston's politicians during the late-nineteenth and early-twentieth centuries. By 1905, though, leaders of the "metropolitans" had come to predominate in Houston's government. After a futile attempt to strike a middle course, they created a commission form of government and a strong mayor, and shielded the utilities in private firms and as "natural" and therefore necessarily regulated monopolies. Under the metropolitans, Platt concludes, the new technologies cohered with the politics of the New South, creating a secure foundation for economic growth in the age of oil, and a "politics of exclusion" involving not only the disfranchisement of blacks and poor whites but also a government policy of service delivery which "hardened traditional patterns of racial and class discrimination into rigid lines of geographic segregation" (p. 208).

This book lends full support to none of the conventional wisdoms in urban and technological history. Those seeking determinisms, whether technological, scientific, social, economic, or demographic, will not find them in Platt's Houston. By starting in the 1830s, moreover, he reminds us that the era of the municipal corporation as an agent for promoting commerce and manufacturing stretched well into the nineteenth century, and that external transit linkages seemed the critical urban service technologies in that period. He reminds us too that the era of the municipal government as purveyor of services for the health, comfort, convenience, and welfare of city residents began only in the mid- and late-nineteenth century. And while he argues that the courts, the national utilities themselves, and "outside" experts loomed large in the counsels of Houston's government after the mid-nineteenth century, he notes that it was, after all, the leaders of the city who decided to encourage the development of urban services. The lively debates and conflicts that took place centered around tactics and goals rather than the larger question of the desirability of more electricity, gas, water, and rapid transit. Nor did the technologies and the firms that housed them respond willy-nilly to the demands of urban residents and their elected leaders. Creation of a city commission and a strong mayor, for example, provided the buffer long-sought by utility operators against the vicissitudes of the urban market, especially voters and elected officials anxious to employ political apparatus to force service improvements at lower cost. As a case in the history of technology, planning, politics, and city building, Platt's study of Houston contends that there existed a political, indeed an urban and political conditioning of the service technologies, and that none of the results were inevitable.

The Technology and Urban Growth Series attempts to focus on the critical role of technology in the city-building and urbanization processes and to explore the complex interrelationships between technology, society, and ways of living and thinking in the urban setting. This is the second volume in the series.

The Editors, Technology and Urban Growth Series

Preface

This book is about the efforts of the American people to build cities in the nineteenth and early twentieth centuries. Moving across the land, they erected a nation of cities which continues to furnish most of us with our homes and places of work. But to describe the creation of man-made environments upon the natural landscape of frontier America would tell only half of the story. The other half involves the ways in which urban surroundings and institutions created city people. For the types of artificial environments Americans constructed changed markedly as urban conditions altered their perceptions, experiences, and aspirations. This interplay between city building and city people forms the heart of the process of urbanization and the subject of my case study of Houston, Texas.

A focus on the growth of public services illuminates the interactions between the urban environment and its inhabitants in two unique ways. First, urban utilities and public works—streets, sewers, water supplies, artificial lighting, and mass transportation—were essential parts of the city building process. Without them, the unprecedented rise of incredibly dense centers of population during the second half of the nineteenth century would not have been possible. Running under, on, and over the streets, these essential services comprised the infrastructure of a new type of built environment, the industrial city. Second, the history of public services is unique because it alone reveals the critical nexus between city people and city building with unambiguous clarity and precision. In contrast to the willy-nilly construction of homes, shops, and factories by individual decision makers, government policy largely determined the growth and distribution of public services in the community. The shifting politics of utility franchises and public works projects accurately mirrors the evolution of city dwellers' efforts to upgrade their physical surroundings.

Beginning in the 1840s, the provision of public services played an increasingly important role in defining the issues of municipal politics. City builders first voiced demands for paved streets, pure water supplies, artificial illuminates, and horsecar lines as community requirements, vital to public health and commercial enterprise. Only the rich could initially afford the luxury of installing plumbing and gas lighting in their homes. Gradually, however, more and more city dwellers came to regard modern amenities as individual as well as collective necessities of urban life. The resulting formation of neighborhood groups around calls for service extensions and improvements gave ward level politics a life of its own, independent from traditional party affiliations. By the 1890s, or Progressive Era, local battles for municipal reform reached national proportions, fueled by an emerging mastery of city building and the introduction of a revolutionary group of electrical technologies, including telephones, light bulbs, and rapid transit. The universal demand of city people for better public services underscored needs for comprehensive planning on a metropolitan scale. At the dawn of the twentieth century, urban progressivism represented a major turning point in the history of the United States from its rural-agrarian origins to its urban-industrial future.

In the nineteenth century, city building was no easy task for either the managers of privately-owned utility companies or the officeholders in charge of government sponsored services. Today, we take the pipes, poles, and wires of public utilities largely for granted, except when an unexpected breakdown causes us a momentary inconvenience. However, their original development took over eighty years of frustrating trial and error by city boosters who were mostly businessmen, but rarely trained experts. The pioneers of the urban frontier faced almost insurmountable problems of environmental engineering in unfamiliar terrains and unfriendly climates. Civic leaders also had to forge new structures of government and business in order to create viable institutional frameworks for the financing and administration of inherently expensive public utilities. Until the 1880s, each community groped alone in virtual isolation from one another in the search for ways to make its physical surroundings more healthy, comfortable, and attractive places to live and work. The settlers of the Texas Gulf Coast confronted as many of these environmental and institutional hurdles as other aspiring city builders who participated in the great westward migration across North America.

This case study examines the efforts of Houston's residents to construct a commercial metropolis at the gateway to the Southwest. It was an arduous task, performed by amateur city builders, that helped to transform them into city people. Part One sketches the founding of the town in the 1830s, and more fully explores the community's initial attempts at environmental engineering after the Civil War. Facing unprecedented challenges, Houstonians applied rule of thumb methods in building paved roads, bridges, streetcar lines, and a system of gas lighting. They also had to contend with the thorny problem of drawing borderlines in grey areas of the political economy between governmental duties and entrepreneurial opportunities to supply public services. For example, was street and sidewalk paving a responsibility of the municipal government or of the abutting landowners whose property values would be enhanced by the improvements? Should city officials or businessmen manage the water supply? Nor was it clear how either the public or the private sector could best design institutions for the economical financing and efficient administration of an expanding array of essential urban technologies.

Until the mid-1880s, the 25,000 inhabitants of the provincial entrepôt made little headway in their efforts to create a modern city. On the contrary, Houstonians mostly fought a losing battle against the forces of ecological decay, municipal bankruptcy, and business failure. Nonetheless, twenty years experience of trial and error produced an accumulating expertise at reforming the institutions and techniques of city building. In addition, local isolation was being steadily supplanted by powerful agencies of national integration such as utility equipment manufacturers and trade associations, stock and bond markets, and a growing body of federal court decisions on urban public services. Together, local experts and extralocal infusions of financial and technical assistance started to overcome the hurdles of the past. The critical issues of public policy also began to shift dramatically from *How* do we supply basic services to *What Kind* of urban environment and society do we want to create? City people became municipal reformers because comprehensive planning and electrical technologies promised to uplift the community to new levels of modern convenience and civic harmony.

Part Two analyzes the resulting political struggles among Houstonians over alternative approaches to city planning. At the center of urban progressivism was a debate over the extent of governmental responsibility for the improvement of the social environment as well as the physical one. In Houston, this pivotal question of social justice was contested within peculiar, albeit not uncommon, local and regional contexts. During the mid-1880s, a ward-based system of politics emerged that reflected a final transformation of Houston's city people into a mature urban society. The ward politicians began to pose a serious threat to the leadership of the city's traditional civic elite. It continued to place top priority on the promotion of urban growth, but the insurgents now gave greater emphasis to the upgrading of the neighborhoods. In the late 1890s, the planning debate over different visions of the coming city turned into a bitter duel for control of city hall that took on ominous racial and class overtones. These social tensions amplified the political contest into a full-blown civic crisis. In 1905, Houstonians resolved the crisis of city planning with the inauguration of a commission form of government. It was not only an indigenous creation but also emblematic of the outcome of urban progressivism in the New South.

Of course, a history of Houston's city builders shares both the advantages and the shortcomings of any test case. Scholars have adopted two strategies for bridging the gap between local studies and more general analyses of American urban development. One approach compares the test case with other cities which have similar origins, functions, or characteristics. The other approach places the local study within regional and national contexts. I have chosen to employ the latter strategy because of the increasing importance of national forces of interdependence in directing the course of city building in the nineteenth century. To a great extent, extralocal influences were responsible for overcoming the pitfalls of environmental engineering in Houston, besides helping to correct its institutional deficiencies. Outside forces were also decisive in determining the winners of the local battle for municipal reform. In the early 1900s, these city planners made critical choices that have led to Houston's current roles as the regional center of the Southwest and the national headquarters of the oil industry.

Over the past several years, I have accumulated a long list of debts in bringing this project to completion. My greatest obligation is to my teacher and friend,

Harold Hyman. He has never ceased to give me support, encouragement, and inspiration. Several other historians at Rice University provided intellectual stimulation, including Tom Haskell, Al Van Helden, Joseph DiCorsia, and Gale Stokes. The chairperson of the History Department, Katherine Drew, proved to be tireless in securing financial aid. The Southwest Center for Urban Research supplied a fellowship during my last year of graduate work.

Librarians and archivists have made this study possible. I am grateful to the staff of the Fondren Library at Rice University. I owe thanks to Mrs. Orgain of the University of Houston Archives. I also appreciate the cooperation of the City Secretary of Houston, and the Clerk of the Court of Harris County. More recently, Louis Marchiafava of the Houston Metropolitan Research Center has furnished invaluable aid in locating and reproducing historic photographs of the city.

In turning a dissertation into a publishable manuscript, I have received help from another group of supporters. Lew Erenburg provided critical commentary and friendly encouragement. Editorial assistance came from Janet Simms who patiently read several drafts of the manuscript. Tom Bennett, the director of Research Services at Loyola University, helped to ease clerical burdens. Mark Rose, series editor, Ken Arnold, and Karen Fasano of Temple University Press were instrumental in the final process of revision. The two people closest to my heart cannot be repaid in words alone. My daughter, Abbey, has had to share her father with this project for her entire life. My wife, Carol Woodworth, has kept the faith by never faltering in her support of me or my work.

Part I

City Building
by Amateurs

1 "The Commercial Emporium of Texas"

The City Building Process

In the nineteenth century, the growth of cities triggered a succession of novel demands for better public services. As a restless people pushed across a continent, urban pioneers kept pace with and often preceded agrarian settlers. The westward movement gave rise to a profusion of new towns, each vying with its neighbors for hegemony over the surrounding hinterland. An intense rivalry for regional preeminence spurred city fathers not only to secure transportation links to outside markets but also to supply all the modern urban amenities. This wild race to upgrade every frontier outpost to the standards of the biggest cities of the East would eventually become a national mania.[1]

In the 1830s, one of the fingers of westward settlement moved along the Texas Gulf Coast. To get around the impenetrable swamps and pine thickets of Louisiana and Arkansas, the frontiersmen sailed from New Orleans to establish a new beachhead at Galveston Bay, the only good natural harbor between the Crescent City and Vera Cruz. Town promoters wasted little time in claiming the most strategic sites of transshipment on the bay (see Map 1.1). There were two superior points of control where transportation breaks interrupted the flow of trade between outside ports and the cotton and sugar lands of the interior. Galveston, at the eastern tip of the island bearing the same name, guarded the entrances to the bay. Two townsites, Harrisburg and Houston, were started at the headwaters of navigation on Buffalo Bayou, forty-five miles inland. They stood next to each other at the center of a fan-shaped pattern of settlement to the west and north.[2]

The voyage between Galveston and the interior strongly impressed early explorers like Frederic Gaillardet, who observed that

> the mere sight of the busy steamboat navigation is enough to instruct the foreigner . . . as to the kind of people he will meet here. The channel of Buffalo Bayou is so narrow and the steamboats which ply its waters are so hemmed in between its two banks that the trees growing close to the water tear into the hulls of the plucky crafts and sweeps their decks. . . . It arrives, however, and that is all that an American insists upon.[3]

Until the Civil War, steamboats and cotton directed the American settlement of Texas. The extraordinary soil of the coastal plain between the bay and the Brazos River to the west produced some of the richest yields in the entire cotton kingdom. Sugar, that aristocrat of Southern agriculture, also thrived in the semitropical climate near the Gulf. Relatively easy access to such highly rewarding

3

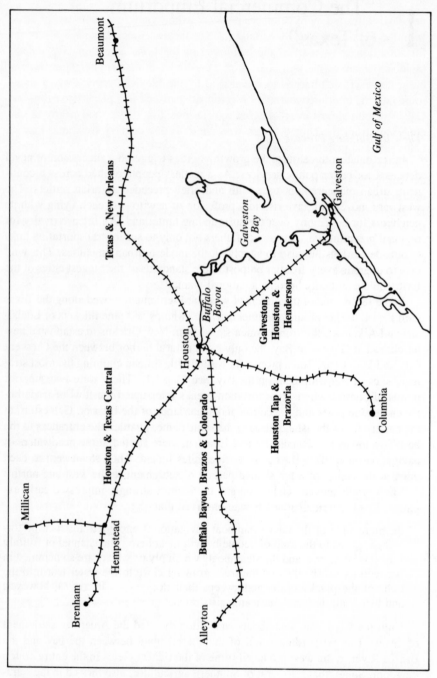

MAP 1.1   Texas Gulf Coast, 1861

new lands attracted many Southern pioneers, who soon wrestled control of Texas from the Mexicans. The 1836 Battle of San Jacinto, fought near the top of the fifty-mile-long bay, marked the beginning of the Lone Star Republic and the rapid settlement of the gulf coast area. Houston's unfortunate neighbor, Harrisburg, however, was burned to the ground by the Mexican army. Only a single route into the interior remained. "Steamboats between this place [Houston] and Galveston run almost every day," a traveler noted in 1839, "and nearly all the emigrants from the United States who come to this country by water, land at Galveston and pass through Houston."[4]

The economics of the cotton trade influenced not only townsite locations in antebellum Texas, it dominated life inside these frontier communities. Like hundreds of other urban places in the South, the sister towns on Galveston Bay grew in tandem with their agricultural hinterlands. The natural cycles of the crops on the cotton and sugar plantations also set the rhythm of urban activity. From 1836 to 1839, a clever promotional scheme by Houston's brother founders, Augustus Chapman Allen and John Kirby Allen, briefly turned their real estate venture into the Republic's first capital. Yet commerce, not politics, most impressed Houston's early observers. A visitor in 1838 recorded that

> many strangers . . . congregated here because it was traversed by the main roads from the interior to Galveston, the place of embarkation. Its trade, too, was considerable. Wagons from the country, therefore, came and went daily, loaded with country produce and, on the home journey, with household requirements.[5]

Over the next twenty years, the business of cotton transformed Houston from a beachhead settlement into a well-established frontier community. By 1840, the original tent town of San Jacinto revolutionaries already had been supplanted by about 400 wooden homes and business houses, a few public buildings, and many saloons, but no churches. Perhaps a thousand people lived there, but population statistics are only guesswork before the U.S. Census enumerated 2400 persons in 1850 and 4800 a decade later.[6]

This was the beginning of a process of urban growth that would turn the frontier outpost into a modern city of over 78,000 people by 1910, when Houston emerged victorious over all its rivals in the Southwest. City building involved a complex interplay between Houstonians and the artificial environment that they erected along the banks of the Buffalo Bayou. The built environment, in turn, worked on the residents of Houston, changing their perceptions, aspirations, and relationships. The clearest illustration of this reciprocal process was the growth of public services, because they alone were built by conscious social effort. The city government either directly supplied essential services or regulated utility companies that needed special franchises. Elected officials largely decided the availability, quality, and cost of the social necessities of urban life. In effect, the policy decisions that determined the distribution of public utilities mapped a political and social geography of the community.[7]

Before 1865, locally spawned transportation facilities constituted a truly urban utility that must be included in any model of public services. The first prerequisite of city building in a non-industrial economy was capturing and nurtur-
ing an agricultural market area. There was neither reason nor money to build up
an extensive urban space without a commercial exchange. The most efficient way
tradesmen could bind farmers to their particular locality was to supply the cheap-
est routes to and from the marketplace. Urban growth depended upon enlarging
the productivity and the size of the hinterland. The mutual interdependence of
town and country explains the rivalry among neighboring communities as well as
the urban "imperialism" of more distant great cities for regional domination.

Competition among communities during their formative period made good
economic sense. Only a few could claim the top levels of the pyramid-shaped
hierarchies of cities that were emerging in each region. Town promoters hurriedly staked out strategic sites along rivers and lakes because the cost of transporting bulky agricultural products overland had long been prohibitive. They
also seemed to realize that winning an advantage first as a center of trade, government, or possibly manufacturing would bring accumulating benefits. Once
rooted in a town, an economic activity would tend to attract related enterprises,
while simultaneously stifling their growth in places nearby.[8]

A major revolution in overland transportation further intensified urban rivalry
just as pioneers began reaching the Texas Gulf Coast in large numbers. The construction of canals in the 1820s and railroads a decade later threatened to overturn urban hierarchies in older sections and promised to build them up in newer
ones. Railroads effectively freed the city (and the commercial farmer) from a
close proximity to the waterways by drastically reducing the cost of moving
goods and people overland.[9] Houston's founders, the Allen brothers, expressed
an early appreciation of the profound impact that this technological breakthrough
would soon make on the growth of cities and their surrounding market areas. In
1836, at a time when less than 200 miles of track traversed the entire country, the
Allens' first promotional advertisement of Houston envisioned that

The City . . . is located at a point on the river which must ever command
the trade of the largest and richest portion of Texas. . . . When the rich lands
of this country shall be settled, a trade will flow to it, making it beyond doubt,
the great interior commercial emporium of Texas.
It combines two important advantages: a communication with the coast and
foreign countries, and with the different portions of the Republic. As the
country shall improve, railroads will become in use, and will be extended
from this point . . . and in a few years the whole trade of the upper Brazos
will make its way to Galveston through this channel.[10]

The coming of the railroad to Texas in the 1850s sparked an intense rivalry
between the sister cities on the gulf. Before then, the natural topography of the
bay area dictated a symbiotic relationship in order to maintain the flow of trade.
The exorbitant cost and uncertain pace of transporting cumbersome bales of cotton overland by ox-team funnelled most traffic to the nearest land-water trans-

shipment point, Houston. There the bulky 400-pound bales were transferred onto flat bottomed steamers for passage to Galveston across sandbars that blocked ocean navigation from the bay. At Galveston, a second transfer to coastal and transatlantic shipping occurred. Since shallow sandbars also skirted the island, a two-step process of handling could not be avoided in either direction. But conflict over the plan for Texas railroads began a half century of rivalry. Each city would keep trying to effect the right combination of water and land improvements to bypass the other.[11]

Houston was typical of urban places in the antebellum South. Geography, transportation technology, slavery, and cotton agriculture cast the Gulf Coast town and its society into a decidedly Southern mold that has remained unbroken to the present. Establishing a commercial economy that promoted urban growth dominated city building efforts during Houston's frontier stage. The initiatives of town boosters to improve water routes to outside markets and to forge overland links to interior customers totally eclipsed parallel plans to upgrade public services inside the community. Before the end of the Civil War, Houston contained few urban amenities of any kind, public or private. It did not have a waterworks, an artificial lighting system, public schools, or mass transit facilities.

In contrast, the older seaport cities of the East were learning that urban growth could not be sustained without undertaking environmental improvements on a large scale in addition to upgrading their transportation systems. As pioneers settled the Texas Gulf Coast in the 1830s, American cities were death traps: mortality exceeded births. Fearsome epidemics forced city dwellers to take collective action. To protect the public health, communities had to find pure water supplies, construct pumping stations, and lay distributor networks under the streets. The need for additional social foundations of city building became painfully evident in the 1840s, when influxes of rural and foreign immigrants overwhelmed traditional spatial arrangements. The bigger cities began creating municipal fire and police departments, paving streets, and installing sewer, horsecar, and gas lines. Whether to promote the general welfare or to boost the local economy, the upgrading of public services came to occupy a central place in the life of the American community.[12]

Until the end of the century, however, the difficult and costly task of environmental engineering rested on a generation of amateur city builders. Houstonians and other city dwellers could draw upon neither a corps of trained experts nor a stock of institutional mechanisms to help impose man-made environments on unfamiliar terrain. Instead, rule-of-thumb methods in the field of engineering were emblematic of an era when professional training was rudimentary at best. It took more than a generation to gain a mastery of city building. Moreover, each townsite presented a different set of ecological problems and a unique configuration of social, economic, and political forces. In a nation of island communities, budding cities had to face the technical and policy issues of supplying public services in virtual isolation from one another.[13]

In Houston and other towns in the urban South, a regional culture fostered a distinctive group of city builders that one historian has called a "commercial-civic elite."[14] Of course, almost every American metropolis and fledgling village had its persistent businessmen whose personal fortunes became tightly interwoven with the future of their locality. It is not surprising that these city boosters drew few borderlines between their private interests and the public welfare. But in Southern towns, the almost complete domination of trade over other economic activities such as manufacturing narrowed the composition of the community leadership to those involved in commerce. Deep-seated regional customs of intermarriage among the best families further limited membership in the urban elite to a close-knit group. After the advent of the railroad, its decisions, more than the founders' choice of location, determined success. Most Southern towns remained paper dreams or obscure hamlets, in spite of their boosters' earnest attempts to achieve metropolitan greatness. In Houston, however, a far-sighted commercial-civic elite emerged in the 1850s to take command of the town's future.

Thomas W. House, for example, personifies the archetype of the first generation of Houston's most successful businessmen. Born in Somersetshire, England, on March 3, 1814, House immigrated twenty-one years later to New York and began working as a baker. He soon met the owner of the St. Charles Hotel of New Orleans, who invited the young man to seek his fortune in the South. In 1838, after two years in the Crescent City, House sought "ground floor" opportunities in Houston, where he established his own bakery. The entrepreneur's business quickly expanded into banking, commission sales of cotton, and real estate, through extensions of credit to farmers in exchange for liens on their crops and land. Marriage with the daughter of one of the town's leading citizens and merchants, Charles Shearn, also played a part in House's rising fortunes as well as guaranteeing him an elite status in a Southern society.

By the mid-1850s, House transformed these diverse but related activities into an economic empire. He managed the state's largest wholesale firm, major warehouse facilities in both Houston and Galveston, separate banking and real estate operations, and substantial investments in water shipping, toll roads, and railroad corporations. The businessman still found time to engage in such civic undertakings as helping to organize the city's first volunteer fire company in 1848, founding Houston's Methodist Church with the Shearn family, serving as an alderman in 1857 and 1861, and occupying the mayor's chair the following year.[15]

House and his fellow members of Houston's commercial-civic elite helped to ensure the continuing growth of a community with social patterns closely resembling those common throughout the urban South. Although located on the periphery of the region, Houston's linkage to the outside world through New Orleans made Houston a cultural as well as a commercial satellite of the South's largest, most cosmopolitan city. A demographic profile of Houston in the 1850s reveals the basic source of its sectional orientation: eight out of ten white residents had been born in the South. If only the adult males in this group are considered (in order to highlight immigration trends), two-thirds still had originated in the South, 20 percent in the Atlantic states, and 10 percent in New England. Native-born white Americans made up about half of Houston's inhabitants, whereas 20 percent were black slaves and another third were foreign born, mostly German. These figures are almost identical to those found further east in Alabama and Mississippi cities that were being established at the same time.[16]

The structure of society in Houston, like its people, duplicated the typical features of town life on the Southern frontier. An economy based almost exclusively on commerce created a distinct set of occupational opportunities and ordered them into a well-defined hierarchy by the 1850s. At the bottom of the economic ladder, blacks formed a permanent underclass of the unskilled. They were engaged mostly in domestic service or in the back-breaking jobs of transferring goods from one mode of conveyance to another. Black workers freed whites from the worst menial tasks. Only 20 percent of the whites labored at unskilled and semi-skilled positions, compared with 25–30 percent in skilled occupations. Many in this latter group enjoyed a middle level social status on a plane with the relatively large proportions of men who were employed as clerical personnel (11 percent) and small proprietors (15 percent). Less than one in ten Houstonians stood among the top ranks of the city's wholesale and commission merchants. Because Texas outlawed banks before the Civil War, these men's activities as cotton dealers and tradesmen naturally spilled over into the financial affairs of their customers, the planters. Merchant wealth was most easily converted into sizable holdings of city and rural land and slaves.[17]

During the 1850s, an established order of status and wealth gradually replaced the frontier stage of social flux in Houston. The primitive outpost where unmarried and untrained young men were almost alone on the Texas beachhead gave way to a more normally balanced demographic community. A contrasting influx of unskilled youths filled jobs opened by the start of railroad construction, but the general trend was unmistakable. Social and geographic mobility in Houston had come closer to matching the patterns of much older cities to the east. Houston's social structure became increasingly stratified, the division of wealth more unequal, and the climb to the top more difficult. As land values tripled over the decade, for example, the proportion of property holders among skilled and white-collar workers dropped by half. The holding of the richest tenth, on the other hand, rose from 53 to 67 percent; the six wealthiest Houstonians owned 17 percent of the town's real estate in 1850, 25 percent ten years later. The crystallization of a more mature social structure was not the only sign of change in Houston.[18]

Urban Services on the Texas Frontier

The formative period of urban settlement on the Texas Gulf Coast was fast drawing to a close at the outbreak of the Civil War. American pioneers, mostly Southern in origin, had travelled along available coastal routes in search of virgin lands suitable for the cultivation of cotton and other marketable crops. Town speculations at Houston and Galveston became successful frontier settlements by joint efforts to overcome the problems of the bay's shallow waters. Two decades of uninterrupted immigration indelibly stamped a Southern culture onto the social fabric of both communities. The coming of the railroad, however, ushered in a new phase of urban development. It marked the beginning not only of urban rivalry on the Texas Gulf Coast, but also of Houston's subtle transition from town to city.

To city boosters like Thomas House, unmet needs for intracity services and amenities were secondary, compared with the overriding imperative of forging better transportation links into the countryside and out to the gulf. Pursuing the vision of the Allen brothers, they organized a community-wide campaign to win and hold claim to the title of the railroad center of the state. The developmental priorities of city boosters in Houston and other frontier places warrant the incorporation of transportation improvements reaching out from the towns into models of public services. To accomplish their primary goal, Houstonians experimented with a far more sophisticated array of public and private structural arrangements than the existing makeshift of city service institutions. The experience gained in this enterprise became the basis for the reconstruction of the town's environment after the Civil War.

The creation of viable institutional structures of city building was a second prerequisite of urban growth. The municipal charter and the utility franchise in particular formed a constitutional, political, and economic framework for undertaking the costly and uncertain task of environmental engineering. Unless this framework was properly designed, improvement projects were doomed to fail because of inadequate financing and/or authority to achieve success. For example, the ability of the city government to provide essential services hinged on its power to levy taxes and its efficiency in collecting them. In a similar manner, the willingness of entrepreneurs to risk scarce venture capital in public utility enterprises depended on the political security and the financial incentives contained in their franchises. In both the public and private sectors, the construction of institutional frameworks comprised a crucial first step in the city building process.

Study of the formative phase of settlement of the Texas Gulf Coast confirms the usefulness of examining Houston's institutional history. It reveals the interplay between a frontier environment and a pioneer society that generated novel ideas of municipal progress. The uneven growth of the town's structural foundations closely correlates with its boosters' developmental priorities. At first, informal means of voluntary cooperation served well enough. Crude institutions sufficed for all three aspects of city building—social services, environmental improvements, and transportation systems—until the beachhead was secured in the early 1840s.

Thereafter, the boosters' preoccupation with expanding their market area meant that the institutions of intracity services were left in a comparatively primitive condition. Houstonians chartered no urban utility companies before 1860. And the municipal corporation remained a "weakened spring" of government without the authority or the fiscal resources to respond vigorously to community needs for better public services.[19] Yet, even as the townsite was being surveyed and platted during 1836–37, the founders were designing institutional mechanisms to capture the fast-growing wealth of the countryside. In the following decade, private, mixed, and public transportation corporations proliferated, creating a continuum of structural forms and public policy alternatives. Houstonians experimented with a series of structural blueprints that were fashioned from well-tested precedents.

The architects of Houston's public services were regional people, but they were schooled in a national system of law. This rich heritage was undergoing a dynamic transformation of its own during the first third of the nineteenth century. The forces of liberalism set loose by the upheaval of 1776 and reamplified by the transportation-market revolution changed America's traditional concepts of the common law. Judicial and legislative craftsmen increasingly wielded the law as a policy tool, converting an immutable body of first principles into a malleable instrument of social and economic reform. Throughout Jacksonian America, lawmakers helped encourage a "release of energy," a spirit of capitalism that was turning a continental wilderness into a productive garden. Texas immigrants, too, shared in this ambitious task of promoting growth within a flexible system of law and order.[20]

The functional elasticity of the corporation, public and private, made it the most important institutional mechanism carried by the urban pioneer to the frontier. It was being wrought into a singularly powerful vehicle for harnessing men and money in common enterprise. All American corporations had originally served public purposes, and almost all had been delegated special privileges or franchises to exercise powers that traditionally belonged only to the sovereign. In the early years of the nineteenth century, however, judges began discovering distinctions. The judicial wedge driven between public and private corporations widened into a constitutional gap during the first third of the century, but the overlap of their functional arenas persisted. Municipalities still invested in such profitable proprietary interests as waterworks, wharf and market facilities, and various transportation schemes. Business firms, armed with franchises, also continued to supply public services, such as toll roads, ferries, banks, water, and gas lighting. The practical utility of these mixed enterprises in pursuing America's developmental goals directed legislators to leave the vague boundary lines dividing public and private corporations drawn with an erasable marker.[21]

The decentralized organization of government in frontier Texas gave even greater practical effect to the dynamic use of the law. City officers and entrepreneurs enjoyed broad latitude from the legislature to draft proposals that supposedly enhanced public services in their locality. A dispersed populace and a primitive communications network largely dictated a semi-autonomous structure of intergovernmental relations. These centrifugal conditions, however, only reinforced an already solid Jacksonian faith in local self-rule and an equally strong abhorrence of centralized controls. Municipal and county subdivisions not only initiated most official urban policy, they financed and administered it as well.

Houston had little trouble gaining passage of nine successive versions of its city charter between 1837 and 1853. Civic leaders could follow this ad hoc routine in coping with the shifting exigencies of local government because they could confidently predict the lawmakers' approval of their reforms.[22]

The belated manner of amending city charters in Texas exposes contemporary tensions between conventional attachments to notions of laissez-faire and pragmatic attractions to current ideas of legal instrumentalism. Houston's part-time officers, like other Jacksonians, held the conviction that government's cost to the taxpayers, and hence its social welfare responsibilities, should be kept to a minimum. The revision process testifies to an unflagging resistance to add extra burdens on the city government. It also expresses a reluctant willingness to resort to the legislature for greater institutional support for the public sector when private efforts to supply an acknowledged urban necessity had broken down. Thus, the progressively more complex structure of Houston's municipal corporation furnishes a reliable measure of the town's public priorities as well as its evolution from a primitive outpost to a thriving frontier community.

The elaboration of city authority over bayou navigation exemplifies how municipal institutions marched in close cadence with the expanding demands of the commercial interests for better transportation. Houston's original charter of June 1837, passed in the waning days of the First Congress of the Republic, conferred corporate status and little else. A year and a half later, charter drafters extended the regulatory jurisdiction of the city far beyond its borders, to protect the flow of trade along the narrow shipping corridor. Houstonians soon turned this vital task into a self-financing and hopefully profitable municipal service. In February 1840, the legislature approved a charter amendment that gave the municipal corporation a right to construct a wharf and to levy a tax on each user of the town's only docking facility. The following month, a sunken boat in the shallow bayou posed new questions about the city's liability for damages that could result to the craft while removing it from the blocked traffic lane. The immediate problem was resolved informally, but additional amendments were enacted in 1842 to immunize local government from civil penalties in similar situations.[23]

The organic growth of municipal institutions that augmented transportation outward from Houston presents an opposite pattern from the stunned development of public services inside the city. The only exception was the erection of a second proprietary venture, a market house, and the enforcement of standard regulations that went along with it to insure fair and orderly retail transactions. By the mid-forties, the wharf and the market began generating significant surplus revenues, but the aldermen earmarked them almost exclusively for bridge building and road grading on the outskirts of town. The city council sought neither charter authority nor additional taxes to supply contemporary urban services such as waterworks, paved streets and sewers, schools, asylums, and fire and police departments. Public health and sanitation efforts rose and fell spasmodically with the seasonal tide of epidemic diseases, especially the dreaded yellow fever, that washed over the gulf coast region.²⁴ Houstonians restricted the business of the municipal corporation to business. Their narrow vision of its functional role in improving the physical and social environment remained traditional even while they opened imaginative new vistas on the structural relationships between the public and private sectors.

The sharp dichotomy in the priorities placed on transportation and intracity services was also reflected in the unofficial public activities that town residents sponsored. Given the absence of both municipal concern and public utility companies, voluntary associations (two fire companies and a lyceum) and individual enterprises (various schools and a newspaper) offered the only city services enjoyed by the community before the Civil War.²⁵ In contrast, spontaneous volunteerism and formal institutions, government and business, coexisted easily together, when focused on the common goal of establishing the town's commercial domination over the hinterland. The attention devoted to the bayou again serves to illustrate this point. Although the city assumed responsibility in 1840 for keeping the channel unobstructed, a hundred men were readily organized to unsnag a vessel five years later. This was a small but typical instance of a cooperative spirit that characterized early Houston. In a similar vein, merchants contributed $5000 in 1856 to a special fund raised to take advantage of a grant to be matched four-to-one by the state for river and harbor improvements.²⁶

Public and private institutions working to improve Houston's transportation facilities frequently complemented each other. In 1851, the town's emerging merchant princes, William Marsh Rice, Paul Bremond, B. A. Shepard, Thomas W. House, Cornelius Ennis, and William J. Hutchins, organized the Houston Navigation Company to operate boats between the gulf and the municipal wharf. The growing success of this shipping firm meant a steady increase in wharf tax revenues to the city, which in turn could afford to purchase a specially designed dredge five years later to widen and deepen the waterway. Analogous schemes to share the burden of road building proved less successful in the short run. Local government began substantial work on overland routes in the mid-1840s. At about the same time, entrepreneurs chartered a number of toll road companies. The city poured considerable resources into the project, but the private ventures never materialized. They were soon overshadowed by railroad construction.²⁷

Texas railroad promoters had experimented without success from 1836 to 1850 for a structural formula that could tie government and business in a fruitful balance of economic and political power. The first railroad incorporation west of the Mississippi River in 1836 and a second charter in the late thirties failed to attract outside capital. Wary Jacksonians had overloaded them with reservations of public controls. An 1841 grant to the Harrisburg Rail Road and Trading Company had lifted the burden of restrictions on private enterprise. However, sectional antagonism caused a stormy political climate throughout North America. Manifest destiny, annexation, and war against Mexico had forestalled actual construction. After the so-called Compromise of 1850, which seemed to signal a period of national calm, Texans debated anew the question of whether business or government should bear the chief responsibility for building the state's railroad system. The rising commercial elites of Houston and Galveston were drawn to opposite sides of the controversy, pitting the two formerly cooperative towns in an enduring rivalry.[28]

Merchant princes from both cities at first backed institutional mutations that fused the public and the private sectors together. Yet each group supported similar proposals for different reasons. Houstonians acted from expediency to turn a threatened loss of their hinterland into an opportunity to solidify their hold on it. By 1850, Houston's nearest competitor, Harrisburg, three miles downstream on the bayou, was admitted to be a failure by its Boston underwriters. They switched from townsite to railroad speculation by petitioning the Third Legislature to charter the Buffalo Bayou, Brazos, and Colorado Rail Road Company (BB, B & C). The incorporation act duplicated the Bostonians' earlier 1841 grant, except for a section added by their new partners from Houston. Five of the towns' most prominent merchants, four of whom were simultaneously forming the Houston Plank Road Company, joined the venture to prevent a potentially disastrous rerouting of the region's richest trade area along the Brazos River. They reacted defensively, tacking on a friendly amendment to the private incorporation charter that authorized the City of Houston to build and manage a branch line to tap into the company's main route. In exchange for letting Houston become the terminus of the projected railroad, Eastern investors gained the political support of the town's influential merchants. The mutual benefits resulting from the partnership strongly impressed local tradesmen because the BB, B & C became the state's first operational railroad. In 1853, a locomotive ran over twenty miles of track between Harrisburg and Stafford's Point.[29]

Galveston's commercial interests also sought to create new institutional frameworks for transportation projects to the Brazos sugar and cotton lands. They, too, blended city government and private business in a joint enterprise. Island merchants won approval from the productive Third Legislature of a bill to permit their municipality to become a direct shareholder in the Galveston and Brazos Navigation Company, a canal dredging scheme aimed at diverting trade away from Houston. Unlike the opportunism that had prompted bayou city businessmen to propose a public-private fusion, however, Galveston's boosters acted with conviction. They formed a tight circle, a closed group that had promoted the townsite as a "family" affair from its beginning. Their structural hybrid simply formalized a familiar arrangement that did not divide the public welfare from personal interests.[30]

Pursuing these institutional directions even further two years later, the islanders officially wedded the public and private sectors in the Galveston Wharf and Cotton Press Company. It merged seven of the port's ten dock facilities into a legitimate monopoly and exempted the firm from municipal taxation in exchange for making the city a one-third partner.[31] It was natural, therefore, that Galvestonians championed a railroad plan for Texas that was balanced heavily on the side of governmental involvements to guarantee the island's prosperity. As economic competition between the two trading posts intensified in the 1850s, it spilled over into state politics. Houston and Galveston became the respective advocates of two radically different alternatives to the railroad question, the most important public service issue of the antebellum period.

The Houston or "corporate plan" triumphed over the Galveston or "state plan" because the prescription of the inland merchants for fostering railroad building—private ownership aided by generous state subsidies—coincided with transcontinental projects. Of course, Houston stood the most to gain: it was the natural site for a regional hub on a through line between New Orleans and the west coast. Nevertheless, city boosters argued effectively that financing rapid development throughout the state would be impossible without forming an alliance with Eastern moneymen on the one hand, while the costs to Texas from extending loans to the railroads would be negligble on the other. They pointed out that the government had already been offering land grants since 1852 to encourage private investment in Texas railroads.

Galveston's representatives played upon sectional prejudices against Yankee capitalists to advance their proposition for a state-centered network of government-owned transportation improvements. They rejected national linkages and instead called for an independent fan-shaped pattern of rail lines, which would radiate from a fulcrum point on the island. Although the appeal to local self-rule touched a responsive chord among the lawmakers, they reached a more realistic conclusion that such an autonomous course was infeasible with current state resources. They also feared that an antagonistic posture toward private enterprise was likely to retard an inevitable integration of Texas railroads into a more unified system.[32]

The self-confidence displayed by Houston's city boosters helps explain the victory of the corporate plan. The financing of railroad building was probably the most decisive factor, but the political acumen of the town's merchants should not be discounted. Houston's most respected businessmen, including Rice, House, and Bremond, travelled to Austin in 1856 to confront the legislators with a solid front in favor of the mixed enterprise alternative. Galveston's spokesmen also lobbied hard, but their position contained an internal weakness that eventually undermined their determination. Practical requirements of the state plan to swell the powers and the administrative machinery of the central authority to construct a railroad system for an area almost as large as Europe contradicted the Galvestonians' ideological commitment to preserve localism. They could not advance a convincing answer to the key question of how sufficient taxes could be raised to finance construction without destroying the decentralized structure of state government. Faced with this difficult dilemma and viewing the Houstonians' alternative, which promised to accelerate economic growth with a stroke of the pen, the legislators chose to support private companies with loans from the state school fund.[33]

An extensive list of regulations acted as a counterweight to the legislature's 1856 endorsement of the corporate plan. The legislature strove to balance government subsidies to private enterprise by incorporating a large measure of public control into the structural formula. Drawing upon past experience with ferries and borrowing from states that had already curbed common railroad abuses, Texas lawmen already had passed a general regulatory law in 1853, before a locomotive had even reached the state. The February 1853 Act required every railroad company to conform with state standards on such varied matters as public crossings, employee uniforms and conduct, time schedules, rate review procedures, and annual reports that had to be filed with the state comptroller.

The anticipatory timing of this law indicates that the "promotional era" of railroads in Texas always included substantial government checkreins on the private sector. Once the legislature launched a program of land grants and loans to business corporations, they tied these incentives to compliance with additional demands for the financial integrity of each company and for the personal accountability of its directors. Four more laws in 1860 supplemented earlier regulations. They suggest that state representatives were responsive to the problem of enforcement and to the particular needs of conflicting interests for orderly arbitration.[34]

Easy access to the state legislature by private parties subtracted from the importance of the judiciary in antebellum Texas. The impressive flow of public and private statutes from the legislature reflected a fluid interplay of business and government that paralleled the creation of urban policy on the local level. An open door at the capitol meant that few significant controversies were directed to the courts for resolution. The self-restrained posture of the Texas Supreme Court further narrowed the judiciary's role in making state and local policy. Before intense partisan politics boiled over into every branch of government during the Reconstruction period, the bench pursued a policy of deference to the legislature.[35]

Under the structural framework wrought between 1850 and 1860, railroad building proceeded at a quickened pace until the outbreak of civil war abruptly cancelled expansion plans (see Map 1.1). The state's most important new transportation artery, the Houston and Texas Central, extended eighty miles to the north from the inland port. Two special state acts and a taxpayers' referendum in 1856 inaugurated Houston's municipally owned tap line. Public funding, not ownership, was apparently intended because still another piece of legislation created a private corporation, the Houston Tap and Brazoria Railroad Company (HT & B) to buy the venture from the city. When the seven-mile feeder road was completed two years later, Houston cemented its commercial ties with Brazos planters by selling the profitable public works project to the HT & B, a consortium of plantation owners and local merchants. A third highway stretched south to Galveston, and a fourth line reached ninety miles to the east. With an overland transportation network radiating in all four directions, the city was without question the railroad center of the state. Houstonians had built 350 miles of track in the 1850s, or three fourths of the state's entire system. A small group of city boosters deserves the major credit for this considerable achievement.[36]

As might be expected, these railroad promoters were also Houston's leading citizens. During the prewar decade a near identity had developed between the town's incorporators of urban service institutions, its largest property owners, its municipal officers, and its most prominent socialites. The names of the commercial-civic elite appearing on almost every one of these lists included William Rice, Thomas House, William Hutchins, Cornelius Ennis, Paul Bremond, B. A. Shepard, James H. Stevens, and William R. Baker. They personified the coherence of the urbanization process in antebellum Houston.

Their interactions with the law had been instrumental, even if not entirely unique or original. They had found the corporation to be an especially flexible institution because it could be fashioned from so many different combinations of public power and private initiative. They had used corporate devices to create an evolving series of public, mixed, and private structures that had provided the formal supports needed to sustain orderly growth. Their top priority, growth, determined how much attention local leaders had devoted to developing the town's physical environment, public services, and social organization. An energetic pursuit of transportation improvements and a general willingness to experiment with the law had led them to champion institutional arrangements that were in close accord with the contemporary structure of the American political economy.

The percolation of transportation in the fifties to the state, if not the national level, however, spelled the end of the railroad's tutelage as an urban public service. In marked contrast to the legislature's earlier delegation of supervision over canals, ferries, and toll roads to local subdivisions, the state capital monopolized official decision making on the railroad. In the fifties, Texans came to view all modes of transportation as extralocal. The resulting centralization of power in Austin accurately reflected the tightening net of interdependence that had been binding town and country together since the founding of the Republic. In an analogous manner, the victory of the corporate plan testified to the inexorable gravitation of Texas into national orbits of railroad finance and politics. The large pecuniary benefits that Houston's commercial elite reaped in the 1850s came in part from spurning parochialism for a more cosmopolitan outlook.

Houstonians could take pride in their successes. Probably the best measure of the town's rising prosperity was the volume of cotton passing through it. The amount shipped annually climbed from less than 10,000 bales in the early 1840s to 45,000 bales in the mid-1850s, when railroad construction began a rapid extension of the town's hinterland. Within five years, 350 miles of completed track were carrying over 115,000 bales to bayou city wharves. Inside Houston, now securely positioned as the rail center, the value of town lots tripled during the decade.[37]

Nonetheless, the future remained full of uncertainty. If the inland trading post had won the initial advantage as the rail hub of the region, Galveston had not lost its natural superiority as a port facility. Their relative positions had not changed from 1840 to 1860 because neither had been able to bypass the other. On the contrary, the striking number of similarities in their growth patterns strongly indicates that they continued to develop in tandem in spite of a basic switch in their relationship from cooperation to competition. Although this heated rivalry promised to subordinate irreversibly one place to another, contemporaries could only guess which town would emerge the winner.

The gathering clouds of sectional conflict also cast a dark shadow over Houston's future prospects. The townspeople voted almost unanimously for secession. Yet the South's bid for independence could not have sustained for long the confidence of local boosters or outside investors in the nascent urban centers of the Confederacy. The shots fired at Fort Sumter in April 1861 severed Houston's budding partnership with Eastern investors, while national plans for government aid to transcontinental railroads were hurriedly shelved. Moreover, the men and material employed in building Houston's transportation projects were soon drained into the war effort. The first generation of Houstonians had witnessed the transformation of a swampy boat landing into a prosperous center of commerce. Whether they would watch Houston continue to prosper or to stagnate in the backwaters of American urban development remained an open question.

2 "The Chicago of the South," 1865–1874

Houston profited handsomely from the Civil War. Rather than causing a sharp break with the past, the conflict accelerated the town's growth, strengthened the wealth and power of its established elite, and reinforced confidence in the future of the rail center. Applying new riches to delayed opportunities, Houstonians renewed their efforts at a quickened pace after the war. Public and private sector activities to boost urban growth evolved smoothly until August 1868, when Reconstruction finally reached the community. The ensuing period of political and social disruption, however, did not immediately overturn conventional notions of what constituted the public interest.

The wartime career of Thomas W. House illustrates the special opportunities offered to entrepreneurs on the fringes of the conflict along the Texas Gulf Coast. This English immigrant had emerged before secession as a member of Houston's elite as well as a leading proponent of its corporate plan of railroad development. At the same time, House cautiously had kept a residence and his main warehouses in Galveston because the rivalry between the two towns clearly had no predictable winner. However, Galveston's exposed military position had highlighted its vulnerability to attack not only by hostile armies but also by violent coastal storms and dreaded epidemic diseases that were known to travel aboard ships from port to port. After the Yankees' uncontested invasion of the island in December 1862, House permanently shifted his operations inland. House supported and supplied the Confederacy, but he exchanged the proceeds from his far-flung smuggling ring into gold, over $300,000 worth by war's end.[1] This vast fortune in specie would soon help underwrite the restoration of Houston's depleted transportation system and the modernization of its central business district.

Many Houston businessmen had pursued similar wartime maneuvers. Their combined activities produced significant new accumulations of wealth, which could supply crucial "start-up" capital for postwar expansion projects. In addition, Houston's role as a military supply depot had maintained, and perhaps strengthened, its trade ties with the hinterland. In contrast to many places in the Confederacy, this Texas headquarters had suffered neither direct physical destruction nor indirect damage to its economic base, the surrounding countryside. A prosperity spawned by war reinforced an earlier urban frontier spirit of optimism. To be sure, Lee's surrender at the Appomattox Courthouse spread uncertainty throughout the defeated South. But like the muted blows of war itself, the impact of Reconstruction would reach the Gulf Coast provinces softened by its long journey from a distant national capital.[2]

19

New Dimensions of Environmental Engineering

At the end of the war, Houstonians immediately returned to their reliance on a pragmatic combination of private, mixed, and public means of promoting city growth. In the absence of any imperative reasons to distinguish more sharply between self-interests and civic purposes, local leaders continued to experiment freely with a wide range of structural forms. From 1865 to 1869, a search for the most productive legal instruments of urban development occupied their prime attention. Established railroad corporations quickly began restoring and extending their now dilapidated networks, while a variety of new companies launched additional rail and shipping enterprises.[3] Moreover, officials and entrepreneurs embarked on novel city building schemes in anticipation of the boundless urban growth that would surely accompany the promised enlargement of Houston's hinterland.

Although limited in scope and purpose, Houston's first substantial city building program led to important managerial and structural reforms of its municipal corporation. Civic leaders initially applied informal procedures to familiar instruments of governmental power. But to construct paved roads, sidewalks, bridges, sewers, and a new market house required the transformation of local government from an ad hoc affair to an ongoing business with established routines and fiscal integrity. After 1866, officials worked steadily to institute regularity in the collection of taxes, the budgeting of expenditures, and the administration of public works projects. The granting of franchises to street railway ventures and a gas and light company made additional demands on city officers to reshape the framework of government. By mid-1868, the town's best men, Republicans and Democrats, reached a consensus on a new approach to public administration. Their ambitious city building plans promised to put Houston on a permanent course of self-sustained growth.

Private enterprise revived swiftly after Appomattox. Businessmen hastened to conclude war-related commercial transactions and to restart operations that had been interrupted by the conflict. Raised levels of confidence in Houston's future meant that its backers more willingly risked their capital to fuel the city's growth. For example, a complex of industries that included foundries, machine shops, lumber yards, cotton mills, and warehouses began rising along the northeast bank of Buffalo Bayou. Many of these businesses provided materials for the reconstruction of worn railroad systems, which were already being refinanced by their Houston managers in Eastern money markets. The resumption of transportation, commerce, and immigration, in turn, gave encouragement to other entrepreneurs to open neighborhood stores, small-scale manufactures, and amusements that could serve an expanding pool of wage earners.[4] The buzz of private sector activity in the streets was soon reverberating inside city hall. At an early point, businessmen seeking special privileges from government began petitioning the council for franchises to supply public utility services.

The origins of the town's gas light franchise provides a good example of the new dimensions of city building in postbellum Houston. Between 1858 and 1867 entrepreneurs filed a succession of petitions for the gas franchise. The first effort was led by C. C. Bier of New Orleans, who introduced the city dwellers to the advantages of gas lighting:

> [n]ow here is a chance for comfort, convenience, economy, and progress, all in one operation. Persons who have ever used gas-lights know how much superior they are in every respect to having any other light known. They are a saving in expense, a saving in trouble, and an advantage to the eyes.[5]

Bier failed completely to enlist local subscribers, but he sold Houston on the civic necessity of modern urban utilities. In February 1860, the same month that the streets were lit in Galveston, a group headed by A. M. Gentry formed the Houston Gas Company. Although Gentry was quick to reclaim his gas franchise after the war, he was slow in putting the project into operation.

Finally, in September 1866, Thomas House organized the Houston Gas Light Company (HGLC). The council was soon encouraging the newest venture "to immediately proceed to erect their works, and lay their pipes within the city in accordance with the provisions of their act of incorporation." In January 1867, the HGLC purchased land to erect a plant and holding tank on the southeast edge of the emerging business district along the western bank of the bayou. This central station began manufacturing coal gas fourteen months later.

The preliminary success of the HGLC rested upon the corporation's solid institutional underpinnings as much as on House's bankroll. To reduce investment risks, company organizers carefully structured the legal relationships of their enterprise with state and municipal authorities. Houston businessmen obtained an attractive array of future-oriented concessions from the public sector to offset the currently limited earning potential of the utility service. In the 1860s, the gas business represented a considerable gamble, even though this urban utility had been illuminating American cities for a half century. Yet its economic viability was still doubtful in all but the largest metropolitan centers because the high cost of gas (compared with cheaper alternatives) kepts its use confined to commercial buildings, public streets, and upper-class homes.[7] A franchise inherently enlarged an enterprise's liability to the exercise of government's ample, though poorly defined, police powers. Nevertheless, special privileges guaranteed that the firm established first would reap the long-term profits from gas lights and the promised evolution of gas from a luxury item to a mass necessity.

The HGLC's incorporation charter contained several provisions that protected the venture from economic loss and political attack. Of first importance, the Texas legislature directly granted a right-of-way for the firm's distribution system of pipes and fixtures in the streets of Houston. The crucial need for this franchise distinguished gas light and other urban utilities from ordinary businesses. By possessing special street-use privileges from the state rather than the municipality, the HGLC was protected against the ultimate political recourse of a hostile community, franchise repeal. The charter also guarded the company's property against malicious damage by declaring such assaults a criminal offense.[8] Fortified with a strong institutional position in state law, the HGLC organizers turned to the city government for equivalent economic concessions.

Gas company and municipal officers cooperated fully to ensure that the fledgling urban service would reward its backers for their financial gamble. A month after a building site was selected in January 1867, the council gave the HGLC a monopoly. An ordinance provided that the enterprise would have the "exclusive . . . privilege of supplying the City of Houston for the term of their [sic] [twenty-five year] charter. . . ."[9] True, a public shield against competition could not create a market for gas, but this key concession did force any and all consumers to rely upon a single supplier. It was also assumed from the start that a generous contract for street lighting would make the city government the foremost customer of the company. Altogether, the HGLC forged an impressive group of structural links with the public sector.

Houstonians laid a legal foundation for street railway services that was quite different from the gas franchise. Yet the underlying motives and end results of both city building ventures were the same. Both private ventures sought and obtained a legal monopoly to supply the city with a public utility. However, the business success of mass transit systems elsewhere strongly affected local horsecar developers. Moreover, because steam trains had chronically obstructed intraurban movement, city fathers had in 1862 secured the sole power to regulate rail technologies.[10] Thus, the municipal charter directed aspiring streetcar entrepreneurs to city hall, where from 1866 to 1869 they competed vigorously for right-of-way privileges along the town's principal pathways.

In contrast to the cautious posture of businessmen toward gas lighting ventures, their active rivalry for streetcar franchises reflected an accurate assessment of the potential profitability of mass transit enterprises. The replacement of the omnibus by rail-borne cars during the prewar decade in the big cities had brought immediate and rapidly climbing returns to investors. Relatively small capital needs and simple technologies also encouraged local businessmen to seek franchise privileges in established young communities like Houston. By 1865, this utility enterprise must have appeared to be a golden opportunity to contemporaries.[11]

The debate among city officials on the structure of streetcar grants expressed a clear preference for "development now" over efficiency or economics. An overriding urge to get the job done quickly surfaced during the debate over the first application for a franchise. In May 1866, a council study committee reported favorably on a petition from two local businessmen, Robert Lockhart and John Carey, because "such an enterprise properly carried out would be highly beneficial to the city at large. . . ." Mayor H. D. Taylor also looked to the future, yet with an eye on the present:

[t]he city of Houston is, as it were, in her infancy. A system of street railroads might, under proper conditions, be of advantage in hastening her immediate growth.

In exchange for a twenty-five year exclusive privilege on designated streets, the franchise required the two partners to build at least one mile of track annually, keep the streets in good repair, and pay the city a $1000 bonus.[12]

After Lockhart and Carey rejected the proposal in August 1866 as too restrictive, Houstonians renewed a competitive search for a structural formula that would give birth to a mass transit service. Over the next two and a half years, the council progressively stripped away reservations of public authority while adding incentives to stimulate capital investment and construction activity. Motivated to initiate development, local officials issued liberalized grants for four similar small-scale projects in the spring of 1867, approved a third grant design for Francis Allen's city-wide venture in August, and passed yet another franchise variation for a limited enterprise in March of the following year. Choosing among these alternatives, entrepreneurs combined their interests under the most favorable, the Allen grant, which then provided the foundation for the August 1868 chartering of the Houston City Railway Company (HCRC).[13]

From 1866 to 1869, the city had let few opportunities pass in its drive to encourage the private sector to build urban public services. With both gas and streetcar utilities, the prior necessity of establishing viable institutional relationships had produced a series of experimental forms. In the case of artificial lighting, a group of business leaders had taken and held the initiative after two previous failures to obtain material results. Basing its enterprise on state authority, the HGLC had received additional safeguards from local officials and had proceeded smoothly in the construction of its facilities. Street railway services had followed an independent course. The city council had given entrepreneurs their choice among four different franchise variations. In the case of both utilities, however, the final outcome had been the same: the emergence of a single company with a legalized monopoly.

The dynamic opportunism that epitomized franchise politics also fueled the drive by public officials to upgrade Houston's environment to metropolitan standards. They shared with the businessmen a new level of confidence in the city's prospects. It could hardly be otherwise, since any dichotomy between the two groups was almost entirely artificial. Only substantial property holders could run for office under municipal charter rules, and the taxpayers alone could vote. In addition, the aldermen and the mayor held part-time, unpaid positions that made relatively minor demands on their energies in comparison to their private lives. That Houston's prominent entrepreneurs and its city managers were virtually one and the same guaranteed a large overlap in the interests and outlook of the public and private sectors. In early 1866, as the restoration of the state government got underway, town leaders eagerly resumed the task of building a modern city.

At first, the search for the ways and means to implement public works projects followed conventional patterns of administration. Ad hoc methods of government management, which still relied on private volunteerism for legitimacy, characterized the conduct of local affairs. But in the postwar atmosphere of boundless expansion, an informal process of decision making about the allocation of limited resources soon developed chronic shortcomings. Discovering worthy reasons for extending public credit and spending proved far easier than finding reliable mechanisms for raising additional taxes. Familiar managerial reforms repeatedly failed to solve the inexorable breakdown of the city's money machine. These fiscal difficulties gradually prompted town leaders to reevaluate the relationship between the municipal corporation and the taxpayer. The Republican takeover of city hall in August 1868 furnished the occasion for the commercial-civic elite of both parties to articulate their new understanding of municipal economics. They agreed to reorganize Houston's government in order to finance an emerging list of city building priorities. The broad consensus reached at the taxpayers' meeting would direct the course of public policy over the next six years.

From February to August 1866, the city council adhered closely to traditional concepts of public sector responsibilities and to piecemeal approaches to the management of government. At an early point, the council's finance committee reported that current revenues were wholly insufficient to fund essential improvements. The pressing needs listed in the report—enlarging the police force, dredging the Buffalo Bayou, paving the main streets, and building a new market house—all related directly to the commercial well-being of the town. The city council also tied municipal sources of revenue to commerce. Houston imposed license fees on various occupations, rental charges on food retailers in the market building, and a "merchandise" or sales tax on goods sold in local stores. Without seriously trying to curb widespread evasion, the city collected comparatively negligible amounts from a one-half percent, ad valorem levy on real estate (see Table 2.1). The finance committee believed that small adjustments in the tax structure would close the gap between anticipated expenditures and revenues. Yet the council hesitated to enact even minor managerial reforms before gaining the approval of the taxpayers.[14]

Official responses to taxpayer protests against the report confirm the small scale, informal nature of Houston's local government immediately after the Civil War. A "large and respectable portion of our citizens," the finance committee discovered over the next few weeks, objected to any increase in the license or merchandise tax. Pointing to a meager income of $35,000 in 1865, the aldermen reiterated their belief that fiscal reform was an "absolute necessity" in order to launch public works programs. To buttress their claims, the councilmen pointed to a second group of petitioners who appealed to city hall for financial aid in buying a new steam fire engine. Although the aldermen presented a sound defense of their position, they chose to defer to the merchants. The city council

TABLE 2.1   Municipal Budget, 1866

Revenues ($)			Expenditures ($)	
License Tax	63,137		Streets and bridges	21,426
Ad valorem tax	5,620		Salaries	19,785
Market fees	11,860		Police department	15,980
Wharf fees	3,472		Dredge boat	9,217
			Fire department	3,200
Gross tax receipts		84,089	Interest	2,389
City Marshall's office	(4,150)		Miscellaneous	16,242
Gross receipts		88,239	Total expenses	88,239

SOURCE: "Financial Statement of the Secretary-Treasurer for the Year Ending December 31, 1866," as reported in W. A. Leonard, comp., *Houston City Directory* (Houston: Gray, 1867), p. 108.

concluded that, in future years, new tax burdens should be shifted onto the property holders.[15]

In the meantime, the council borrowed money by issuing municipal bonds in order to meet the long-standing need for public improvements. The aldermen supplemented long-term, interest-bearing bonds with a variety of scrip issues that collectively accounted for the city's unfunded or "floating" debt.[16] As tax collections fell further and further behind expenditures, the council increasingly resorted to these unsecured IOUs to cover municipal salaries and bills from local contractors. Expansion of public indebtedness proved an easy, short-term expedient for part-time officials who worked without a budget or a plan, with only a vision of Houston's future greatness.

Now that management of Houston's outward thrust into the hinterland had gravitated elsewhere, facilitating movement inside the town assumed chief importance. At first, public officials recognized little need for structural or managerial reforms to achieve this goal. The council devoted an increasing amount of its resources to overcoming the environmental impediments to efficient and convenient transportation within local boundaries. The granting of franchises to gas lighting and horsecar firms represented a part of this effort to ease the flow of people and goods throughout the commercial center. But the main business of government became the grading, drainage, and paving of streets with shells from the nearby gulf, and the construction of bridges across the Buffalo Bayou. Intraurban transportation dominated civic attention between 1866 and 1869, although two other public works projects received special consideration by city fathers.

A new market house and a ship channel assumed a major importance in the emerging plan to steer Houston onto a path of self-sustained growth. The need for a new market facility, which could also house the city government, appeared obvious. However, the expense of the structure envisioned by the aldermen worried taxpayers. In September 1866, after finance chairman John Reichman reported from New York that the iron skeleton for such a building would cost $150,000, a public meeting was called to rally citizen support. Instead, physician Ingram S. Roberts and other large property holders advised the council to delay selling bonds in the North because "political chaos rules rampant and the vast masses of the voting population are yet unfriendly to the South." The aldermen disagreed, but they again deferred to the opinion of the electorate.[17] The market house project remained shelved for over two years.

In contrast, any delay in cutting a direct water route to outside markets posed a more serious and immediate threat to the town's ambitions for metropolitan status. A ship channel loomed as a crucial necessity when Galveston began tightening a monopoly grip on Texas shipping after the war. The port's semi-official Wharf Company increasingly controlled the flow of traffic by cementing ties with the two shipping giants of the region. Favored treatment helped Charles Morgan to take command of the coastal trade west of New Orleans and allowed the Mallorys to crush all competitors who engaged in ocean-borne travel with New York and Europe. Unless Houston opened an alternative route to outside markets, its merchants would have to pay tribute to the Wharf Company and, in effect, enrich their island rivals. To forestall this potentially crippling situation, Houston sponsored a series of ever larger ship channel schemes to complement private efforts to bypass Galveston.[18]

The institutional structure of the ship channel evolved quickly, recapitulating previous experience with the spectrum of public and private sector instruments. In 1866, the councilmen earmarked $9200, about one tenth of city revenues, for dredging the bayou. Although coastal craft could navigate this narrow waterway, deep-bottomed ocean ships remained blocked from its entrance by two sandbars that stretched across the entire width of Galveston Bay. To open a channel through these formidable barriers, local officers appealed to the community the following year to subscribe voluntarily to a $75,000 bond issue. After failing to sell more than a third of the securities by June 1868, the council turned in a new direction, the creation of a joint, public-private corporation. The proposed Houston Ship Channel Company (HSCC) bore a significant resemblance to the Wharf Company, but the purpose of the former was to raise investment capital, not to establish an official monopoly. The city government would underwrite the HSCC with a $300,000 bond issue. In exchange for the receipts of the bond sale, the HSCC would give the city an equivalent amount of company securities.[19]

The effort to finance a ship channel confronted town leaders with the inescapable conclusion that a complete reform of municipal finances could be delayed no longer. By mid-1868, the gradual expansion of the public sector had outstripped city resources to the point where local businessmen refused for the first time to heed their own government's appeal for financial support. The alternative of securing outside investors for such expensive projects as a waterway and a market house highlighted the already glaring inadequacies of the city's money machine. The commercial-civic elite's growing realization that the restoration of the fiscal integrity of the municipal corporation was a prerequisite to further progress happened to coincide with the intrusion of Reconstruction politics into the community. In July and August 1868, the removal of many local officials by military authorities aroused vocal Democratic protests.[20] The removal also provoked a concerted attempt to maintain a consensus on the need for municipal reform. Thirty-five of Houston's richest men issued a call for a meeting to liquidate the government's "burdensome debt" in order that improvements essential to the "health, prosperity and general good" of the city could be initiated.[21]

The taxpayers' meeting marked a critical turning point in the city's history. Fiscal and political crises had combined to draw together many of the 101 citizens who possessed $10,000 or more worth of property. Collectively, these holdings accounted for at least 75 percent of the town's assessed valuation.[22] Furthermore, six of the next seven mayors were among the participants in the debate over the best remedy for the city's insolvency. The pivotal importance of this gathering of the elite cannot be overemphasized. The decisions they reached became the foundation of public policy until the depression of 1873–1874 and were a source of major influence in the politics and economics of the city for over twenty years.

The chairman of the meeting, George Goldwaithe, made an astute analysis of the municipal government's fiscal difficulties. Goldwaithe was the chief counsel for the Texas Central Railroad and would exert a continuing influence in local and state politics into the 1880s. Too much city scrip, the prominent Democratic lawyer argued, had created an inflationary spiral that eventually caused a breakdown. According to Goldwaithe, "the city has made itself a machine to grind out paper [scrip] to be shaved at enormous rates. This is all wrong. This is the great evil. . . ." He explained that the overgrown size of the floating debt had reduced the value of Houston scrip to only forty cents on the dollar. Contractors forced the council to pay them higher compensatory charges, and city employees had to take whatever cash the money dealers would give them for their discounted paychecks. In turn, these speculators sold the paper to the large taxpayers who obtained full value for it in paying their city dues. By issuing more and more scrip to make up for increasing cash deficits, the council inadvertently added to the problem by diminishing the amount of cash the treasury received in taxes. Until this vicious cycle was broken, Goldwaithe concluded, the credit of the city could not be restored.[23]

There was general agreement that a solid credit rating was the spark needed to ignite the engine of self-sustained urban growth. Rebuilding confidence in Houston's fiscal integrity, several speakers asserted, required the replacement of ad hoc practices with a systematic policy. Led by Goldwaithe, they outlined a plan that supposedly applied business principles to the administration of government. First, the council would have to eliminate the scrip evil, the $40,000 floating debt. Then, based on current property valuations of about $5,000,000, city officers could sell up to $1,000,000 in long-term municipal bonds for improvement projects. The taxpayers believed that these urban utilities would attract new industries and settlers to the community, while the railroad drew more and more of the surrounding hinterland into Houston's trade orbit. Rising prosperity would swell the tax base, guarantee the faithful payment of the debt, and permit the funding of additional city building projects. According to the Goldwaithe plan, growth would finance itself, so to speak. As long as the city promptly honored the bonds' interest coupons, Houston's borrowing potential seemed unlimited.[24]

Creation of this blueprint for progress signalled the end of the town's reliance on informal, volunteristic methods of public administration. The three years from 1865 to the gathering of the taxpaying elite in 1868 had been a period of experimentation, of drawing plans and searching for the most efficient instruments to realize them. Competition for the municipality's meager resources had narrowed the alternatives to a fixed list of allocation priorities and franchise holders. To be sure, the unchallenged position of the merchant after the war had meant that public priorities had been chosen within a limited context. The need to strengthen the town's commercial vitality dominated thinking about the proper functions of the government sector. But at the same time, this single-minded pursuit of prosperity had led civic leaders to advocate several unique dimensions of city planning, including public utilities, street improvements, a market house, and a ship channel. Local leaders hoped that these urban services would act as a pump primer to accelerate Houston's climb to metropolitan greatness.

The town's neophyte planners had learned important lessons in the process of transforming the municipal corporation into a central agency of urban development. The proposals advanced at the taxpayers' meeting reflected these insights. The failure to sell the voluntary ship channel bonds at home taught the leadership that the city had to seek outside capital for large-scale public works projects. This conclusion paralleled earlier solutions to the thorny problem of railroad finance. However, establishing investor confidence in a municipal corporation involved far more complicated calculations than those needed in gaining support for a privately-owned transportation company. In addition to a promising economic future, the ability of local governments like Houston's to secure investment capital depended on the appearance of social consensus, or at least political stability. As finance chairman Reichman had discovered in New York, the cost of borrowing money was prohibitive in the absence of these signs of community cohesion. In August 1868, the threat of divisive partisanship posed by the Republican ascendency prompted the commercial-civic elite to formalize their new understanding of city planning in concrete terms.

Republican adherence to the Goldwaithe plan became the sine qua non for taxpayer support of the incoming administration. At the August 1868 meeting, the participants made a long-range commitment to divert a part of their income to the public sector. In effect, the large property owners agreed to mortgage their present and future holdings to the city's bondholders. The taxpayers completed the transition from a commercial to a property based tax system that the council had begun two years earlier. In exchange for the voluntary sacrifice of local self-sufficiency to foreign capitalists, the local elite insisted that whoever ran city hall must accept their priorities and implement their plans without deviation. To them, a ship channel and a metropolitan appearance would ensure regional hegemony for Houston, especially as its railroads fanned deeper into the Texas countryside.

It was not difficult for the newly installed Republicans to adopt the Goldwaithe formula. From 1868 to 1874, they dutifully followed its prescription of fiscal reforms and allocation priorities. Since large property holders filled the positions of power in both parties, Houston's Democratic and Republican chieftains shared the same optimistic outlooks, economic aspirations, and public policy objectives. On the other hand, the spokesmen of the two parties diverged more sharply in their social status and their attitude toward racial accommodation. Nevertheless, these differences had little impact on the plans of the community's city builders. They had faith that the main agencies of urban growth in the New South were trade and transportation, modern amenities and attractive surroundings, fiscal integrity, and political stability.

City Building: The Entrepreneurs

The translation of the Goldwaithe plan into actual services and utilities confirms first impressions that the commercial vitality of the town dictated the parameters of the public welfare concept. Between 1868 and 1874, Houstonians created an urban environment that to our eyes, more closely resembles a Hollywood movie set than a thriving metropolis. The making of this physical geography graphically reveals the political economy of city building in Houston. Public and private managers devoted great attention to the corridors between the railroad depots and the market square in the center of the town. These three or four main pathways of trade received paving, drainage, gas lighting, and horsecars, but behind this impressive facade, frontier conditions prevailed. Emerging residential areas enjoyed none of these services, nor others essential to public health such as a pure water supply or a sewage system. During the Reconstruction period, the proper functions of city government remained restricted to the promotion of commerce.

In spite of the great amounts of money and toil that were expended on even limited objectives, Houstonians made little headway in furnishing the town with urban services and durable improvements. Street railways and lighting services were intermittent at best; roads paved with shells were constantly deteriorating to mud and dust. The establishment of a deep water ship channel continued to elude the combined labors of government and business. A magnificent market house was finally opened in 1874, but cost overruns seriously upset the municipal corporation's fiscal equilibrium. By 1875, the entire enterprise of constructing an artificial island of modernity ground to a halt, bankrupt and broken down.

The reasons for the miserable performance of Houston's city architects lay simply in their inexperience. Although the Democrats would later charge the Republicans with incompetence and malfeasance, the efficacy of the Goldwaithe plan was unquestioned until well after the Redeemers' return to power in January 1874. During the postwar era, city building depended on local talent and material, except for outside infusions of capital. Traffic planners, coal gas chemists, highway engineers, government financiers, and other experts had to be recruited from within the community. On-the-job training by trial and error was not only inherently expensive, but often resulted in outright failure. In this respect, government and business managers accumulated an equally poor record of achievement in creating lasting improvements and efficient services. The plan to uplift Houston to metropolitan standards and regional hegemony proved too ambitious and eventually overwhelmed its designers.

The preliminary stages of construction indicated just the opposite conclusion: city building seemed easy. By the spring of 1868, the early accomplishments of franchise holders and public officials were already evoking metropolitan images of Houston. A visiting Brownsville journalist, for instance, took note of the sharp contrasts that these improvements could make in an urban landscape:

> Two months ago, you might plod your way home, through the dark and mud, to the great danger of being knocked down, or garroted at every corner, or else hire a hack at heavy expense to obviate the difficulty and danger, but now the streets are illuminated with gas, making the night perambulations rather a pleasure than a terror; and now two of the principle streets of the city are traversed with street railway cars, which offer cheap facilities for those who would travel from necessity or pleasure; besides these, other [street] railroads are in progress.[25]

Local newsmen, too, became enthusiastic observers of these projects. In June 1868, as transit company workers graded Main Street, the *Telegraph* boasted that "it will present the appearance of a metropolitan street and will really be a credit to the city. . . ." When the company inaugurated service the following month, the paper crowed

> It [the streetcar] was an object of admiration, not only because of its rare beauty, but on account of its being an entirely home enterprise. . . . The appearance of a passenger car on Main Street this morning creates an interesting chapter in the history of Houston.[26]

The following month, the taxpayers would verify the reporter's claim that the city was entering a new era. But like the plans formulated at the meeting, the initial triumphs of the city builders were based on a keen appreciation of past experience. By exploiting preexisting land use patterns, they raised the probability of success to the point where no difficulty seemed insurmountable. A single-minded pursuit of growth left little doubt that public improvements should serve to enhance the efficiency, convenience, and attractiveness of conducting business inside the city. Within this context, decision making about where to begin construction seemed obvious because the effects of a commercial economy had already shaped the general contours of Houston's topography. A brief look at this process of segregating the land into specialized, functional districts largely explains the location of the town's first urban services.

By far, the single most powerful influence in determining the pattern of land use and the distribution of public utilities in Houston was transportation.[27] An overriding dependence on the steamboat in antebellum Texas had decided the very location of the townsite at the headwaters of navigation. Moreover the primacy of water shipping had persuaded the Allen brothers to orient the town plat, or street grid, in accord with the path of the Buffalo Bayou rather than with the points of the compass. For example, the central axis of the municipality had been laid out from the original docking place at Allen's landing, perpendicular to the waterway, in a southwestern direction. The town's fledgling merchants had in turn erected their stores along this "Main Street" and the intersecting roads near the public docks. In contrast, the northeastern portion of the city had remained virtually deserted before the Civil War because no bridge spanned the bayou. Thus, the steamboat and its water highway had demarcated the use of land into specialized areas: a central business district as well as a residential one that sprung up in a semi-circle around it. In the 1850s, the decision had logically followed to put the two new railroad terminals close to the waterway, but on the outskirts of the built-up section.

Although rail and water systems evolved beyond local control after Appomattox, they still exerted a singular force in molding Houston's physical contours. The location of the Houston and Texas Central depot and repair shops was decisive in turning the northeastern side of the bayou into an industrial-worker district. In addition to the establishment of numerous manufacturing concerns directly related to the construction and maintenance of the railroad, it brought Houston more and more agricultural products from the north. These required storage, and perhaps processing, before being transferred for export onto waterborne shipping. In the late 1860s, grain elevators, cotton compresses, and lumber yards began rising in a cluster between the rail depot and the bayou.[28]

On the other side of the waterway, railroads from Galveston and southwestern plantations terminated at the Union Depot, the southern anchor of the central business district. Imported goods and settlers sifted through downtown shops, outfitters, and hotels before moving deeper into the interior. Houston served as a launching pad for immigrants who came in record numbers after the defeat of the South. To a great extent, these existing land use patterns informed the locational choices of the postwar city builders.

Houstonians adhered tightly to established lines of development in drawing their blueprints for progress. The scramble for horsecar franchises most explicitly pinpointed the routes that contemporaries considered of outstanding importance. Competition for street right-of-way privileges focused on three crucial pathways of trade: one, about a mile long, from the center of the business district to the Union Depot; a second, shorter route across the bayou to the Central Depot; and a third on Main Street itself. Gas company officials similarly chose to lay distribution pipes only under Main Street and one crossroad, Congress Street, which ran from the Union Depot past the town's finest hotel and the market square to the bayou.[29] The council's relatively quick action on constructing four iron bridges to tie the divided city together further acknowledged the importance of the burgeoning industrial area near the Texas Central terminal. Moreover, the aldermen's list of street paving projects coincided almost completely with the franchise holders' judgments about where services should be provided first.[30] Public and private policies combined to reinforce, rather than reshape, the configuration of urban growth that was being wrought primarily by the impact of transportation technology.

A sound understanding of past experience helped order locational priorities, but it offered hardly any guidance on how to conduct a successful urban service. Consider that if the much impressed reporter from Brownsville returned for another visit two years later, he would again have to plod through unlit streets. In less than a year, the owners of the street railway abandoned their enterprise at a total loss; the gas company kept the lights flickering dimly until 1872, when they were extinguished indefinitely. The practical problems involved in setting up a viable urban utility go far towards explaining why the level of public services in Houston remained so low for over a decade. To be sure, the unquestioned domination of the community by a commercial-civic elite accounted for the limited range and scope of services initially found in the town. Nevertheless, the serious difficulties encountered in operating even this small group of utilities acted independently to inhibit the expansion of existing services and to preclude the adoption of additional ones.

The case of the street railway presents a good example of the economic and managerial hurdles that had to be overcome in creating a workable urban service. In July 1868, the HCRC began running a horsecar up and down Main Street on a single-line track with a turntable at each end. Four or five months later, the company folded because it could not attract enough patrons. Only 800 to 1000 passengers a month were willing to pay ten cents for a ride, which extended for no more than eight blocks. The horsecar took twenty minutes to complete a round trip, whereas a pedestrian could walk the length of the route in half that time. In June, the *Telegraph* had correctly anticipated that "no person will wait twenty minutes to ride even ten blocks. The oftener the cars run, the more travel will be stimulated." Unless the transit firm could supply a "momentary accommodation," the paper warned, success would be denied.[31]

The community waited five years before wary local businessmen poured chronically scarce capital into another urban transit venture. Despite the ground-floor opportunities still attached to this public utility, the example of the defunct company proved difficult to offset. Finally, in 1874, leading merchants such as Thomas House and William T. Brady committed enough of their capital to give Houston an adequate transit network.

Avoiding the mistakes of the past, their venture, the Houston City Street Railway Company (HCSRC), built a coordinated system of routes that immediately attracted substantial numbers of riders. "The different lines of street railways," the city directory reported, "have been extensively patronized from the beginning, much to the chagrin of the . . . 'bull whip' old fogies."[32] During April and May 1874, the company opened four routes between the Market House and the two train stations, the Houston Central railroad shops, and the state fair grounds at the end of Main Street, where an annual exposition and weekly festivities were held. Twelve stylish cars picked up and discharged passengers along three miles of track for five cents a ride, the standard American fare.[33]

In comparison to the previous effort, the HCSRC offered more extensive service, greater convenience, and reduced fares. These differences paid off handsomely in terms of consumer acceptance and profits. For instance, the new Congress Street line to the Union Depot carried about 6,000 passengers per month, or more than six times the entire patronage of the old enterprise. In 1875, this route alone cleared approximately $13,000 above operating expenses.[34] The company's promising statistics support the contention that the street railway became a quick success as soon as sufficient resources were invested in the construction of a network of transit services along Houston's principal arteries of movement. Subsequently, the company made only minor improvements until challenged by competitors in the late 1870s.

Starting a street railway after the Civil War meant overcoming the economic and managerial pitfalls common to all nascent urban utility services. Entrepreneurs in the Texas city struggled to find a workable balance between providing enough services to attract customers and too many to pay dividends. Other utilities, those of gas and water, encountered many of the same problems in setting up satisfactory service arrangements and remunerative distribution networks. On the other hand, a horse drawn railroad was easy to build. The fact that both of Houston's transit ventures were largely homespun affairs is itself a good indication of a relatively simple technology. Even in this small provincial town, a work force existed that possessed sufficient skills to fashion lightweight roadways and cars that fit local needs.

In marked contrast to streetcar and water supply enterprises, gas companies faced unprecedented technical problems. Both gas and water services were delivered directly to the consumer through underground pipes and special fixtures. But the extent of the similarity in their technologies ends here. Lighting firms had to cope with a highly complex manufacturing process involving a series of precise steps that transformed coal into a gas that exhibited a brilliant flame, masked an intolerable odor, and resisted an explosive propensity. The secret of this chemical metamorphosis posed a troublesome enigma that puzzled the gas industry throughout most of the nineteenth century. However, as company managers searched for a way to make a safe and efficient product at a reasonable price, gas lighting slowly evolved into a unique urban technology. Between 1870 and 1890, a completely integrated type of system emerged out of the necessity to invent almost everything from the coal retorts to the fixtures on the consumer's wall. Although most innovations in the gas business originated in cities with the biggest mass markets, the ingenuity displayed in supplying smaller places with artificial illumination was also impressive. The early history of the Houston Gas Light Company (HGLC) exemplifies the kinds of technical dilemmas that hamstrung efforts to boost the level of modern comfort in budding cities just behind the frontier.

An inability to master the science of gas making prevented the HGLC from enlisting more than a few hundred customers during its first decade. After the trial test of the facilities in March 1868, perceptions of Houston began altering. As the journalist from Brownsville noted, gas lighting gave the town an urban appearance. Illuminating a town with street lamps could suddenly liberate an urban society from the age-old tyranny imposed by the natural rhythms of day and night. Yet Houston, the *Telegraph* admitted in August, was "not particularly heavy on gas, judging from the amount burned during the month just closed." Shortly afterwards, the paper suggested a reason for the apparent rejection of this remarkable utility. An editorial stated, "The light [from the street lamps] could not possibly struggle through the thick coat of filth." Eight years later, in 1876, little had changed. "The gas furnished now is about as miserable an apology for gas as anyone was ever afflicted with," the newspaper revealed.[35]

The chronically poor performance of the company stemmed chiefly from its failure to recruit an experienced technician, an expert in the art of manufacturing the illuminating gas. The futility of the HGLC's search is not surprising, since contemporaries of the postwar period composed the first generation of coal gas "experts." In this instance, large and small cities alike essentially went through the same learning process. The cost of operating a complex technology by such rule-of-thumb methods was high. In 1873, the second superintendent of the HGLC, Charles P. Russell, conducted a tour of the works that gives an insight into the nature of these problems. Arriving a year earlier, Russell had found the plant in the "worst possible condition imaginable." His predecessor had purchased such inferior equipment that most of it had to be scrapped, even though it was only five years old. For example, Russell was in the midst of replacing the original set of twelve iron furnaces used in heating the coal into a gas with clay retorts that cost one third as much and lasted four times as long.[36] Troubles at the central station were a part of a related group of technical shortcomings that continued to plague the company for several more years.

Unreliable supplies of high-grade coal also impeded efforts to make a superior artificial illuminant, one that most Houstonians could afford. Because the gas was burned as an open flame in Bunsen burner-like devices, the brilliance of the light ultimately depended on the chemical properties of the coal. Unsuitable raw materials probably caused the dirt encrusted film that spoiled the effectiveness of the street lamps. The town's reporters periodically commented that the HGLC's coal supply was "finer than that which you could find in the North, even to blacksmiths, and as such was in every respect unfit for gas purposes . . . gas in large quantities cannot be made from such slack."[37] Occasionally the company shut off the gas after running out of supplies; more often it used low quality materials. Far from coal mining regions, the Houston firm either could not find or refused to pay for the appropriate fuels.

Unsophisticated in many technical fields, Houstonians did solve some complicated problems with considerable acumen. Local genius helped the public utility secure a virtually inexhaustible and cheap supply of the lime needed for "washing" the gas of noxious odors. A way was discovered to adjust the machines to accept crushed oyster shells, which contained a wealth of the required ingredient.[36] But innovations like this adaption to special circumstances could not correct all the basic flaws in the gas making system. Technical drawbacks not only depressed popular demand for the inferior illuminant, but also raised the price of service beyond the reach of the ordinary home consumer.

During the post-Appomattox decade, company officials seemed unable or unwilling to break out of a tightly confined market position. At seven and eight dollars per thousand cubic feet, all but a handful of Houstonians continued to rely on candles and kerosene for their artificial lighting needs. In any case, a total of only two to three miles of gas mains extended from the works into the central business district.[39] An unreasonable rate and a restricted distribution narrowed the use of gas to commercial establishments, theaters, hotels, and a few homes of the wealthy, besides the public street lamps that consumed about a third to a half of the firm's entire output. Undoubtedly, the poor performance of the plant made company investors reluctant to enlarge their financial commitments by laying expensive pipelines in the uncertain hope of enlisting more customers.

Traditional business attitudes also worked to forestall the expansion of services throughout the community. The price of service remained prohibitive for almost everyone until the HGLC adopted an aggressive policy to make gas widely available to householders later in the 1880s. The creation of a mass market offered the only way to counteract the effects of an inefficient technology and an expensive fuel supply. As with the street railway, the extraordinary fixed and operating costs of the gas company had to be spread out among a large number of consumers. Only then could the gas rate be cut to a level at which it could compete with lamp oils. Centuries of scarcity economics ill prepared contemporaries to deal with equations of mass marketing and consumption. In the postwar period, economists were just beginning to appreciate fully the inverse ratio between the price of public services and the number of customers that they attracted.[40]

Yet, perceptive persons could be found who understood these general principles, even in Houston. The tour companion of superintendent Russell was one of those individuals. After his inspection of the plant, he argued that the company needed to keep expanding in order to give Houston "a full supply of good gas in quantities sufficient to enable us to light the streets, extend the mains, and to use gas for household purposes, as is done in the North." In this analysis, Russell's guest describes a cumulative process in which consumption increases as economies of large-scale production allow reductions in the rate for home use. But the conservative attitudes of the utility owners prevented the inauguration of the new economics. "[W]e are satisfied," he concluded, "that unless liberal views of certain gentlemen are carried out, the Houston Gas Works will be declared a failure and a nuisance, and the citizens will find means of dispensing with its services. . . . In this company, as in many others, there are many men who desire to draw great dividends without the expenditure of a dollar."[41] Actually, the lighting firm represented an investment of between $50,000 and $100,000.[42] In the mid-

seventies, however, neither the stockholders nor the public received much benefit from this still premature enterprise. The confident expectation of the city
builders that public utilities would dramatically transform the urban environment
had fallen far short of its mark. Instead, the first decade of modern utilities had
served as an incubation period, a time of fumbling experiments and uncertain
strivings, that gave birth to viable, self-supporting corporations.

A fair assessment of the unfulfilled hopes of the planners requires a weighing
of prevailing business practices and attitudes against unprecedented technological and managerial challenges. On the one hand, investments in public utilities
by House and his fellow merchants had constituted a logical extension of their
primary activities in trade and transportation. Lighting and transit services along
the main corridors of commerce had enhanced the attractiveness of conducting
business in Houston. The utilities had helped give the town at least the appearance of a prosperous urban center.

On the other hand, unanticipated difficulties in several areas had frustrated
efforts to uplift Houston to a new level of urban modernity and comfort. Ten
years after the granting of gas and streetcar franchises, utility services had only
marginal effects on the daily lives of most citizens, whose perceptions of the environment had nonetheless been altered. The utilities had been provided for the
convenience of tourists and travellers, not the permanent resident. On balance,
the private ventures had laid a foundation that would sustain a more mature
growth in the quality and availability of utility services over the course of a second decade. But judgment of the accomplishments of the utility entrepreneur
should be reserved until compared with the results of analogous government
programs.

City Building: The Officeholders

From 1868 to 1874, basic deficiencies also undercut the efforts of local government to pull Houston up by its bootstraps to the prominence of a regional
center like New York or Chicago. Inexperience in management, defects in technology, and inadequacies in finance characterized the city building exertions of
public officials as well as private businessmen. The Goldwaithe plan provided an
outline of public policy goals, but officeholders had to fill in the details that
would spell the difference between success and failure. Following the taxpayers'
prescription for accelerating the town's growth, the Republicans strove to restore
the credit of the municipal corporation, raise the capital for a ship channel project, organize the improvement of the streets and bridges, and direct the construction of a market house. At first, the administration achieved striking results
in its vigorous pursuit of these objectives. After 1872, however, unforeseen flaws
caused a series of setbacks that, by 1875, multiplied into a profound civic crisis.

The wellspring of this community trauma stemmed from fundamental, but
hidden, weaknesses in the economic resources of the city government. In contrast to the utility companies, the municipal corporation depended on the collection of taxes to pay for its capital outlays and current expenses. In August 1868,

the taxpaying elite accordingly assigned top priority to devising a method to ensure that more revenue flowed steadily into the public treasury. By eliminating the scrip evil, they argued, a 1 to 2 percent levy on property values would generate an ample and reliable source of income. This proposition initially worked well enough to establish a solid credit rating for the city. However, the plan rested entirely on the shaky premise of the citizens' voluntary compliance with city hall. The need to install administrative machinery to enforce the collection of tax bills remained unrecognized until the depression of the mid-1870s. Then it was too late; the fiscal structure of the government tottered and collapsed under the economic hardships and partisan pressures that snapped the bonds of community consensus.

The initial confidence of outside capitalists in Houston also tended to blind officials from seeing the weak links in the city's fiscal apparatus. The failure to raise funds locally for ship channel improvements had driven the commercial-civic elite to conduct a municipal housecleaning in the first place. A deep water canal would supersede cargo transfers at sea and thus permit shippers to bypass Galveston and its odious Wharf Company. Under the arrangement worked out in June 1868, the city would act as the underwriter of an essentially private venture to be called the Houston Ship Channel Company (HSCC). Two months after its incorporation in January 1869, the firm exchanged $100,000 worth of its bonds for an equal amount of municipal bonds, which promptly sold in New York money markets. The agents of the HSCC negotiated the loan on favorable terms, because a second $100,000 exchange and sale followed a year later.[43]

Houston's financing scheme highlights the key role of municipal bonds in the city building process during the second half of the nineteenth century. The leap in local indebtedness from $200 million in 1860 to $820 million in 1880 is testimony to the cities' widespread resort to government securities to cover the cost of developing transportation improvements, utility systems, and other public works. Urban communities everywhere turned to municipal bonds in a calculated move to cut the high price of borrowing investment capital. As a result of landmark decisions by the U.S. Supreme Court, the promissory notes of local governments throughout the country became preferred over the analogous securities of private companies. In the 1860s, a series of strident, moralistic rulings made it perfectly clear that the national judiciary would wield the full extent of its power to force recalcitrant cities to pay their debts. In spite of evasive tactics and even outright repudiations, the high bench left local governments and their taxpayers no room for escape from eventually fulfilling their contractual duties.[44] In contrast, the law limited the obligations of business corporations and their stockholders to redeem their bonded indebtedness. After the bankruptcy courts liquidated a firm's assets, the liability to the creditors ended.[45]

With the Supreme Court acting as a nationwide collection agency, municipal bonds became relatively more secure "securities" than those of private enterprise. Market forces translated these differences in law into economic terms. As investment banker and lawyer J. A. Burhans noted from the perspective of the late eighties, "It is especially to the Supreme Court of the United States that is due the present importance, stability, and value of the municipal bond as an investment security."[46] As early as the 1860's, however, policy makers in Houston and other cities recognized that public financing could significantly reduce development costs. Three variables measured the degree of risk investors attached to a bond issue: the interest rate, the length of time until the principal fell due, and the sale price. For example, City of Houston Ship Channel Bonds promised to pay 8 percent annual interest for twenty-five years and sold originally for about 80 to 85 percent of face value. This meant that when the bonds matured in 1894, the city would have paid out $200,000 in interest plus $100,000 more to return the principal. This amount seemed a reasonable price to pay in exchange for the financial resources to keep the town commercially competitive with its island rival.

In 1869 and 1870, the smooth progress of the ship channel scheme encouraged the Republicans to pursue the other two prime goals, paved streets and a market house, along similar lines. But before the next steps could be taken, a complete changeover of the council occurred. In August 1870, the recently elected governor, E. J. Davis, elevated Timothy Scanlan to the mayor's chair and appointed fellow "Radicals," including four blacks, to fill the ten aldermanic seats. Although the integration of city government in Houston marked a sharp departure from the past, the new administration adhered closely to the taxpayers' plan.[47]

In large part, the commanding force of Scanlan's personality maintained continuity in public policy. He clearly dominated the council until it was again replaced by state officials three-and-a-half years later. The neophyte mayor was an upstart compared with his predecessors. The immigrant Scanlan had arrived in 1855, after the first wave of businessmen had established themselves. Nevertheless, the twenty-year-old Irishman had gotten into the lucrative cotton smuggling trade during the war, emerging as an independent merchant after the conflict. Heading the council's pivotal committee on finance since August 1868, Scanlan had received valuable training in running city hall by the time he took the reins of power.[48]

Equally important, perhaps, was the education in city building that Scanlan gained while conducting a wide ranging tour of urban America. For two months during the summer of 1871, the chief executive visited metropolitan centers from New Orleans to New York. Shortly after his return in September, the mayor submitted a highly revealing report, an analysis of the mechanics of urban growth and progress. For instance, the mayor tested the financial strategy hammered out at the gathering of the taxpayers by surveying Houston's credit position on Wall Street. He found that the town's unblemished record of meeting the semi-annual interest payments was indeed making a favorable impression on the bond dealers. They viewed Houston as a solid credit risk, especially since the town stood at the gateway to a region that was undergoing tremendous immigration and expansion. Speculative fever ran so high, Scanlan told his local audience, that "some New York capitalists have Texas 'on the brain.'"[49]

However confident the mayor may have felt about the city's standing in the money markets, his report counseled a cautious approach to turn Houston into the "Chicago of the South." His inspection tour of public works in several places left him with an overriding sense of the need for moderation. "My observations," the mayor stated, "have shown me that solid and substantial improvements, in which permanence and utility have been sought, rather than expensive and often decaying ornamentation, are the characteristics of the progressive cities of the United States." [50] Scanlan's conclusions provide a useful yardstick for measuring the performance of his administration. Moreover, they express some of the strands of thought that would gradually come together to form what historian Paul Gaston calls the "New South Creed." His rejection of fashionable style for functional efficiency was becoming common currency among New South spokesmen. They too strove to lift their region out of the past to reach a level of urban prosperity and modernity comparable with that of the North. [51]

The mayor's report offers not only a philosophy of city building but also a handbook, rich in detail, on environmental engineering. Scanlan's findings include an intelligent discussion of the merits and drawbacks of different kinds of street pavement, for example. He believed that stone blocks were the best materials for durability and strength. Stone pavement, however, was very expensive as opposed to alternatives that Houstonians could better afford. The mayor declared wooden roads useless and expressed a decided preference for asphalt, a "first class pavement." [52] Scanlan's practical approach to street construction was typical of his attempt to achieve a balanced ideal between costs and benefits, as well as between moderation and uplift.

Guided by these perspectives, the Republicans issued $300,000 in municipal bonds over the next two years to pay for street, sidewalk, and bridge improvements (see Table 2.2). Working through private contractors, the city supervised the grading and paving of the central business district, which encompassed about a fifty-block area in the mid-1870s. [53] The administration continued the practice of using shells, the least expensive material available, for street paving. However, more permanent sidewalks made out of asphalt, brick, and stone graced the fronts of prosperous commercial establishments. Throughout the rest of the downtown, low cost plank sidewalks became so popular that residential "suburbs" nearby began laying connecting strips of their own. In addition, four bridges gave areas surrounding the business district to the north and east easy access to the center of town. [54]

A stubborn environment, however, proved more than a match for the combined expertise of the mayor, a full-time Street Commissioner, and the contractors. Situated only forty feet above sea level, Houston literally floats on a sandy crust of constantly shifting soils. Even today, any pedestrian in the city immediately notices the deformed and twisted state of many of its thoroughfares. A semi-tropical climate also worked ceaselessly on them, turning avenues of convenient movement into impassable hazards to health and safety. These conditions created one of the imperative reasons for installing a network of street lights.

TABLE 2.2   Houston Bond Issues, 1866–1874

Date	Name of Issue	Amount ($)	Interest Rate (%)	Tenure (Years)
Feb. 14, 1867	J. A. Stevens [Tap Railroad]	44,000	8	25
Mar. 28, 1867	J. H. Bower [Tap Railroad]	10,000	8	10
Jan. 28, 1869	M. Reichmann	1,000	8	10
Mar. 25, 1869	Ship channel—first series	130,000	8	25
Apr. 22, 1869	Houston Tap & Brazoria Railroad Company	30,000	8	25
Mar. 3, 1870	Ship channel—new series	100,000	8	25
May 20, 1871	Market House	100,000	8	30
June 5, 1871	Road and improvement	100,000	10	30
Nov. 7, 1871	Market House	150,000	8	30
Jan. 27, 1872	Road and improvement	200,000	10	30
May 24, 1873	Matured indebtedness—second series	100,000	10	30
Aug. 16, 1873	Road and improvement—second series	150,000	10	30
Jan. 17, 1874	Funding	75,000	10	25
July 25, 1874	Funding	100,000	8	25
Oct. 10, 1874	Western Narrow Gauge Railroad	100,000	7	30

SOURCE: Council Minutes, Books: B–G (1867–1875).

"People living off Main Street," the *Houston Daily Union* observed after a long blackout in 1870–71, "can now venture out at night without fear of breaking their necks or some other portion of the body, in going over some of the dreadful street crossings."[55]

In large part, the answer to Houston's intractable environment rested upon devising a comprehensive system of drains and sewers. Without it, street improvements actually exacerbated the problem. In May 1868, for example, the newspaper had been quick to praise the horsecar venture for grading Main Street from curb to curb. But the first torrential storm replaced the street's "metropolitan appearance" with sights of little boys floating down it on jerry-built rafts.[56] The levelled surface soon filled with rainwater because it lacked runoff drainage.

In the seventies, the erosive effects of the elements on public improvements posed an insoluble dilemma for the city builders. Although they fully appreciated the importance of the problem, limitations of money and expertise hamstrung efforts to overcome it. Mayor Scanlan understood that good drainage was a prerequisite to street paving with hard surfaces such as asphalt or stone. A system of drains and sanitary sewers, his report asserted, was the "true mark of the 'live' towns" he visited. However, cost factors kept Houston's progress along these lines restricted to a few pilot projects. The city spent at least $100,000 just to protect the market house square from storm damage and to supply the building with sewers.[57] Elsewhere, the administration took a more expedient course, which applied primitive methods to minimize capital outlays.

The story of the Preston Street bridge reveals the low level of technical skills that typically were brought to bear against the town's semi-tropical surroundings. Opened in 1869, this public works project spanned from the downtown section to the upper rim of the city and its major highway to the north. Following the instructions of the bridge's East Coast architects, local contractors constructed the iron structure on solid concrete piers that were sunk deep into each bank of the bayou. Houston's civil engineers, however, failed to take sufficient account of the fluid characteristics of the environment. The sides of the bayous were especially plastic, since the waterways served as nature's drainage system. Runoffs of rain-water ate away at the embankments, leaving the span standing higher and higher above its access roads. The steady decay of the ground around the bridge forced its closing only three years after it had been erected. City authorities restored the approaches to the span in about a year. The new causeways suffered from the same defects in design and became noticeable almost immediately.[58]

The battle to retard the constant deterioration of Houston's public works loomed as a prominent feature of government administration in the 1870s. Unable to afford the best available talents and materials, municipal officials were left to solve perplexing technical riddles on their own. Under these circumstances, Scanlan diverged from his practical guidelines in order to get the job done, more or less. Shelled pavements, plank sidewalks, and similar projects of relatively small initial expense undoubtedly enhanced the movement of people and goods within town borders. But "bargain basement" approaches to city building entailed special costs. For example, these approaches demanded that city hall maintain a battalion of workers to hold back the forces of erosion. As long as city managers kept paying the repair crews, the town's precarious facade of modernity would remain intact. However, even a temporary breakdown of the city's money machine would soon turn the whole public works program into a rear guard action against the forces of decay. The abandonment of the mayor's insights into environmental engineering meant that pressures mounted steadily on a public treasury that was already straining under a growing weight of bonded indebtedness.

The swelling burden of fixed and current obligations was increased still further by the huge price tag of the Market House. The fulfillment of this final part of the taxpayers' plan proved the one grand exception to the bargain budget policies of the administration. The Market House became much more than a functional emporium; it gradually assumed the proportions of a civic monument to the community's faith in Houston's coming greatness. At first, Scanlan's cautious posture towards public improvements prevailed. During his inspection tour in 1871, the mayor rejected several bids in the $240,000–300,000 range by Eastern iron works as an extravagance that the city could ill afford. He argued in favor of a cheaper building that could be made out of bricks produced by industries at home. Scanlan pointed out that his proposal would not only save money but keep tax dollars circulating within the local economy. Yet by 1875, he would authorize the expenditure of a minimum of $300,000, and perhaps as much as $450,000, to complete the structure.[59]

The Republicans created a truly magnificent edifice that epitomized Houstonians' belief in progress. The three-story building occupied the middle of a full city block that was landscaped into a well-manicured park. In addition to facili-

ties for a meat and produce market on the ground floor, the facility contained
ample room for a city hall and extra space for retail shops and professional offices. Although adorned by twin bell towers, the real centerpiece of the Market
House was its beautiful theater. With a seventy-foot lobby in front, the gargan-
tuan auditorium held a thousand seats. In May 1874, the grand opening of this
culture palace provoked a giddy sense of success and uplift even from the Galveston newsman who covered the event. Houstonians, he reported, "have serious doubts whether the Grand Opera House of Paris is not a little mean one-horse
affair besides the grandeur of the Market House which the theater surmounts.
Well, the truth is, I do not blame them a bit for being proud, as the theater is a
good one, creditable to its builders and an honor to the city." [60]

The ornate structure was exceptional not only in its expensive design and
pleasing results, but in its utility to the entire community. In effect, the building
combined early versions of today's civic centers and shopping malls under one
roof. By serving several purposes, it functioned as a meeting place for a wide
range of social, economic, cultural, and political activities. Even if the project
cost twice as much as its anticipated price, nobody, including the Democrats,
seemed to mind. In 1875, the Redeemers did not hesitate to pay out $30,000 to
cover some final bills from the prime contractor, William Brady.[61] For all Houstonians, the Market House symbolized the postwar goal of reaching metropolitan
stature and renown.

Although the Scanlan administration deserved praise for the community center, dubious achievements in the areas of municipal finance and environmental
engineering increasingly overshadowed the officeholders' unique accomplishment. The Republicans had faithfully pursued the Goldwaithe strategy for urban
growth. They had applied large infusions of outside capital to programs that had
enhanced Houston's transportation facilities and commercial attractiveness.
However, the amateur city builders had not discovered the underlying flaws in
either the concept or the execution of the plan. By the time the theater opened,
the city had accumulated a million dollar debt, which was generating approximately $90,000 annually in interest claims. Moreover, the government's com-
mitment to maintain such services as street repair and police protection had
grown proportionally in the budget to about $60,000 annually.[62] At the same
time, tax receipts had remained virtually unchanged from their $100,000–
120,000 level of the late sixties. By mid-1873, the fate of both the Republican
party and the municipal corporation hinged precariously on an overloaded public
treasury.

The impending crisis in Houston government stayed hidden from the view of
town leaders until it was far too late to take corrective actions. In 1868, the taxpayers' agreement on the means and ends of public policy had encouraged the
Republicans to rush headlong into the task of transforming a frontier landscape
into an urban condition. Glued to a vision of expansive uplift, the Scanlan administration never wavered from the Goldwaithe formula, in spite of an accumula-

tion of setbacks from inadequate finances, makeshift methods, and shoddy results. After 1872, the opposition grew apprehensive about the city's declining credit position but they too seemed mesmerized by the use of the municipal government as a promotional instrument of economic development. The Democrats expected to find a plundered treasury when they re-entered city hall in January 1874. Yet they did not seriously question the master plan for another nine months. The realization that the city was hopelessly in debt finally struck them like a hammer blow.

The amazing consistency among public policy makers during the postwar decade stems from their single-minded pursuit of growth as the cardinal goal of urban planning. The swelling size of the city debt little worried town leaders because they saw it as the pump-primer that would soon set a process of self-sustained expansion into motion. In the meantime, their dream of Houston as the Chicago of the South was grand enough to inspire them to plunge ahead while disregarding any number of signs to the contrary. Not that Houston's civic elite were visionaries; rather, they seem to have been caught up in the infectious spirit of progress that gripped the nation's cities after the Civil War.

The new dimensions of public policy that were wrought in Houston were not unique. In fact, the fateful decision to finance growth with municipal bonds gives a good indication of the increasing extent to which Houston was being drawn into larger webs of interdependence. By the mid-1870s, the Gulf Coast port had been securely linked with national networks of commerce, finance, transportation, and party politics. Decision makers did not so much create an original blueprint of city planning as adapt current trends to local conditions. Analyzing the reasons for the remarkably fast 300-percent jump in the size of the country's municipal indebtedness, one perceptive commentator argued that "each [city was] in a sort of rivalry or race with all its neighbors for outward Renown." This competition, he continued, spurred the attempt "to outfit every large town or city, within a period of a single generation, with all the conveniences and comforts and luxuries that elsewhere have required centuries to accumulate." [63] It is not surprising therefore that Houston's chief promoters of urban development—its railroad managers and lawyers and its merchant princes—were correspondingly those men who had most fully tapped into outside channels of communication. Their ambitious schemes for Houston's coming greatness neatly fit into the emerging aspirations of the region for the rise of a New South.

But the practical problems of actually erecting a modern city dragged heavily against these hopes. As economic life revived after the Civil War, the continuing success of Houston's entrepreneurs in directing the flow of trade and immigration through the town created additional needs to facilitate movement within it. Despite concerted effort, the task of superimposing a man-made environment over the natural one frustrated and baffled them. Experienced businessmen were neophytes in the difficult art of city building. Their smallest advances occurred in the areas where precise, technical solutions were demanded. City efforts to overcome the erosive effects of a semi-tropical climate were especially crude and shortsighted. The exertions of the gas company to operate a complex technology produced analogous results.

Driven to get the job done now, but lacking trained engineers and sufficient resources, Houstonians resorted to trial and error. For the most part, these home-spun experiments proved costly lessons in what not to do. Perhaps little more could be expected in any provincial town in an era when the rule of thumb still prevailed. The basic similarity in the fumbling techniques that were employed by city officials and utility managers alike suggests just such a conclusion. In any case, their first ventures in upgrading the environment and providing urban services laid a groundwork upon which more substantial achievements could be built in the future.

3 "The Very Life and Existence of the City," 1874–1880

On March 18, 1873, two crews of railroad workers met near the border of Texas and Oklahoma to perform an historic mission that, paradoxically, was fast becoming commonplace in the United States. As construction teams joined converging sections of track, they opened a new era of direct rail service between Houston and the North. Similar projects designed to connect the town to other major transportation networks culminated seven years later with the long awaited completion of a route through the swamplands of Louisiana to New Orleans.[1]

Houston's linkage into the continental system of transportation epitomized the general process of integration that was knitting America's "island communities" in tightening webs of interdependence. In the second half of the nineteenth century, urbanization occurred to an increasing extent within a national context. Rapid demographic growth and geographic sprawl posed a number of common challenges to the country's urban centers.[2] Yet each community had to adapt uniform solutions to the problems of city building to fit its own particular setting. The evolution of each locality remained inherently unique; Houston was no exception.

The period from 1873 to 1880 marked a crucial turning point in this city's history. National influences began redirecting Houston's course in such areas as race relations, social organization, government finance, and the delivery of urban services by private enterprise. Radical shifts in the direction of public policy created an era of crisis and conflict. Out of this turmoil, a new self-image of the community emerged—an abstract conception of the public welfare. At the same time, agents of modernization were absorbing Houston into the mainstream of national development.

A large measure of autonomy as well as isolation had characterized Houston's relationship to the outside world before the depression of the 1870s. Amateur city builders had helped speed up the growth of the rail hub soon after the end of the war. The influx of settlers had sustained belief in the Goldwaithe plan, because the immigrants had nearly doubled the population to 9,400 persons in the 1860s and added another 7,000 permanent residents over the next ten years.[3] Yet after years of concerted effort, the transformation of Houston from town to city remained problematical. Houstonians had made only tentative steps toward the creation of a modern city in such diverse areas as environmental engineering, public utilities, municipal reform, and political organization. While the Texans had been relatively free from outside restraints, they also had been cut off from whatever practical advice more experienced experts could offer. At most, a pervasive spirit of progress, reinforced by easy money on Wall Street, had encouraged local leaders to pursue ambitious plans for the promotion of Houston's growth.

After the Panic of 1873, on the other hand, powerful external forces shaped the course of Houston's transition from a frontier town to a modern city. Outside influences created intense pressures within the community that sharply accelerated this transformation: first, the federal imposition of Reconstruction politics; and second, the economic downturn, which pushed the municipal government into virtual bankruptcy. When the incessant demands of the city's creditors shattered the town's solid reputation for upholding the public trust, many traditional bonds of civic cohesion were smashed. They had already been weakened by the growth of interparty competition, but now conflicts of interest inside the town became endemic.

During the contending parties' ensuing struggles, which often took place in the courts, Houstonians made clear separations between the public and private sectors for the first time. While prosperity lasted, there had been little incentive to question the wisdom of the growth strategy implemented by the commercial-civic elite. However, once the fiscal plight of the city forced local leaders to distinguish the collective needs of the townspeople from the particular claims of the bondholders and the taxpayers, new concepts of the city and the public welfare soon followed. These fresh perspectives signalled not only the final passing of Houston's frontier community, but also its replacement by a far more complex matrix—an urban society.

A second set of extralocal forces attracted Houston into the spreading webs of interdependence. During this period of rapid urbanization, the breakdown of the cities' money machines and their public services became commonplace. Municipal bankruptcies like Houston's, for example, were so widespread that they collectively represented the first truly national urban crisis in American history.[4] In the 1870s, the judiciary took the lead in coping with the bewildering dilemmas of public finance by limiting the number of policy alternatives to a fixed mechanical formula. Utility company managers also took steps to discover uniform solutions to the cities' crying needs for better public services. Beginning in 1873, utility executives formed national trade associations that significantly accelerated the diffusion of managerial expertise and technological innovations across the urban landscape. By the end of the decade, standardized systems of water supply, communications, and lighting were being installed in cities of every description.

Taken together, the forces of centralization created a potent configuration, or field of influence, that gave shape and direction to Houston's metamorphosis from town to city. In 1880, the inaugural group of rail passengers from New Orleans would disembark to find few visible signs of recent progress in the Texas city. Hard times had stunted its physical and demographic expansions; city building seemed to have been suspended long ago. But underneath these surface appearances, Houston had become a fundamentally different place. When the economy revived strongly a few years later, Houstonians would turn once again to take up the burdens of constructing a modern city. Now, however, they would be armed with vastly improved tools and, equally important, an abstract image of themselves as an urban society.

Federal Connections

Before the Panic of 1873, continuities with the past had been the primary sources of reference in the formulation of Houston's public policies and social attitudes. Extralocal forces had influenced the development of the coastal entrepôt more as harbingers than as spearheads of reform. Of course, in some respects, the postwar years had been transitional, constituting a period of change characterized by tentative starts towards the creation of an urban environment and polity. More remarkable, however, had been the resilience of older modes of thought and action. The Redeemers could even roll back most of the advances made by the deliberate and forceful interventions of the national government, whose forward thrusts in practical democracy, political organization, and race relations were no match for the deep-seated prejudices and fears of the Southern community.

Reconstruction politics deflected the town's course only tangentially. From 1866 to 1872, the downward flow of political issues, leadership, and authority from Washington and Austin gave the original impetus to organize the townsmen into the two major parties. Once realignment began, political rivalry took on a life independent from national and state organizations. In the municipal elections of the early seventies, an indigenous urban politics that reflected the electorate's racial, ethnic, and class composition gradually appeared.

Although a dual party system of urban democracy lasted only briefly in the period between 1872 and 1875, the intrusion of outside forces caused permanent, if unfinished, changes in Houston's political and social contours. The expression of self-conscious group identities may have been suppressed politically for a decade, but it endured in other organizational forms such as religious congregations, social clubs, and benevolent associations. For the ex-slave especially, the era of Reconstruction provided a badly needed respite from the crushing burdens of repression. The crucial value of black voters to the Republican party gave these Houstonians a "breathing space" in which indigenous leaders and group solidarity were nurtured. New structures of internal cohesion took shape that could extend private aid to supplement a meager share of the city's public services.[5]

The Republican party also carried a number of its white leaders into the top echelons of the commercial-civic elite. Despite the coining of local myths about mismanagement and waste by the Radicals, individuals were not personally branded with corruption or scandal. To the contrary, Mayor Timothy Scanlan and several of his lieutenants gained acceptance in the inner business and social circles of the established families.[6] Yet the flowering of a truly urban polity awaited the late 1880s, because the inertia of tradition and localism still outweighed the accumulating forces of change.

In contrast, the hammerblows of the depression tipped the scales towards a preponderance of outside agents of innovation and reform in the city building process. After 1873, the Houstonians' responses to the urbanization of their community cannot be understood outside of the broader contexts of regional and national interdependence. Local institutions, previously integrated into larger networks of finance and transportation, became the conduits for the heavy shocks of economic collapse that began buffeting the provincial trading center in the winter of 1873–1874. Already in the midst of political upheaval, the hard-pressed taxpayers revolted in mass. Public officials struggled futilely to uphold the city's honor and credit with the bondholders. The resulting municipal insolvency acted as a catalyst, precipitating an acute civic crisis that shattered belief in the Goldwaithe plan of urban growth.

Virtual bankruptcy forced town fathers to embark on a search for a wholly different approach to the fiscal dilemmas of their suddenly beleaguered city. Discovering answers to Houston's problems was difficult because they were not amenable to internal solutions. Breaking with the past, Mayor James T. D. Wilson, a banker, led the ruling elite in discarding outdated concepts and in grasping for new directions in public policy. Wilson's conceptual breakthroughs represented essential prerequisites to the formulation of managerial and structural alternatives that could cope with a perplexing set of new social and economic conditions. But the translation of the mayor's new perspectives into a concrete course of action, which would return the city to the path of progress, remained elusive.

At first, the profound implications of these reorientations in the urban political economy overwhelmed most members of the commercial-civic elite. The Texans' confused responses characterized the uncertain reactions of Americans everywhere to the wrenching dislocations that followed the seven-year slump in the business cycle. The urban-industrial revolution fostered new perceptions of self-awareness and self-interest among formerly cooperative segments of the society.[7] Whether Grangers and railroad companies in Illinois, taxpayers and municipal bondholders in Texas, or butchers and slaughterhouse monopolists in Louisiana, more and more self-conscious groups were colliding in bitter struggle. In the 1870s, as one scholar contends, "the simultaneous emergence of regulation, repudiation, and revulsion against corporate privileges threatened a multitude of vested interests on an unprecedented scale."[8] Many of these clashes occurred because of large grey areas in the political economy where the perimeters of the public welfare and the private sector had long overlapped without apparent conflict. During the Gilded Age, conflicts between nascent organized groups similar to those forming in Houston occasionally erupted in violence. More frequently, competing groups turned to the courts for peaceful settlement of their disputes.

"To the degree [that] a general government policy existed in the years following reconstruction," Robert Wiebe notes, "the Federal courts . . . usually supplied it."[9] Inherently, the judiciary is the most passive branch of government. It cannot initiate reform; it can only respond to the controversial issues that others

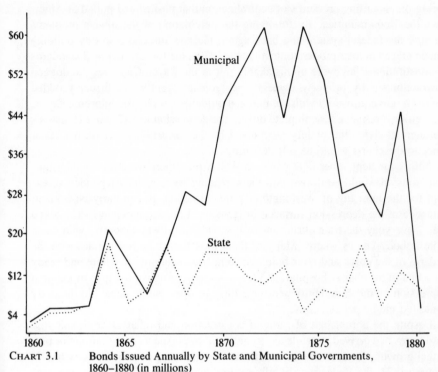

CHART 3.1   Bonds Issued Annually by State and Municipal Governments,
1860–1880 (in millions)
Source: A.M. Hillhouse, *Municipal Bonds* (New York: Prentice-Hall, 1936)

bring before the bench. But compared to the chronic political stalemate in the national executive and legislative branches during the late seventies and the eighties, the Supreme Court provided vigorous leadership in the "search for order."

This conclusion has special relevance for the cities. In the 1870s, municipal bond cases, more than any other item of court business, filled federal dockets. More than one fifth or $100,000,000 worth of these securities fell into default (see Chart 3.1).[10] The Supreme Court's determined interventions in this area of urban policy making cast the bench and bar into the role of municipal reformers. Under the direction of the high court, the legal profession was given broad jurisdictional authority to settle the perplexing controversies that arose among the major groups involved in the city building process. Through the federal system of courts, the legal reformers brought a new degree of uniformity to the direction of municipal reform.

Research on the changing course of jurisprudence in the Supreme Court is well underway, but the local origins and impacts of these structural reforms have received little attention. Houston's travail furnishes a reliable test case for measuring the mounting pressures of centralization that pushed and pulled at America's local communities. By following the percolation of the town's problems through the federal system and back again, the new directions in city building can be placed in their proper context. In the 1870s, the force of national standards of constitutional law were unmistakably felt in the Bayou City. Despite dogged obstructionism by property owners, the judiciary gently but firmly prodded the town into conformity with the national guidelines set by the Supreme Court. This process remained incomplete during the depression of 1873, but Houston's commercial-civic elite plainly recognized by the early 1880s that further resistance to the courts would be self-defeating.

Before the September 1873 panic on Wall Street, there were few visible signs that Houston would be drawn into the spreading webs of interdependence, except for the faint tug of Washington's political bonds. But in early November, evidence of the depression surfaced in Houston. Local commentators remarked that, "everyday the trains bring in fresh squads of railway laborers, who came from nobody knows where. Many of them look the worse for contact with the malaria of the creek and river bottoms; some are apparently destitute and ready for a bed in the charity hospital." [11] Within weeks, the tightening grip of national depression on the community became a topic of open public debate in the hotly contested municipal elections.

Despite the abrupt halt of railroad construction and other clear signals that hard times had arrived, town leaders continued to pursue a fading mirage of perpetual growth. For at least nine months after regaining possession of city hall in January 1874, the Redeemers blindly refused to accept the fact that the city was hopelessly in debt. They quickly took steps to make a full accounting of the municipal treasury, which they expected to find drained empty by the Republicans. And yet, belief in the Goldwaithe plan was persistent; the incoming councilmen clung tenaciously to its formula for urban progress. In a special appeal to the taxpayers, just after assuming office, the Redeemers declared, "that the fair name and good faith and credit of the city of Houston in regard to the just and legitimate liabilities of said city are of paramount importance and must be preserved; and that it is the determination of this council to adhere to a prudent and economic management of the affairs of the city." At the same time, the officials "kindly but urgently" requested immediate payment of overdue tax bills so that improvement projects would not have to be interrupted. [12]

At first, older modes of thought obscured awareness of the city's grave fiscal situation. The size of the debt, $1.4 million, was finally disclosed in the week following the mid-March 1874 elections. [13] But the Wilson administration was not deterred from the path of their Republican predecessors. Only a month later, for example, the council passed an ordinance exempting manufacturing concerns from city taxes for two years. In August, a proposal to loan $100,000 in municipal bonds to a new railroad scheme also received favorable treatment from the aldermen. [14] These dysfunctional responses compounded the basic problems of inadequate public revenues and overwhelming financial burdens. Houstonians had great difficulty in inaugurating a reassessment of their growth-oriented strategy. Before the council could take action on the Western Narrow Gage Railroad subsidy, however, the plain facts of the town's virtual bankruptcy suddenly dawned on Mayor Wilson.

The mayor led the council into a dead end before the inherent defects of the perpetual growth plan struck him as a revelation. Shortly after meeting the semiannual payment of $50,000 in interest due on the bonded debt, the banker Wilson realized that this sacrosanct practice was self-defeating. Since volunteristic appeals to the taxpayers had fallen on deaf ears, every effort of the administration had failed to raise enough funds to fill the bond account. Even severe cutbacks in public services, which were now paid for in scrip, left a $30,000 cash deficit on the eve of the July deadline. Closely identifying his honor with that of Houston's, Wilson was forced to reach into his own pockets to satisfy the demands of the creditors. Although the mayor successfully saved the reputation of the community for the moment, he boldly called for a complete reevaluation of the city government's priorities.[15]

Once the mental barriers of the past were breached, new ideas flooded readily into Wilson's mind. In a dramatic speech to the council on September 12, 1874, the mayor argued that the city must scrap the Goldwaithe plan. "I felt in common with you all [the councilmen], a personal pride in our city and its credit," he recounted, "and I was possessed with the desire to do everything possible to preserve its good faith and credit." By July, however, it was "painfully evident" that this policy was a bad mistake because the municipal debt was accumulating interest faster than the city could collect taxes.[16]

Simple calculations showed that the expected annual revenues of about $90,000–$100,000 were only half the amount required to pay the bondholders, while still maintaining a bare minimum of essential services. Additional issues of either scrip in the local economy or bonds in distant markets, Wilson asserted, could only exacerbate an already desperate situation. An accurate diagnosis of Houston's financial condition was a breakthrough in itself; the conclusions drawn by Wilson from this assessment revealed an extraordinary insight into the general urban crisis of the 1870s.

The importance of the policy alternatives outlined by Wilson in his analysis of the fiscal plight of the local government cannot be overestimated. These alternatives mark a key turning point in the history of the Texas community that ranks on par with the formulation of the taxpayers' original plan for city building. For the remainder of the decade, Wilson's proposals became the central issues around which all other political questions revolved. Rejecting the resource allocation choices of the past, the mayor gave top priority to such day-to-day service functions as police and fire protection, street lighting and repair, and public health and sanitation. Initially, only a few fellow members of the commercial-civic elite shared Wilson's views. However, the national courts exerted pressure that mounted and eventually pushed Houston's leadership into finding the ways and means to implement the mayor's proposals.

Wilson envisioned a world of conflict in which, for the first time, distinct battle lines between the public welfare and private interests were drawn in the urban community. He recognized that the current policy of contracting new debts to pay the accrued interest of the old was "fraught with disaster to every best interest of our people." Instead, highest priority should be given to the maintenance of vital urban functions. Wilson stated that these

> constitute the machinery of city government, organized for the purpose of preserving the good order of society, the safety of the lives and property of the people, the general sanitary condition and welfare of all, in fact the very life and existence of the city, which must be preserved at all hazards, and rightfully and properly deserve the first consideration at our hands as essential to self-preservation.[17]

By identifying interests of the general welfare as separate from those of the city's property owners and creditors, Wilson opened up a whole new range of policy options. Reversing his earlier course, the mayor proposed that the bondholders take second place in the allocation of public revenues, subordinate to the immediate needs of the community for government services. Moreover, he no longer equated the legitimate purposes of the municipal corporation with the enhancement of the taxpayers' estates. On the contrary, a much broadened concept of the common good allowed Wilson to demand that property owners contribute to the support of essential public services in spite of personal sacrifice. Since property owners were already straining under current tax loads, according to the mayor, the council should direct its attention to extracting a compromise from the city's creditors. They could expect to receive little payment in the future unless they agreed to consolidate the bonded debt at a much lower rate of interest. The city executive admitted that revealing Houston's fiscal embarrassment might tarnish its reputation, but that the survival of the community must take precedence.[18]

The reaction to the mayor's path-breaking proposals was a mixture of disbelief and reproach. While a journalist applauded "the moral courage of the mayor in being mentally strong enough to tell the truth," most regretted that he had done so.[19] The council's finance committee took the lead in denouncing the publicity given to the debt problem. A week after Wilson's address, its reply discounted the gravity of the situation. The aldermen retorted that prospects looked promising in the near future for a renewal of rising land values. Sticking closely to the Goldwaithe formula, the committee called for a funding of the floating debt and the enactment of charter amendments to augment tax collections. The committee specifically recommended that a Board of Appraisers be created to help increase the tax base from the present $6 million assessment to a full market value of $10 million. Other structural changes would shift the burden of paving expenses onto adjoining property owners, besides adding a vehicle tax to defray street repair costs. In any event, the committee optimistically projected that a $30,000 surplus would remain after paying the January 1875 interest on the debt (see Table 3.1).[20]

TABLE 3.1   Mayor Wilson and the Council Budget Plans for 1875

	Mayor Wilson's Budget		The Council's Budget	
	Liabilities		Liabilities	
Bond interest	103,600*		51,800†	
Floating debts	64,000		64,000	
Scrip	23,400		23,400	
City expenses	84,000		28,000	
Total liabilities		$275,000		$167,200
	Assets		Assets	
Ad valorem tax	44,000		64,700	
License tax	19,800		21,600	
Market fees	13,200		6,000	
Back taxes	33,000		96,500	
Sidewalk tax	0		12,000	
Total revenues		$110,000		$200,800
Final balance		−$165,000		$ 33,600

SOURCE: Council Minutes, Book C:405–07, 419–20.
*Calculated on a one year basis.
†Calculated on a one-half year basis.

The stark contrast between the two reports stemmed from different perspectives on Houston's relationship to the larger economies of the region and nation. On the one hand, the councilmen saw the historic development and the current well-being of their town as independent of outside forces. Created by the absence of strong ties of economic interdependence before the war, an illusion of local autonomy was reinforced afterwards by the seeming success of policies to upgrade the commercial center to urban standards. From this point of view, the urban planning of the taxpayers still retained all of its original efficacy. On the other hand, Wilson connected the city's virtual bankruptcy directly to the nationwide depression. The economic slowdown would in the short run stunt the growth of the municipal tax base, and strenuous administrative efforts to collect the $100,000 in delinquent taxes would be unsuccessful. From the mayor's standpoint, a chronic shortage of tax resources made a basic shift of public priorities a necessity. In retrospect, Wilson proved to be the better prognosticator; business on the Gulf Coast and elsewhere did not revive for another six years.

Yet a majority of the chief executive's contemporaries joined the council in rejecting his analysis of Houston's fiscal dilemma. Ironically, the voters were approving a special referendum on the railroad bonds at the same time that the mayor was delivering his far-sighted speech. Although it came too late to influence this poll, the citizens registered an 11–1 preference for the subsidy in a second vote at the end of October.[21] In December, ominous signs for Wilson appeared when a "considerable party" bolted from the regular organization of Democrats. Irwin C. Lord, one of the Redeemers and the owner of the Eagle Iron Works, headed the ticket of independents. On election day in early January 1875, Lord's slate of candidates emerged victorious; Wilson and his platform had been repudiated by the community.[22] To an extent, the mayor's personality lost him the election because he was "not accounted a personally popular man, he being a rather retired and distant sort of disposition."[23] For the most part, though, Houstonians lagged behind Wilson in accepting the city's interdependent relationship with the national economy. He had failed to persuade them that he had a better policy alternative than the opposition.

While Houstonians removed Wilson without great trouble, the problems that he had identified were not so easily dismissed. Little by little, the new administration found that the counterproposals of the finance committee could not lift the town out of its deep depression. An ad hoc group formed to revise the municipal charter had already disbanded after failing to come up with even a single suggestion for institutional reform. A second gambit to meet the January interest payment of $52,000 by selling $80,000 in "Funding Bonds" brought a disappointing $48,000 return, or approximately sixty cents on the dollar. The incoming council averted default at the last moment by securing a very costly loan from Thomas W. House. More discouraging, perhaps, were the monthly reports of the tax collector, who was receiving less than 5 percent of the city's revenues in hard currency and the rest in scrip.[24] Without any hope of raising enough cash for the July deadline, the alderman turned reluctantly to examine Wilson's idea of consolidating the debt. By mid-April, a disheartened council was willing to admit that a "very full estimate" of the government's annual resources—about $150,000—would cover only half of the city's needs.[25]

Faced with a huge deficit, public officials prepared a carefully worded "Circular" to induce Houston's creditors to accept a compromise. The announcement admitted that the January interest had been paid with receipts from more bonds rather than the "legitimate [tax] resources of the city." Declaring this policy "suicidal and disastrous," the council asked the bondholders to exchange their present holdings for new, thirty-year securities. Unless they agreed, the circular transparently implied, no further payments could be expected. The main feature of the consolidated notes was a much lower 5 percent annual rate of return, which would cut interest payments in half for the city (see Table 3.2). To guarantee the new notes, the council promised to pass legislation earmarking a 1 percent ad valorem tax for a special account. Property owners would be required to discharge this part of their dues in hard currency only.[26]

Over the next several months, the process of negotiation brought the city and its creditors into open conflict. The bondholders were willing to accept the consolidated notes, but only at a 7 percent annual rate of return. They calculated that what they lost in the short run, they would regain eventually by receiving payments for an extended period of time. Moreover, the bond exchange would preclude any future attempts to repudiate the debt in court, while giving the creditors a secure legal claim in case of default. After they presented their response in August, the council refused to budge from its original offer.[27] The stalemate had the effect of pushing the dispute from behind the closed doors of city hall into the streets.

Public debate over the compromise moved the community much closer to Wilson's advanced position on the urban political economy. The proposal of a compromise represented a step forward in the recognition of Houston's dependence

TABLE 3.2   Council Debt Refunding Plan, 1875

		Current revenues	
Ad valorem tax		90,000	
License tax		35,000	
Market House fees		24,000	
Ship channel fees		15,400	
Total Revenues			164,000
		Current expenses	
City expenses		123,000	
General interest payments			
891,400 @10% =	89,100		
47,500 @ 8% =	3,800		
100,000 @ 7% =	7,000		
Subtotal		99,990	
Special Interest Payments			
250,000 @ 8% =	20,000		
Market House			
230,000 @ 8% =	18,400		
Subtotal		38,400	
Floating debt payments			
17,400 @10% =	1,700		
Subtotal		1,700	
Total debt payments		140,000	
Grand total liabilities			263,000
Final balance			− 98,600
		Refunding plan	
City expenses		123,000	
General interest payments			
1,094,300 @ 5% =	54,700		
Special interest payments			
Subtotal	38,400		
Floating debt payments			
Subtotal	1,700		
Total debt payments		94,800	
Grand total liabilities			217,800
Final balance			− 53,800

SOURCE: Council Minutes, Book C: 630.

on extralocal forces. The clash with the bondholders helped to separate more sharply the interests of the general public from those of private individuals. By September, community frustration over the stalled negotiations triggered bitter denunciation of the creditor's claims in favor of local improvements. The *Daily Telegraph*, for example, argued that "[w]e must put the streets in order, no matter whether our creditors are willing to take a five percent bond or prefer to invoke the engines of the law." [28] A week later, the newspaper echoed Wilson's call for the elevation of public services to the top of the city's budget priorities. According to the daily, "The taxes collected and being collected belong to the improvement of the city, so to speak. Our motto is to pay debts, but to do so we are not called upon to forget our immediate necessities." [29]

Against the mounting pressures for settlement, from the community as well as from the bondholders, the council's resolve to hold steadfast to its 5 percent offer weakened and finally crumbled. While the press clamored for a renewal of city building projects, the creditors threatened to break off the negotiations.[30] In November, the creditors' representative warned in an open letter that the holders of a sizeable minority of the debt, mainly large brokers, were preparing to split off and seek redress in the courts. However, the majority were willing to accept a 6 percent compromise if Houstonians acted with dispatch.[31] On December 10, 1875, the council relented; it passed an ordinance embodying this proposal. To offset the bitter taste of defeat, the aldermen inserted a proviso that converted the three interest payments from July 1875 to January 1877 into the new consolidated bonds.[32] With a year's respite, they looked forward to a complete restoration of the city government's fiscal health. But the councilmen's elation was short-lived.

Instead of rising out of the depression, Houston plunged to the nadir of despair. In 1876, a series of events undermined the plans of the Lord administration to return the city to a cash basis and to accumulate funds in the bond account. First came the crisis of the Market House bonds. These securities were not included under the terms of the compromise because they provided for separate funding out of the receipts generated by the civic center.[33] The economic slowdown, however, cut revenues to the point where they barely covered the costs of the building's upkeep and insurance. In May, finance committee chairman John C. Thomas reported that the interest fund was short $6,500 of the $10,000 needed by July. To the alderman, a default

> will culminate in a calamity from which it will be almost impossible to recover and most certainly will produce a decided tendency to defeat the negotiations now pending for the exchange of the old [funding] bonds. . . . [A]ll the fond hopes of Houston will be shrouded in gloom and uncertainty.

Agreeing with Thomas, the council authorized the creation of additional short-term debts to meet this important deadline.[34]

On the eve of making the payment, a true calamity struck when the Market House burned to the ground. On July 8, a fire started beneath the theater stage. Before volunteer fire fighters arrived to battle the blaze, the entire structure was engulfed in flames. With only small reservoirs of water stored in clay cisterns, the firemen were practically helpless.[35] The council hurriedly printed a circular to assure the bondholders of the city's determination to honor the new securities. Yet the loss of the town's centerpiece was a severe psychological blow. The part-time officials were about ready to give up the struggle for solvency. A month later, for instance, the council passed a resolution that promised to disband the police, fire, and street repair departments unless the taxpayers began to support the administration.[36]

As weary public officials struggled to keep the city government on its feet, the courts pushed it to the brink of total collapse. Riveted to the problem of restoring Houston's reputation abroad, city officers had long neglected many outstanding obligations closer to home. For example, in August 1874, Judge James R. Masterson of the state district bench had ruled that the city's failure to redeem $11,800 worth of bonds for a parcel of land known as the "hospital block" would result in a sheriff's sale.[37] After the auction had brought a mere $4,000, landowner Mary Duer futilely petitioned the aldermen for over two years to levy a special tax. Finally, in December 1876, the city's blatant refusal to comply with the state bench so angered Masterson that he ordered the sheriff to jail the entire council until Duer received her money.[38]

The forceful intervention of the state district court into municipal matters completed the polarization of interests into three distinct categories: the creditors, the city government, and the taxpayers. The bond negotiations had already driven a permanent wedge between the city and its distant creditors. The contempt decree now opened a wide breach between public officials and the non-compliant property owners. Feeling beleaguered on all sides, the aldermen's reaction to the sheriff's appearance betrayed a sense of resigned desperation. The council protested that after the property owners' refusal to support even a bare minimum of essential services, Masterson's directive represented "an unjustifiable, arbitrary, and tyrannical exercise of judicial power, calculated to . . . destroy the dignity and sovereignty of City Government." Public officers resolved to adjourn the council until they were released from the custody of the sheriff.[39] An appeals court quickly overruled the district bench, but the judicial challenge to local self-government made a lasting impression on Houston public officials. Displaying their alienation, the chief executive and four out of five incumbent aldermen declined to seek reelection. The only exception, John C. Thomas, was defeated by a better than two to one margin.[40]

In January 1877, the return of Wilson to the mayor's office signalled the start of a new, quasi-official system of tax evasion. As the bondholders correctly asserted in court, it was "the predetermined and studied policy" of the administration neither to collect city dues in U.S. currency, nor to enforce the law against tax delinquents.[41] A tacit alliance between city hall and the property owners allowed the council to create a local circulating medium of municipal scrip. These unsecured notes permitted Wilson to achieve his top priority of maintaining basic public services. City employees and suppliers accepted the scrip because it had special worth to the taxpayers. They could buy the paper from money dealers at highly discounted rates and turn around and receive full face value for the scrip when they paid their municipal dues.

There were two major drawbacks in the scrip system of tax evasion for the city. The city suffered substantial losses from the circular path of the paper. In effect, the government received only 40 to 80 cents on the dollar for the paper, depending on fluctuations in the rate of exchange. Moreover, the scrip system completely precluded the issuance of municipal bonds. The public sector could not finance large-scale city building projects until Houston resumed paying its creditors in hard currency. Nevertheless, the mayor's policy temporarily solved the problem of a chronically overdrawn treasury. From the outset, the Wilson administration decided to make a commitment on the side of the community's "immediate necessities."

By 1877, with the reelection of Wilson and his decision to default on the city's bonded indebtedness, the lines of conflict had become tightly drawn. What the mayor had failed to bring about by his September 1874 speech, three years of unrivaled national depression had accomplished. The economic and legal pressures generated by Houston's fiscal crisis had delineated a separate general welfare concept that did not coincide with the private interests of either the property owners or the bondholders. Within the small world of municipal politics, Wilson pragmatically chose to favor local taxpayers over distant creditors. However, he ignored the staunch determination of the state and national courts to enforce the legitimate claims of the bondholders. The mayor's scrip system of tax evasion left little room for a reconciliation. With the help of the judiciary, the creditors would foreclose the mayor's program to deliver a minimal level of governmental services to the community. With the scrip system in shambles, Houston had to submit to outside arbitration in the settlement of the controversy.

For over a decade, the U.S. Supreme Court had assumed an unusually rigid posture against bond defaults and repudiations by local units of government. Beginning with the landmark case of *Gelpcke* v. *Dubuque, Iowa* (1863), the high bench had been leading a vigorous campaign, bordering on a holy crusade, to uphold the public morality and the sanctity of contract obligations.[42] Debt defaults by city governments threatened to erode the moral fabric of the entire nation, according to a majority of the Supreme Court, as well as influential law writers such as Thomas M. Cooley and John F. Dillon. With the heresy of state secession fresh in their minds, the lawmakers reacted in a knee-jerk manner to fasten strong checkreins on local communities. To ensure that cities could not escape the reach of federal law, the Supreme Court opened broad opportunities for the judiciary to intervene in the management of municipal debt problems. Often disregarding its own rules of decision, the high bench became almost "fanatical" in defending the rights of city creditors, justice Samuel Miller complained.[43]

Two cases, *Von Hoffman* v. *Quincy, Illinois* and *Galena, Illinois* v. *Amy*, have special relevance for Houston. The decisions directed the judiciary at every level of the federal system to exercise ceaseless pressure on the cities to uphold the public trust. The bench outlined the procedural steps that the judiciary should take in enforcing the legitimate claims of city creditors. The first remedy was a writ of mandamus ordering the city to pay bondholders from any account earmarked for servicing the debt. Although funds set aside for current expenses would not be touched, demands by the courts for municipal funds could exceed the available tax receipts. Then the city could be ordered to pay a pro rata share to each petitioner. In addition, according to the *Von Hoffman* ruling, the courts were empowered to order the city to levy a special tax to pay the bondholders.[44]

Between 1878 and 1882, however, the bench and bar in Texas seemed unwilling to apply the stringent remedies that the Supreme Court had prescribed in the *Von Hoffman* decision. Instead, local members of the legal profession patterned their petitions and rulings after the less drastic *Galena* ruling. To an extent, the

Texans' inexperience with the law of municipal bonds probably accounts for their caution. The state's lack of full conformity with national guidelines also stemmed from the uncertain reactions of the property owners to a court imposed special tax. To enforce this kind of relief would have created a direct confrontation with the already recalcitrant taxpayers. Rather than face the strong possibility of direct resistance at the outset, the bench and bar pursued a more restrained approach.

Counsel for the creditors asked the courts to issue two different kinds of orders to strike at both ends of Houston's money machine. The main line of attack was aimed at draining all existing bond funds by tapping into every special account. A second group of suits petitioned the bench to compel the tax collector to accept unredeemed bond coupons for any city dues. A flood of this paper in the local economy would destroy the efficacy of the scrip system of evasion. Both types of litigation attempted to force public officials to reinstitute vigorous collections of current and back taxes in U.S. currency. Until then, the taxpayers could resist paying the bondholders, but this course of action would also result in a deprivation of government services from city hall. The creditors entered their complaints against Houston at the county, state, and federal levels. Two of these cases in the chambers of State District Judge James Masterson will serve to illustrate the general pattern.[45]

In October 1878, J. E. Reynold's lawyer requested that the court order the city to pay the New Yorker $1200 in overdue interest on several precompromise bonds from the early 1870s. According to Reynold's suit, the council refused to pay him while hoarding over $20,000 in the market house and the consolidated bond accounts. Only a writ of mandamus, the petition concluded, could provide the bondholder with a remedy. The city attorney pleaded that the separate accounts should not be violated because their funds were held in trust for particular groups of bondholders who were now owed almost $200,000 in unpaid interest. Adhering to the *Galena* precedent, however, Masterson directed the council to honor Reynold's claim out of market house funds.[46]

After the courts completely drained the city's bond accounts dry, they applied a different remedy that would prevent the council from favoring special groups of creditors in the future. In March 1979, R. M. Chapman, a citizen of Maine, entered a suit similar to Reynold's. Since the city owed Chapman $3400 but its treasury contained only $400, Masterson could no longer give full relief to the bondholder. Declaring the maintenance of the consolidated bond account illegal, the state jurist ruled that every legitimate creditor had an equal claim to any existing debt funds and uncollected taxes. Masterson directed the council to pay Chapman a pro rata share of the remaining money in the bond account. For the next two and a half years, this kind of holding action disarmed the city from using the bond funds as a lever to force the creditors to accept a new bond exchange.[47]

The first set of court decrees meant that the council lost independent control of the collection and distribution of city revenues. Until the interventions of the judiciary, the mayor and the aldermen had acted as the exclusive gatekeepers of the municipal coffers. They had exercised these powers through ordinances that defined the size of the annual levies, the mode of their payment, the duties of the assessor-collector, and the amount of scrip in circulation. Now, the court stripped local officials of whatever leverage they could exert on the creditors to accept compromise deals by withholding payment from those creditors who refused to exchange their old notes for new issues.

The court orders produced incredible strains within the council as well as between city hall and the taxpayers. In levying taxes for 1878, the council protested against setting aside one-half of the city's inadequate revenues for the bond-holders. Such a policy, the aldermen declared, "will very materially impair, if not utterly paralyze the efforts of the city government to properly care for the needful and rightful expenses and necessities of the city." [48] Two weeks later, the mayor reiterated that "our people feel the utter impossibility of handling the debt as it is."

The first bond compromise of 1875, Wilson explained, proved to be of minor benefit in relieving the city's fiscal distress. Although $850,000 worth of the old bonds had been exchanged by the end of 1877, another $350,000 worth of the higher interest-bearing notes remained in circulation. The resulting demand on the municipal treasury was almost double the anticipated amount of $50,000 annually. On the other hand, the tax collector was receiving virtually no cash from the property owners. Many paid in scrip; many others (enough to fill fifteen columns of newspaper print with their names), did not pay at all. [49]

Houston's shrinking tax base epitomized the combined effects of the national depression, the federal law, and the local crisis of public finance. Declining by 30 percent from 1874 to 1878, the assessment rolls of city property lost $2,000,000 in value, dropping to a figure of $5,000,000. Over those four years, delinquent taxes amounted to a $150,000 shortfall. [50] Powerless to control critical parts of the tax machinery, the council could neither maintain minimal levels of government services nor satisfy the creditors. Houston was broke and Wilson's scrip system of evasion lay in ruin (see Chart 3.2). His successor, A. James Burke, was left the unenviable task of paring down day-to-day expenses to about $50,000 per year, or half the budget of recent years. Until the council discontinued the use of scrip and put the municipality back on a cash basis, the courts would not remove their powerful hands from the financial affairs of the city government. There was no escape; the judiciary would hold the public sector hostage until the taxpayers ended the revolt. Houston would stay in an impoverished condition until its creditors' claims were honored by a resumption of the semi-annual payments or a conclusion of a satisfactory compromise. [51]

Caught in the middle between the courts' orders and the taxpayers' revolt, the administrators of the city government were left with few options other than pursuing a new agreement with the creditors. The proposed compromise would scale the debt burden down to a reasonable share of the city's total receipts. Then, perhaps, the taxpayers would be more willing to cooperate in the restora-

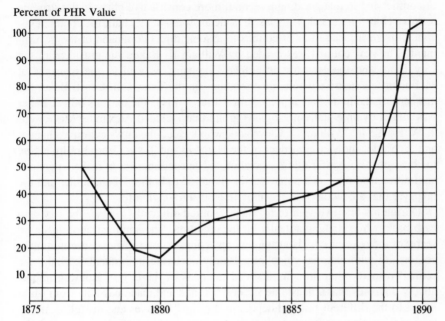

CHART 3.2   Trading Prices of Houston Six Percent Bonds, 1875–1890
Source: *New York Commercial and Financial Chronicle* 23–51 (1875–1890): passim.

tion of the fiscal vitality of the public sector. In addition, a successful compromise plan would eliminate a major loophole in the tax system, the unredeemed bond coupon. The retrenchment programs of the Burke administration were already drying up the other source of tax receivable paper, city scrip.[52]

In the late 1870s, the costs of the stalemate in the coastal entrepôt weighed more and more heavily on the large property owners, who comprised the city's commercial-civic elite. As the national and local economies revived, the business community began to demand a renewal of city building projects. Most of the past improvements in the central business district, such as shelled roads, drainage ditches, and plank sidewalks, had long since washed away. Moreover, rickety wooden bridges needed replacement, streets required better lighting and sewerage, and the installation of a water supply network in the built-up sections was deemed essential.[53] As the pressure for improved arteries of commercial movement mounted, the resistance of the taxpayers diminished.

The municipal elections of April 1880 proved pivotal in ending this first period

of conflict and in inaugurating a second, more constructive phase in the struggle
to solve Houston's fiscal problems. In a clean sweep of city hall, the commercial-
civic elite resurfaced in local politics to assume direct command of the government. The new council was headed by William R. Baker, the president of the
City Bank and the Houston Insurance Company, as well as the manager of
McIlhenny's extensive wholesale operations on the Texas Gulf Coast. Baker began serving the first of an unprecedented three terms in the mayor's office. Baker
was joined by an equally prestigious group that included Alexander McGowen,
T. W. House Jr., William D. Cleveland, who headed the city's cotton exchange,
and J. Waldo, the vice-president of the Houston and Texas Central railroad and
the boss of the Texas Traffic Association.[54] Their willingness to make a personal
commitment to the city's public sector signalled to both the bondholder and the
taxpayer that a new day was dawning in Houston's civic life.

During his first two-year term, Baker worked diligently to place the city on a
cash basis while striking a deal with the creditors. The administration made no
secret of the reasons why Houston was reversing its course from confrontation to
conformity with national guidelines. Boldly declaring its immediate goals, the
council resolved that "the commercial interests of the city of Houston imper-
atively demands that at least one street be graded and made passable from Main
Street to the different railroad depots in the city."[55] Baker and his fellow members of the ruling elite now seemed ready to admit that without making concessions to the nearby courts and the distant creditors, these objectives would fail. If
the tax revolt continued, court orders would arrest support of governmental services at substandard levels. Moreover, the deterioration of the urban environment
would continue to go unchecked.

Consequently, the Baker administration moved vigorously to conclude a settlement with the bondholders. In May 1880, negotiators from both sides hammered out the basic outline of an acceptable compromise. The bondholders refused to sign a final agreement, however, until city officials established the good
faith of the community by completing the uncertain transition from a scrip to a
cash system of taxation.[56] After a year in office, Baker and the council were
ready to launch a policy of accepting cash only for all city dues. Public revenues
for 1881 dipped to a record low of $70,000, but only 9 percent of this amount was
script and coupons.[57]

By December 1881, these reforms were proof enough to convince a majority
of the bondholders to undertake a second exchange. They agreed to turn in their
old notes and coupons on a scaling formula of fifty cents on the dollar. The creditors would receive new thirty-year securities that paid an annual interest rate of 4
percent.[58] However, a minority of the bondholders held out against making any
further concessions to the city. A month before the signing of the compromise,
the dissenters started a second round of litigation. They asked the courts to enforce their rights by bringing the full force of the Von Hoffman ruling to bear on
Houston.[59] Although these suits threw a dark shadow over the city building plans
of the Baker administration, the government remained confident that the compromise would ensure a steady restoration of the city's fiscal abilities.

As we have seen, between the election of Wilson in 1874 and the elevation of another financier, Baker, into the mayor's office in 1880, Houstonians resisted pressures to conform to the national standards set by the Supreme Court. After the Panic of 1873, a deep and intractable depression drove the previously cooperative groups of urban taxpayers, local officials, and city creditors into sharp conflict over the future direction of government policy. Mayor Wilson offered valuable insight into the city's fiscal dilemmas by clarifying the separate and superior claims of the public welfare from the competing interests of various private parties. By 1877, he had persuaded Houstonians that first priority must be given to sustaining a minimum level of essential governmental services. He designed an ingenious system of local scrip to keep up the flow of these public services to the community, while evading the incessant demands of the bondholders. The courts closed this policy option at the end of 1878, demonstrating the flaw in Wilson's strategy. With the election of Baker, the commercial-civic elite acknowledged that Houston could not maintain a position of autonomy outside of the federal hierarchy. At best, further resistance to national law would only prolong the stalemate in city government, which was fast becoming a self-defeating proposition for the property owners.

During the 1870s, the Texas bench and bar handled the delicate task of imposing constitutional checkreins on Houston with a propitious blend of restraint and determination. Following the procedures laid down in the *Galena* decision, local members of the legal profession extended a broad jurisdictional reach over the city government's finances. The first phase of litigation conclusively proved to the community that the federal connections pulling it into conformity with national standards were inescapable. Yet at the same time, the lawyers did not ask the bench to impose the severe remedies allowed by the Supreme Court. Before an economic recovery was well underway in the early eighties, none of the creditors' petitions demanded that the courts order the city to collect a special tax above the charter's 2 percent limit. Such a decree would have brought the judiciary into a very risky confrontation with the town's recalcitrant property owners. During the hard times of the 1873 depression, the legal profession avoided tugging so hard against the inertia of localism that the traditional bonds of respect for the law were stretched beyond the breaking point.

The inexorable, if begrudging, integration of Houston into the national system of law highlights the central role of the legal profession in the process of urban reform. From the mid-1860s, the leadership of the Supreme Court inspired the bench and bar to take an active part in solving the problems of municipal government. The legal reformers of the Gilded Age strove to draw indelible constitutional borderlines between the conflicting rights of urban taxpayers, city governments, and their creditors. In the decisions of the Supreme Court on municipal bonds, this mechanical jurisprudence acted directly as a centralizing force on America's cities. The high bench threw a wide net of federal jurisdiction over the finances of local units of government. Other expressions of legal reform such as Cooley's and Dillon's influential treatises also helped create a new degree of uniformity in the constitutional relationships between the states and their local subdivisions. To be sure, diversity from place to place and from state to state was by no means wiped out in the 1870s. But the range of urban policy alternatives was substantially limited by the structural reforms of the lawmakers.

The federal connections forged by the legal profession were the most prominent of several conscious forces of urban reform that were emerging on a national scale. The fiscal crisis of American cities during the depression provoked novel perceptions that the nation's fast-growing urban centers were suffering from a common set of chronic ills. Across the country, reformers began forming local clubs and organizations to address the problems of supplying the cities with more honest and efficient government, better public services, and improved utility systems. By undertaking comparative studies of the city, these groups began to communicate with one another, preparing the way for the appearance of a nationwide alliance of urban reformers. Among the earliest and most important of these organizations were the associations of utility company executives.

Organizational Links

In the 1870s, conscious forces of national integration began to influence not only the cities' municipal governments but also their utility enterprises. The origins of their shifts from autonomy to interdependence were similar because in both cases the Panic of 1873 triggered reform movements that reversed older patterns of local isolation. Under the impact of the depression, conflicts of interest in American communities broke out over the franchising of essential services to private companies as well as over the financing of city governments. In the mid-1870s, moreover, legal reformers started to draw parallels between the municipal and the utility corporation as they mapped the constitutional spheres of the two sectors. Yet by the end of the decade, reforms at the national level were producing opposite results at the local level in the two institutions most directly involved in the city building process. In pulling urban governments into compliance with constitutional standards, lawmakers narrowed the range of policy options available to the public sector. On the other hand, in forging organizational links in the utility industry, business leaders expanded the ability of the private sector to supply the cities with essential services.[60]

Beginning in 1873, national meetings of the various utility industries helped local operators surmount many common obstacles that had always belied promises of low cost, high quality city services. Before the founding of the American Gas-Light Association (AGLA), businessmen who supplied urban utilities had worked in virtual isolation from one another. Utility companies in local communities everywhere had long been hamstrung by a shortage of trained technicians, an absence of information on equipment improvements, and a lack of managerial expertise in handling the unique political and financial problems that accompanied operating a business under a special franchise. The managers of gas companies took the lead in organizing nationwide trade associations, because the depression suddenly confronted them with hostility from consumer-voters and competition from alternative lighting technologies. These two new threats combined with existing deficiencies to pose a potentially fatal blow to the coal gas industry.

To reform and upgrade their inefficient ventures, the gasmen created a central institution that could serve a dual purpose. The AGLA became a clearinghouse to speed up the diffusion of the latest advances in the industry to the hinterlands. The trade association also provided a forum to coordinate the mutual interests of the scattered companies into a concerted strategy. By sharing experiences and innovations, the executives were able to sponsor the adoption of a uniform package of reforms to overcome their business' chronic drawbacks and current challenges.

At the first annual meeting in New York City, speakers stressed the value of a central institution in breaking the isolation of the past. One of the organization's prime movers, William H. Price of Cleveland, recalled how most gasmen came "accidentally" to the industry, rather than by training or education. Several utility pioneers confirmed that each company operated in a cloistered environment; without help or advice from others in the same trade.[61] Similar confessions reinforce the conclusion that the lonely and frustrating experiences of the entrepreneurs who introduced coal gas in Houston were typical of gasmen throughout the country. A lack of trained engineers and a complex chemical process are factors that go far in accounting for the persistence of poor quality, albeit expensive, lighting services in American cities for over fifty years.

The emergence of the AGLA reflected a new maturity in the entire utility industry. Soon the managers of the city's waterworks, street railways, and electrical systems would each form similar self-interest groups on a national scale.[62] The organizational ties wrought among the utility executives fulfilled the need for a centralizing force, a shared sense of direction. In smaller cities like Houston, public officials and private entrepreneurs alike eagerly sought to make contact with outsiders who could help solve local problems. Through the trade associations and other channels of communication, city builders found a growing pool of managerial and technical experts, specialized publications, and equipment manufacturers whose businesses were devoted exclusively to producing hardware for the city's utility systems. By the early 1880s, Houston and provincial centers across the nation would receive the latest innovations almost as fast as the biggest metropolitan areas would.

Although solutions to economic problems occupied the attention of association leaders in the 1870s, they also kept a close watch on important developments in the courts. Conflicts of interest that generated unprecedented concepts of the public welfare also fostered related changes in the attitudes of city dwellers towards their franchised utility companies. After 1873, city governments frequently shifted their posture from shielding the monopolies of the established firms to encouraging competition in essential services by granting additional franchises to new ventures. The resulting struggles between rival concerns and between the public and private sectors often landed in the courts. Judges at every level of the federal system began contributing to the clarification of the recently troublesome grey areas of the political economy. The ratification of the Fourteenth Amendment in 1870 gave the Supreme Court ample opportunity to set national standards that defined the constitutional status of the urban utility corporation.

In the decade following the Panic of 1873, however, economic problems seemed to worry urban utility executives more than the changing course of the law. Most judicial diversions from tradition were barely noticed before the mid-1880s because only a few of these precedents directly affected the self-interest of local operators, whose attention was riveted to the immediate challenges of interfirm rivalry and technological competition. To overcome these pressing threats, local utility managers sought mutual aid and support by organizing national self-interest groups. Their associations acted as clearinghouses of trade news and as a forum to hammer out a united front against current and future enemies.

Houston provides a litmus test to gauge the successes and failures of the organizational links that were being forged in the various utility industries. By the early eighties, rapid advances in the quality and availability of urban services were being recorded in the areas of artificial lighting, water supply, and mass transportation. Even the HGLC began to prosper in spite of the use of kerosene and electricity. But the gas company and other established firms were singularly unsuccessful in keeping upstart rivals out of the city. If Houston was at all typical of American cities, the reasons for the failure to thwart competition are easy to explain. At least in this coastal entrepôt, the utility men's theories of the baneful effects of competition proved just the opposite. Even the threat of entrepreneurial rivalry stimulated vigorous responses by the established firm to maintain control of its consumer markets. Assessing the impact of these contests upon the community, Houstonians concluded that franchise bidding was the most effective way in which to bring about better services at lower rates.

In the late 1870s, Houstonians were attracted magnetically to extralocal influences, which seemed to possess superior solutions to the community's utility problems. Both public officers and private businessmen sought outside assistance in overcoming chronic deficiencies in the town's urban amenities. At the same time, increasing numbers of representatives from national manufacturing companies arrived to sell complete utility systems. Competition between new and established firms allowed the city council to extract concessions from each franchise bidder. Armed with a broadened concept of the public interest, officials acted to protect not only the municipal corporation, but also the general welfare and the individual consumer.

The struggle for the street lighting franchise demonstrated the powerful effects that outside forces were beginning to exert on Houston's utility services. The termination of the gas company's contract in 1877 was greeted by several rival bids for the local government's patronage. Promoters of a variety of patented oil lamps offered to supply service anywhere in Houston for $4 or less monthly for each lamp. In comparison, the HGLC served only a few streets in the central business district and charged $7 per month for each gas light. By entertaining the oil lamp proposals, the city was able to assume the initiative. Confronted with the loss of its largest customer, the HGLC capitulated to several council demands rather than forfeit from a third to a half of its total sales. For the first time, the city imposed regulations on the utility to safeguard the public welfare in addition to winning an immediate 28 percent rate reduction.[63] In this instance, extralocal competition helped to break the monopoly hold of the established firm. However, the superiority of gas lighting over oil lamps helped the local company to retain its market position.

The origin of the waterworks represented a different case, one in which outside influences dominated in the solution of a local problem. Between 1871 and 1875 a succession of salesmen from the North offered to build Houston a water supply system, but the municipality's financial embarrassment forced officials to reject every proposal. After the Market House disaster in July 1876, however, the council turned to explore practical ways of attracting private investors to underwrite the project. The aldermen proceeded slowly through correspondence with other city governments, besides commissioning engineers to study local needs.[64] A policy of caution and comparison attempted to exploit the advantages of not being an innovator in a fairly complex technology.

Rivalry between local businessmen and outside experts for the waterworks privilege brought substantial benefits to the community. Based on comparative research, in November 1876, the council rejected the bid of a locally organized venture whose terms were monopolistic and too expensive. The aldermen continued to study various offers over the next two years until they quickly and unanimously awarded James M. Loweree of New York with a franchise contract. It was by far the most detailed and comprehensive grant ever adopted by Houston's municipal authorities, who characterized the outsider as an experienced engineer who had installed waterworks in cities across the land.[65] In less than a year, Loweree constructed a complete system that included damming an upstream bayou to create a reservoir, erecting a pumping station and a standpipe tower, and laying four miles of distributor mains. Only after conducting a pressure test that shot water through a fire hose more than 100 feet into the air did Loweree sell the operational plant to local interests. Timothy Scanlan became the biggest investor in the Houston Water Company (HWC) and its first president.[66]

The contrast between the early beginnings of Houston's gas light and water supply services could not have been more complete. Although the two utilities possessed some important differences, their central stations and distribution networks that went directly into shops and homes gave them even more essential similarities. These similarities made the contrast in their early histories even more striking. On the one hand, the lighting firm was started not by trained engineers, but by local businessmen who remained without the benefit of outside expertise until they joined the AGLA in the late 1870s. Isolated and plagued by difficulties, the gas company grew hardly at all. From 1868 to 1881, it increased at an annual rate of less than 3 percent, or from $16,000 to $22,000 worth of business. During this bleak period, the utility halved its rates and doubled its output. But in a city with 17,000 people and 200 miles of streets, the HGLC served only 300 customers along a mere ten miles of mains in the central business district.[67] After thirteen years of operation in a technical vacuum, the gas company was barely surviving on public contracts; it was a long way from becoming a "prime necessity" to Houstonians.

On the other hand, the waterworks at the outset was put on a solid technical footing by an accomplished expert. Loweree, the New Yorker, brought to the city what was then its largest steam engine (70 horsepower), in order to pass the crucial pressure test. After only two years of service, distributor pipes of the HWC already exceeded the length of the gas company's mains.[68] The striking contrast between the foundations of the two utilities accurately reflected the changing pattern of technological diffusion. Moreover, the council's attempts to learn about urban water supply systems in other cities and its familiarity with equipment supplier offers helped produce a comprehensive agreement with the HWC. Unlike the earlier grant by the state to the HGLC, the water franchise adequately protected municipal and community interests.

By the early 1880s, the city government's growing sophistication and ability to turn interfirm competition to the advantage of the general welfare had reached a new stage. The public sector now held the balance of power over private enterprise. Official responses to a series of bids for street railway privileges mirrored the aldermen's improved understanding of the value and importance of utility franchises. Having only four miles of track in 1882, the Houston City Street Railway Company (HCSRC) had allowed a potentially large consumer market to go undeveloped. Over the next three years, three different groups of local and foreign promoters intervened. Reacting to the first of these competitors in October 1881, the council asserted that

> other municipalities throughout the country, mindful of the vast benefits accruing to the street railway companies through the use of occupancy of the streets have derived great pecuniary aid from the sale of the right for a specified time. In light of the surrounding circumstances, it is reasonable to believe that this city, increasing in size and population, will be able in a very few years to support three or four horse car companies and it is no less reasonable to suppose in view of such demand that there will be no lack of application for such privileges by capital seeking investment and willing to compensate the city for such rights for a term of years.[69]

Directed by these fresh perspectives, the Baker administration encouraged new entries into the horsecar business, but on terms that protected "the rights of the people . . . and the reserved rights of the City." A process of hard bargaining ensued between the council and the franchise seekers. After the city dropped a very expensive street paving clause in August 1882, a second group of local entrepreneurs immediately began construction. They chose to compete directly against the established firm by building a line that paralleled the HCSRC's most lucrative route to the Union Depot.[70]

Consolidation by extralocal ownership soon ended this unstable state of affairs. During 1883, both Houston companies were purchased by William Sinclair, a member of Galveston's inner circle and the president of the island city's sixteen-mile transit network. By the end of the following year, the outsider's money and managerial talents combined to triple the length of the street railway to twelve miles of track (see Map 3.1).[71] Although interfirm rivalry endured only briefly in the horsecar business, it lasted long enough to produce a significant expansion of transit services. Local residents also gained from franchise stipulations that went far to regulate the private concern in the public interest. The switch in council policy from monopoly to competition in utility enterprises resulted from an astute assessment of the rising value of urban franchises.

As a test case, Houston demonstrates that the organizational impulses of the utility industry during the 1870s had strong and direct influences on local communities. Faced with perplexing shortcomings in public services at home, businessmen and officials alike turned enthusiastically to open channels of communication with the emerging array of national institutions that specialized in urban utility systems. In each service examined—artificial lighting, water supply, and mass transit—Houstonians benefited in a variety of ways from their ties with this spreading web of national agencies. Competition and technical advances from extralocal sources worked to upgrade the service levels of the private companies as well as to strengthen the abilities of the city government to promote the general welfare. The overall impact of the growing network of organizational links in the utility industry must be judged a success for all concerned (except established firms that fell to superior rivals).

The experiences of Houston also suggest that the interactions between localities and national institutions fostered a fluid economic and technological situation throughout the utility industry. In the mid-seventies, broader entrepreneurial opportunities to introduce services or to compete against established firms opened in hundreds of smaller places like Houston. In the large cities, too, where utility services were recognized necessities, public policy often encouraged competition. In this relatively unrestrained atmosphere, the electrical inventors began installing their new technologies. The solid organizational foundations laid in the 1870s inspired the electrical manufacturers to forge even tighter bonds between scientific research, technical innovations, and market management of local services.[72] Within a decade, these new organizational relationships would overturn the entire pattern of supplying urban public services, a configuration that had evolved slowly over the course of the nineteenth century.

The Urban Matrix

Between the inauguration of rail service to the North in 1873 and the day when the first train from New Orleans rolled into the Union Depot seven years later, Houston grew from a town to a city. The completion of this critical transformation involved a change of mind as well as a remaking of the physical environment. It was not accomplished solely by city building activities that

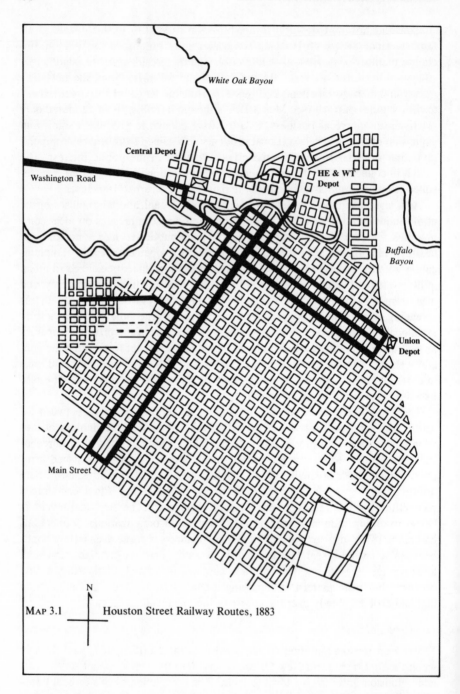

White Oak Bayou

Central Depot

Washington Road

HE & WT
Depot

Buffalo
Bayou

Union
Depot

Main Street

N

MAP 3.1   Houston Street Railway Routes, 1883

imposed an artificial environment over that of the natural. In fact, residents witnessed a depressing erosion of their jerry-built surroundings during the hard times of the 1870s. Instead a profound change occurred in the community's image of itself that marked the full emergence of an urban society. The crisis in government finance drove a permanent wedge between previously overlapping public and private interests and spawned an abstract self-image of the community, a concept of the general welfare. Although local aspirations for metropolitan greatness were the original causes of the fiscal collapse, extralocal forces subsequently gave shape and direction to Houston's travail.

During this wrenching transition from town to city, Houston became enmeshed in a tightening network of American cities that formed an urban matrix. Conscious forces of integration were pushing and pulling the centers of commerce and industry into a web of national interdependence. In addition to the existing ties of most urban centers to far-flung markets and transportation systems, cities became more and more bound to each other by political, federal, and organizational links. The accumulative effect of these centralizing influences was the adoption of uniform solutions by an increasing number of municipalities, both large and small. At the same time, the steady outreach of urban centers like Houston into their hinterlands was inseparably binding town and countryside together. The metamorphosis of the American city's position in regional and national settings was not fully apparent to Houstonians, who were distracted by personal hardship and civic crises. Nevertheless, the linkage of their provincial city to the urban matrix furnished them with a solid foundation to support a rapid revival and expansion of their local economy when a general recovery began in the late 1870s.

Paradoxically, the most obvious intrusion of national influence, Reconstruction politics, seemed to have produced the least enduring impact. A decade after the war, the inertia of race prejudice and the tradition of localism appeared to have rolled back any initiatives from Washington. The Congress had attempted to reorder the structure of party politics and race relations in the Southern community. But partisan affiliations, which had their origins in the antebellum debate over slavery, stubbornly retained their regional character in the old Confederacy and elsewhere. Other factors also weighed strongly against any major realignments of political power, especially an urban-based alliance of city dwellers. The state-centered nature of federalism and the preponderance of voters in rural areas forestalled the formation of a distinctly urban coalition until the late 1920s.

Yet the lessons from interparty competition at the ward level were not lost in Houston, only submerged temporarily under the more pressing burdens of municipal bankruptcy. The imposition of bipartisan politics by the Congress may have been premature, but it encouraged the organization of Houston's largest ethnic minorities—Afro-Americans and German and Irish immigrants—into self-interest groups. In spite of the depression, the community continued to grow and diversify, fostering a proliferation of neighborhood, benevolent, religious, labor, and trade groups, as well as local affiliations with national associations.

When prosperity returned to the Texas Gulf Coast in the mid 1880s, Reconstruction's legacy of ward level democracy would resurface full-blown as a more mature style of urban politics.

The ambiguous record of reform in Houston, coupled with the unbroken political continuity of its public policies, suggests that the term the "Renewed South" described the process of Reconstruction better than the label the "New South." At least in this Southern community, and perhaps in others, there were no sharp breaks in city planning between the antebellum and the postbellum periods and among the several administrations during the decade following the war's end.[73] In 1868, the articulation of the Goldwaithe strategy of city building gave explicit expression to the implicit practices of the past. The use of the municipal corporation as a promotional instrument of urban growth and the assumption of perpetual progress went unquestioned by Democrats, Radicals, and Redeemers alike. To be sure, Reconstruction brought reform to Houston. It gave the city's blacks a chance to organize their community, and it opened opportunities at the top for ambitious white newcomers. However, Congressional intervention in local affairs was too weak to force any significant departures in either race relations or public attitudes towards the proper functions of city government.

In contrast, the power of the federal courts to influence the city grew steadily in response to the consensus-shattering blows of the nationwide depression. Following the lead of the Supreme Court, the legal profession took an aggressive stand in setting constitutional limitations on the discretionary powers and policy options of municipal authorities. While each ruling of the U.S. bench acted directly as a centralizing force, the treatises of Cooley and Dillon also brought a new degree of uniformity among the state laws that governed local subdivisions. For the American city, the interventions of the legal reformers came at a time of alarmed reaction against the heresies of state secession and the sins of urban corruption by Tweed-like "machines." The reformers saddled the municipal corporation with a heavy load of constitutional restrictions on its fiscal strength. These structural shackles permanently crippled the ability of city governments to meet constantly rising demands for better public services.

The expanding involvement of the courts in the fiscal affairs of local governments were typical of the broad extension of judicial supervision over many critical aspects of public policy in the second half of the nineteenth century. Intractable conflicts of interest among Houston's bondholders, officials, and taxpayers epitomized the pervasive sense of malaise that accompanied the urban-industrial revolution. Given the absence of leadership from the legislative and the executive branches in Washington, the judiciary was left virtually alone at the national level to respond to the endless stream of controversies percolating through the federal hierarchy. These cases raised important new questions about the very foundations of the American political economy. By applying a mechanical jurisprudence, the Supreme Court hoped to clarify the ambiguous grey area between the public and the private sectors.

In the process of drawing these boundaries, the judiciary became a full partner in shaping the course of the great transformation of the United States into an industrialized nation of cities. Despite its state-centered rulings of the 1870s, the Supreme Court acted as a nationalizing force. The mere fact that it accepted jurisdiction over urban issues established the precedent for the next generation of justices to take an even larger part in directing the outcome of local conflicts of interest. Armed with the militant textbooks of the legal reformers, state jurists also began to play a more creative role in defining and standardizing urban law. From the 1860s to the 1880s, municipal bond disputes pressed hardest for solutions. But the high Court's preliminary rulings on public utility franchises set the stage for the next pivotal area of urban decision making by the judiciary. While these early controversies little worried the owners of utility enterprises, the challenges of competition after 1873 gave them a common reason for immediate urgency—economic survival.

Breaking down the barriers of local isolation, the utility men banded together in voluntary associations of national scope to overcome the potentially fatal defects in their businesses. An awareness that urban service operators from cities across the land shared such similar problems as interfirm rivalry, managerial inefficiency, and technological displacement was in itself a significant discovery for the industry. More important, however, was their impulse to organize, to create national institutions as the best vehicle to effect essential internal reforms. The gasmen set up a badly needed clearinghouse of information and an open forum to debate policy questions and political strategies. Judging from the profitable exchanges at these initial meetings, there is every reason to support historian Samuel Hays's succinct explanation for this choice of means to save the utility industry, "organize or perish." [74] Whether national trade associations or local neighborhood clubs, the institutionalization of special interest groups became one of the most common responses that Americans employed to cope with the bewildering series of intrusions into their local communities.

The organization of the national trade associations underscored the coming of age of the entire urban utilities industry. From an odd collection of homespun enterprises, it reached a new maturity with the wedding of local operators and the specialized equipment manufacturers who had begun marketing their appliances across the urban landscape. During the 1870s, the Houston experience of successful competition from traveling salesmen with complete utility packages was becoming commonplace throughout the country. By the end of the hard times, moreover, equipment promoters simultaneously started to install the telephone and the electric street lamp in the central metropolis and the provincial town. By 1890, the pattern of diffusion would be reversed. The tremendous cost and complexity of new urban technologies would force their inventors to prove the feasibility of their innovations in test markets such as Richmond, Virginia, and Montgomery, Alabama, before introducing them in major cities.

Compared to these expansive trends in the business sector, the thrust of structural reform in city governments pointed in just the opposite direction. As the utility industry became an increasingly vital component of the spreading urban matrix, constitutional shackles on the municipal corporation narrowed the range of policy options in the public sector. Of course, as a Chicago bond expert claimed in 1889, "[I]t is especially to the Supreme Court of the United States that is due the present importance, stability, and value of the municipal bond as an investment security." [75] But the tight restrictions that the legal reformers had placed on their issue precluded local governments from engaging in city building projects like the creation of public utilities, which required huge capital outlays. Since the efficacy of the municipality as a promotional instrument of development was severely circumscribed, franchise regulation assumed a more central role in urban planning. In this area, the judiciary seemed to offer hope of a broad interpretation of the city's police powers. Yet, in the early 1880s, no one could easily foresee how far the courts would go in extending this vague concept over private business enterprises.

Economic recovery, not legal theory, was uppermost in the minds of Houston's citizens. The revival of trade and commerce brought relief from personal hardship and held the promise of new city building improvements. In 1880, the election of the Baker slate (a virtual *Who's Who* of the city's commercial-civic elite), signalled that Houston had indeed survived the depression and the crisis of fiscal collapse. Four years later, good times had sufficiently returned to allow even the epitome of civic boosterism, the *City Directory*, to admit that

> there have occurred periods in its [Houston's] history when internal improve-
> ments seemed to be at a stand and its pulse as a city presenting urban facilities
> and advantages of life beat with a very feeble stroke. The shadow of its great
> debt darkened its future and enforced a current of economy which was pain-
> fully realized in darkness and mud. But that point of depression is happily
> past forever. . . . The boom of a great population is in the air, and the whir of
> machinery, the shrieks of locomotives and the din of workshops tell the story
> of progress and prosperity. [76]

4 "Everything Is Becoming New," 1880–1888

In 1886, the Reverend John Green disembarked at one of Houston's rail depots to assume new duties as a Methodist minister. His arrival is notable because he kept a journal of his first impressions of the coastal entrepôt. Green's graphic imagery of Houston offers an important commentary on the most striking characteristics of the city. "We were carried . . . in a little mule street car," the Reverend recorded in his diary, "which was Houston's only reliable means of transportation, slow, but sure. . . . All south [of Main Street] was deep mud, in which danger signals were displayed to keep folk out of a bottomless pit."[1] The newcomer's report certainly does not correspond with the "metropolitan" center that local boosters saw (apparently only in their minds' eye) emerging out of the improvement projects of the past six years. Instead, Green's impressions of the conveniences of public transit services were largely offset by vivid confirmations of the city's dubious reputation for "cotton, hospitality, and mud."

But the minister also detected the presence of an infectious spirit of self-confidence that gave a sense of reality to the boosters' wishful dreams. To the perceptive newcomer, "[t]he big, muddy town reminded me of an overgrown, burly boy having a good time wading in the mire and rejoicing in his rapid growth and his 'great expectations.'"[2] This "burly boy" metaphor might also apply to the feeling of the town's citizens. Houstonians believed that they had reached a new level of mature urbanity as well as a new mastery of city building.

The rail center was no longer the bare frontier settlement of five thousand people who lived in the Texas town at the conclusion of the Civil War. The city builders had largely fulfilled the Allen brothers' promise that a "commercial emporium" would arise at the headwaters of Galveston Bay. Despite the persistence of an unwanted reputation for muddy thoroughfares, the built environment had undergone great alteration over the intervening twenty years. Both the local government and the utility enterprises had focused their efforts to construct a man-made environment in the central business district. They had placed an overriding priority on facilitating the mercantile transactions that formed the basis of the city's economy. In the 1880s, the rapid growth of separate industrial and residential areas completed this supplantation of a frontier town by an urban environment. Moreover, all the modern amenities of urban life provided by current technology were available to those consumers who could afford them. The material advances wrought within a single generation offered Houston's twenty-five thousand inhabitants striking proof that progress depended upon man's conscious efforts.[3]

As the Reverend Green sensed, social change was becoming as characteristic of the Texas city as environmental improvement. In fact, the two went hand-in-hand. The final transition from town to city not only reordered land use patterns but also altered the social geography of the community. In addition to the sheer increment in the number and diversity of Houston's population, the unplanned sprawl of home construction created needs for more formal centers of social interaction. The streetcar and the telephone pushed city boundaries outward, dispersing different social, racial, and ethnic groups over an enlarged area. At the same time, steady gains in the speed of intraurban movement wove the community more closely together. Increasingly, the urban-industrial process channeled community activities into associational frameworks.

In the 1880s, a dual structure of organizational life gradually replaced older, less formal patterns of social intercourse. Although many causes other than environmental change contributed to this urge to organize, they all seem intimately tied to the emergence of an urban-industrial nation during the second half of the nineteenth century. The physical expansion of Houston helped stimulate a proliferation of neighborhood and special interest groups. Over the course of the decade, for example, the number of benevolent clubs almost tripled from twenty-one to fifty-eight; labor unions increased from one to eleven. Simultaneously, Houstonians responded to related needs to coordinate the activities of groups that served similar functions. A second set of city-wide associations, such as the Women's Exchange and the Labor Council, began forming.[4] (See Table 4.1 for a summary of these patterns.)

As environmental alterations caused social realignments, the reverse process became manifest in political reform movements bent on changing the course of city building policies and priorities. Local politics provides the best reflection of the crystallization of Houston society into a multitude of self-conscious interest groups. Municipal elections allowed the community to exert direct influence on the city government's improvement programs and to wield indirect influence on the franchised utilities' service standards. The proliferation of formal associations greatly amplified the potential strength of political pressures that the ordinary city dweller could exert on both aspects of public policy. While serving many different functions, organized groups could forge their members into blocks of voters who stood united behind particular issues or candidates. When enough of these groups joined together in concerted action, they formed coalitions that could ultimately win control of city hall.

By the mid-1880s, the reciprocal interactions of environmental and social change in Houston began fermenting a major political upheaval that would continue for the next twenty years. Until the mayoralty contest of 1886, the maturing of an urban polity had remained below the surface of popular expression at the polls. Then several organized groups shattered the long prevailing consensus of leadership by the commercial-civic elite. The insurgents rallied together to defeat the incumbent, William Baker. In part, the success of his administration in restoring the municipal government to an active city building role inspired the up-

TABLE 4.1   The Growth of Associational Activities, 1880–1890

Type of Activity	Date 1880	1890
Social-benevolent clubs	21	58
Fraternal institutions	4	13
Religious groups	7	26
Labor unions	1	11
Local business corporations	5	28

SOURCE: Morrison and Fourmy, *General Directory of the City of Houston* (Galveston and Houston: Morrison and Fourmy, 1890), pp. 54–70.

rising. The insurgents' "great expectations" initially centered on expanding the scope of public works projects from the central business district to the residential neighborhoods. As the quickening pace of technological innovations affected the daily lives of more and more Houstonians, however, the focus of politics broadened to encompass a wide range of public utility issues. Without diminishing concerns about municipal reform, partisan rivalry eventually evolved into a general struggle for control of city hall. The contest pitted those who favored growth-oriented policies against those who placed greater emphasis on upgrading conditions in the neighborhoods.

Town and Country

Before a new phase of urban reform, progressivism, emerged in the 1890s, the drive to fulfill the Allen brothers' vision of Houston as a "commercial emporium" reached a successful culmination. With the virtual completion of the Gulf Coast's network of transportation ten years earlier, the founders' dream of a bustling center of trade and industry, linked inseparably to a rich agricultural hinterland, finally became a reality.[5] Despite the depression, the first generation of city planners had doggedly pursued their growth formula, fueling the urban economy by increasing the flow of goods and people through the coastal entrepôt. During the hard times of the 1870s, this had required relinquishing control of local rail and water enterprises to national corporations. But Houston stood to benefit handsomely from the wedding of town and country, of region and nation. If Galveston and other budding cities in Texas could be definitively surpassed, the Bayou City would become the commercial hub, the heart of the entire Southwest.[6] In the 1880s, civic leaders continued to believe that the enhancement of transportation, both through the city and inside it, was the best way to harness the forces of urban growth and prosperity.

The wellsprings of Houston's prosperity in the eighties originated in the previous decade when city, region, and nation became inseparably bound together. On a smaller scale, some Houston businessmen were able to take advantage of the hard times to consolidate and extend their city's control of the rich natural resources of the hinterland. The depression converted many cotton and grain farmers into indebted tenants of the merchant-financier. On a larger scale, however, Houston had to compete against Galveston and budding rival cities of the interior, such as Dallas and Fort Worth, for the support of the nation's transportation leaders (see Table 4.2). Although neither entrepôt on the Texas Gulf Coast outpaced the other, both formed fruitful alliances that ensured the cities an enlarging role in the development of the Southwest. By 1884, the industrial offspring from this marriage of town and country was clearly perceptible to the editors of the *Houston City Directory*. "A second city—one of workshops, of mills, of manufactures—has already sprung up," they observed, "and within a few years [it] will bid fair to rival the older [commercial] portion in population and wealth." [7]

In spite of Houston's dim prospects during the seventies, its men of commerce never lost sight of the Allen brothers' vision. Throughout the decade, they took vigorous steps to turn the Bayou City into the capital of a vast agricultural empire. To keep a rising stream of goods and people funneling through the coastal entrepôt, Houstonians reached out, bringing vast tracts of the hinterland under their control or ownership. Urban-based Texans not only promoted the opening up of new lands but also assumed responsibility for the management of established plantations. In these ways, the businessmen helped neutralize the danger that direct connections to the North and the East would rechannel the flow of commerce away from the Gulf ports. Within Texas, Houston and Galveston acted like national centers of influence, pushing and pulling the spreading settlements around them into an intimate relationship of interdependence.

Houston's position as the rail hub of the state cemented its ties to the countryside. In the 1870s, the railroad spearheaded the drive to weld farm and market together. Construction workers added over 2599 miles of track to the patchwork of 700 miles that fanned out from the coastal cities. Overland lines penetrated the Southwest from every direction, opening up huge areas of virgin soil to native and foreign immigrants. A flood of settlers 800,000 strong poured in behind the advancing edge of the railroad. By the end of the decade, they almost doubled the population of the state. Even more impressive, Texans old and new expanded the acreage under cultivation by 327 percent. To an extent, better tools and methods accounted for this leap in agricultural productivity. But an uninterrupted decline in the prices of cotton, corn, wheat, and oats also forced farmers to plant more and more just to keep even. [8] Although this response ultimately did little to relieve the farmers' plight, steady increments in the volume of products moving through the commercial centers had just the opposite effect on city dwellers.

At first glance, it might appear that urban Texans played only supporting roles in the rush to banish the frontier. Yet a more careful inspection reveals that Houston businessmen often took a leading part in the settlement of the state's rural areas. The growth of communities in the "piney wood" region, for example, had its origins not in the westward tide across the Mississippi, but on Main Street. In the early 1870s, contemporary observers were already describing the reciprocal interactions that would bind town and country. Local booster William Brady could foresee that, "Houston, situated in the intermediate position with the vast

TABLE 4.2   Population of Southern Cities, 1890*

Southern Rank	National Rank	City	Population
1	7	Baltimore	434,000
2	12	New Orleans	242,000
3	20	Louisville	161,000
4	34	Richmond	81,000
5	38	Nashville	76,000
6	42	Atlanta	64,000
7	43	Memphis	64,000
8	44	Wilmington	61,000
9	53	Charlestown	53,000
10	69	Savannah	43,000
11	77	Dallas	38,000
12	81	San Antonio	38,000
13	82	Covington	38,000
14	88	Norfolk	35,000
15	90	Augusta	33,000
16	97	Mobile	31,000
17	106	Galveston	29,000
18	112	*Houston*	27,000
19	119	Birmingham	27,000

SOURCE: U.S., Department of Commerce, Bureau of the Census, *Compendium of the Eleventh Census—1890*, pp. 434–36.
*Cities with more than 25,000 residents.

timber lands of Texas east of her parallel and the vast expanse of country where that timber can and will be utilized west of that parallel, must become the great central depot for the lumber trade of Texas." [9]

In 1875, Paul Bremond, the pioneer railroad builder, gathered impressive backing to launch a new venture from the city's saw mills and docks into the heart of the forest. A substantial subsidy from the municipal government helped the Houston East and West Texas Narrow Gage Railway reach the Trinity River three years later. In 1881, gangs of loggers filled twenty cars a day for shipment to Houston. By decade's end, the thoughtless depletion of timber reserves in the Midwest created an insatiable national demand for Southern pine from the East Texas area. Quickly becoming the state's largest industrial pursuit, the lumber business remained centered in Houston, where a new breed of land and timber barons would emerge in the 1890s. [10]

Outright purchases of working farms also helped steer the wealth of the countryside through Houston's factories, markets, and shipping facilities. Thomas House's career again serves as the best illustration of this process because of the broad range of his business endeavors. In 1872, for example, House bought a 8750-acre sugar plantation southwest of the city. Five years later, during the depth of the depression, his ample gold reserves allowed him to acquire an entire railroad, the original Sugarland line, for a mere $1100 at a sheriff's auction sale. Employing black convict labor for the arduous tasks of cultivating and milling the cane, House fed both the finished products and his fat profits back into the urban economy. When Houston's most eminent city builder died in 1880, he held a total of a quarter-million acres in sixty-three counties. Although the enormous extent of these holdings was exceptional, the practice of landowning among merchants and bankers was common in an era of rising farm tenancy.[11]

Yet the integration of town and country on the Gulf Coast would have only minor significance if the bulk of the state's resources was to be siphoned off by new rail lines to the industrial centers of the Northeast. This potentially crippling diversion of the flow of trade through Dallas and Fort Worth equally affected the two port cities on the gulf. In the 1870s, both cities formed successful alliances with national shipping interests in order to maintain a hold on the regional economy. In the case of Houston, Charles P. Morgan, the commodore of the coastal trade, unified rail and water connections at the Texas terminal. Moreover, in 1882, Colis P. Huntington of the Southern Pacific designated Houston as the regional headquarters of his sprawling transportation empire. From 1873 to 1890, then, the deadlock between the coastal rivals remained unbroken.[12]

A comparison of the two cities provides compelling evidence that town and country progressed together as integral parts of a single regional history. Because of the stalemate in their commercial rivalry, Houston and Galveston present an exceptionally clear case of parallel development. Of course, each place had individual qualities and unique characteristics. Nevertheless, from 1870 to 1900, the evolution of the sister cities remained remarkably similar in such basic variables of urbanization as demographic composition, economic activities, property values, and housing patterns (see Charts 4.1–3). Their tandem growth testifies to the mutual dependence of city and hinterland in the Southwest.

By the late 1870s, the rapid expansion of the railroad throughout Texas had bound town and country sufficiently to support a strong revival of the urban economy. The best indicator of the return of prosperity was still the cotton trade. Although commodity prices continued to decline, the upsurge in the traffic moving from farm to market signalled better days ahead, at least for the cities. In the five years following the depression's nadir in 1876, the amount of cotton flowing through Houston increased by nearly 500 percent, amounting in 1881 to 200,000 bales.[13] The transportation promoters and the rural settlers provided the underpinnings upon which the city dwellers built their new, man-made environment.

The industrialization of Houston was based on the railroad and its cargoes of cotton, lumber, and grains. The manufacture of finished goods such as wagons, furniture, and saddles for sale to rural customers made a smaller but not unimportant contribution to the erection of a "second city" on the north side of the bayou. As more and more cotton funneled into the rail terminal, the opportunity to process the commodity during its transfer to waterborne carriers attracted local and foreign businessmen. The first large compressing operation had been set up in 1875, shortly after the city's traders organized the Houston Cotton Exchange. But in the early 1880s, three more major facilities arose in the fifth ward, including one built by the Atlanta firm of Inman and Company. New technologies also created a secondary industry by turning the previously discarded seeds

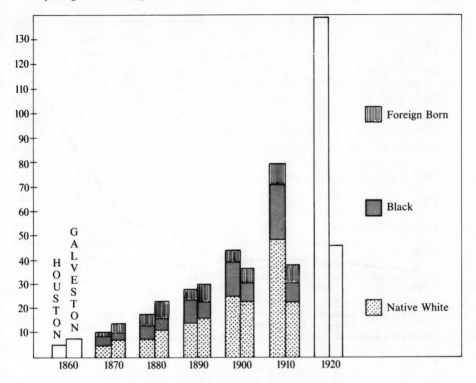

CHART 4.1   Growth of Population, Houston and Galveston,
               1860–1920 (in thousands)
Sources: U.S. Bureau of the Census. *Census of the United States, Population: 1860, 1870, 1880, 1890, 1900, 1910, 1920.*

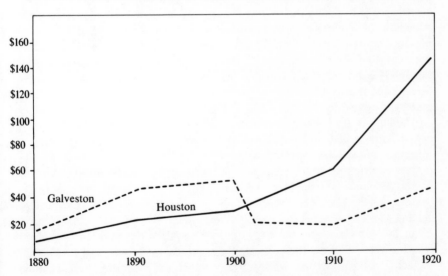

CHART 4.2   Growth of Property Values, Houston and Galveston,
               1880–1920 (in millions)
Sources: U.S. Bureau of the Census. *Census of the United States, Report on the Valuation, Taxation and Public Indebtedness in the United States: 1880, 1890, 1900; ibid., Special Reports, Financial Statistics of the Cities: 1910, 1920.*

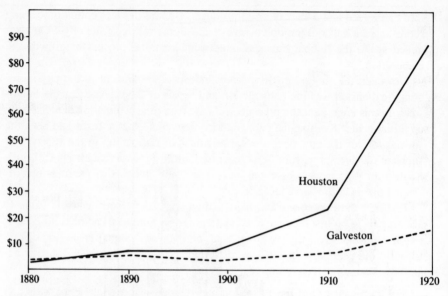

CHART 4.3   Growth of Production of Manufactured Products, Houston and Galveston,
              1880–1920 (in millions)
Sources: U.S. Bureau of the Census. *Census of the United States, Manufacturing: 1880, 1890, 1900, 1910, 1920.*

into cattle feed and a variety of oil products. By mid-decade, cotton processing represented a half-million dollar investment in the future of the city.[14] On a reduced scale, the lumber business underwent a similar process of growth and elaboration.

However, the single most important industrial component in the city's economic expansion was the construction and repair of the railroads of the Southwest. In this area, Houston presents a classic case of accumulating benefits from an initial lead.[15] Keeping the cars and locomotives rolling in Texas had been the special role of the city since the earliest days of railroading in the 1850s. The shops of two former mayors, Alexander McGowen's foundry and Irwin C. Lord's Eagle Iron Works, were essential parts of a rising complex of facilities that attracted others to the same location.

In 1882, these factories and their skilled workers helped persuade Colis P. Huntington to build a regional headquarters for his Southern Pacific railroad system in Houston. Over the next few years, he spent over a quarter-million dollars to build the railroad's regional headquarters. The *City Directory* astutely described the anticipated coming results:

> The establishment of the Texas and New Orleans depot in the Fifth ward and its use practically as a union depot has had a powerful effect in crystalizing population around it and opening business. . . . But it is to be reasonably expected that the establishment of the great workshops of the Southern Pacific Railroad in the Fifth Ward will give that portion of the city such an impulse that imagination may paint a bright scene for the future without incurring the charge of extravagance.[16]

The railroad leader's fateful decision, in turn, convinced still others to locate in the one place with so many related advantages. Five years later, for example, John F. Dickinson of Marshall, Texas, set up a plant for manufacturing car wheels.[17]

The clustering of the transportation industry across the bayou from the commercial business district broadened the base of the urban economy and diversified the composition of the work force. Before the discovery of an ocean of oil under the coastal plain in the 1900s, the lack of a cheap source of energy severely restricted the growth of heavy industry in the region. Houston's railroad complex proved a rare exception. By 1891, the repair shops of the Southern Pacific alone employed 1250 men; who comprised about half the number of skilled workers in the city. Along with many other railroad linemen who called Houston their home, the skilled and well-paid white worker was often a member of a union. In the 1880s, the rail hub became the undisputed center of the organized labor movement in the state. As we shall see, the presence of substantial numbers of Knights of Labor and trade unionists amplified political and social overtones in the community, which were barely heard in most cities of the South and the Southwest.[18] The industrialization of Houston added new dimensions to the city's social geography during the eighties. Steady increases in the flow of trade did even more to reinforce preexisting patterns of urban growth.

The revival of commercial traffic through the city touched off a building boom that pushed Houston's boundaries outward in every direction. By mid-decade, 300 new buildings were changing the face of the urban environment. The central business district sprawled in the southwest along Main Street, besides filling in vacant land in the older portions near the bayou. The downtown area took on a more urban appearance from the clustering of additional business houses and the construction of impressive structures such as the Houston Cotton Exchange, the Masonic Temple, and the County Court building. Yet the railroad depots and the Market House, the perfect symbols of the commercial city, continued to anchor the central business district and to define its major axis of movement.[18]

The solidification of the central business district moved most residential construction to the periphery, where houses spread in a broad arc around the downtown area. The most rapid buildup occurred on the north side of Buffalo Bayou in the fifth ward, but the southwestern portion of the city also experienced considerable new construction. The great majority of Houstonians lived in single family dwellings. Most families rented these wooden houses and cottages because few workers, less than 10 percent, could afford to buy their own homes. And despite the swelling size of the city, it remained small enough to forestall residential segregation by either class or race.[20] Taken as a whole, land use in Houston was becoming increasingly specialized into industrial, commercial, and residential zones.

Prosperity in Houston during the 1880s was based on the rising productivity of the countryside. The railroad laid these foundations by opening up the fertile lands of Texas for the farmer, rancher, and logger. Town and country developed together; each influenced the growth of the other in the Southwest. At the same time, the nation's transportation leaders were binding the region into even larger systems of interdependence. Unfortunately for the rural settlers, the linkage of local economies into centralized international markets turned their productive gains into losing propositions. Fortunately for Houston and Galveston, the integration of water and rail modes of transportation placed the coastal ports in an intermediary position in the two-way flow of commerce between the interior and the outside world. In the inland entrepôt, the constant upsurge in the volume of trade fueled an economic expansion that lifted the city out of the depression and the mud.

Rules and Regulations

In the 1880s, urban growth was paralleled by a mastery of city building for the first time. Houstonians began to tackle the chronic environmental problems of the last quarter-century with a growing sense of self-confidence and accomplishment. Buoyed by the rapid expansion of the region's economy and guided by the sound advice of the nation's experts, urban Texans made steady improvements in the administration of their government, public facilities, and utility services. Each of these advances still involved a difficult, step-by-step series of reforms. But this process went forward more smoothly because new institutional channels helped to overcome the stumbling blocks of the past. A decade of remarkable achievements in environmental engineering would not only restore Houstonians' faith in progress, but it would also stimulate fundamental changes in the community's social geography and political aspirations.

A strong institutional framework was an essential prerequisite to city building. As prosperity returned in the late 1870s, the painful lessons of the city's fiscal crisis pointed out to the Baker administration the necessity of strengthening the two major structural tools of environmental engineering, the city charter and the utility franchise. These instruments created a legal, economic, and political framework that could either support the financing and management of urban services or inhibit their improvement. Without engaging in a process of structural reform, Houston would not be able to finance public works projects or to persuade private investors to risk scarce venture capital in utility enterprises.

During Baker's six-year administration, municipal reform was focused almost exclusively on the goal of improving the streets. The successful linkage of the Gulf Coast to the transcontinental economy in the 1870s turned urban rivalry inward during the 1880s. Easing movement in the city's streets completely overshadowed other concerns such as better health and sanitation measures, parks and recreational facilities, and even police and fire services. Houston's single-minded goal may seem myopic today, but to contemporaries, it was neither a unique nor a foolish choice. In fact, this spatial orientation to city building was so common in the postbellum period that historian John B. Jackson has observed "a growing tendency in [urban] America to interpret every civic improvement in terms of linear design, in terms of more and better streets." [21] Increasingly, the conditions of the city's streets and their employments determined land use and values. In addition to pavement, the prices and rentals of adjoining parcels of property—especially in the newer sections of town—depended on whether they were served by water, sewer, gas, electric, and mass transit lines. As arteries of transportation and as conduits of urban services, the streets became a major focus of city building activities.

In the government sector, the general welfare concept provided a legal and political framework for the reconstruction of the municipal corporation into an effective instrument of public policy. Conceived of during the civic crisis and born out of the struggles among conflicting parties, new notions of public and private interests emerged. The division of the political economy into two separate spheres set the city builders on a new course. To be sure, Mayor William R. Baker and his colleagues still adhered to the traditional goals of the commercial-civic elite: more trade and more growth. But they enacted a far-reaching series of reforms in the methods of government finance and administration that were used to obtain these ends. Following the implications of the general welfare concept, the city council became engaged in a regular succession of managerial and structural adjustments in the city's charter and utility franchises. As a result, a powerful administrative machine was erected for financing the improvement of the streets and regulating their use. Both sets of reforms tended to centralize power at city hall, where more and more members of the community looked for solutions to their social and environmental needs.

The primary focus of Mayor Baker's reforms revolved around the rehabilitation of the city's taxing authority. Road-building projects were so expensive that they required separate long-term financing. But the deadlock with the bondholders precluded any immediate reliance on public credit and sharply curtailed other policy options. To sidestep these hurdles, the structural reformers designed a self-contained system of special assessment taxes. To restore the city's full fiscal strength, public officials would ultimately have to break the stalemate with the city's creditors. Baker began the preliminary work of refurbishing the machinery for levying and collecting the general property tax into an inescapable administrative apparatus.

The reformers also had to pay close attention to private uses of the public streets that impeded commercial intercourse. The Baker administration initiated the training of a corps of employees to police, clean, and repair the city's arteries of movement. Long-term utility grants created special relationships between the public and the private sectors. The council needed to find practical ways of exercising a constant vigilance over the operations of the companies. The reformers sought to establish the government's authority to regulate the firms and to discover the proper mechanism of enforcement.

The main tool in the reconstruction of the public sector was the municipal charter. Actually, tinkering with the structure of city institutions began a year before Baker's election in 1880, when a joint committee of citizens and politicians sent a reform package to Austin for the perfunctory approval of the legislature.[22] The Texas lawmakers' attitude of self-restraint in deference to local autonomy carried over to the state judiciary. During the 1870s and 1880s, the Texas bench usually upheld municipal charters in test cases that sought to limit public control over the lives and property of private individuals. In addition, state and national courts heard a series of loud complaints from urban service companies against government regulations and franchise policies. In the mid-1880s, these suits culminated in the formulation of a constitutional doctrine of public utilities by the U.S. Supreme Court. At each step of Houston's charter reform movement, the latest rulings of the courts were incorporated in the next reworking of the city's structure of government. Every two years, the charter writers were back at the capital, strengthening the powers of the public sector over the urban environment.

By the end of Baker's unprecedented third term in 1886, the accelerating momentum of municipal reform threatened to sweep beyond his original intentions. The mayor and his elite companions in the council pursued a relatively narrow vision of the government's legitimate functions, which were restricted to promoting Houston's growth and influence in the region. To reach these goals, the council restored the city's tax powers and established an absolute authority over all private uses of the streets. The epitome of the administration's limited point of view was its exclusive focus on the needs of the central business district. The councilmen virtually ignored the industrial and the residential areas. Baker's priorities remained essentially traditional, but the machinery of government was assuming the form of a modern bureaucratic organization. The very success of the reformers in gaining a mastery over the physical environment stirred hopes in the community that similar public controls could be extended to improve the social environment.

In 1879, Houstonians began the restitution of the municipal government to a full role in the city building process. However, their early attempts at reforming the charter continued to embody vague distinctions between the public and private sectors. There had long been an ambiguity in American cities as to whether street improvements primarily enhanced the general welfare or the value of private property. Special assessment schemes of taxation contributed to this traditional confusion by shifting the burdens of paving costs from the general community to the specific property owners whose lands fronted the improved roadways.[23] At first, Houston's charter provisions on street paving relegated the council to a minor, ministerial role. The reformers, for example, specified that the council could not initiate paving projects; instead, it could only act after receiving a petition from 75 percent of the affected property owners.[24]

Under Baker's leadership, charter amendments soon began reflecting a more precise and comprehensive understanding of the public welfare concept. In the early 1880s, the municipal charter became a virtual catalog of urban activities in the public areas of the city. As the diversity and pace of these activities increased, the charter writers learned how to redefine the public authority in broader terms. The process of structural reform by the council and its legal advisors involved a progressive series of adjustments. Usually the aldermen reacted to specific problems as they arose by enacting local ordinances or by instructing city officers to deal with the situation. If the council's responses adequately managed the problem, they would be incorporated in the next round of charter revisions. Later, the new sections of the charter might be challenged in the courts, leading to another series of institutional adjustments in the city government. In this manner, Houston's public officials and their allies in the legal profession built up expertise as structural reformers.

In the 1880s, the reformers made greater and greater assertions of the public authority over the pulsating movement in the streets. The enumerated list of regulated activities grew longer at the same time that the government's power became more encompassing. In 1881, the charter declared for the first time that "the city council shall have the exclusive control and power over the streets."[25] To a large extent, the swelling flow of goods and people in these public areas created the need to impose more government controls in order to prevent a breakdown of commercial intercourse. Gradually, however, the charter also expressed a public interest in the health, safety, and well-being of the community.

The shift of discretionary authority over street improvements from the property owners to the councilmen illustrates the step-by-step trend towards a centralization of power in the public sector. After two years without results under the 1879 charter, Houstonians ramrodded an "emergency" measure through the legislature because "the streets and sidewalks . . . are in a dreadful condition." Now the initiative rested with the aldermen, who could designate road projects to be in the "public interest." They still needed the consent of a majority of the abutting property owners, but special assessments became a normative method of taxation. The charter also armed the city with power to enforce the tax through court proceedings that could foreclose a tax lien on the affected property. Moreover, the reformers added drainage, sewage, and grading projects to the list of public concerns about the urban environment. Under the 1881 amendments, paving in the downtown area got underway, but glaring deficiencies in the structure of government power soon became obvious.[26]

Two years of experience taught Mayor Baker that the need to establish bureaucratic regularity required a complete centralization of power at city hall. The municipal charter took on the appearance of a codebook of administrative procedure as well as a catalog of urban activities. After 1883, the council alone decided which streets and sidewalks would be improved, besides all the specifications of the paving projects themselves. The reformers outlined in minute detail each procedure for levying and collecting special assessments. As in most cities, they were apportioned according to the length of the land fronting the improvement.[27] Individual property owners had little choice except to pay the tax or to face certain court actions that could lead to the loss of their land.

Charter reforms represented the end product of a complex interaction among the council, the courts, and the private interests affected by the public authority. Most changes in the system of street improvements, for example, evolved out of the council's reactions to the practical problems of managing the public works program. Every aspect of administration needed clarification—from the drawing of paving contracts to the inspection of completed work and from the first notification of property owners to the final collection of their dues. In response to these managerial problems, the council enacted local ordinances, which later appeared in the charter to give them the sanctity of state law.[28]

The accumulating success of the reformers in manipulating the structure of city government rested mainly on the institutional channels of arbitration that had been recently forged by the legal profession. Judicial involvement in municipal problems made a major difference in the pace and efficiency of reform, because the courts provided an orderly procedure for establishing the legitimacy of innovations in urban government. By the late 1870s, the courts had become full partners in making decisions about the nature of local government and the future of the city. Increasingly, the courts served as active mediators in conflicts between the public authority and the rights of private individuals.[29]

By the mid-1880s, for example, the law of special assessments seemed harmoniously settled on all fundamental issues in Texas and national forums. Jurists consistently refused to intervene between property owners and local authorities in the determination of tax burden equities. The courts offered taxpayers only procedural protections. If local administrators deviated from their city charters, the courts might intervene on behalf of the taxpayer.[30] Litigation protesting special assessment levies continued throughout the decade, but the predictability of the judiciary's deference to the legislature encouraged public officials in Houston to execute their road building plans.

Together, Houston's charter reformers and the courts created a stable and useful method of financing public improvements. Judicial rulings implied that local lawmakers needed to institutionalize each step in the taxing process. The council also embodied practical solutions to administrative problems in charter provisions. Similar structural and managerial adjustments were rebuilding the general property tax machinery. It was becoming a reliable system for financing the growing array of urban services provided by the city government. The interactions of the reformers and the judiciary tended to centralize decision-making power in the public sector. Structural reforms were strengthening the authority of the city council over the urban environment.

By 1886, travelers like the Reverend Green could travel over four miles of wood, gravel, and stone pavement. Special assessments raised 78 percent of the $167,000 cost of these improvements. Moreover, city and county officials paid about $100,000 from general tax funds to bridge builders from the East who erected two iron spans across the bayou. These links to the fifth ward had been essential parts of the deal that had attracted Huntington's railroad repair center to Houston.[31] To be sure, the scale of Baker's achievements seems small in a city with over 200 miles of streets. Yet, measures of his accomplishments cannot be limited to material progress alone. They must also include the major reorientation of power in the community back towards the public sector. Under his leadership, the council took the first difficult steps to reverse the depression legacies of environmental decay and fiscal collapse. Reinforced by the courts, the mayor's structural reforms translated the public welfare concept from an abstract idea into a practical guideline for government action. Moreover, the steady (albeit slow) success of the Baker administration in paving the central arteries of commerce eased the way for other reformers with different goals and priorities.

The general welfare idea also influenced government representatives to assert regulatory controls over private uses of the streets. Public highways, whether paved or unimproved, had little utility when clogged with obstructions and filled with dangers to life and limb. By their nature, the chief offenders were the utility companies, with their underground pipes and mains, railway tracks and cars, and electric poles and overhanging wires. Keeping the city's streets clear of impediments was the job of both the policeman on the beat and the policymaker at city hall who decided the terms of the utilities' franchises. These grants of special privilege permitted the companies to make extraordinary uses of the streets. In the mid-1880s, however, the Supreme Court announced in the name of the general welfare that the public retained an inalienable right, if not a duty, to exercise a constant vigilance over urban service enterprises. Houstonians were already exploring the broad but vaguely defined boundaries of the evolving public utility doctrine in the state courts. For the most part, Texas jurists supported the claims of local authorities that the companies must submit to government scrutiny and supervision.[32]

The repercussions from the judiciary's closer involvement in urban affairs were substantial. In Houston, the most immediate and visible impact was evident in the city's changing posture towards its utility enterprises. Citizens turned to their local government with increasing frequency to correct deficiencies in the public services supplied by the private companies. As these services became household necessities for more and more members of the community, government regulation loomed as a potentially explosive political issue.

In 1886, for example, a fire consumed an important cotton seed mill, while firemen stood by helplessly because the hydrants were dry. Outraged Houstonians quickly formed a committee to demand action from the city council, including a thorough investigation of the entire water supply system. The committee reminded their aldermen that

> [t]here is no principle better established in law or equity, than that the holders of any franchise, granted by a government shall be responsible to that government for a faithful performance of the obligations . . . assumed with said franchise."[33]

The council responded by ordering the water company to demonstrate an ability to fulfill its franchise specifications. In addition, the aldermen explored new ways to ensure that future water supply needs would be adequately met by the company. Although the utility passed a water pressure test, the council enacted a comprehensive reform measure that tightened its controls over the company's service standards.[34]

Between the early and late 1880s, a dramatic change occurred in the attitudes of the councilmen about the right of the government to regulate private interests in order to advance the general welfare. In part, this reorientation flowed naturally from the council's efforts to protect its costly street improvements. But this new direction in city policy also reflected a deeper understanding of the public welfare concept and a renewed confidence in the government's ability to improve the urban condition. Consider that in 1881, respect for the property interests of the streetcar company completely inhibited legal action by the council against the utility's numerous violations of street repair ordinances. Elected officials agreed with alderman William Shaw's judgment that enforcement of the law was "bad policy" because it would "clog the investment."[35]

Six years later, the council brazenly wielded police power against the same company. The council attempted to force the street railway to comply with policies only remotely related to regulating the use of the streets. After the company removed its tracks along a principal trunk line to allow paving contractors to improve the street, the council hurriedly passed a new "regulation." The ordinance prohibited the company from replacing its equipment until it paid its fair share of the public works project.[36] Similar clashes between the local government and the public service companies were duplicated many times after the mid-1880s.

However, this incident sufficiently outlined the implications of the law's altered configurations for government-business relationships in the city. After 1885, Houstonians began exhibiting more confidence in their local government's ability to control the direction and quality of urban life. The water company investigation was just one example of an increasing tendency of the community to look to the public sector to solve environmental and social problems. Many other influences besides street improvements and legal reforms were acting to produce similar perceptions about the strength of municipal institutions. Yet the growing mastery of public officials in managing city building programs marked a watershed that reinforced current attitudes and added a separate momentum of its own.

Light and Power

Until the late 1880s, Houston's public utility enterprises were devoted almost exclusively to the same goals as the municipal government—enhancing the flow of people, goods, and information through the city streets. The rail hub's gas lights, omnibuses, and horsecars were each designed specifically to aid intra-urban movement. As the decade opened, businessmen began installing telephones, electric arc lamps, and more railway tracks to augment further the level and ease of linear motion within the commercial center. Even the waterworks was joined to this task by its function of keeping the streets clean and the drains clear.

But in contrast to step-by-step reforms in city government, urban service enterprises were undergoing a revolution. The pace of change differed radically because the modernization of municipal institutions was still locally centered, while national influences were sharply accelerating the metamorphosis of the utilities industry. Before the nineties, on the one hand, municipal reform remained essentially an isolated experience without central direction or concerted action, despite the unifying force of the federal court system. On the other hand, "engineer-entrepreneurs," investment bankers, and trade association leaders were joining together to create a nationally integrated structure in the private sector.[37] By the 1890s, the utilities industry would be in a position far superior to that of the public sector in meeting a massive upsurge in demands for better urban services.

The transformation of public utilities during the 1880s fully warrants the label "revolutionary" for four closely related reasons. At base, a rapid-fire series of innovations in the commercial application of electricity to long-standing urban needs amounted to a major technological breakthrough. In a remarkably short period between 1876 and 1890, many of the public services that we still depend on today—such as telephones, electric lights, gas appliances, and transit facilities—were introduced in American cities, both large and small. An almost simultaneous pattern of diffusion resulted from the widespread realization by both consumers and investors of the new technologies' significance. Americans pumped vast amounts of their surplus savings into these ventures.[38] Virtually overnight, investment bankers helped create a rich market in utility securities. Rapid infusions of capital, in turn, fueled a complete reorganization of the industry that stretched from the board rooms of Wall Street to the research labs of the electrical manufacturers and the sales offices of the local operators. Finally, and perhaps most important of all, the electrical utilities had a profound impact on the daily lives of the average city dweller. Although local governments were also contributing to the erection of an artificial environment in the public areas of the city, utility services alone were penetrating deeply into the private homes and workshops of the ordinary citizen.

In Houston, the widening gap between the institutional strengths of the public and private sectors was not obvious at first. During the 1880s, in fact, the opposite trend appeared to be shifting the balance of power to the city government. The revival of the economy and the movement of people into the city underpinned steady increases in the tax rolls. In addition, structural and legal reforms seemed to lift the general welfare of the community above the interests of those peculiar private enterprises that supplied public necessities. But by the end of the decade the rapidly building momentum of the technological and organizational revolutions in the utilities industry would begin to outdistance the improvements being wrought in municipal government.

The transformation of street railway services in Houston gives strong indications that key aspects of the utilities revolution were already underway at the local level. In 1882, the city's most profitable utility venture was the first to face stiff competition for underdeveloped markets in the central business district, as well as in the newer residential and industrial areas.[39] In March of the following year, Galveston's William Sinclair purchased the rival firms, beginning the transfer of local ownership to outside investors. The experienced operator of the island city's mass transit facilities immediately applied his managerial talents to consolidate and expand the new enterprise. By July, Sinclair's plan to coordinate the three existing circular routes evoked comments that he was "establishing a very convenient system."[40]

With the opening of horsecar services to the industrial fifth ward in September 1884, the impact of the new "system" made an even more striking impression on contemporary observers. "This company," a journalist noted, "has revolutionized travel in this city and has made our town really metropolitan in its appearances and conveniences."[41] No longer devoted strictly to commercial intercourse, the transit network of fourteen and a half miles began to change the contours of urban life for most city dwellers. For instance, merchants in the previously isolated fifth ward had to lower prices or watch their customers commute to downtown stores.[42] At the same time, track extensions into cheap suburban areas accelerated the geographic sprawl of the city, the functional specialization of land uses, and the purchase of homes by middle-class families. On the eve of the railway's conversion to electric traction in 1891, Houstonians well understood that the thirty-five miles of additional trackage laid since 1884, "vastly expedited both urban and suburban growth. It has been the first cause of the enhancement exhibited in real estate generally . . . and the tendency is, while this street railway extension continues evenly in all parts of the city, to equalize both rents and realty valuations." [43]

Yet the truly revolutionary force in city services came from distant centers of technological innovation, not local sources of business reform. The origin of electric lighting in Houston illustrates these changing patterns. The initial organization of an electric company closely paralleled the beginnings of the waterworks, but the management of the newer enterprise soon diverged from conventional pathways. In both cases, local investors invited outside experts to build a complete facility, including a central station and a distribution network. However, only the electric venture retained a corps of technicians who kept in contact with their home offices, the patented equipment firms. As a result, channels of communication that promoted rapid improvements in the quality of services were opened among consumers, operators, and central manufacturers. In contrast, the water supply system became more and more outdated, falling far behind the fast-growing needs of the community.

In February 1882, just three years after Charles Bush successfully introduced electric arc lamps on a commercial scale,[44] Mayor Baker inaugurated local efforts to bring these brilliant 2000 candle power devices to Houston. A few months earlier, he had witnessed the new system of illumination in the Middle West, while returning from bond negotiations in New York. In a city with few sidewalks or paved streets, Baker told the council, public lighting was a special concern because the pedestrian needed to see every step of the way. However, the high cost of gas services, even along a few arterial thoroughfares in the central business district, had meant that Houstonians had suffered without any street lighting for the past two and a half years. Bush arc lamps offered a superior solution to gas, and one that was also cheap enough to fit within the city's tight budget. In Aurora, Illinois, the mayor had viewed Bush's inventions on 150-foot towers, which, "causes the illumination to issue by broad floods, from a few fountain points, instead of an endless multiplicity of gas jets, or taper flames that serve like the star light, more for fancy than for use." [45]

The fiscal weakness of the city government foreclosed the public ownership alternative. Private ownership would have to underwrite the capital costs of the new utility. According to Baker's calculations, a public lighting system could be built for the relatively small amount of $15,700 (see Table 4.3). Yet this investment could be made only by diverting funds from other essential services such as fire and police protection. "We have need, urgent need for more income than we have," the mayor admitted, "[but] we have not the means for many pressing necessities . . . as well as light and we have not the ability to carry out our wishes, except very slowly and gradually." [46] Baker himself became a major stockholder in the Houston Electric Light and Power Company (HELPC), which was organized a few months later, and called upon citizens to subscribe to the new enterprise. Before the end of the year, Bush engineers had installed the facility and were ready to throw the switch, lighting up about forty lamps for private customers along five miles of wire.[47]

At first, Houstonians reacted to the new technology with a mixture of astonished delight and angry disappointment. The mid-December 1882 test trials of the arc lights drew large crowds that seemed "to be completely enraptured with them." One reporter described the light as "a perfect burst of sunlight, for that is the only thing the brilliancy and power of the light can be compared with." But at the same time, the community became frustrated; the city could not afford the improved system of illumination. "[C]ity fathers should take the hint," the *Post* chided, "and . . . help us through the muddy and slippery streets these winter nights. Let us have light!"[48] Moreover, like any new complex technology, the utility contained a number of annoying defects such as power blackouts and unreliable appliances. These drawbacks prompted some of its charter customers to have the faltering lights immediately removed from their stores, hotels, and workshops.[49] By March 1883, however, private demand had already outstripped the fifty-lamp capacity of the original equipment.

Under the direction of outside experts, electric services for private and public use improved by leaps and bounds over the next few years. Trained engineers of the HELPC were constantly adding updated equipment, besides perfecting the performance of the entire system. Between 1883 and 1887, these gains in the quality of services were reflected in a five-fold increase in both the number of arc lights and the length of circuitry. During this period, the city also became a customer by contracting with the company for thirty-two street lamps, a figure that crept upward to forty-seven by the end of the Baker administration.[50]

In December 1883, less than two years after Edison opened New York City's Pearl Street station, the incandescent bulb arrived in Houston. This invention marked a major advance in electric lighting that quickly surpassed the importance of its predecessor technology. Although the very brilliance of the arc lamp restricted its use to large open spaces, the softer incandescent bulb could be flexibly adapted to fit practically any need. Whereas rates remained too high for home consumers, applications of the light bulb in commercial establishments kept demand running well ahead of the company's generating capacities. By 1887, the HELPC could provide enough electrical power to light approximately 1,000 bulbs at the same time.[51] But in spite of the utility's steady progress in services and marketing, the venture did not prosper.

On the contrary, the HELPC failed as a business enterprise. In March 1887, the company defaulted on its debts and entered the first of several bankruptcies and reorganizations. The basic problem with the electric utility stemmed not from the technical shortcomings of its outside supervisors, but rather from the financial deficiencies of its local owners. Before the introduction of motors, fans, and other appliances, electric plants operated at peak loads for only a few hours each night. Profits alone simply could not cover the heavy expenses of purchasing additional equipment to keep up with surging consumer demand. Under local

TABLE 4.3   Municipal Electric Light and Power System Proposal, 1882

Item	Cost ($)	
Power plant		
Central station building	1,500	
25 h.p. steam engine	2,500	
Bush dynamo and light machine	2,200	
Subtotal		6,200
Distribution system		
6 light towers @ $1250	7,500	
200 poles; 5 miles of wire	1,000	
Subtotal		8,500
Light fixtures		
16 arc lamps	1,000	
Subtotal		1,000
Grand Total		15,700

SOURCE: Council Minutes, Book E: 575–76.

ownership, the electric plant was chronically on the brink of breakdown from either insufficient generating capacity or inadequate financial resources in meeting its capital charges.[52]

Efforts to stabilize operating companies in many other cities were showing that solutions to the utilities' organizational problems, as well as their technical ones, lay beyond the local setting. In the late nineteenth century, there was an increasing correlation between improvements in utility services and extralocal financing and management. Houston's most isolated enterprise, the water company, presented the most glaring case of retarded development.[53] In contrast, the modernization of the city's other utility services closely matched the degree of their integration into national business structures.

The gas industry, for example, probably reaped the greatest benefits from new inventions and their far-reaching social impact. Although the appearance of brilliant arc lights initially seemed to strike a fatal blow at the gas companies' future, just the opposite resulted. In 1888, the president of the gas light fraternity reported happily that consumer demand for gas products was soaring in most cities. These recent leaps, he admitted, were due largely to the influence of electric lighting. The new source of illumination was "almost compelling people to have more light." Four years later, New York's William H. White confirmed that arc lamps "have taught the everyday people of our times that a good volume of artificial light in their shops and homes was a necessity, not a luxury."[54]

In the gas industry, a revolutionary innovation helped fulfill the rising expectations of consumers for better utility services. In the mid-1880s, an Austrian chemist accidentally discovered a process for making an incandescent mantle for gas fixtures. The "Welsback mantle" radically changed the production of coal gas to maximize its heat-generating properties. Local operators were supplied with an increasingly inexpensive product, which was suited equally for heating, lighting, or cooking. Moreover, since the new energy fuel allowed companies to employ their equipment on a more full-time basis, rates began to drop dramatically in the nineties. The price of gas fell to the point where the majority of working class urbanites could afford the utility service.[55] In Houston and hundreds of other American cities, the revolutionary transformation of the gas business from a lighting to an energy industry could be keenly felt by company managers, public officials, and private consumers alike.

Beginning with the introduction of electric light and power in the early 1880s, wave after wave of innovative improvements swept over the urban landscape. No longer tied exclusively to aiding the flow of commercial movement in the streets, utility services were fast becoming individual and collective necessities in the late nineteenth century industrial city. Turning on the lights, finally overcoming the age-old problem of darkness, made a profound impression on a whole generation of city dwellers. Predicting that electricity would "revolutionize" Houston, one witness exclaimed, "old things are passing away, all things are becoming new."[56]

The rapid-fire impact of public utilities and their mounting influence on the daily life of the city dweller brought an increasingly intense focus of attention on these enterprises. Because their modernization and internal reform ushered in a series of profound changes in the life of the urbanite, public utilities would be a root cause and form an integral part of urban progressivism. In effect, the franchise acted as a fulcrum that gave consumers unusual political leverage over the companies. The utility grant turned customers into voters who elected the regulators of the urban service ventures. In the 1880s, this peculiar relationship began to take on ominous overtones for local operators.

Bankers and Brotherhoods

Although the origins of progressive reform are complex, a growing mastery of the city building process must be considered one of the cardinal underlying causes. During the 1880s, Houston gained 11,000 new residents, an increase that boosted its population to 27,600 people.[57] Demographic increments, geographic expansion, and economic diversification went hand in hand with a general reorganization of society into formal self-interest groups. As an urban matrix became superimposed over the small town, the nature of the community changed. A proliferation of neighborhood clubs, city-wide federations, and local chapters of national associations replaced older, more informal patterns and relationships. Social reorganization also fostered a resurgence of ward-level grassroots politics that reflected a new appreciation of the vital nexus between city building and community welfare.

Reconstruction's legacy of bipartisan ward-level politics was not forgotten in Houston, only suppressed for a decade under the heavy burden of the city debt. In February 1886, the city's Knights of Labor pressed the elite leaders of the Democratic party to schedule early nominating conventions in each ward. To head off a possible protest movement behind the Republican James G. Tracy, party executives acceded to the demands of the brotherhood, which claimed about 750 members. On the eve of the March 1 meetings of the wards, a ground swell of opposition to Baker broke loudly out into the open. A preliminary caucus of businessmen and professionals had endorsed the mayor after a heated debate, but the Young Men's Democratic Club fell to the insurgents when a full gathering of the organization assembled. The name that resounded triumphantly there and in all five of the party conventions was that of Dan C. Smith.[58]

The two candidates, Baker and Smith, personified the changing nature of an urban society that was promoting political realignments within the community. An early pioneer, Baker accumulated a considerable fortune in commerce, railroad building, and banking. After turning over the management of the Houston and Texas Central to the Huntington interests, Baker divided his time between public service and such private ventures as the HELPC and the city's leading newspaper, the *Daily Post*. In contrast to this steward of Houston's inner circle of families, Smith grew up on a farm in Ohio and later became apprenticed as a locomotive engineer in nearby Cincinnati. In 1858, the 22-year-old machinist immigrated to Houston, where he worked for Baker's railroad until after the war. For about a decade, Smith ran his own machine shop, but he was eventually hired by Southern Pacific to help supervise its repair center.[59] The master mechanic stood out as an ideal representative of the newly organized working class in much the same manner that Baker had emerged earlier from the city's traditional elite of commercial businessmen.

Neither Smith nor his leading supporters, however, advocated a proletarian revolt against capitalism. On the contrary, each active group of insurgents had good reason to believe in the Horatio Alger myth of upward mobility.[60] The Knights of Labor, who sponsored Smith's candidacy, were highly skilled and relatively well paid. Employed mainly by the railroads, these blue-collar workers comprised a respected middle layer of white society on a par with the small entrepreneur. The true proletariat positions were occupied exclusively and permanently by blacks. As in other segregated communities of the South, Houston's Knights began organizing in the early 1880s as social fraternities, not bread-and-butter trade unions. Like Smith, other labor-supported candidates were manual workers on the way up, such as the first ward's George Underwood, a painter at the Houston and Texas Central shops, and the fourth's Ben Riesner, a German-born blacksmith who had recently opened a carriage manufacturing company.[61]

While the Knights formed an organized block of voters, a second group of ambitious young professionals actually managed the hard-fought campaign. Mostly native Houstonians, a new breed of lawyers, corporation executives, and nascent entrepreneurs was making its debut in municipal affairs. These men would dominate local politics, besides playing an enlarging role in state government, for the next quarter century. Attorney H. F. Ring, for example, plotted the takeover of the Young Men's Democratic Club and would soon join the Smith administration as its legal expert. Another lawyer, Oran T. Holt, was a leading spokesman for the insurgents, a budding chieftain of the Texas Democratic party, and a future mayor of the city in the early 1900s. In addition, a journalist, William H. Bailey, provided crucial institutional support by starting an opposition newspaper called the *Houston Herald*.[62] Although more informally organized than the Knights, these white-collar reformers were becoming members of an interlocking network of social, business, and political associations. And even though they were different from Smith's working-class followers, the professionals shared with them a common faith in the upward progress of their careers and their community.

Indeed, Smith's managers exploited widespread feelings of frustration over Baker's inability to strike a final settlement with the bondholders. With public credit in a legal limbo, the insurgents recognized that the rising expectations of the community for better public services and facilities could not possibly be realized. Next to this central theme, Ring and other campaigners attacked the secrecy and the almost "autocratic power" of the Baker administration. Prodded relentlessly by the *Herald*, Mayor Baker finally issued a public disclosure of the city debt, the first such statement since the compromise four years earlier. Bondholders had exchanged over $900,000 worth of the old securities. But a handful of creditors, mostly large dealers, retained another $750,000 worth of the old issues, plus $350,000 worth of outstanding court judgments for unpaid interest.[63] Nevertheless, Baker stubbornly refused to budge from his original position. Until the city's credit was restored, Smith's supporters told the voters, the municipal government could take only half steps toward the creation of a modern city.

Baker's inconclusive bond strategy probably cost him the election. Only 4 out of 4500 votes separated the two contestants in the final talley. Chronicler Benajah Carroll recalled that, "[the voters] had seen that the great financiers could do nothing so they went to the other extreme and turned the city's affairs over to what was facetiously called 'the short hair' element. . . . [T]he city had been turned over to the labor element."[64] For the upwardly mobile, the standpat nature of the established elite was no longer tolerable. Poll watchers also confirmed that class and race were again important factors in municipal politics. Smith decisively carried only the adjoining first and fifth wards, the most industrialized sections of the city. On the other hand, Baker won sizable majorities in the "aristocratic looking" third and fourth wards, which contained the city's most preferred and segregated housing. Race-conscious observers implied that blacks chose Smith over Baker, but it is uncertain whether blacks voted as a unified block.[65] In any case, the elections of 1886 demonstrated the strength of organized group action in urban politics. The upset victory of the Knights taught a lesson that many other special interests and reform groups would attempt to repeat in future campaigns.

Solving the debt problem became Smith's chief accomplishment and accounts for his easy reelection to a second term in office. The few remaining dissatisfied bondholders left the new administration little choice. As soon as the courthouses opened in the fall, the creditors launched a double-barreled assault on the city treasury. In both state and national arenas, the bondholders asked the judiciary to force Houston's officers to levy a "sufficient tax" to cover their overdue coupons.

However, State District Judge James Masterson followed the established practice of simply ordering the city to pay the petitioners their pro rata shares of available bond funds. But in a departure from past strategy, the creditors now appealed to the Texas Supreme Court for a full remuneration of their claims.[66] Similar petitions in the U.S. District Court immediately received favorable treatment. Although the same requests had been denied only three years earlier, Judge Chauncy Sabin finally brought the Gulf Coast district into compliance with the ruling precedent of *Von Hoffman* v. *Quincy, Illinois*. In December 1886, Sabin issued a mandamus writ ordering public officials to levy a "special tax."[67]

The immediate responses of the community to this new turn in the bond controversy ranged from near hysteria to the formulation of an ingenious counter strategy. "This seemingly arbitrary ruling of a Federal judge," the *Post* protested, "has caused considerable feeling among our people, setting the precedent, as it does, for unlimited taxation at the sweet will of a United States Court."[68] Emotional, knee-jerk reactions prompted a few aldermen and wealthy taxpayers to propose that Houston abandon its city charter and become a direct ward of the state. In January 1887, against the advice of the council, Baker and other diehards introduced such a bill in Austin, which interrupted the normal pace of charter revision for another two years.[69] Led by the mayor and the city attorney, the council acted to comply with the court orders, while simultaneously avoiding additional tax burdens. Throughout the year, the Smith administration shrewdly employed a variety of legal tactics to delay actually collecting any special taxes above the regular 2 percent ad valorem levy. In the meantime, the city's tax machinery generated enough revenues to meet the demands of each specific court order, which by the end of 1887 amounted to well over $80,000.[70]

Smith responded to the creditors' maneuvers in the courts by attempting to reach a permanent settlement with the largest bondholder, the New Orleans brokerage house of Fazendi and Seixas. In March 1887, the administration sponsored a bill in the legislature that provided for the creation of state commissions to guarantee the enforcement of municipal bond compromises. Smith's use of these "Boards of Liquidation" reflected a shift from the personal orientations of the past to a reliance on institutions and administrative solutions. The council also flexed its muscle by lowering the assessment rates by an average of 15 percent. This demonstration of the council's control of the tax machinery was aimed at shaking the securities dealers' confidence in the ability of the courts to enforce their claims.[71]

However, the centerpiece of the Smith plan was to refund the outstanding indebtedness in thirty-year, 3 and 4 percent bonds. An August 1887 circular offered a "plain business proposition" that promised the creditors the security of the new state liquidation board. Moreover, by reducing the interest burden to an amount that the municipality could realistically handle, the bondholders could expect faithful payment of their coupons.[72] In the midst of negotiations and on the eve of the April 1888 elections, the Texas Supreme Court announced its decision on the bond controversy. The high bench brought the state into conformity with national law by ordering Houston officials to levy the special taxes. Under tremendous legal and political pressures, Smith agreed to Fazendi and Seixas' demands to refund the debt at a higher 5 and 6 percent rate.[73]

The bond settlement carried Smith to victory, but not without a difficult uphill struggle until the last days of the campaign. The reinvigoration of urban politics in Houston shifted the locus of political power back into the wards. In some of these subdivisions, five or six aldermanic aspirants vied for the endorsement of the nominating conventions. The Smith forces controlled neither these ward level meetings nor the city-wide gathering of the Democratic party. After two days and eight-eight ballots, a deadlock between the incumbent and the challenger, Henry Scherffius, ended with both being endorsed by the convention. In addition, the divided Democrats faced a serious threat from H. D. Johnson on the Republican ticket. The outcome remained in doubt until just four days before the election, when Smith announced the agreement with the New Orleans brokers. A consensus of approval among the city's big taxpayers assured Smith a comfortable margin of Democratic votes over Scherffius. However, the mayor won only by a plurality of 47 percent of the 4835 total vote.[74]

In a brief period, from 1884 to 1888, a mature urban polity emerged full-blown to sweep Houston's traditional leaders out of office. After a decade of suppressing partisan rivalry under a guise of racial fear and fiscal crisis, Democratic chieftains suddenly confronted a broad-based revolt against city government by the elite. The insurgents gained widespread support because they promised to give the whole community a role in translating the general welfare concept into concrete programs. Significantly, the already organized segments of the urban matrix now spearheaded the drive to revive a ward-centered politics. Dramatic changes in the occupational profiles of Houston's elected officials epitomized these shifting patterns of power and influence. In sharp contrast to the predominance of the commercial-civic elite in the Baker administration, Mayor Smith's colleagues on the council represented a much fuller spectrum of community interests (see Table 4.4). The elevation of workers, managers, and professionals to positions of power signalled the beginning of a major reevaluation of public priorities and civic goals.

However, the new configurations of social organization and political power in the community did not immediately produce a radical departure from the growth-oriented policies of the past. After a short period of resistance to the Smith administration, the old guard found that it had little to fear from the insurgents.[75] The unresolved debt controversy, compounded by a general business recession, tightly restricted Smith's fiscal options during his first term. Yet, reallocations of the city's limited resources revealed the coming of age of a ward-based politics. For example, a new lighting contract gave the aldermen an opportunity to alter the locations of the street lamps. Rather than giving top priority to the central business district, the councilmen divided services proportionally among the wards.[76] Although similar readjustments seemed equally minor at first, the re-

TABLE 4.4   Occupational Profile of Houston City Council, 1882 and 1888

Ward	Name	Occupation
	Council of 1882	
	Mayor William R. Baker	President, Houston Insurance Company
		President, City Bank of Houston
		Manager, McIllheny Company
1	Alexander McGowen	Owner, Bayou City Iron Works
	John Kennedy	Owner, Kennedy and Miller
		Real Estate
2	William J. Hutchins	Hotel owner, Land agent
	Martin Curtin	Owner, metal works shop
3	William D. Cleveland	Wholesale cotton merchant
	J. Waldo	Vice president, Houston and
		Texas Central Railroad
		Commissioner, Texas Traffic Association
4	Thomas House, Jr.	Owner, private bank, Cotton broker
		President, Houston Gas Light Co.
		Vice president, Houston Water Co.
		Vice president, Houston East and
		West Texas Railroad
	William Shaw	Clerk, T. W. House's private bank
5	John C. Thomas	Politician (?)
	Sam Allen	Wholesale lumber manufacturer
	Council of 1888	
	Mayor Dan C. Smith	Master mechanic, Southern
		Pacific Railroad Shop
1	Hugh Hamilton	Owner, Crystal Ice Works
	George Underwood	Painter, Houston and Texas
		Central Railroad Shop
2	John Kennedy	Owner, Kennedy and Miller
		Real Estate
	Henry Freund	Superintendent, Houston City
		Street Railway
3	M. G. Howe	Superintendent, Southern Division,
		Houston and Texas Central Railroad
	James Meyer	Owner, wagon supply store
4	Henry Koch	Saloon keeper
	Benjamin Riesner	Wagon manufacturer
5	John T. Browne	Owner, grocery and bakery store
	James Pruett	Yardmaster, Houston East and
		West Texas Railroad

SOURCE: Morrison and Fourmy, *General Directory of the City of Houston* (Galveston and Houston: Morrison and Fourmy, 1882–1889).

orientation of public policy toward neighborhood improvements would eventually splinter the Texas community into bitter partisan factions.

The rebirth of municipal politics in Houston was typical of the dawning of a new era of city building throughout urban America. During the Baker years, city dwellers were awakening to the great potential of urban institutions to advance the general welfare. By the mid-eighties, Baker's steady gains in easing linear movement within the central business district raised common hopes that city hall could solve other pressing environmental as well as social problems caused by urban-industrial growth. The accumulating mastery of the city builders, both public and private, encouraged an increasingly self-conscious, diverse, and organized society to demand a larger voice in the determination of public policy. As more and more urbanites came to depend on utility services, the movement for better city government would cut across all segments of society and give city dwellers a common cause that would bind the urban polity into a powerful engine of reform. By the mid-nineties, political battles over utility franchises were erupting in so many localities that the city again attracted national attention.

Unlike urban planning in the past, a solid infrastructure of institutional supports gave a rising generation of municipal reformers an unparalleled mastery of the city building process. The physical and social maladies of rapid urbanization continued to mount, but now civic leaders could rely on an impressive array of structural mechanisms and administrative procedures to help solve these chronic shortcomings. After twenty years, the period when amateur city builders worked in virtual isolation from one another had come to a close. They had created more or less integrated systems in both the government and the business sectors, which were designed specifically to cope with America's urban problems. By the late 1880s, moreover, another recent innovation—the graduate school—was training an expanding corps of experts from electrical engineers to political scientists to manage and improve these systems. In many respects, the most important legacy of the passing generation of amateurs was an impressive group of national institutions devoted to making the cities efficient, harmonious, and comfortable.

Robert Wiebe's image of a nation of "island communities" seems especially appropriate for describing the condition of the governments of American cities during the Gilded Age. The legal reformers alone penetrated this isolation by creating a constitutional framework that outlined the limits of the city's legitimate powers. Cooley's and Dillon's influential theories of the municipal corporation practically stripped localities of any inherent right to self-government, making them dependent wards of the state. The federal judiciary also tied severe restrictions on the public sector's fiscal powers. However, the courts' expansive general welfare concept still left local subdivisions considerable leeway to shape the quality and direction of urban life. Civic leaders in their communities learned how to work within these guidelines, which pinpointed the municipal charter as the pivotal instrument of reform. City attorneys and other structural reformers became expert at tapping the authority of the state in order to impose public controls on the city building process.

In contrast, businessmen constructed a much fuller set of institutions to bind urban service companies into a single national framework. Beginning in the 1870s, local utility operators banded together in trade associations to overcome technical problems and to develop defenses against the challenges of competition. Over the next twenty years, industry leaders forged an integrated structure that gave the private sector a degree of unity and strength far greater than the public's federal connections could match. By 1890, the utilities industry controlled access to technological advancement, commanded vast sums of investment capital, possessed flexible mechanisms for vertical and horizontal reorganizations, and advocated concerted strategies to deflect popular hostilities. The comprehensive scope of this modernization and internal reform created a structure of economic and political power that would outmaneuver, if not overwhelm, civic leaders in the coming battles over utility franchises.

If the institutionalization of city building by government and business ended one phase of American urban history, it also opened a new period of intense political struggle for the reins of power at city halls across the nation. A command of the technical aspects of supplying most public services and utilities shifted the central question from How do we make improvements? to Who gets them first? Questions of priorities in the allocation of the city government's limited resources, including the expensive option of public ownership, assumed first importance. A growing dependence on utility services as basic, individual, and social necessities of urban living also contributed to sharpening the focus of attention on elected public officials. The broad but still vaguely defined concept of the general welfare left unsettled the boundaries of the public's right to regulate the rate and service levels of the private enterprises. Policy makers at the helm of municipal governments in the 1890s were in the crucial positions of setting the course of the city for at least a generation.

In Houston, a heady sense of mastery over the urban environment was proving infectious. Smith's settlement of the debt controversy finally lifted the restricting weight of bondholder suits from the municipal treasury and set loose waves of optimism rippling through the community. "A new era of feeling in regard to public improvements is dawning," the newspaper proclaimed. By the end of 1888, the Texas urbanites were engaged in a vigorous debate over charter amendments to take full advantage of the restoration of the city's credit. Ambitious plans to expand the scope of paving and sewerage projects received enthusiastic support, even from large taxpayers. "The public improvements of a city," the *Post* explained, "are a very good index to the character of the inhabitants for thrift and enterprise." [77] Compared to the depressed state of affairs in Houston just a decade earlier, these expressions of hope and progress gave voice to widespread feelings that all things were indeed becoming new.

Main Street at Congress Avenue, 1860s. The beginnings of the central business district include the Morris Building (center), the Houston Telegraph Office (left), and the Van Aslyne Building on the corner of Congress Avenue. Courtesy Houston Metropolitan Research Center, Houston Public Library.

Main Street at Congress Avenue, 1860s. The be-
ginnings of the central business district include the
Morris Building (center), the Houston Telegraph
Office (left), and the Van Aslyne Building on the
corner of Congress Avenue. Courtesy Houston
Metropolitan Research Center, Houston Public
Library.

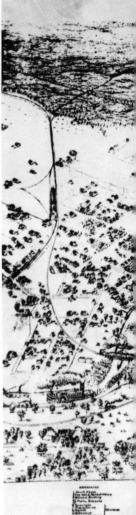

Bird's-eye view of Houston, 1873 (looking south).
A commercial city emerges from waterborne traf-
fic, railroad depots, and business establishments.
Courtesy Houston Metropolitan Research Center,
Houston Public Library.

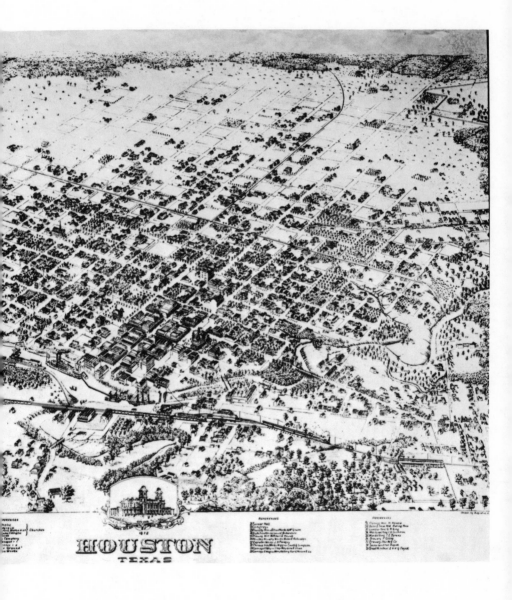

Bird's-eye view of Galveston, 1885 (looking south). The sister city shows similar land use patterns of waterfront docks, railroad yards (right), and beach front resorts (top). Courtesy Amon Carter Museum, Fort Worth.

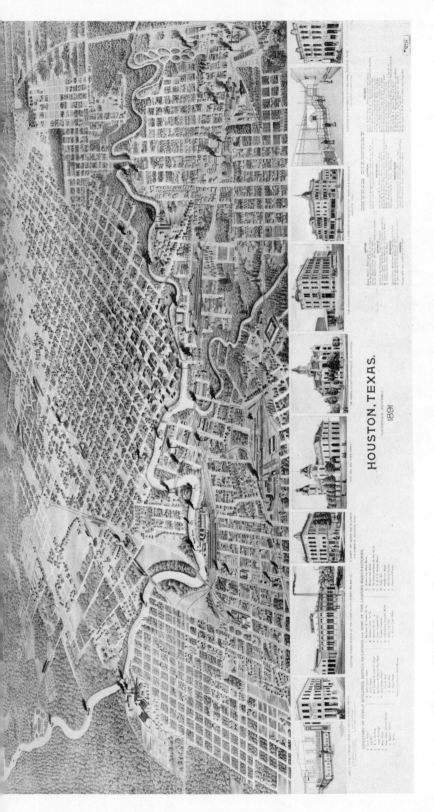

Bird's-eye view of Houston, 1891 (looking south). Metropolitan scale results from the sprawl of homes and factories around the central business district. Courtesy Amon Carter Museum, Fort Worth.

Houston, looking northeast from the Courthouse,
1880s. Commercial buildings dominate the downtown area. Note the Farendon Building, lower right
corner. Courtesy Houston Metropolitan Research
Center, Houston Public Library.

Congress Avenue at Fannin Street, 1890s. This intersection was in the heart of the commercial emporium. Note the Farendon Building, right center. Courtesy Houston Metropolitan Research Center, Houston Public Library.

Wholesale produce district, 1890s. Specialized
districts gave Houston a metropolitan character.
Courtesy Houston Metropolitan Research Center,
Houston Public Library.

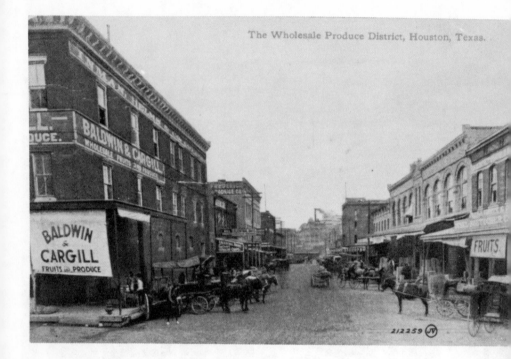

Second Ward waterfront, 1890s. As this post card
shows, the ship channel had deteriorated into an
industrial slum by the 1890s. Courtesy Houston
Metropolitan Research Center, Houston Public
Library.

2ⁿᵈ· Ward. Houston, Texas.

*Many thanks for card, Vincant Px.
712 Chenevert St, Houston, Texas.*

88

Fifth Ward panorama, 1890s. The Fifth Ward was
an industrial district of factories, smokestacks, and
warehouses. Courtesy Houston Metropolitan Research Center, Houston Public Library.

Fifth Ward seen from Southern Pacific R. R. Office Building,
Houston, Texas.

Southern Pacific Railroad Shops, 1890s. The single
largest employer of skilled, blue-collar workers.
Courtesy Houston Metropolitan Research Center,
Houston Public Library.

Main Street at Franklin Avenue, 1890s. By the end
of the century, Houston was a modern city with
trolley cars, paved streets, and the ubiquitous tan-
gle of overhead wires. Courtesy Houston Metropolitan Research Center, Houston Public Library.

Part **II**

Urban Planning by Experts

5 "The Spirit of Progressive Municipal Legislation"

The National Outlook

In 1893, Chicago's Columbian Exposition announced to the world America's ascendancy in industrial progress. Millions visited the great White City, with its dramatic displays of modern science and invention, its dazzling electric lights, and its urbane titillations along the Midway.[1] Among the tourists was Henry Adams, the brilliant if cynical student of the West's metamorphosis from a religious to a technological culture. To Adams, the White City asked "for the first time whether the American people knew where they were driving."[2] His self-demeaning attitude restrained him from openly venturing an opinion, but the question disclosed the bewildered state of his contemporaries. Within a single generation, a vast continent of rural communities had undergone a profound transformation into an interdependent nation of industrial cities. Certainly Adams was not alone in questioning whether there was a sense of order and direction to this unsettling experience.

The Chicago world's fair provoked imaginative questions about the future because it demonstrated that the United States possessed the skills and tools to get just about anywhere it wanted. Touring the grounds, Adams paused a long while inside the exposition's electric palace. To him, its silently spinning dynamos epitomized the final triumph of technology over the forces of nature. He believed that the whirring machines were fast replacing the Virgin—for him, the universal totem of fertility—as the modern symbol of energy and life.[3] Yet the grand panorama of the plaster of paris city that enclosed the fair's machines probably impressed visitors more than any particular exhibit. The neo-classic style of architecture embodied an optimistic faith that an urban-industrial civilization would endure for centuries. Reflecting the city builders' expertise in environmental engineering, the exposition reinforced hopes that similar achievements in the social sciences could ameliorate the most glaring deficiencies of modern life. In any case, the fair left little doubt that the United States was moving through a transitional period between a fading rural past and a dawning urban future.[4]

During this transformation in the 1890s, Americans hotly debated Adams's quandary: Which path would best lead the nation into the twentieth century? The accumulative legacy of the Gilded Age infused an entire society with a spirit of pragmatic experimentation. Americans became caught up in a searching examination of themselves and the national purpose. In the cities, the focus of reformers began shifting from one of solving technical problems to one of raising political issues about social goals and community priorities.

119

Contemporaries built programs of reform on the foundations of the recent past. In the late 1880s and early 1890s, the process of reassessment produced original modes of thought, novel principles of political economy, and a wide range of alternative social visions. After the Panic of 1893, however, groups as divergent as the Populist farmers and the organized workers punctuated this intellectual ferment with militant demands for radical change. The bitter struggles of the depression years narrowed the political options to a single choice—that of urban progressivism. This new national order directed the course of reform for the next two decades. The debate over the reorientation of American society at the onset of the new era offers an important key to the answer of Henry Adams's question about where the country was heading.[5]

Although the progressives soon opened new frontiers of social theory, the path of reform in the cities traced an unbroken line of continuity with the past. The amateur reformers of the 1870s and 1880s left an enduring legacy, a solid foundation of reform skills and institutional tools at each level of the federal system. These technological, economic, and constitutional structures of the Gilded Age not only shaped the issues at the start of the debate but also largely determined the final outcome of municipal reform at the conclusion of the Progressive Era.

After the mid-1880s, the virtually instantaneous diffusion of electric inventions into cities across the country helped trigger a massive ground swell of political insurgency. For the first time since the fiscal crisis of the 1870s, municipal reform attained national momentum. In effect, the electric utilities revolutionized consumer demand for essential services. Technological breakthroughs in rapid transit, communications, sanitation, and energy systems promised to end chronic social pathologies and to uplift metropolitan living to unprecedented levels of mass convenience. The introduction of the electrical systems sharply accelerated the transformation of public services from personal luxuries to collective necessities of urban life. Mounting pressures for more essential facilities and better social services fueled the drive to organize broad-based political coalitions that struggled for control of city hall.

A major legacy of the Gilded Age—the electrical innovations of the engineer-entrepreneurs—ensured that the utilities industry would be both a root cause and an integral part of municipal reform in the Progressive Era. By 1890, the recast configuration of urban institutions gave the private sector a leading role in supplying essential services. It had welded the legal, organizational, and technological developments of the postbellum period into a strong, integrated position. The leaders of the utility associations were well prepared to manage the coming revolution in consumer demand for public services. They had already formulated and tested a political strategy to channel reform currents toward a favorable outcome. The mid-1880s experiment of Massachusetts gasmen proved so advantageous to private enterprise that regulated monopoly by a state commission eventually became the overwhelming choice of the entire industry.[6]

Structural continuities from the Gilded Age also framed the configuration of the public institutions in the subsequent period. But municipal reform efforts had not paralleled the growth of modern business structures. Civic leaders had not forged the divided authorities of local government into a flexible and responsive arrangement of federalism. On the contrary, the legal reformers had moved in the opposite direction, to confine the municipal corporation under debilitating restraints. State and national limitations had hamstrung city hall's fiscal powers, placing many reform goals beyond its reach. Constitutional checkreins dragged against the political upsurge to obtain extensive improvements in public utilities and social services. Collectively, the structural changes wrought in government and business during the 1870s and 1880s set the stage for the political contests of the 1890s.[7]

It is not surprising that the major battle for municipal reform in Houston and in most American cities pitted insurgent coalitions against the utility companies. The evolving pattern of the technological, economic, and constitutional structures of city building each pointed toward this very result after the mid-1880s. Reflecting the rich legacy of the amateurs, new issues were superseding older questions about how to solve the technical shortcomings of environmental engineering. After the utilities industry ushered in the electric technologies, an unprecedented emphasis on social planning and resource allocation priorities began to permeate discussions of municipal reform. The enormous investment costs of the electric systems put the relationship between government and business at the center of the debate over the future direction of public policy. Political alignments as well as city budgets revolved around the pivotal issue of supplying essential utilities by either public or private means.[8] A growing corpus of constitutional law on the cities defined the alternatives and shaped the framework of the contest to prove the superiority of one option over the others.

During the Gilded Age, the U.S. Supreme Court had narrowed the previously fluid range of city-utility relationships to three distinct choices: regulated competition, regulated monopoly, and public ownership. Yet the nascent doctrine of urban public utilities kept posing new dilemmas in the process of resolving old ones. Under private enterprise options, state and city governments were not only authorized but also duty bound to protect the public interest. The courts charged municipal officials with the task of maintaining a constant vigilance over their franchisees. In 1890, however, local officials could only vaguely discern the parameters of this police power. State and national jurists had made a good start in demarcating the permissible areas of environmental supervision, but no limitations yet circumscribed critical areas of regulation such as service standards and rate limitations. Public ownership, of course, neatly eliminated all these problems. However, a different set of equally perplexing issues arose from other high bench rulings on municipal finance. Although the courts' state agency theory of urban utilities fully justified public ownership, their restrictions on municipal indebtedness seemed to foreclose this expensive option.

Gilded Age decisions about the city's fiscal and regulatory authority ensured that the structural renovation of local government would become an imperative precondition of reform in the Progressive Era. In order to promote the social welfare, urban reformers first had to rehabilitate the institutions of city government. The three alternatives presented strikingly different ways to supply public utilities. Each required substantial changes in the institutions of government, either to create efficient regulatory mechanisms or to finance public ownership. Moreover, the option of regulated competition imposed additional requirements to restructure the law and the economics of public utilities in such a way as to guarantee the continuous operation of market forces.

In any case, municipal reformers had to overcome the legacy of the Gilded Age before they could achieve significant improvements in their physical surroundings and their social welfare. By the 1890s, city dwellers no longer questioned the need for modern public amenities. Instead, they asked how public utilities could best provide high quality services at low cost. Even the essential services in most obvious need of repair formed a long list: constructing schools, roads, and sewers; upgrading police, fire, and sanitation departments; and securing up-to-date utility facilities. To accomplish these tasks, reformers first had to realign the municipal corporation in the federal system. Only then could the city reinvigorate its fiscal strength and build a regulatory power over the business sector.

Initially, an infectious spirit of progress fed contemporary hopes of overcoming any structural reform hurdle. From the avant-garde graduate schools of public administration to the smoke-filled ward meetings of provincial places like Houston, Americans eagerly discussed their plans for the modern city of tomorrow. A budding faith in American know-how, which found such vivid expression in the neoclassicism of the White City, raised expectations that the physical and social sciences could discover remedies for all the maladies of an urban-industrial civilization. Although this innocence did not last long among seasoned reformers, it infused the progressive dialog with a fresh, expansive sense of the future.[9] The federal character of the government produced a triple-tiered debate on local, state, and national levels. At the same time, national and state leaders were constantly interacting, exchanging ideas, and testing their model programs against the practical results of local politics.

On speakers' platforms throughout the federal system, the coming role of big business in modern society dominated the debate over the direction of progressive reform. This choice of topics represented the culmination of a political argument that stretched back to the antebellum period. The legitimacy of the business corporation first attracted serious attention in the 1830s. The Jacksonians had expended a great amount of rhetoric on the proper structural relationships between the public and private sectors. But they had left the question open ended because these powerful instruments of development seemed to be fulfilling their economic promise. A half century later, however, the threat of big business to the constitutional ideal loomed large. By the late 1880s, the influence of private corporations appeared to have grown so enormous as to belie the fundamental proposition that "all organized power be [held] responsible by measures of utility and of justice."[10]

Americans everywhere believed that the future of democracy in the United States hinged on the same point of political economy. Big business had a critical impact on urban workers striving to obtain essential services from the utility companies, small entrepreneurs trying to survive competitive challenges from giant trusts, and rural sharecroppers attempting to escape from debt peonage to the banks, railroads, and commission merchants. While Americans applauded the efficiencies of large units of production, they simultaneously feared the social consequences of monopolistic power. More liberal interpretations of the social welfare only accentuated political demands to resolve this persistent dilemma of American capitalism in favor of the public interest. Nowhere did the growth of the business corporation appear more ominous than in the essential service sectors that comprised the infrastructure of the emerging urban-industrial society.[11]

On a national level, a new breed of European-trained social scientists spearheaded the drive to impose a sense of order and direction on the coming age of the giant corporation. Repudiating the mechanistic formulas of the recent past, the academic-activists devised new methods of analysis that employed statistics and research to construct normative models of society. But in spite of this rejection of formalism, the pragmatists relied on untested theories from the Gilded Age to explain the alarming trend toward monopoly in essential services. Social scientists assumed uncritically that "natural monopolies" inevitably resulted in capital-intensive industries such as urban utilities and interstate railroads. Business leaders agreed wholeheartedly with the assertion that economies of scale inexorably reduced competition in public services to a sole supplier. However, the two groups came to opposite conclusions from a similar analysis of the problem. The social scientists advocated public ownership of natural monopolies, whereas the leaders of big business called for the creation of state regulatory commissions as the best way to maintain a fair balance between public interests and private rights.[12]

A different kind of ferment was brewing in the states. Rural-based solutions to the problems of big business were generating radical economic reforms and major political realignments. Throughout the South and the West especially, hard-pressed sharecroppers were drawing together in cooperative movements. The Populists tried to break the economic stranglehold of a variety of business corporations that provided crucial marketing, financial, and transportation services. The farmers' struggle for economic democracy soon turned into a political revolt, because their hopes rested on the enactment of structural reform measures. In Texas, the insurgency of the farmers stirred a thorough reevaluation of the state's relationships to its corporate creations, including the municipal corporation.[13]

Led by Governor James G. Hogg, Texans renovated their state government in the early 1890s. Under Hogg's leadership, modernization of the state government meant restricting the freedom of corporations, but without destroying their utility or their vested rights. Ironically, the revolt of the farmers, which initially lifted Hogg to prominence, shifted political power to a coalition of industrial agriculturalists and city-based financial leaders. For instance, Hogg received early and continuing support from members of Houston's commercial-civic elite such as Thomas W. House's son, Edward M., lawyer-politician Joseph Hutchinson, and railroad manager E. P. Hill. Their help in electing Hogg governor gave Houston new importance within the Democratic party.[14]

Hogg's brand of reform was emblematic of the New South approach to big business. The New South strategy attempted to restore balance and stability in government-business relations in order to attract Northern capital into the region. The new generation of urban-based leaders of the Texas Democracy did not share their rural brethren's fear of corporate power. Instead, they were more concerned with sharing in the economic growth fed by industrialization. The city of Austin, for example, promoted industrial diversification by providing cheap energy. Houston sought to stimulate its growth as an agricultural processing center through similar schemes to encourage rice planting and timber harvesting in the surrounding hinterland. The help of investment capital from the North was essential to the achievement of these goals. To attract this support, cities throughout the region tried to establish financially sound local governments with low tax rates and at least the appearance of sociopolitical stability.[15]

On a local level, Houston and other urban centers experimented freely with the three alternative means of supplying essential services. Buoyed by the growing mastery of the city builders, Houstonians also paused to take stock of themselves and the future of their community. While the commercial-civic elite still adhered to a New South strategy of urban growth (a public policy of promoting Houston's hegemony over the regional economy), the newly organized segments of the urban society began challenging this choice of priorities for the allocation of the public sector's limited resources. The insurgents placed greater emphasis on upgrading the quality of life in the neighborhoods. They hoped to realize the promise of the modern city in the immediate future. They also reacted against the loss of local autonomy and the growth of national interdependence. Houstonians with narrow neighborhood perspectives attacked the most convenient manifestation of big business, the utility companies, which were owned by outside investors. The insurgents forged new directions in public policy by granting competitive franchises to native sons and by exploring options for municipal ownership.

The United States stood at a crossroads of reform in the late eighties and early nineties. During this transitional period, continuities from the Gilded Age played a configurative role in shaping the framework of intellectual discourse. In the area of municipal reform, the legacy of the amateur city builders laid a solid base of practical experience and institutional structures that helped to guide a rising generation of urban planners into the twentieth century. If Americans did not know in which direction they were headed in 1893, at least they possessed a good idea of the various routes they might follow. During the depression of the mid-1890s, public policy alternatives began to polarize around opposing positions staked out earlier in the debate. From these ideological moorings, local leaders charted the course of urban politics. For the next two decades, reformers moved along plainly marked pathways of social theory and economic dogma.

The Local Viewpoint

A close inspection of a single city presents a test case to measure the influence of social scientists, utility leaders, and state reformers at the local level. The battle for municipal reform in Houston, moreover, provides a comparative context to weigh the theoretical remedies of national experts against the practical results of structural change in government-business relations. In Houston, the late 1880s and early 1890s represented a period of reorientation in public policy and of experimentation in city building. Already enjoying home rule from Austin, the urban Texans ambitiously opened several frontiers in the structural dimensions of local government. The technological revolution in urban services also gave municipal reformers a fresh opportunity to reassess the city's approach toward its utility enterprises.

After the mid-1880s, a mastery of city building left little doubt in the minds of Houstonians that progress and public improvements comprised two sides of the same coin. Renewed faith in the future stimulated discussion on city planning and structural reforms to accelerate the modernization of the community's public services. Reformers also explored how the three franchise options could be used with maximum effect to upgrade the level of services delivered by private companies. Houstonians went about revising their city charter with confidence because they drew freely on the reform legacy of the Gilded Age and the current practices of other localities. These adjustments rapidly increased the scope and range of Houston's public services as well as the administrative costs of city government. With the onset of a severe economic depression in 1893, local officials began searching for ways to make better use of the public sector's limited resources, including its utility franchises. Reformers hoped to shift a larger share of the economic burden of improving the urban environment onto the utility firms, and they hoped to cut the high cost of utility bills by embarking on the path of municipal socialism.

The final settlement of the third bond compromise in June 1888 set off a provocative public debate on city planning. Mayor Dan Smith's restoration of the public credit opened fiscal options that had long been closed to the debt-ridden municipal corporation. Few Houstonians questioned the equation between "paving and progress," [16] but they argued furiously over alternative schemes of paying for a rapid expansion of the improvement program. Two related issues at the center of the debate reveal a process of reorientation in community attitudes about building a modern city. Structural reformers had to decide whether to begin financing public works projects with municipal bonds or to continue the old system of issuing assessment certificates to the contractors. The prospect of a significant increase in special assessment taxes also raised new questions about the adequacy of existing checks and balances between the local government and the property owner. Over the next three years, Houstonians embodied their city planning philosophy in a succession of structural revisions in the municipal charter.

After the bond settlement, public improvement planning quickly became the "all absorbing topic" within the community.[17] Houstonians were typical city dwellers of the late nineteenth century. The mastery of environmental engineering that was gained in the Gilded Age turned the physical condition of each community into an index of its civic spirit, if not its moral character. On the Texas Gulf, an intense urban rivalry for Southern migrants and Northern capital further accentuated the importance of city building activities that would enhance Houston's attractiveness. Civic leaders therefore emphasized that the debt compromise marked the beginning of a bright new era rather than the conclusion of a dark and difficult one. A prominent citizen, George Porter, expressed the common assumption that

> [o]ur people . . . all know that without good roads and a sewerage system we cannot build a modern city. The present horrible condition of our streets and the lack of drainage and sewerage will not attract live and intelligent people to make this their homes unless they have every assurance that this condition will be gradually changed to meet the requirements of modern civilization.[18]

Porter's addition of sanitation and drainage projects to the list of essential public improvements reflects the sophisticated level of contemporary debate over city planning. A long history of painful lessons in ecological decay had taught Houstonians a great deal about managing an artificial environment in a semitropical climate. Recent insights by medical experts added urgency to the civil engineer's call for a comprehensive city plan. The coastal entrepôt had always been vulnerable to epidemic attack, especially from the dreaded yellow fever. However, Louis Pasteur's studies of the transmission of germs gave scientific backing to the old suspicion that contagious diseases often spread through contaminated water supplies. The experts' linkage of public health and sanitation was just one example of a growing complex of urban functions that seemed to fall within the government sector. During the community-wide debate of the late 1880s, Houstonians also pointed to the need to establish a network of municipal parks and a system of street numbering. "All these improvements," a newspaper editorial concluded, "go to make up a metropolis. They are just and necessary and give a town a business-like appearance, not only to our own people but to strangers."[19]

Houstonians sought outside advice from a variety of professionals and practitioners before committing themselves to a concrete plan of public improvements. On the one hand, resident experts informed the planning debate with the latest findings of their colleagues. A spokesman for the local medical association, Dr. Flewelen, warned of dangers to the public health not only from sewage but also from wooden paving materials. The doctor argued that bois d'arc blocks and plank stripping were both disease breeders in a semi-tropical area. On the other hand, local policy makers travelled more frequently to inspect public works projects in other locales. Shortly after the first set of charter revisions sailed through the legislature without opposition in March 1889, the mayor and the city engineer toured nearby rival cities. Investigating their paving and drainage programs, Mayor Smith returned home "almost overzealous for permanent improvements in Houston as the best means to assume city airs and proportions." [20] For Smith, the inspection tour reinforced belief in a formula for municipal progress that equated public improvements and urban growth.

Moreover, Smith and his fellow Houstonians believed fervently that they possessed the tools and training to implement their plans for the city's future. They relied on their skills as structural reformers to translate policy goals into institutional terms. An expertise in revising the municipal charter represented a vital legacy of the amateur city builders. Houstonians agreed in general to boost the pace and scope of public works projects, but they argued over the specific details of financing the expanded program. Despite these minor disagreements, most participants in the public debate expressed a new sense of confidence in themselves and in the abilities of the expert to fulfill their visions of the coming city.

Surprisingly, the heated debate on alternative mechanisms of financing the city plan did not pit the taxpaying minority against the propertyless masses. In January 1889, a series of public meetings on the city council's proposals for charter reform exposed a division of opinion along different lines. None of the spokesmen for the property owners questioned the continued use of special assessment taxes to pay for streets, sidewalks, sewers, and drains. The constitutional stability of this taxing system established its practical utility. However, some taxpayers advocated municipal bonds as the optimal instrument of long-term public finance. Interest rates would be 2 to 3 percent lower than the charges levied by the current scheme of contractor certificates. In contrast, others worried that such a policy would soon put Houston back on the old road of excess, which led to municipal bankruptcy. [21]

To prevent deadlock and delay in launching the expanded program of public improvements, Houstonians compromised their differences. They initially accepted the position of the conservatives and retained the certificate system. Two years later, however, a more liberal posture triumphed after an uninterrupted boom in real estate values boosted the tax rolls by 50 percent, to over $15,000,000. [22] Structural reformers again amended the charter, permitting the council to issue up to $150,000 per year in street improvement bonds. Local lawmakers did not exercise this option before the depression, but they took advantage of other new powers that substantially extended the public authority over the urban environment. Two unique provisions in the charter of 1889 illustrate the expertise of the city builders in translating planning goals into public policy. Reformers had little trouble modifying the special assessment method of taxation to fit the needs of their sanitation program. From the original linear design of street improvements, they created a system of taxing districts to pay for sewerage improvements. A second and related extension of governmental authority gave the council far-reaching powers to remove stagnant water and other health hazards from private property at the owner's expense.[23]

In large part, a spirit of compromise prevailed in Houston because reformers felt assured that they could restructure the municipal government to safeguard private rights against abuses of power. In the 1889 revision of the charter, for example, Houstonians created a Board of Public Works that was composed of three citizens appointed by the mayor. The board acted as a watchdog over the council's public improvement program. Each proposed project had to pass through the advisory body before the aldermen could solicit contracts. The 1889 as well as the 1891 revisions of the municipal charter further elaborated the procedural rights of individual property owners who became subject to special assessments. Additional protections of private rights against excesses by the council took the form of structural changes in the selection of the city's administrative officers. Reversing the trend of the Baker years, reformers inserted amendments requiring that nine of the most important department heads, such as the assessor-collector, city attorney, and street commissioner, be elected.[24]

A sense of mastery in city planning and charter reform extended easily to embrace franchise relations with the city's utility companies. But Houstonians seemed to flounder in these troubled waters, compared with their steady advances in expanding the public works program of environmental improvements. Since franchise politics forms the central theme of the following chapter, one example will serve here to highlight the dilemma of choosing among the three alternative forms of utility services: regulated competition, regulated monopoly, and municipal ownership. It is fitting that the best illustration of the utility problem begins in March 1889, when a syndicate of Northern capitalists purchased Houston's street railway monopoly. Heading the group was Charles B. Holmes, the promoter of mass transit on Chicago's south side who had built the largest system of cable cars outside of San Francisco. The timing of his move into Texas and the disclosure that his group was also buying streetcar lines in several other places suggests that Holmes anticipated a breakthrough in electric traction.[25]

In April, however, the city council completely upset the Chicagoan's plans for the Southern community. After a month of bitter debate, an evenly divided council finally granted a rival franchise to William Boyd, a paving contractor. The old adage that "competition is the life of trade" apparently convinced Mayor Smith to cast his tie-breaking vote in favor of the Boyd grant. To Holmes, this unexpected "slap in the face" represented an understandable but outmoded approach to public policy.[26] He launched a publicity campaign that combined promises of massive aid from the North with threats of an abrupt pullout of the syndicate from the Texas city. Holmes tried to persuade the Texans of the folly of competition in the public utility sector. Echoing the public service strategy of national utility leaders, Holmes called for the mutual cooperation of business and government as the only way to guarantee urban growth and prosperity.

The expertise in urban planning displayed by Holmes during his public relations effort epitomizes the difference between the new and old generations of city builders. Investments in urban utilities, the Chicagoan argued in a series of letters to the mayor, had an impact on the city that went far beyond mere improvements in public services. Mass transit extensions in other cities were creating streetcar suburbs, enhancing real estate values in general, and rapidly boosting city population. His syndicate's $300,000 investment in Indianapolis, Holmes pointed out, had triggered the greatest building boom in the city's history. Moreover, indirect benefits to the city's economy amounted to at least four times the initial investment. Holmes predicted that similar multiplier effects would also accelerate Houston's growth, if only "the people would gladly unite with us in developing the interests of the city." Instead, Holmes chided, Houston had already lost $500,000 of the syndicate's money, while the Southern community was gaining the dubious reputation as a parochial center of anti-Yankee sentiment. Holmes declared that competition in public utilities was a bad mistake. It would result in a decline of services and a boycott of the city by Northern capitalists.[27]

Although Mayor Smith denied the charge that Houston looked upon the foreign-owned company as "something to be seized and destroyed," his protests did little to reassure the Chicago investors.[29] Over the next year, Boyd's Bayou City Company built a sixteen-mile network of belt lines that extended services for the first time into several parts of the city. The utility's purchase of $75,000 worth of real estate indicates that local businessmen also recognized the intimate connection between transit services and city growth. In fact, Houstonians specifically created a third transit firm to tie the downtown area to a distant suburban development by means of steam or electric traction.[29] This "new agency of city building," the *Houston Daily Post* confirmed from a study of rapid transit in other cities, "bring[s] outlying fields and resorts within easy and cheap reach of the citizens and busy workers, and builds the suburbs with a truly magic development."[30] The urban Texans accepted Holmes' analysis of the new urban technology, but they rejected his advocacy of utility monopolies. Unable to convince public officials to reject the regulated competition option, the Chicagoans delayed their original plans to convert Houston's streetcars to electric traction. Instead, the Holmes syndicate sold out in early 1891 to another Northern speculator, Oscar M. Carter, who simultaneously purchased Boyd's Bayou City line.[31]

For Houston, the decision to have regulated competition in mass transit brought mixed results that made this public policy difficult, if not impossible, to evaluate. On the one hand, the Boyd grant stimulated an immediate expansion of transit services, almost doubling the existing trackage. With over 27,500 inhabitants listed in the U.S. Census of 1890, Houston had several neighborhoods without public transportation until the Bayou City Company built extensions into these neglected areas.[32] Competition between utility firms also gave the city council better leverage to extract tax and regulatory concessions from the private companies. On the other hand, granting rival franchises discouraged Northern investment in the local economy and delayed the installation of a modern electrical system of rapid transit. Moreover, the council's policy unintentionally marked the Texas community with a stigma of the old South—xenophobia. Finally, the alternative of regulated competition ultimately failed when both franchise holders sold out to a third party. On the eve of the city's belated conversion to electric traction in mid-1891, the two-year experiment in competition left no clear answer as to which franchise option best promoted the general welfare.

The dilemmas of utility franchises comprised only one part of an interrelated set of problems that collectively defined Houston's agenda of municipal reform. Civic leaders were discovering from their experiments in planning that government and business were increasingly dependent on each other for success in city building. The dismal experience of the Chicago syndicate perfectly illustrates the deleterious effects of a utility company taking a stubborn position of opposition to public policy. At the same time, city hall's improvement program suffered too from lost revenues that the streetcar venture would have paid to defer the costs of paving between its tracks.

In a similar manner, public policies to provide fire hydrants and street lights in previously neglected neighborhoods affected government and business in different but related ways. While these improvements contributed substantially to the economic well-being of the utility firms, each service extension permanently added new pressure on the municipal budget. With water and electric light bills mounting to over $30,000 annually (or about 20 percent of the city's operating funds in 1891), officials began exploring the public ownership alternative.[33] Although they reached no conclusions before the onset of the depression of 1893, they gained a better appreciation of the mutual interdependence of government and business in the area of municipal reform.

Between the bond settlement of 1888 and the national economic crash five years later, Houstonians made bold commitments to upgrade their physical surroundings and their public services. According to Mayor Smith, this consensus was the "spirit of progressive municipal legislation." At the dawn of the 1890s, he confirmed that "[t]he City of Houston is fully awakened to the fact that in this progressive age a liberal policy in regard to public improvements . . . is absolutely necessary to its growth and prosperity."[34]

The mayor's definition of urban progressivism from a local viewpoint underscores the importance of the Gilded Age's legacy of mastery in city building. This rich heritage had transformed public facilities and utility services from luxuries to necessities of urban life. Rapid transit, gas, telephones, and electric lights were now considered as essential as the water supply. Houstonians increasingly depended on utility companies to get to work and move information, to operate their businesses and keep their homes sanitary, and to uphold the public health and safety. These "captive" consumers could exert leverage on their utility suppliers only indirectly; that is, through city hall.

The shifting perspective on utility services—from personal luxuries to community necessities—was causing fundamental realignments in the political relationships among city residents, municipal governments, and utility companies. Regardless of their initial attitudes toward municipal reform, city dwellers in

Houston and many other locales were becoming captive consumers of the utility enterprises. The rising importance of the utility franchises put elected officials into pivotal positions of power brokers between the consumer-voter and the utility supplier. Mayors and aldermen also gained new opportunities for personal and party graft. The growing dependence of the utilities on local policymakers for franchise and regulatory concessions gave the companies a strong incentive to maintain a constant lobby at city hall. Utility managers had good cause to create a permanent "sphere of influence" in the public sector.[35]

But despite utility industry campaigns to defuse popular hostility, the crucial importance of public services to the community often sparked explosive battles over franchise policy. The speculators' scrambles for electric concessions, muckraker exposés of franchise bribery and corruption, and corporate arrogance towards consumers triggered reform coalitions into action. From the local viewpoint, perceptions of the essential nature of urban utilities broadened the issues involved in the provision of these public services from a simple question of economic expediency to a perplexing array of ideological, political, and social quandaries. The electrical revolution presented local communities with a fresh but essentially irreversible chance to choose among the three alternative franchise policies. After government or business committed large, nonliquid investments to utility fixtures, policy inversions would become extremely impractical from both a legal and a financial standpoint.

The city builders of the Gilded Age created a paradox for their successors in the Progressive Era. Finding solutions to the problems of environmental engineering generated a whole new set of more difficult puzzles about social goals and public priorities. The Gilded Age left behind it a legacy of reform skills and institutional tools, but the past could not tell contemporaries how to put this expertise to the best use in an urban society. In the city hall of Houston and in the electrical palace of the White City, the question was the same: where was American society heading? While national figures like Henry Adams were probing for answers on the highest level of metaphysics, provincial Houstonians were looking for solutions on the more mundane level of practical politics. In fact, Americans at every level stood at a historic crossroads, searching for a sense of direction, at the turn of the twentieth century.

6 "The Thin Edge of the Wedge," 1886–1896

On March 18, 1889, the battle for the streets of Houston began. While a huge crowd of spectators looked on from a safe distance, two opposing armies, with seventy to eighty men each, collided in a wild melee outside of the Union Depot. The city dwellers were not confronting the first wave of a foreign invasion; rather, they were fighting among themselves over which mass transit firm would get to lay its tracks along disputed thoroughfares between the railroad station and the downtown hotels. A few days earlier, the upstart railway builder William Boyd had marshalled his crew into the streets in a mad rush to meet his franchise deadline, but the established firm retaliated with a construction drive of its own. Vowing to fight competition with competition, Superintendent Harold F. Mac-Gregor of the Houston City Street Railway Company (HCSRC) ordered his team of workers to cut off the Boyd forces by laying tracks across their path at a strategic intersection. Although many citizens still carried pistols and knives, Houston was no longer a wild frontier town, and the sheriff arrived to stop the brawling men before they suffered serious injury. He delivered separate court injunctions against further construction to both private enterprises.[1]

The following day, the battle for the streets shifted into the chambers of State District Judge James R. Masterson. Before a packed courtroom, legal experts for the two firms and the city continued the heated controversy over who had the right to decide which utility could use the contested public highways. According to the established company, Boyd's imminent crossing of their tracks would cause "irreparable injury and damage," besides violating their right to an "exclusive use" of the streets. At the same time, Judge Masterson heard City Attorney Henry F. Ring defend the government's complaint against the HCSRC. Without a construction permit from the city engineer, Ring argued, the transit venture's sudden construction activities constituted an unlawful obstruction of the streets. Boyd's counsel concurred, adding that the established firm had begun laying track to "harass" the new rival and to maintain a monopoly of the mass transit business.[2]

There is little doubt that public transportation in Houston had become a lucrative business. In 1888, the HCSRC had grossed $80,000 and made a $25,000 profit carrying 1,500,000 riders over its fourteen-mile network of belt lines. In comparison, the next largest utility venture, the Houston Water Company, earned about $10,000 on $50,000 worth of business. Frank Sprague's solution to the problem of mechanical traction during the summer of 1888 meant that the profitability of mass transit would increase enormously in the immediate future.

When Boyd first applied for a franchise in March 1888, he had planned to install a battery powered system. However, both Sprague's breakthrough in electric traction and a rainy winter delayed the inauguration of construction until the following spring. Boyd had to build an operational system within four weeks or forfeit his franchise.[3]

As a large audience listened, the lawyers asked Judge Masterson to decide the critical issues of public policy. The competing firms attempted to persuade the jurist that the merits of free enterprise and monopoly in urban utilities were on trial. To the established firm, Boyd's rivalry represented a "great embarrassment" to Charles B. Holmes and the other new owners from Chicago. On the other hand, Boyd argued that the older company had "no exclusive right to maintain or operate lines of street railway . . . to the suppression or stifling of competition." However, City Attorney Ring reminded the court that the central issue was not an economic one but whether the municipal government retained the power to exercise a continuous authority over its franchised utilities. Texas law, Ring asserted, placed these issues of public policy in the legislative branch of government, not the judiciary. While Judge Masterson took the testimony under advisement, the battle for the streets shifted to yet another forum, the city council.[4]

The March 25 meeting of the council exposed more than Houston's predominant faith in a market economy. Signs that both parties in the dispute were corrupting public officials surfaced almost immediately. It was no secret that councilman Henry Freund had long served as the general manager of the HCSRC. Less well known was the fact that his colleague, George Underwood, had recently changed his occupation from painter to superintendent of the Boyd enterprise. Not surprisingly, the two councilmen became the opposing champions of a resolution to revoke Boyd's right-of-way along the contested street. After the council split 5 to 5, Mayor Dan Smith cast the decisive vote in favor of competition.[5]

The battle between the two utilities dramatically highlights the perils inherent in franchise policy making at the onset of a revolution in urban public services. Houstonians and their counterparts elsewhere found no easy answers to the question of which franchise alternative best promoted the highest level of services at the lowest cost. Municipal reformers attempted to resolve this problem by experimenting with the different policy options of regulated competition, regulated monopoly, and public ownership. But all three failed to pass the test of economy and efficiency. After Houston decided in favor of Boyd's competitive grant, an outside speculator from Omaha consolidated the two streetcar companies and restored a monopoly. In addition, the resulting uncertainties in government-business relations created a strong incentive for the utility operator to establish a "sphere of influence" at city hall.[6] Without a single, superior solution to the dilemma of utility franchising, the policy debate became emotionally charged with contending ideologies.

At the base of the problem of providing better urban services was a growing gap between rapid city growth and the administrative machinery needed to impose some order on that geographic sprawl. Often the result was a complete breakdown of government and utility services. In Houston, for instance, an earlier reliance on a combined watch tower and alarm bell for fire protection no longer served the city's expanding complex of urban and suburban districts. City fathers had to reformulate the problem on a metropolitan scale before they could find a workable solution. The fire bell had to be replaced by a far more sophisticated central alarm system that could expand with the growth of the metropolitan area. As the interdependent parts of Houston's urban environment grew in size, diversity, and complexity, comprehensive planning became an imperative necessity.[7]

During the 1890s, Houston underwent a metamorphosis, a fundamental change in scale, from a compact city to a sprawling metropolis. Swelling from 27,000 to 44,000 people, Houston passed the threshold where its commercial and industrial foundations could sustain a local boom in the construction and service sectors. To be sure, the coastal entrepôt was no New York or Chicago, but it experienced many of the same problems as these larger urban areas. For example, a municipal jurisidiction that extended only one and a half miles from the city center no longer embraced Houston's expanding community. The coming of rapid mass transit further enhanced outlying suburban development. The bigger cities were also wrestling with the impacts of decentralization set off by the electric street railway.[8]

City building was becoming less of a technical problem and more of a political struggle over urban planning and public policy. After the mid-1880s, a growing faith in technology as the remedy for urban-industrial ills inspired the city dweller to become a municipal reformer. Underlying the reformer's faith was a conviction that reshaping the physical environment of the city would result in corresponding changes in its society. Beginning with Edward Bellamy's visionary novel, *Looking Backwards*, more and more reformers believed in an environmentalist approach to social reform.[9] But even as unprecedented technologies helped to trigger urban progressivism, their great promise of fulfilling dreams of the modern city ensured an intense battle for control of the city building process. Urban planning loomed as a key to the construction of a new social order.

In Houston and many other cities during the 1890s, municipal ownership became the pivotal issue around which swirled the broader ideological struggles over city planning and social reform. The rising cost and complexity of environmental engineering dictated that policy makers set allocation priorities in municipal budgets. The Panic of 1893 further accentuated the need for city planners to coordinate public works projects and utility company improvements. Some reformers turned to municipal ownership as the best way of alleviating mounting pressures on city budgets as well as eliminating a major source of corruption. Other reformers, however, placed greater importance on different sets of allocation priorities for the city government's limited fiscal resources. By the end of the decade, the public ownership issue was moving into center stage in the battle for municipal reform.

The inability of Houston officials to solve the dilemma of utility franchises signalled local reformers to look to outside experts for guidance. But the social scientists offered conflicting testimony, because they attempted to solve this complex issue of social policy on the narrow grounds of efficiency. The very failure of the economists to demonstrate the superiority of one alternative over the others helped turn the franchise question into such an emotionally charged political issue. The warning of a prominent business leader in 1893 that insurgent movements for municipal ownership comprised "the thin edge of the wedge . . . to split our industrial system," epitomized the self-serving nature of the debate over franchise policy. The utility executive's defense of private enterprise underscores the conclusion that this pivotal issue of urban progressivism was intrinsically ideological, not economic.[10]

Regulated Competition

In 1886, of course, there was no dispute in the coastal city about the incomparable advantages of competition. In a city built upon commerce, the civic elite never questioned the dogmas of Adam Smith. Except for the street railway business, however, each of Houston's utility enterprises had always enjoyed an uninterrupted monopoly, and this legacy did little to undermine confidence in the market system. In each case, the city dwellers had been anxious to secure even a single supplier of the different public services: gas lighting, mass transit, water supplies, telephones, and electricity. At the same time, Houstonians had always assumed that these monopolies were temporary expedients. The normal condition, competition, would eventually follow as the city grew in population and wealth. A concept of "natural monopoly" was fundamentally alien in a community where the political leadership was composed of merchants and traders.[11]

Houston's sole experience with franchise competition reinforced belief in the virtues of free enterprise. From 1881 to 1883, a rivalry between two streetcar companies produced a three-fold increase in trackage, extending services into several neighborhoods. Although Galveston's William Sinclair soon restored a monopoly, he consolidated the rival lines into an unified system of mass transportation. In this instance, even a brief period of economic competition advanced the general welfare. In contrast, the uninterrupted monopolies of the other utilities meant that services had been extended slowly while rates remained prohibitive for most home consumers. In a city with 25,000 inhabitants, the gas and the telephone companies served less than 500 noncommercial customers. Electric lighting, also restricted to the central business district, was completely absent from private homes; it was too expensive. The waterworks supplied fewer than 1000 households despite municipal directives to install pipes and hydrants in the sprawling residential sections of the city.[12]

After 1886, the electric revolution presented a fresh opportunity to turn traditional tenets of free enterprise into public policy. During Mayor Smith's four-year administration, entrepreneurs sought municipal franchises to install rival systems of artificial lighting and rapid transit. At first, a policy of regulated competition advanced the public welfare, bringing the community improved services at reduced rates. But the resistance of the established firms to council policy caused a rapid deterioration in government-business relations. Although public officials withstood these pressures, their position crumpled in the face of the backlash coming out of Chicago. The street railway's subversion of the city's paving program forced the council to give recognition to the close interdependence between the public sector and the franchised utility corporation. More ominously, Houston's utility operators conspired to defeat Mayor Smith and his franchise policies in the 1890 elections. Their success in corrupting local politics led almost immediately to a reversal of public policy towards the opposite approach—regulated monopoly.

Only four years earlier, Houston's municipal officers welcomed the chance to test the dicta of free enterprise. In 1886, the Houston Electric Light and Power Company (HELPC) provided the Smith administration with its first opportunity to put a policy of regulated competition into practice. Ever since the utility initiated services in 1883, Houstonians had been complaining about the high price and low quality of the street lamps. The local owners were poor managers because they repeatedly allowed the generating capacity of their central station to fall below the demand for electric power. Consequently, the entire system failed to reach a satisfactory level of performance. Underfinanced and overloaded, the anemic company finally slipped into receivership three years later. When a new corporation replaced the bankrupt firm in 1887, the council seized upon a legal technicality to cancel the remaining portion of the five-year contract. The aldermen decided to solicit sealed bids for a new franchise contract. Embodying the council's growing expertise in the electrical technologies, the grant was a model franchise. It detailed the specifications of company obligations to meet service standards and it carefully reserved the right of the public to regulate the utility.[13]

In November 1887, however, the local company tried to pressure the aldermen into abandoning their plan of seeking competitive bids for the model contract. Threatening to turn off the lights, the utility used its monopoly position to demand that the councilmen give prior consideration to its offer. The council almost capitulated to the local firm, but the company's proposal of $280 annually for each arc lamp differed little from its current rates of charge. In an equally divided council, Mayor Smith's veto saved the original scheme. While the thwarted enterprise enforced a blackout, the city received three bids from outside firms that significantly undercut the terms offered by the local company. The Fort Wayne "Jenny" Electric Light Company submitted the lowest proposal of $150 per light, a 46 percent savings on an expense of $13,800 per year. Moreover, this substantial reduction in rates meant that Houston would be paying only 15 percent more than the national average for arc lamps. The Texas city felt the impact of competition shortly after the council accepted the Fort Wayne proposal. In January 1888, the HELPC restored services at the much lower cost of only $182 per street light.[14]

A policy of regulated competition achieved sizable savings in the city's electric bill and new standards of regulation to safeguard the public interest. In April 1889, the Fort Wayne concern inaugurated services after threats of litigation by the gas company caused a costly delay in the construction of the new facility. Typical of the electrical revolution in urban utilities, the light plant used six different patents. The introduction of daytime services to power fan motors was equally characteristic of the rapid pace of innovation in the electric industry. The company strung almost fifty miles of power lines throughout the city. Reflecting the ward-centered nature of local politics, the aldermen had insisted on an equitable distribution of the city's seventy lamps.[15] The initial success of the Fort Wayne venture proved fatal for its immediate rival, which did not survive without a municipal contract. In January 1891, the HELPC sold its assets to the renamed Citizens' Electric Light and Power Company.[16]

Competition for lighting customers also acted as a powerful stimulant on the Houston Gas Light Company. In January 1889, the utility cut its rates for large customers by 25 percent to $3.00 per thousand cubic feet (mcf), the first such reduction in over a decade. Although this price still remained about twice the national average, the special expense of importing coal from the East kept gas rates above the norm throughout the Southwest. More important, the rivalry of the new electric venture spurred the gas company to start a major publicity and expansion campaign to attract home consumers. Belatedly implementing the strategies of its national trade association, the Houston firm offered to sell gas stoves at cost. Over the next five years, the company extended its mains into residential areas, doubling the distributor network to fifty-five miles. Simultaneously, the utility began converting its manufacturing process to an oil-coal system that made the energy fuel equally suitable for lighting, cooking, and heating purposes.[17]

The catalytic affects of market mechanisms on the mass transit business in Houston have already been noted. It is important here to summarize the results of this competition. Franchise rivalry sharply accelerated the outward sprawl of Houston and forestalled the emergence of a congested urban core that was so characteristic of Northern industrial cities. Instead, continuing growth at the fringes of this New South community produced a basic change in its physical scale and social geography.[18]

During the same period of 1888 to 1892, uninterrupted monopolies in the telephone and water supply businesses produced only marginal gains in public services. For example, the number of telephone customers rose to a mere 450. The monopoly of the water company is more difficult to evaluate, but the conclusion is the same. The quality of service provided by the waterworks remained far below any other utility, in spite of the city's fire hydrant program that extended the mains from twenty-eight to forty miles. The locally owned firm refused to install home meters. Consequently, customers had little incentive to conserve supplies or to fix the leaks that kept pressure levels dangerously low throughout the system. The company's niggardly attitude towards replacing obsolete distributive pipes also helped to deprive fire fighters of adequate water supplies.[19]

The history of franchise competition in Houston disputes the claims of trade association leaders and some social scientists that market mechanisms were harmful in the utilities sector. Interfirm contests as well as confrontations between alternative technologies acted as powerful agents in upgrading the amenities available to the urban community. The most obvious benefits were large improvements in transit services and reduced rates of charge for artificial lighting. The substitution of the experienced Fort Wayne company for the floundering local enterprise had the effect of allowing more and more Houstonians to enjoy better artificial illuminants. Although the electric light bulb had not yet penetrated the mass consumption market, it prodded the gas company to transform its services into a regular part of home living for the ordinary family. The demand for gas increased almost 450 percent in the decade following the inauguration of electric arc lamps.[20] In similar ways, direct competition in the street railway business resulted in more than a doubling of services and insured an early introduction of electric traction.

Yet the competitive policies of the Smith administration were both costly and unviable in the long run. Local government seemed incapable of sustaining interfirm contests. On the contrary, a policy of franchise rivalry was successful only for temporary periods, when either (1) a large market, or (2) technological innovation went unexploited by an established firm. No additional entrepreneurs otherwise entered the utilities field, whereas mergers inexorably followed the elimination of these two conditions. By the end of 1891, each utility service had restored an uncontested position. The natural monopoly hypothesis was unproven, but the experience of several local rivalries adhered to a single pattern of consolidation under single ownership.

The Smith administration's policy of regulated competition also contributed to the appearance of two new serious problems: overcapitalization and political corruption. The first drawback overburdened operating companies with debts, diverting revenues from maintenance and improvement budgets into the pockets of the speculator. Under Oscar Carter's reorganization of the street railway business, for instance, the utility's liabilities jumped from $22,000 to over $71,000 per mile of track. But according to the industry's foremost expert, this amount represented a minimum of $28,000 per mile in watered stocks and bonds, or 40 percent of the company's total capitalization.[21] An analogous leap occurred in the liabilities of the electric company before decade's end. These harmful financial practices would lead to bankruptcy for both enterprises.

The second major drawback of the Smith administration's franchise policy was the corruption of local politics. Conflicts of interest had been a normal part of a government run by amateurs who served on a part-time basis.[22] In the late 1880s, however, utility managers and politicians began to engage in corrupt practices that differed markedly from this custom of dual occupations. Starting in 1890 (and continuing until the establishment of a commission form of government fifteen years later), the franchise holders would try to predetermine the outcome of each biannual general election. A deepening sense of uncertainty about government-business relations drove the utility managers to engage in corruption. Besides the insecurity generated by the city's encouragement of competition, the council's assumption of a more vigilant watchdog role over the utilities' activities in the community was also an important source of anxiety. Unlike other public contractors, the utility companies came under continuous municipal controls that created a reciprocal interest in shaping official decisions on an ongoing basis.

Until the late 1880s, the corruption of Houston politics by the franchise holders remained below the surface of popular awareness. But when the council evenly split on the question of street railway franchises, the Chicago speculators threatened Mayor Smith openly. In a letter to the *Houston Daily Post*, Holmes abruptly cancelled a $500,000 modernization plan and levelled stinging charges of xenophobia at the Texas community, tarnishing its New South image. While these blows were weakening the council's resolve, the Chicagoans hit the aldermen where it hurt most—in the city's improvement program. The railway's new owners not only refused to pay their share of paving the streets, but they also left miles of abandoned track to erode the costly road surfaces.[23]

Holmes's bold attempt to intimidate the city's chief executive was a visible episode in a larger campaign mounted by the utility executives to dictate the policies of the local legislature. With the central issue of who had privileges to use electric traction still undecided as the April 1890 elections approached, rapid transit promoters labored to ensure the selection of friendly candidates. Smith had accumulated a solid record of accomplishment in settling the city debt, forwarding the public works program, and improving the services provided by public utility enterprises. Yet he faced serious challenges from within his own party, which would choose the next administration if the Democrats could avoid factional splintering at their city-wide convention.

By 1890, Houstonians accepted and practiced a ward-centered politics, a distinctly urban form of participatory democracy. It had emerged four years earlier to overturn older patterns of elite leadership. Campaigning now flourished at the grassroots level among the Democrats, with several candidates vying for each aldermanic and executive position. In the months preceding the nominating convention, would-be politicians held nightly meetings at neighborhood stores and gathering places to rally support for the ward primaries. Equally characteristic of the new style politics was the growth of organizational endorsements by special interest groups. An urban polity assumed a modern form as more and more functional interest groups joined traditional ethnic-racial organizations in taking an active part in municipal affairs. The city's two largest minority groups, blacks and Germans, respectively, comprised 38 percent and 5 percent of the population. If the Democrats split into antagonistic factions, a well-disciplined minority group could deliver a decisive block of votes to cooperative candidates.[24]

At the same time, the rise of ward-centered politics did not so much displace the commercial-civic elite as force it to share power with organized segments of the community. Despite the Smith insurgency and the reinstatement of elective officers, Houston's traditional elite remained entrenched in positions of party and civic leadership. The conspicuous absence of skilled workers and small proprietors from the Democratic Executive Committee reveals the slow shift in the balance of political power toward the rank and file. On the contrary, new party officials came chiefly from the offspring of elite families and from young professionals who worked for long-established local firms.[25]

The 1890 elections demonstrated that the commercial-civic elite had adjusted with adroit flexibility to the emergence of a ward-centered politics. Democratic chieftains plotted a strategy aimed at holding the German minority within party ranks. From the outset of the campaign in January 1890, the better classes of Houston society supported Henry Scherffius for the mayoralty nomination. Scherffius, a German immigrant and veteran blockade runner of the Civil War, was a successful businessman. The odds-on favorite of local pundits, he defeated Smith after a protracted struggle at the party convention and went on to win the April elections.[26]

Direct proof of corruption by the streetcar companies in the 1890 campaign is lacking but the great weight of circumstantial evidence points to just this conclusion. Political corruption is inherently difficult to substantiate because the participants usually strike their deals under a cloak of secrecy that the press rarely uncovers. Nonetheless, the historian has the advantage of hindsight to reconstruct the existing evidence into a coherent, or at least plausible, picture of the past.

Although the new mayor's German roots were important, his intimate ties to Northern businessmen was probably the crucial factor in his selection. Scherffius worked as a sales representative, selling agricultural implements and industrial machinery manufactured in the North. More telling circumstantial evidence comes from the fact that the mayor led the drive for a policy change away from regulated competition. In spite of the dogged resistance of a council majority, Scherffius repeatedly rebuffed the bids of potential utility rivals and strove to ensure that the established firms received preferential treatment.

While the mayor cannot be tied directly to the HCSRC, he steered the city onto a new course of regulated monopoly. In September 1890, two different promoters of suburban subdivisions applied to the council for mass transit franchises. But Scherffius vetoed the transit bills, claiming that the city should not encourage "needless competition." Despite a pervasive faith in competition, the mayor considered urban utilities an exception. Scherffius asserted that "once granted, franchises are irrevocable and in each instance a practical monopoly."[27] His administration turned to government regulation as a substitute for market mechanisms. A growing belief that public utilities were indeed unique was also generating a ground swell of support for municipal ownership. It gained momentum as the monopoly option quickly posed policy dilemmas even more intractable than the perils of competition.

Regulated Monopoly

Between 1890 and 1895, Houston officials searched futilely for effective levers of control to enforce a policy of regulated monopoly. Instead, the council found that it possessed neither the political nor economic power to make the established firms comply with the obligations of their franchises and contracts. Without the actual or implied threat of competition, the utility companies brazenly ignored the city's attempts to enforce the law. Even worse, the council discovered that the success of its public improvement program depended upon the voluntary cooperation of the private firms. In the absence of a mutuality of interests, the financing and maintenance of the city's public works projects—the very measure of progress—were thrown into serious doubt. By 1895, the frustrations of civic leaders had mounted to the point where normally conservative men became ready to entertain radical solutions to the utilities problem.

Municipal regulation was an inherent part of the utility franchise, but fundamental changes during the Gilded Age had altered the relationship between government and business in three essential ways. Before Houston began installing expensive pavements and sewers, the council had little interest in supervising the activities of utility enterprises in the streets. The city limited its role to keeping the streets free of permanent obstructions. After the mid-1880s, however, officials had an enlarged public investment to protect. The utility firms were constantly tearing up improved roadways to extend and repair their distributor networks. In the case of the street railway, moreover, the city depended on the utility to bear a substantial share of the assessment tax, up to $20,000 per mile of pavement.

A second basic change in government-business relations was caused by a technological revolution that transformed utility services into collective necessities of urban life. City dwellers were no longer willing to tolerate breakdowns and shoddy quality in government-sponsored services such as the street lights and the water supply. Third, the modernization of Houston society gave the urbanites organizational vehicles by which to express themselves politically on the delivery of both public and home services. In 1894, a typical failure of fire hydrant pressure resulted in tragedy. An aroused community began mobilizing a political movement for franchise reform.

The council's repeated inability to force the transit monopoly to obey local ordinances governing its activities in the streets exposed the pitfalls of regulation. After 1890, the basic problem for the city planners was designing tools of administration to guarantee the efficient enforcement of public policy. But driven and then hounded by his dreams for the suburban development of Houston Heights, Carter blatantly disregarded the municipal authority.[28] Despite the council's ever more stringent efforts, the speculator drained the profitable transit operation in a desperate attempt to keep his corporate empire from collapsing in the wake of the financial panic of 1893. As the utility company sunk into bankruptcy, public officials faced miles of abandoned track and obstructed thoroughfares and a rapid accumulation of unpaid taxes for paving assessments.

It did not take long before the transit company delivered a sharp lesson to the new administration on the limits of governmental power over private enterprise. In July 1890, the aldermen revoked the utility's right-of-way across a strategic bridge linking the business district to the fifth ward. They were retaliating against the firm's stubborn refusal to cooperate with the city in fixing the streets. The following day, the company obtained an injunction in the state district court, prohibiting municipal interference with the construction project.

The Texas Supreme Court upheld the lower bench, although the jurists went out of their way to denounce the evils of monopoly franchises. Building on the constitutional precedents of the Gilded Age, the court set the boundaries of the police power by a process of inclusion and exclusion. In this case, the state bench reiterated earlier rulings that once the company took actual possession of the streets, it gained a vested right. The municipal government could not impair this right of occupancy in wielding its ample power to regulate the utility. In effect, the court ruled out franchise blackmail as a legitimate exercise of the police power.[29]

But the real problem for Houston officials was forging effective instruments of enforcement, not carving out new areas of governmental authority over the business corporation. When Carter purchased the rival transit firms in September 1890, he inherited miles of superfluous track and speculative routes to undeveloped areas. At the same time, he needed to build a six-mile extension to his 1765-acre "new town" north of the city center.[30] Reflecting the mastery of the city builders, Carter reversed traditional priorities between real estate and mass transit. The suburban developer paid little attention to repair and maintenance duties, while displaying a single-minded devotion to programs aimed at installing an electric trolley system to Houston Heights. For the city, the transit company's feverish activities meant long stretches of "dead" tracks, which protruded dangerously like stumbling blocks in the middle of the streets. And in new construction areas, existing road surfaces were ripped out with impunity. But after four years of threats, resolutions, and various schemes to bring the utility into compliance with the law, the council seemed no closer to its goals than when it began.[31]

Although solutions to the riddle of utility monopolies remained elusive before 1896, a definite pattern of regulatory legislation was emerging from the trial and error of the council. Following previous trends, local lawmakers continued to institutionalize the supervisory functions of various city departments. For example, the council charged the street commissioner with the task of reporting obstructions to the city engineer, who had to inspect all construction work by the utilities on their tracks, poles, wires, mains, and pipes. At the same time, the council attempted to hold company officers personally responsible for violations of the city's environmental regulations. Motormen, too, had to obey a growing list of traffic rules or face arrest and stiff fines. The council also moved in new directions to strengthen the enforcement powers of the municipal government. For instance, a series of ordinances authorized the city engineer to repair the companies' damages to the streets and to remove their obstructions to movement at their own expense. To ensure collection, another set of regulations required franchise holders to deposit sizable bonds with the city before they began construction or repair work.[32]

In spite of all this legislative creativity, however, Carter's transit firm fell further out of compliance with its basic franchise obligations. In large part, the utility monopoly became less able to respond to the public authority regardless of the penalties. Overloaded with paper debts, the Houston City Street Railway Company was financially starved to death by Carter. Increasingly, he diverted its income and assets to shore up his faltering conglomerate of land and banking corporations. For example, the Omaha financier built a six-mile extension to Houston Heights with HCSRC funds. Carter sold the line to other corporations (which he also owned) for their promissory notes. The extension route was then leased back to the original firm for $8000 annually.[33]

After the onset of the depression of 1893, transit services declined rapidly and company profits turned into deficits. Three years earlier, Carter had expanded the company's capital stock of $200,000 and bonded indebtedness of $184,000 to $1,250,000 each. Although he used only one third of the new capital to pay for the conversion to electric traction, the modernization program helped to boost the venture's gross earnings sufficiently to cover bond interest payments. In 1893, however, this account absorbed 37 percent of the company's $200,000 gross earnings. In contrast, an efficient enterprise would devote about 75 percent of its revenues for normal operating expenses, according to street railway experts. Overburdened with maintaining its debts, the Houston firm began abandoning service on a number of lines, neglecting track and street repair duties, and defaulting on its special assessment taxes. The following year, the company failed to meet its obligations to the bondholders. Led by Albert N. Parlan, a Boston manufacturer, the investors petitioned the United States District Court at Galveston in July 1895 to appoint John Kirby as receiver of the railway company. A payoff of $5,000 convinced Carter to resign.[34]

Houston's streetcar case was fairly representative of utility receiverships at the end of the nineteenth century. Unpaid mortgage bondholders initiated equity court proceedings in order to restructure finances and to gain ownership control of companies. Urban utility bankruptcies paralleled the growth of a national market for the securities of public service corporations. Consider that in one typical month of the mid-nineties depression, fifty-eight street railway companies with funded debts of over $50,000,000 were in the hands of the receiver.[35] In the Houston case, the protective supervision of the federal court allowed Parlan and Kirby to reorganize the firm's finances within a year. The bondholders received substantially less in interest payments after 1895, but they also became the company's owners.[36]

For Houston officials, the Carter episode was an unmitigated disaster. Five years of searching for workable levers of control over the utility now seemed in vain. In effect, the financial collapse of the company precluded the enforcement of public duties to keep the streets free from obstructions and in good repair. The bankruptcy also forestalled the collection of the firm's assessment taxes. In short, the Carter experience threw the policy option of regulated monopoly into serious doubt. If the aldermen failed to discover effective mechanisms of environmental

regulation, they were equally stymied in their attempts to ensure the faithful performance of government contracts for public services.

The breakdown of the water system tragically demonstrated the limits of the
local government's power to guarantee that the utility companies fulfilled their
franchise obligations. In August 1894, a fire consumed a residential block and
the St. Joseph Infirmary. Two nuns died in the blaze because the volunteer fire
department had to fight the conflagration without water. Again, as the past had
consistently shown, fire hydrant pressure was wholly inadequate. Company
president Timothy M. Scanlan's accurate explanation that compliance with the
pressure levels defined in the original 1878 franchise was virtually impossible did
little to appease an outraged community. Direct pressure methods of fire fighting
were outmoded along the greatly expanded sixty-mile distributive network and
many mains were simply too small. On October 6, officials voiced their reactions
to the tragedy at a hurriedly organized special session of the council. Demanding
municipal ownership, alderman William H. Bailey characterized the city's past
indulgence in the company's chronic violations of its franchise as a "shameful
indifference" to the rights of the citizens. He successfully urged the council to
launch a full investigation, which for the first time permitted home consumers to
testify.[37]

In large measure, Bailey's accusation of official neglect was accurate. Only a
year earlier, a Texas civil appeals court had dismissed a damage suit by Henry
House against the Houston waterworks for a similar breakdown of hydrant pressure. According to the owner of a fire-gutted cotton compressing plant, the utility
corporation's "quasi-public nature" meant that its franchise obligations extended
to all the inhabitants of the municipality. In the state's first appellate decision on
this critical issue, the bench observed that House was neither a party to the government contract nor its direct beneficiary. He could not sue the utility for a
breach of contract; the waterworks was liable to the city alone. The court ruled
that responsibility for enforcing the duties imposed upon the utility rested solely
with the municipal government.[38]

During October 1894, the investigation committee heard from three interested
groups: consumers, corporate officers, and fire insurance underwriters. The universal complaint of the ninety-three citizens who appeared before the council
concerned overcharges. Since only a few heavy users such as hotels and livery
stables could afford the company's high rental fee for a meter, most customers
paid on the basis of the number of rooms and taps in their households. To appease public hostility, the company admitted that its definition of a "room" was
imprecise, by liberally redrawing the rate schedule. For consumers, the public
hearings brought some order to a confused relationship and welcome savings for
their pocketbooks.[39]

The water company based its defense on a recital of current projects to improve services. Utility executives presented considerable proof that neglect was
not among their major faults. For example, corporation attorney and director
James A. Baker, Jr. reported that over $250,000, or 52 percent of the total invest-

ment in the facility, had been expended within the last three years. Superintendent Francis J. Smith displayed plans for supplementing undersized mains, digging more artesian wells, and installing new machinery to double the plant's
pumping capacity. Significantly, however, company officers left an essential part
of any water supply system, the meter, entirely out of the discussion. But Scanlan offered to sell the enterprise to the city for a price to be determined by an
arbitration board.[40]

Fire insurance underwriters supplied the most comprehensive analysis of
Houston's water supply system. Members of the state executive committee
served as outside experts and outlined a series of reforms for both the utility and
the government. Their proposals were enacted because the Texas underwriters
imposed a special tariff on insurance premiums. The insurance men placed
Houston in a second-rate category compared to other cities. This onus of urban
inferiority in the great battle for regional preeminence acted as a powerful incentive for reform. The underwriters concurred with company officers that the utility must expand its distributive network to correspond to the community's enlarging scale and increased consumption. But the underwriters directed their
most scathing criticism at the local government. In order to lift the special tariff,
public officials had to institute a paid fire department, a program for the rapid
installation of an electrical alarm system, and a more stringent building code.[41]

The tragedy of St. Joseph's undermined support for the regulated monopoly
option. Houston's civic leaders no longer believed that secure private monopolies would best promote a rising level of utility services. Despite governmental
supervision, the waterworks had broken its most fundamental obligation to protect the community against fires. City hall seemed equally impotent to enforce
the terms of the street lighting contract. And throughout the first half of the decade, the transit company evaded council directives to remove track obstructions,
to repair the streets, and to pay special assessment taxes. A loss of faith in the
regulated monopoly alternative became manifest in two ways. During 1895, the
council resorted once again to utility competition by granting franchises to new
telephone and rapid transit ventures as well as by permitting the Houston Heights
Light Company to extend services into the city. The second indication of a turn
away from the monopoly option was the appearance of a political ground swell in
favor of municipal ownership.[42]

Municipal Ownership

In Houston, an upsurge of support for municipal ownership grew out of several parallel but related failures of government and business to provide the community with modern public services. In the area of franchise relations, a process
of elimination eventually directed reformers to this remaining policy option. Neither traditional practices of competition nor recent experiments with monopoly
passed the pragmatic test of economy and efficiency. At the same time, a swelling deficit in the city budget created a separate momentum of its own in favor of
public ownership. Beginning in 1892, civic leaders hoped to replace the drain of

utility bills for water and light with a flow of revenue from profitable municipal enterprises. Another important source of political pressure to improve services originated in the rising expectations of an urban society. Although less easy to measure, widespread dissatisfaction with the utility companies brought many newly organized groups into the political arena for the first time. After the St. Joseph Infirmary fire, these groups began to coalesce into a broad-based reform movement.

Serious consideration of municipal ownership as a policy option grew out of efforts to reduce the costs of providing public services. Mayor Scherffius first suggested that the best way to end nagging budgetary deficits was for the city government to become engaged in the electric light and the water supply business. Scherffius, of course, was no radical; his proposal emerged out of the dilemmas of ordering public priorities. Tied to business interests, his advocacy of public ownership represented no basic contradiction with his belief in the tenets of capitalism.

In 1890, the municipal government spent $26,000 over its $145,000 budget, and the following year the deficit grew to $60,000 more than tax receipts (see Table 6.1). By saving $30,000 annually in utility bills, according to Scherffius, the city would more than offset the cost of purchasing the public facilities. Property taxes and consumer bills would be reduced, while the constant hassle of regulation would be eliminated.[43]

For Scherffius, an advocacy of municipal ownership as the answer to budgetary deficits came too late. In 1892, the Democrats passed him over for another prominent businessman and Horatio Alger story, John T. Browne. A united party leadership chose Browne because he promised to restore a balanced budget. Immigrating to Houston in 1852, the 47-year-old Irishman had worked his way up from brick carrier to owner of a large grocery concern. He took little part in local politics until 1888, when he became the chairman of the council's finance committee.[44]

An inability to balance inflexible tax revenues against rising departmental expenditures soon led the new mayor, like his predecessor, to the idea of municipal ownership. Despite a council prohibition on departmental spending above budget appropriations, the city kept falling deeper into the red during Browne's two-year term. By 1894, the municipal corporation had accumulated about $100,000 in floating debts, an amount equal to 40 percent of its annual tax receipts. Browne concluded that large savings could be effected only in one area: the city's utility bills. The mayor was a good administrator but he admitted that there was little hope of holding departmental spending within a budget as long as the city continued its rapid growth. A need for planning also became manifest as the council began serious inquiry into the ways and means of building municipal utilities.[45]

During 1893–1894, the council's explorations into public ownership showed that initial expectations of large savings at a small cost were optimistic. In less than a year, even Julius Hirsch, the council's staunchest advocate of this policy option, revised his estimate upward from $500,000 to $900,000 for the construc-

TABLE 6.1   Allocation of Public Revenues, 1877–1892

Year	1877	1880	1887	1892
Population	14,000	16,000	25,000	30,000
Interest				
Amount	$11,700	$25,100	$142,000	$109,400
Percentage of total	12.5	30.0	50.0	38.1
Per capita expenditure	$.84	$1.57	$4.48	$3.64
General Expenses				
Amount	$24,600	$18,500	$24,400	$30,000
Percentage of total	26.2	22.0	12.8	10.4
Per capita expenditure	$1.76	$1.05	$.98	$1.00
Public Safety*				
Amount	$26,600	$5,600	$27,800	$37,000
Percentage of total	28.3	6.7	12.3	12.8
Per capita expenditure	$1.90	$.35	$1.11	$1.23
Health				
Amount	$7,800	$3,600	†	$10,000
Percentage of total	8.3	4.3		3.5
Per capita expenditure	$.56	$.23		$.33
Roads and Bridges‡				
Amount	$23,300	$22,000	$30,000	$40,000
Percentage of total	24.8	26.2	13.3	14.0
Per capita expenditure	$1.67	$1.37	$1.20	$1.33
Utility Services				
Amount	§	$9,700	$26,800	$30,000
Percentage of total		11.5	11.8	10.4
Per capita expenditure		$.61	$1.07	$1.00
Education				
Amount	§	§	$2,800	$30,000
Percentage of total			1.2	10.4
Per capita expenditure			$.11	$1.00
Totals				
Amount	$94,000	$84,000	$225,000	$286,000
Percentage of total	100.00	100.00	100.00	100.00
Per capita expenditure	$6.71	$5.25	$9.00	$9.05

SOURCES: Council Minutes, Books: D–H: passim; U. S. Bureau of Census statistics, as listed in *Texas Almanac* (Dallas: Dallas Morning News, 1972), p. 163.
*Includes expenditures for police and fire services.
†No funds reported in this category.
‡Includes only current budgetary appropriations.
§None.

tion of a waterworks and a light plant. The Board of Public Works advised the aldermen against such a move, since increasing the municipal debt by 50 percent during a depression would involve considerable risk for the city as well as for the creditor. The representatives of the large taxpayers recommended that the aldermen first investigate the cost of purchasing the existing two facilities. Together the council and the board learned that the task of appraising the worth of the companies and the future needs of the community were beyond their abilities. After two years of study, the Browne administration decided to hire a planning expert who could estimate the coming public service demands of a city of 75,000 people.[46]

In the midst of hard times, the difficult questions raised by the utility investigation undoubtedly diminished support for a costly experiment in municipal ownership. With a city debt approaching 10 percent of the tax base, selling a large bond issue in a tight market at unfavorable terms seemed to foreclose this policy option. On the other hand, Browne was holding budgetary deficits down to a rate of 7 to 8 percent, while slightly increasing tax revenues.[47] This record of achievement probably accounts for his quiet reelection in April 1894 to a second term. The public ownership issue languished until the St. Joseph's fire jarred the council. But again nothing was accomplished until the city received yet another unsettling blow. In April 1895, a state court ruling threw Houston into a full-fledged civic crisis.[48]

"The decision this morning fell upon the community like a clap of thunder from a clear sky, and today the whole situation which was yesterday so serene, is all turmoil and commotion," a journalist reported.[49] In *Higgins* v. *Bordages*, the Texas Supreme Court held that special assessment tax liens were unenforceable against urban homesteads. Neither litigant contested this issue, but a newly reconstituted bench of Hogg Democrats seized the opportunity to reverse a position that had been settled conclusively twelve years earlier in *Lufkin* v. *Galveston*. This sharp departure from legal precedent and traditions of self-restraint signalled the beginning of a new, activist role for the Texas judiciary in state and local decision making. In effect, the court ended the efficacy of assessment taxation. Financing street and sewerage projects with special levies was impractical without the power to force every abutting owner to pay or face certain loss of his property.[50]

The *Higgins* decision created an immediate "public calamity." Houston's chief road builder, Richard Storrie, and other contractors brought all work in progress to an abrupt halt. Property owners also stopped making any further payments on their assessment dues. Over $300,000 in unpaid taxes stood in the balance, besides the possibility that levies of $586,000 collected since 1881 might be declared invalid.[51]

In Houston, the fiscal crisis forced a thorough reexamination of the basic goals of city government in the New South. Over the next few months, a divisive debate about allocation priorities shattered the 1880s' consensus on public improvements. At city hall, the aldermen dropped their investigation of the public ownership option because the anticipated shift of fiscal resources to street improvements would logically preclude the purchase of a utility plant with municipal bonds. Instead, the Browne administration attempted to continue financing paving and sewer projects by proposing a long-term plan.

But Browne's five-year plan provoked several organized groups to propose alternative long-range plans of their own. For the first time, a broad spectrum of people was not only participating in the political process, but also demanding a direct voice in the determination of public policy. The controversy over fiscal priorities remained unresolved because the taxpayers defeated a bond referendum endorsing the administration's views. After the September poll, the planning debate became a full-blown political conflict, splintering the Democratic party into three antagonistic factions. An independent party movement proved to be temporary, but the focus of a mature urban polity on the related issues of budget priorities and municipal ownership produced lasting effects. The crisis pitched Houston into a search for a new definition of community and the role of government in that vision of an urban society.

During July 1895, the Browne administration rapidly reassessed the financial position of the municipal corporation. City officials calculated that $1,000,000 in new bonds could be issued safely over a five-year period. These funds, according to the council, should be earmarked exclusively for paving and sewer extensions. To justify this restricted use of public resources, the finance committee reasoned that "five years of assured activity in improvement and development of the city will not only tend to inspire confidence and stimulate activity at home but will invite capital and enterprise from abroad." [52]

The administration's priorities largely reiterated earlier equations between paving and progress. The council report also embodied the New South creed, by paying homage to Houston's need for investment capital from the North. Since any bond issue over $100,000 required the approval of a two-thirds majority of the voting taxpayers, the aldermen placed their proposal in the form of a referendum. [53] "There is patent reason for assuming street paving means growth," the *Houston Daily Post* editorialized in support of the official plan. Northern bond investors were looking for a "spirit of progress," for a "prosperous and growing and public spirited community. They will pay more for such investments than for those in a slow-growing [and] slovenly looking town." [54]

The upcoming bond poll presented many of the recently organized groups with a first opportunity to express an opinion on a policy issue. The St. Joseph's fire had made an indelible impression that led several special interest groups to begin linking the municipal ownership option to larger questions of city planning. In June, for example, the Houston District Medical Association intervened in the management of the water supply. The doctors reported that the company's water was "detrimental to the public health" and advised consumers to secure alternative sources. Armed with scientific procedures to analyze microscopic organisms, the medical experts found the utility's bayou reservoir dangerously contaminated. [55] Urban expansion above the dam had made the old system obsolete. This shocking report, following on the heels of the infirmary tragedy, spurred the Labor Council to sponsor a series of educational programs on utility services, municipal franchises, and public finances. The federation of local unions concluded that the municipal ownership of the waterworks should receive top priority, not street and sewer improvements. [56]

Towards the end of July, union leaders met with city officials to persuade them to change their list of priorities. Alderman James McAughan, a blacksmith from the fifth ward, voiced the objections of the Labor Council to the administration's allocation proposal. To Houston's skilled workers, the purchase of essential public services overshadowed the need for additional improvement projects that would primarily benefit private property owners. McAughan argued that the people ought to be given a chance to decide between the two alternatives. The councilmen admitted that they had confirmed the allegations of the medical association through an independent study by state scientists, but that they preferred to rely upon Scanlan's promise to circumvent the pollution hazard by digging more artesian wells.

Mayor Browne, however, began to doubt whether present policy makers could ethically commit future administrations to a long-range plan. Without tomorrow's experience, he thought, a short-term "experiment" was the prudent course of action. Yet only a veto stopped a determined majority of the council from proceeding with the larger scheme. Eventually, the politicians worked out a compromise that would authorize the sale of $500,000 in municipal bonds over three to four years.[57] In response, the Labor Council organized an ad hoc "citizens' committee" to campaign against the measure. By the time of the September poll, few taxpayers turned out to support the administration, spelling the defeat of its plan by a 525 to 497 majority.[58]

In the days following, contemporaries advanced various reasons to explain the defeat of the referendum. Its supporters bitterly characterized the majority as "mossbacks," opponents of progress. The losers also singled out the suburbanites, who allegedly believed that the proposed service extensions would never reach the peripheral areas. More neutral observers pointed to a small but resolute band of property owners. They had already paid special assessments and now resented the idea of being taxed to pave others' streets. In a handbill, these taxpayers asked the electorate who would have to pay the $300,000 in uncollected assessments that were thrown into legal limbo by the *Higgins* ruling.[59] Without a more comprehensive approach to the city's allocation dilemma, the effort to order fiscal priorities resulted in confusion rather than acceptance of the official plan.

Unresolved, the planning crisis quickly spilled over into the approaching contest for control of city hall. In December, the first of two independent factions emerged, aimed at removing the regular Democratic leadership from power in the April 1896 elections. The small response to the referendum disguised powerful political reactions against the administration's policy orientations. The planning debate triggered a process of polarization that tore the community into antagonistic camps. Municipal ownership became the central policy issue, but an inability to solve the franchise question on economic grounds soon turned the controversy into a bitter ideological struggle for political power among the community's various socioeconomic and racial groups. For the next ten years, Houstonians fought over opposing concepts of the general welfare. The winners would determine what part government would play in fulfilling the city's needs for better public services.

The first visible indications of deep-seated resentment against the Democratic leadership appeared at a meeting to organize a Good Government League. This independent party was a political vehicle for a portion of Houston's middle class. An occupational profile of the organization's seventy-five founders shows that they were mainly professionals, managers, and retail proprietors. Typically, the fledgling party chose for its president a lawyer and Democratic loyalist since the 1870s, Norman Kittrell, and for its secretary, bookstore owner Benjamin P. Bailey.[60]

In January, the League issued a manifesto that announced the position of the party towards the role of government in an urban community. The paper asserted that, "the laws of God are immutable. Cities like individuals are under the law of right and wrong. . . . It [the city] must be self-restraining, law-abiding and inviting as a home for legitimate business operations and for the family alike." [61] Significantly, the Leaguers drew a close parallel between the Protestant work ethic and successful government administration. Traditional worries about public morality retained a strong hold on middle-class reformers, in spite of calls for the study of municipal administration by Woodrow Wilson and other experts at the national level. The independents found the council's neglect to enforce laws on lotteries, saloons, and gambling halls to be almost criminal. Licentiousness had to be suppressed, according to the manifesto, or American liberty might be lost. An emphasis on moral rejuvenation, however, did not exclude a concern about the need for the structural rehabilitation of the city goverment.[62]

A solid platform of institutional reforms provided a counterweight to the strident moralism of the manifesto. In February 1896, the League outlined methods to tax property values more equitably, charter amendments to revive a vigorous public works program, and ways to eliminate the corrupting influences of the old fee system with a new schedule of fixed salaries. Moreover, the platform advocated the eventual municipal ownership of the waterworks and the immediate reduction of utility rates for street lights.[63]

But a truly independent party was too radical for Houston. The resignation of President Kittrell illustrates the continuing strength of the Democracy, the party of the fathers. As the election approached, the League decided to name a separate ticket on a nonpartisan basis, rather than merely endorse selected Democratic candidates. Kittrell withdrew in protest; he refused to support any Republican. His dramatic gesture signed the death warrant of the League. In Southern cities like Houston, reform had to triumph first within the Democratic party before it stood any possibility of becoming enacted into public policy.[64]

The stillbirth of a nonpartisan party contrasted with the growing vitality of a splinter movement among the Democratic rank and file. Henry Brashear, a rich landowner and the clerk of the criminal district court, led the insurgents. Other dissidents included Aldermen William Heinze, Jules Hirsch, and William Bailey, besides Brashear's nephew Sam, who was serving as the city attorney. While the revolt was sparked by differing opinions on the proper course of government policy, the Brashear faction found its most compelling appeal in denouncing the lack of democracy within the party. The insurgents charged that the elections of the recent past had been a fraud. A small group of insiders, they charged, had manipulated the selection of Browne and other candidates, in addition to juggling the final election returns. The recent reapportionment of the city from five to six wards did little to appease the insurgents. By March 1896, a struggle for party control had submerged the policy debate beneath a revolt against the directives of the central executive committee.[65]

This intramural conflict generated two separate primaries and slates of candidates. The Brashear faction conducted a primary during daylight hours to underline its demands for fair and open elections. Led by H. Baldwin Rice and five incumbent aldermen, the regulars held a primary at the usual time—at night. Unlike the only notable upset since the Reconstruction era, when workingman Dan Smith displaced banker William Baker in 1886, both mayoral hopefuls were the offspring of successful urban pioneers. Brashear and Rice belonged to families of great wealth, social prestige, and political influence.[66] Their contest focused less on policy issues than on questions of party organization and leadership. Brashear's ticket polled an impressive 2800 votes, but the Rice slate swept the April elections with over 3600 supporters. In comparison, the candidates of the Good Government League collected a mere 300 votes.[67]

The election returns mirrored deep divisions in the electorate that were quickly polarizing the community into two antagonistic camps. In 1896, the blending of policy disputes and leadership quarrels prevented the crystallization of a positive mandate on either question. Organizational loyalty seems to have determined the outcome of the first round of the contest for political power. As the unfinished task of defining a city plan again moved into the forefront of the civic crisis, factional warfare became endemic. On the one side, the regulars continued to place top priority on urban growth. They believed that the city should devote public resources first and foremost to street improvements, which were considered a primary engine of progress. On the other side, the dissidents seemed more concerned with upgrading the quality of life in the neighborhoods. They demanded immediate improvements in the delivery of public services. Municipal ownership became the rallying cry and symbol of the insurgents.

After 1896, Houstonians were no longer willing to tolerate the many glaring deficiencies in their physical surrounding and their public services. An array of promising technological innovations further heightened expectations that every modern amenity would soon become available to the average city dweller at affordable prices. But mounting pressures for better services and more facilities only exacerbated the problems of extending them over an expanding metropolitan area. Piecemeal approaches resulted in the frequent breakdown of overtaxed utility networks, operating budgets, and bureaucratic systems. The failure to find a franchise policy that worked deepened the community's sense of frustration and crisis triggered by the unexpected loss of Houston's major source of public improvement funds. New limitations on the city's fiscal resources turned contending city plans into mutually exclusive political platforms. These positions soon hardened into opposing ideologies, setting the stage for a protracted battle for the reins of power.

The origins of municipal reform in Houston lay rooted in the gap between the city's metropolitan scale and its outmoded structure of government administration. After the advent of rapid transit in the early 1890s, this gap became a chasm that widened to a crisis in public administration. Until the need to restructure the machinery of government took first place on the agenda of municipal reform, solutions to the problems of public services remained elusive. To be sure, new technologies and the experts of environmental engineering promised to cure many chronic ills of city life. But ad hoc solutions simply did not work any longer. The complexity and cost of city building now demanded comprehensive planning on a metropolitan, if not a regional scale. To govern the coming city of the twentieth century required systematic approaches and central direction.[68] Although Houston had expanded at a fairly consistent rate, by the early 1890s, it had reached a turning point in the scale of administration needed to supply modern public services.

In addition, new perceptions about living in an urban environment further increased the consumption of public services, making the task of administration even more difficult. In the 1880s, Houstonians considered an ample water supply a necessity only for the protection of property against fires. A decade later, however, advances in medical science and mass education made a pure source of water a prerequisite for public health and sanitation. Paved streets also required regular washing where dirt roads had needed only occasional cleaning. Per capita consumption of water also rose in proportion to city size. Consumers in large cities used more water than their counterparts in smaller urban centers.[69] Similar changes in the scale of demand for public services were occurring in other areas, such as mass transit, street lighting and paving, education, fire protection, and communications. Each ward, moreover, expected its aldermen to secure a full share of each service extension.

Urban growth imposed needs not only for unprecedented technologies, but also for new levels of administrative sophistication. In the case of the water supply, simply adding one extension to the next eventually overtaxed the entire network of distributor lines to the breaking point. Water pressure at the hydrants fell dangerously low throughout the city, remaining at that level until the city builders reformulated their concepts of the utility as a single integrated system. Only a comprehensive plan could hope to meet all the diverse needs of the community. As the insurance underwriters pointed out, this approach had to include the coordination of company and city efforts. In May 1895, the council finally brought the fire fighters under a centralized administration. Only then could Houston begin to implement a technological solution to the fire hydrant problem on a citywide basis by converting from direct pressure methods to the use of steam pumpers. The more general problem of insufficient water pressure awaited the universal installation of meters.[70]

By the mid-nineties, in fact, problems of administration assumed center stage at city hall. Like the jerry-built waterworks, the government bureaucracy had grown piecemeal until the reins of control over the municipal work force slipped from the hands of the council. In the first half of the 1890s alone, the aldermen created several new positions—fire inspector, sewer inspector, building inspector, and city electrician—in addition to expanding the established departments.[71] In short, the city builders had to become city planners. They needed to think about the techniques of management in novel, holistic ways that encompassed the scale and the complexity of the urban environment. These planning concepts could then direct reformers in the renovation of the machinery of government and in the implementation of more systematic approaches to public administration.

City dwellers elsewhere were as confused and dissatisfied as the Houstonians. In the mid-1890s, only a few dynamic leaders such as Detroit's Mayor Hazen Pingree possessed a compelling vision of the coming city. On the contrary, most municipal officials were still trying to mobilize their chain of command and regain a handle on their depression-torn budgets. The reorganization of city government and the institution of "sound business methods," often became requisites for further reform. Of course, some progressives argued that the structural reform of city government was just a beginning, not a final solution for America's municipal problems. The mayor of Boston, for example, pointed out that "municipal corporations are organized not to make money but to spend it; their object is government, not profits."[72] But until reformers imposed levers of control on city bureaucracies, attempts to reconstruct society would remain problematical.

7 "Those Comforts and Conveniences of City Life," 1896–1902

In 1895, the national government acted as a catalyst in the crystallization of a metropolitan vision of city planning in Houston. The formulation of a modern version of the New South strategy for urban progress began in earnest when Galveston won congressional support to become a deep water port. After years of fruitless agitation, the island city finally cemented a regional coalition of trans-Mississippi states strong enough to gain passage of a $5,000,000 appropriation. The Army Corps of Engineers would cut a path through the sandbars blocking entrance to Galveston Bay. In contrast, the Army experts consistently scotched Houston's supplementary proposal to refurbish the decaying ship channel at the same time. The engineers pointed out that the island city was undeniably the superior site for a modern port, while the duplication of facilities would be a wasteful extravagance. Besides, urban-industrial growth had turned Houston's shallow waterway to the Gulf into a dangerously polluted open sewer. Cleaning it up, government experts insisted, would be a prerequisite to further federal action in any case.[1]

Galveston's designation as the region's entrepôt posed a potentially lethal blow to the future growth of its inland rival. The dire implications of Galveston's victory in the long contest over transportation facilities were not lost on Houston's commercial-civic elite. One of its most influential spokesmen, Rene Johnson, observed that the deep water challenge had rekindled the "spirit of enterprise" quenched by the *Higgins* case on special assessment taxation. Johnson's commentary is important because he was both the editor of the elite's chief organ, the *Houston Daily Post*, and the founder and guiding light of its associational vehicle, the Houston Business League.[2] While applauding the renewal of planning efforts, he urged his fellow municipal reformers to take a broad metropolitan perspective. A modern ship channel was essential, he wrote in 1896,

> [b]ut there must be an attractive city here at the same time. People can find so many progressive towns in which to locate these days that there must be a bid for population by supplying those comforts and conveniences of city life without which now the more desirable kinds and accessions of population cannot be secured. The city must not only present advantages, but comforts, modern improvements of every description, indicating a care for health and easy transaction of business and betraying a broad public spirit.[3]

The decisive influence of the U.S. Congress in the Galveston harbor controversy comprised only one of several external forces that were directing the course of urban progressivism. The involvement of Washington in setting public policy at the local level was emblematic of a spreading national matrix that stretched from the capitals of government and business to the provincial centers of the Southwest. In the late nineties, municipal reform increasingly took place within a context of this national framework of law and economics. Urban reformers still had to formulate individual city plans that took into account each place's regional setting and local circumstances. But the national matrix narrowed the range of policy options; it channeled the path of urban progressivism within acceptable parameters of the American political economy. On the Texas Gulf Coast, the direct involvement of the Congress was a relatively new aspect of an expanding federal partnership.[4] In comparison, the national judicial system, utility equipment manufacturers, and money markets played a more consistent and powerful configurative role in shaping the outcome of the battle for municipal reform in Houston.

The mediating role played by the federal hierarchy of courts illustrates the growing impact of outside forces on urban policy formation. The upsurge of franchise reform battles in cities across the country allowed jurists to sit as the final arbiters in disputes over the limits of the public authority to regulate service standards, set "reasonable" rates, and levy special taxes on utility companies. These decisions, in turn, guided city governments and the utility companies as they negotiated the specific terms of new franchises. More important, perhaps, was the courts' tendency to enlarge their own jurisdiction over a broad range of government-business relationships.[5] But the courts could not settle the political debate in Houston and other cities over the basic goals of municipal reform. On the contrary, decision making at the local level was becoming more difficult as each policy issue became enmeshed in larger ideological conflicts over municipal socialism and the meaning of progress.

After 1895, Houston's failure to resolve the dilemmas of city planning exploded into a full-blown crisis. Powerful undercurrents of social, class, and racial tension broke through the shattered consensus on public improvements, touching off bitter clashes at the polls and violent confrontations in the streets. Mounting demands for better public services far exceeded the institutional and administrative capacities of the municipal government. A deepening depression further compounded the thorny problems of choosing budget priorities. Between 1894 and 1899 the tax base remained frozen, while population growth and geographic sprawl continued at a rapid rate. Conflict pervaded the community, throwing its organized interest groups into a protracted struggle for the reins of political power and social control. Practical needs to draw up comprehensive plans polarized the city dwellers around two ideological positions towards municipal reform.[6]

At the center of the crisis stood the enigma of franchise relationships and the pivotal issue of public ownership. A tightening web of interdependence between the city government and its franchised utility companies exacerbated the already difficult task of policy formation on a metropolitan scale. Each sector's current finances, ability to deliver urban services, and long-term investment planning became inflexibly linked to decisions made by the other. Locked together in a financial balancing act after the onset of the depression of 1893, each sector attempted to maintain its footing by shifting the heavy burdens of extending services onto the other. On one side, the utility firms sought to resist pressures for rate cuts and tax increases while making their franchises more secure. In Houston, this posture set off a political backlash against corporate arrogance and tax dodging.

On the other side, the city government tried to reduce its utility bills while raising additional revenues. Taxing the franchises of unpopular corporations offered politicians an attractive alternative to hiking the assessments of the hard-pressed property owners. Yet, public raids on the out-of-state utility companies seemed to undercut efforts to attract Northern capital and industry to the New South metropolis. The double-edged nature of the city's policy alternatives in the question of utility franchises accelerated the process of political polarization within the community. From 1896 to 1902, Houston politicians walked a tight-rope between plunging the city into deep debt and breaking away from the tenets of the New South formula for urban growth and regional hegemony.[7] Eventually the bitter controversy over municipal ownership brought decision making to a standstill. By 1902, the polarization of Houston politics was complete.

But two momentous events on the Texas Gulf Coast forced Houstonians to recall that their intramural struggles could not be divorced from the larger forces of regional and national interdependence. On September 8, 1900, in the worst natural disaster ever to strike the United States, a fierce hurricane destroyed Galveston. Four months later, a vast ocean of a different sort, oil, was discovered just outside of one of Houston's satellite cities, Beaumont. Fifty years of intense rivalry between Houston and Galveston suddenly reached a culmination. For Houston's commercial-civic elite, there was a new urgency to resolving the crisis over city planning. Conscious effort could turn the rail center's temporary advantage into permanent ascendancy. The safer inland city could become the undisputed central city of the region.[8]

Politics and Planning

The primary elections of 1898 marked a critical turning point in the realignment of Houstonians into two antagonistic camps. Campaigning on the issues, rival Democratic factions offered the voters a clear choice between different ideological positions towards municipal reform. Heading the party insurgents was State District Judge Samuel H. Brashear, the nephew of Mayor H. Baldwin Rice's previous opponent. Brashear's brand of urban progressivism implied that the city government should be instrumental in uplifting both the physical and the social conditions of city life. The challenger threw Mayor Rice on the defensive by attacking his meager record of accomplishment in upgrading Houston's public services and facilities. Raising their own banner of municipal ownership, the insurgents appealed to neighborhood values. They expressed the demands of the local taxpayer, skilled worker, and small shopkeeper for improvements in the quality of the immediate environment in which they lived. These voters helped to repudiate the Rice administration and its apparent deference to out-of-state utility companies.

Nonetheless, both candidates placed top priority on meeting the federal government's prerequisites for a modern ship channel. Despite bitter ideological differences, their agreement on the importance of the city's transportation system reflected a common appreciation of Houston's economic dependence on outside markets. Neither man could afford to ignore the congressional decision on a deep water port for the Texas Gulf Coast. An identical emphasis on cleaning up the Buffalo Bayou illustrates the growing weight of national forces on local decision makers. Increasingly, outside influences not only limited policy options and set allocation priorities, but they also gave shape and direction to the resulting city plans.

The Rice-Brashear contest promised to reverse a decade of increasing social tension and political polarization. The challenger and the incumbent shared a remarkably similar upbringing among Houston's most prestigious and wealthy families. Both men were native sons in their mid-thirties. They belonged to large families that were extending the influence of their pioneer fathers through business expansions, kinship networks, and political involvements. Rice, for example, inherited cattle and cotton lands but chose to serve as a public weigher and a county commissioner before his 1896 election to the mayor's office. Pursuing a parallel career in public life, Brashear became a lawyer and county court clerk like his father. In 1892, the 27-year-old official successfully campaigned for election to the district court, becoming the youngest state judge in Texas history. The common backgrounds of the candidates suggest that their perspectives on urban progressivism would mirror the outlook of their class, the commercial-civic elite.[9]

On the contrary, ideological differences on the role of government as an active agent of social reform separated the two young men into opposing camps. On one side, Rice stood for traditional beliefs about the political economy. His administration followed the conventional wisdom that limited the use of government to the promotion of the private sector. The incumbent was a reluctant reformer who tried to retard city hall's deepening involvements in the daily life of the community. In the area of franchise relations, moreover, Mayor Rice reacted courageously against the assaults of the utility corporations, but he actually favored a policy of regulated monopoly. On the other side, Judge Brashear represented a break with the past. He envisioned a much-expanded public sector that would take a leading part in the movement for social justice. The challenger demanded a municipal light plant as well as the subordination of the private companies to the advancement of the general welfare.

The election of 1898 completed the process of polarization by linking political conflict over public policy with deep-seated class and racial divisions in the community. At the outset of the campaign, the Democrats decided to prohibit black participation in the primaries. As we shall see in the following chapter, disfranchisement of the blacks and, later, other poor people led directly to their exclusion from the benefits of the modernization of Houston's public services. In addition to racial discrimination, antagonism between labor and capital moved to the center stage of local politics when transit workers went out on strike against the non-Southern Houston Electric Street Railway Corporation (HESRC) a few days before the Democratic poll. Brashear contrasted his goal of municipal ownership by the people against the incumbent's conciliatory posture towards the utility companies and his anti-labor policies towards city workers. By the time of the voting, the two candidates had become identified with opposite ideological positions towards government-business relations. A rampage of violent destruction against the transit company in the wake of the elections exposed the bitter depths of social discord that a chronic state of crisis had produced.

From the start of the contest in early January, the leader of the party dissidents called for a full debate of the critical issues facing Houston. The daytime primary became the dissidents' symbol of an open, democratic process. The local executive committee agreed to this demand in order to contain the Brashear faction within party ranks. To further guarantee Democratic unity and ultimate control of city hall, committee chairman Ben Riesner also announced that blacks would no longer be allowed to participate in the party elections. The new arrangements not only opened the door to Jim Crow but also reinforced the ward-centered nature of city politics. Under the primary rules, aldermanic hopefuls were chosen on a ward-by-ward basis. In contrast, the general elections required at-large majorities to win a seat on the council. Unless Democratic infighting spilled over from one poll to the next, however, black Houstonians were effectively frozen out of the political process.[10]

While Brashear outlined a comprehensive program for neighborhood uplift and social justice, Rice was forced to defend a lackluster administration. The challenger attacked the incumbent's lack of initiative and his decision to pay city workers in scrip. Constitutional restrictions on the city's taxing and borrowing powers had hamstrung the Rice administration in the wake of the *Higgins* ruling. In 1896, the mayor had inherited a $168,000 deficit or floating debt in addition to two long-term debts totalling $150,000, which had to be refunded in municipal bonds. Coping with rigid fiscal options, the mayor made a vain attempt to hold down budgetary deficits by paying the salaries of municipal workers with city paper. While this stopgap measure saved some money, it earned Rice the enmity of Houston's labor unions. At least, the mayor retorted bitterly on the campaign trail, his policies had "filled men's bellies." Yet Rice's admission that the long-belated start of paving projects had been "the life of this city" for the past six months better captures the anemic tone of his campaign.[11]

Nine days before the March 24 primary, a strike by transit workers brought the clashing positions of the two mayoral candidates into high relief. Their attitudes toward capital, labor, and utility corporations became pivotal after the workers' walkout upset the daily routine of an entire population. Organized six months earlier, the Amalgamated Association of Street Railway Employees now demanded higher wages, shorter hours, and a closed shop.[12] The strike seemed to

crystallize a deep strain of resentment against the loss of local autonomy to outside corporations. Endorsed by the central Labor Council, the demands of the
transit workers were greeted with support by the police, railroad men, and many
small shopkeepers who sympathized more with hometown neighbors than Yankee capitalists. When the transit company attempted to restore operations with a
substitute work force, large mobs repulsed the scab drivers back into the car
sheds. Mayor Rice, too, voiced sympathy with the strikers' demands, but he
pledged to protect the corporation's property. In the midst of this extremely tense
situation, Democrats voted in the primary election.[13]

The voters rejected Rice by more than a three to two margin; moreover, five
out of eight incumbent candidates for the city council also went down to defeat.[14]
The posture of the party regulars toward business-labor relations, as symbolized
by the utility strike, probably accounts for the impressive size of the dissidents'
victory. More importantly, Brashear's concept of urban progressivism went beyond traditional principles of the promotional state to embrace a broader notion
of the welfare state. In 1898, community hopes for ameliorating deficiencies in
the delivery of essential services to the neighborhoods and for regaining local
autonomy rested on Brashear's pledge to turn the city government into an instrument of social reform.

The imminent transfer of political authority to a new city administration
elected with strong labor support helped to dissipate an emotional state of tension. Three days after the primary, riot and armed violence rocked the city despite Mayor Rice's ban on public assemblies and demonstrations. The outburst
was triggered by a tragic explosion at the Citizens' Electric Light and Power
Company plant that left the utility in ruins and four workers dead. Rice had to
call for reinforcements from the state militia and a posse of dependable citizens.
As troops patrolled the city streets and guarded the railway's property, a group of
Houston's best men mediated a compromise between the company and the union.
Yet the dynamiting of several cars three weeks later revealed that the settlement
did not entirely heal the business-labor rift in Houston; deep scars of bitterness
remained on both sides.[15]

The Brashear administration offered real hope that social tensions could be
eased by comprehensive city planning. In contrast to Rice's disjointed and passive approaches, the new mayor possessed a coherent vision of municipal reform. He spearheaded an ambitious drive to expand governmental responsibility
for the welfare of the community. Whether building a metropolitan system of
sanitation, forging untried franchise policies, or buttressing the structure of the
city's tax and regulatory powers, Brashear advanced integrated programs for the
modernization of Houston's services and environment. By the end of a two-year
term, he had fulfilled all his major platform promises, except for a municipal
light plant. This goal continued to elude him because his aggressive posture in
government-business relations met with mounting resistance by the utility companies as well as growing consternation among the commercial-civic elite. By
the 1900 elections, municipal ownership emerged as a symbolic issue, the litmus
test of ideological alignments in the struggle for political power.

Although the neophyte mayor asserted that an 1897 bond referendum represented an "imperative command" to build a city light plant, he gave first attention to securing a deep water ship channel for Houston.[16] Neither contemporaries nor later historians had any doubts about the vital significance of this decision to keep pace with Galveston's new shipping facilities. In *The Port of Houston*, Marilyn Sibley succinctly sums up the city's predicament: "Deep water at Galveston brought Houston to a major crisis in its economic development. Houstonians could either sit still and watch many of their commercial advantages disappear, or they could build a channel that would again put their town on par with Galveston."[17] The Army Corps' reservations about the health hazards from Houston's pollution of the headwaters of the channel focused local attention on the need for a centralized treatment plant. The planning implications were clear to journalist Rene Johnson, who demanded that the new administration make a unified sewerage system its "chief concern." Calling for no radical departures from the past, the editor reminded Brashear that "[w]e have grown and prospered by reason of the steady development of public improvements and we can confidently anticipate continued expansion and profitable return for every dollar expended for paving, drainage and sewerage."[18]

The planning of the sanitation system best illustrates the metropolitan dimensions of city building undertaken by Mayor Brashear. In January 1899, he hired an imaginative city planner from New York, Alexander Potter. Trained as a sanitary engineer, the outside expert soon put Houston's public health problems in a broad context of environmental and municipal reform. Potter showed how most existing sewer pipes could be tied into a central treatment plant that would serve an area of sixteen square miles. Moreover, he introduced an innovative concept of harnessing several municipal services together. The planner presented the council with a unified study of the city's future needs for water supplies, sewer distributors, and electrical power and light. On the same site, he proposed, an electrical generating station would run the pumps of the sewage plant and perhaps a waterworks. Potter also suggested that a municipal incinerator for garbage disposal be included at the public facility. The council responded enthusiastically to the Potter plan because it was far more comprehensive than the blueprints of local city builders.[19]

Brashear realized that fiscal reform would comprise an integral part of any bold scheme for city planning on a metropolitan scale. Almost immediately after taking office, the mayor organized a charter revision committee to restructure the city's finances along with its regulatory powers. By the time Potter presented his plan in February 1899, a far-reaching set of reforms was already before the state legislature. Included among the charter amendments was a provision for a special bond issue of $300,000 to pay for the massive public works project. As soon as the new charter went into effect in May, the council passed a referendum measure for the sanitation system. Two months later, the taxpayers approved it by an overwhelming majority. The Potter plan not only solved major public health and environmental problems but also opened the way for a reconsideration of the ship channel by the Army engineers and the Congress.[20]

In a similar manner, Mayor Brashear aggressively pursued new directions in government-business relations by prodding the utility companies into providing the community with better services at lower rates. During his first year in office, for example, the chief executive began withholding half of the payments due the water and the light companies because of their failure to fulfill contract duties to meet minimum standards. The council cooperated with the mayor in tightening quality controls by establishing a gas inspector, a city electrician, and a permanent waterworks committee. Franchise holders often used government inspectors to deflect consumer complaints. But the creation of the waterworks committee indicates that the Brashear administration intended these regulators to act as public watchdogs for the consumer. The council acted after numerous petitions charged the water company with virtual extortion and fraud in setting water rates. Since overcharges on individual bills remained too small for judicial relief, some type of collective response was needed. Brashear directed the standing committee to investigate each complaint in order to accumulate a persuasive case of franchise violation by the utility firm.[21]

Dynamic approaches to regulating established utilities paralleled franchise policies that employed competition as a tool to enhance public services. For instance, a fifteen-year non-exclusive grant to a telephone venture incorporated a broad range of community welfare objectives. In addition to a detailed list of regulatory concessions, the franchise included a provision to set consumer rates. In March 1899, the Citizens' Telephone Company also agreed to hire only local construction workers, pay them (as well as switchboard operators) a minimum wage set by city hall, provide free services in public offices, and add at least $50,000 worth of property to the tax rolls within eighteen months. The advent of competition stirred the rival Bell affiliate to accelerate improvements in its Houston services, besides reducing its rates to those set in the new grant.[22]

Brashear's politics of confrontation caused one after another of Houston's utility corporations to line up against the administration. By the end of this two-year term, the mayor's vigorous efforts to rebalance government-business relations in favor of the public interest were hitting all the franchise holders where it hurt the most, in their pocketbooks. Moreover, the chief executive used his office to campaign openly for municipal socialism. In his annual message of 1900, for example, Brashear asserted that "municipal ownership of public necessities is a cure for the usual troubles arising with private corporations . . . as well as a financial saving to the city. [This proposition] can no longer be questioned by reasonable, disinterested people."[23] Taken together, Houston's biggest corporations had good reason to align themselves with the opposition in the 1900 elections.

Other large taxpayers also came to harbor deep resentments against the administration. From his inauguration, Brashear unrelentingly prosecuted the collection of delinquent property levies that frequently stretched back to the 1880s, when evasion of the bond tax was semi-official policy. Within a year, City Attorney James S. Stewart had collected over $400,000, while another $140,000 worth of judgment suits were pending against wealthy individuals and business firms. In some cases, the belated collections caused unfair hardships for small homesteaders who purchased their land without knowing about the unpaid tax bills of previous owners. To help alleviate this problem in the future, Brashear inserted a clause in the new charter of May 1899 limiting delinquent tax collections to a four-year period. In Austin, however, a taxpayer's group had the structural reform amended to apply retroactively as well. Brashear successfully contested this "stay law" proviso in the courts, but he also earned the enmity of a sizeable portion of the commercial-civic elite.[24]

Offsetting policies that antagonized the utility corporations and the big taxpayers were innovative programs to enhance the welfare of the entire community. The mayor's brand of progressivism went beyond the traditional belief in a promotional state and wielded government as an agent of social justice and civic uplift. Planning a comprehensive network of city parks was emblematic of Brashear's community orientation toward metropolitan reform. The mayor established Houston's first recreational space in a central location. At the same time, he called for the creation of a system of neighborhood parks before rising land values made these public amenities an overbearing expense on the municipal treasury. In an analogous way, Brashear put greater emphasis on primary level education by shifting funds from the high school, which served only a small elite of college-bound students. A minimum wage ordinance was aimed at raising worker pay scales throughout the urban economy. A pure food and milk law regulated the sale of these essential commodities city wide, not just in the outgrown market house in the middle of downtown.[25]

In this context of social reform, municipal ownership loomed as an ideological symbol, the pivotal issue in the realignment of Houston's urban polity. By 1900, a public electric plant came to represent Brashear's position towards the growth of public responsibility for the well-being of the community. The issue was no longer confined to a simple question of economic expediency, that is, of cutting the cost of providing essential services. To be sure, the mayor's promises of budgetary savings remained an effective political appeal, especially among middle-class taxpayers. But municipal ownership now took on added meaning as a civic instrument for regaining local control over the city's public services and for restoring the primacy of community values over the pecuniary interests of out-of-state corporations. From the mayor's point of view, the franchise holders had been "very negligent and, in some cases, almost defiant" in spite of public grants of special privileges.[26] Municipal ownership offered an appealing alternative to the apparent grip of monopoly power on the welfare of the community.

On balance, Mayor Brashear did not so much reject the traditional outlook of the city booster as embrace new purposes and broader perspectives in order to resolve the civic crisis by comprehensive planning. His priority on the ship channel established an unbroken continuity between the pioneer and the urban generation of Houston leaders. But Brashear's reform program of enlarging the duties of the government to enhance the social welfare marked a departure from the past. Except for the erection of a municipal light plant, the mayor largely fulfilled his platform promises to improve Houston's urban services and metropolitan environment. While few opposed these accomplishments, several powerful interests objected to being forced to pay for this extension of the public authority over the private sector. Moreover, conservative spokesmen like Rene Johnson became more and more worried that Brashear's energetic attack on corporate arrogance and tax dodging was undermining the opportunities of the business elite to attract Northern capital and industry to the New South city.[27]

Courts and Corporations

The uphill campaign of the Brashear administration for public ownership demonstrated that national influences were playing an increasingly predominant role in local movements for municipal reform. In Houston, a national system of courts, manufacturing companies, and financial markets largely shaped the outcome of the political battle to decide who would supply electrical services to the community. The sharp contrast between rigid fiscal limitations in the government sector and flexible institutional arrangements in the business world gave the utilities industry a significant advantage. This economic superiority rested on a national foundation of interstate instruments of finance and management, which furnished local operating firms with ready access to America's rapidly accumulating funds of venture capital. While urban progressives like Rice and Brashear were attempting to loosen constitutional checkreins on the city's taxing and borrowing powers, businessmen were securing their positions as the exclusive suppliers of urban necessities.

In the case of the light plant, the vigorous drive of the General Electric Company to update and expand the local facility removed a sense of urgency from embarking on the uncertain adventure of government competition with private industry. A federal court receivership, moreover, extended an umbrella of protection over the enterprise while General Electric completely rebuilt the plant up to the most modern standards. But to Brashear, municipal ownership still symbolized the grand struggle for social justice. A long list of pressing demands for better governmental services, however, left the reformer little room to pour the city's limited resources into expensive utility systems. Although the mayor used the federal courts to advantage in imposing new taxes on the franchises of the local firms, the constitutional legacy of the Gilded Age kept the public's fiscal options tightly restricted. By 1902, the contrast between the modern plant built by General Electric and the unfunded plans of the administration irreversibly tipped the political balance of power into the hands of Brashear's opponents.

A crucial feature of the mayor's strategy for municipal ownership was the extraction of more taxes from the franchise holders. Without additional sources of revenue, the reformer could not underwrite programs to provide the community with an expanding array of governmental services and facilities. Unprecedented forms of utility taxation comprised a part of a larger progressive current to tap the vast, albeit intangible, wealth of the modern business corporation. In this complex area of public policy, the courts played a central role at every level of the federal system in shaping the direction of reform.[28] Closely following the latest decisions of the bench, Houston officials imposed new levies on every franchise holder.

The struggle over franchise taxes epitomizes the inextricable bonds of interdependence among the cities, utilities, and courts at the turn of the century. Although the judiciary cut off Houston's chief source of special tax revenues in the 1895 *Higgins* case, the courts also helped to widen the tax liability of franchised corporations. The evolving configurations of government-business relations in the courts proved pivotal to Brashear's move to tax the franchises of these companies. In 1897, the U.S. Supreme Court deliberated as a panel of economic experts on the "value" of franchises and other intangible assets. Involving a Fourteenth Amendment controversy, the *Adams Express* case asked the judiciary to determine whether Ohio's tax on these newer forms of corporate wealth constituted a valid levy or an unequal and arbitrary confiscation of property. The state statute directed assessors to calculate the property value of their capital stock and securities. By using this "unit rule" of assessment instead of taxing only physical equipment, the valuation of the Adams Company jumped from $50,000 to $500,000. Attorneys for the firm denied that this tenfold difference represented any actual value, only stock speculators' predictions of corporate success.[29]

The Supreme Court upheld the Ohio law in a 5–4 decision. Chief Justice Melville W. Fuller agreed that a unit rule of assessment measured "use and management" of company property, not just tangible assets. But the market price of corporate securities, Fuller believed, was a valid indicator of a firm's actual value. To the court majority, franchises, managerial skill, good will, and other intangible factors directly appreciated the corporation's worth. Justice David J. Brewer went further in arguing that property in a "complex civilization" consisted of anything that had currency in the market place. The ruling reflected the Court's willingness to recognize the many new forms of wealth created by the nation's transformation from an agricultural to an industrial society.[30]

The high court's approval of the unit rule supplied local officials in Houston with a legitimate method of levying new taxes on the franchise holders, including the steam railroad companies entering the city. In September 1899, the unit rule was applied by the assessor-collector, Julius Hirsch, a former alderman who strongly favored municipal ownership. Admitting that any particular figure was arbitrary, he still felt legally bound by state law to list every form of "property" on the tax rolls. For example, Hirsch doubled the valuation of the streetcar company to $500,000. Every franchised corporation protested the validity of these levies before the Board of Appraisement. One after another, the attorneys threatened protracted and expensive court challenges to prevent the municipality from adding the value of local franchises to their companies' tax burdens. City Attorney Stewart, however, informed the board of the *Adams Express* decision and asserted that the unit rule would ultimately be sustained in the national courts. Faced with this persuasive argument, the franchise holders offered to pay the tax increase if each was reassessed uniformly at $250,000, which would yield

$5,000 per company. This represented an immediate gain of $34,000, besides establishing an important precedent for future tax hikes.[31]

Political pressure to squeeze more tax concessions out of the utility companies illustrates how the franchise was a double-edged instrument of public policy that bound the financial integrity of each sector to the other. While the franchise could shore up the monopoly positions of poorly managed firms, it could also undercut their financial stability. A corporation with a threatened or contested franchise had difficulty raising investment capital to pay for service improvements and extensions. Investor risk climbed even higher if the utility enterprise depended heavily on the government for contracts, as did Houston's water and electric companies. The upsurge of a grassroots movement for municipal ownership further eroded the economic moorings of the affected corporation.

A comparison of government and business during the Rice and Brashear administrations reflects the vital importance of their interdependent relationship with the modernization of urban services. In the absence of mutual cooperation in city planning, each side inflicted financial hardship on the other. For example, the contract strategy of the Citizens' Electric Light and Power Company resulted in disaster. In 1897, the utility's bid for an ironclad contract backfired to the advantage of the proponents of a municipal facility. The arrogance of the electric company provoked Mayor Rice into sponsoring a bond referendum on the construction of a rival public facility. In November, over 1,200 taxpayers appeared at the polls to approve the referendum by a 57 percent majority.[32]

The anticipated loss of the city's business plunged the Citizens' company into a receivership, which lasted for four years. The bondholders had gone unpaid since September 1896. The timing of their suit over fifteen months later in the U.S. District Court must have been directly tied to the local poll on municipal ownership. The reports filed in the case confirm that the enterprise depended on the city for about a third of its revenues, or about $22,000 of its $66,000 annual income. Without the government contract, the firm's bonded debt obligations of over $15,000 per year would jump from 23 to 35 percent of its gross receipts. The insolvency of the utility corporation well before the expiration of the contract underscores the fragility of its financial structure. A closer examination of the receivership reports discloses the sources of these institutional shortcomings.[33]

The origins of the Citizens' Electric case were typical of urban utility receiverships in the late nineteenth century. The dire predictions of industry leaders that fixed capital charges would cripple the operating companies materialized with the emergence of a national market for public utility securities. In the Houston example, the electric company carried a capital burden of $188,000 worth of mortgage bonds although the receiver set the value of its equipment and buildings at less than $35,000. Even after making generous allowances for the utility's land (which was liable to flooding and had to be abandoned), its franchises, and a fifty-mile network of wires and poles, the company's liabilities far exceeded its assets and current earning power. Either the corporation's debts had to be scaled, as in the earlier case of the Houston transit company, or the services provided by the electric plant had to be upgraded to the point where its income was sufficient to cover its capital charges. The creditors of the Citizens' company chose the latter course.[34]

The financial problems of the utility sector stemmed from extralocal sources, which also predominated in finding solutions to these structural weaknesses. For example, the receivership of Houston's electric company illustrates the full extent to which the national judiciary could become responsible for the administration of an urban service enterprise. Less than three months after the bondholders filed their suit in January 1898, a tragic boiler explosion leveled the main plant and killed four workers, touching off a night of rioting by striking transit men. Rather than liquidate the few remaining assets of the company among the bondholders, U.S. District Judge Bryant approved their request to supervise the refinancing and reconstruction of an entirely new plant. Two years later, the electric generators went into operation at an approximate cost of $200,000, but the utility continued under the guardianship of the national court for another two years. During this period, Judge Bryant permitted the creation of an additional $150,000 worth of liabilities for service extensions to keep up with consumer demand. Judge Bryant, moreover, became involved in various managerial problems including the settlement of a strike by the unionized linemen and the institution of a suit against the city for partial nonpayment of its street lighting bill.[35]

A second institution of national importance, the General Electric Company, played an equally influential role in the modernization of Houston's electric light and power services. In December 1901, the U.S. Court's supervision of the utility firm's rehabilitation ended with its sale to the major creditor, the United Electric Securities Company. This interstate financial instrument was a holding company for the giant equipment manufacturer. General Electric had underwritten both of Houston's facilities in order to create a market for its products. Consequently, its holding company controlled almost all of the receiver-related securities, besides two thirds of the original mortgage bonds. In this instance, the judiciary provided a protective umbrella for General Electric while it installed a much larger facility to capture the growing market for energy in the Texas city.[36]

The construction of an updated and expanded central station by the General Electric Company provided a practical solution to the financial and technological shortcomings of the renamed Houston Lighting and Power Company. Improved generators, connected to meters, produced twenty-four hour services as well as consumer confidence in the utility firm. The meter system ensured that each household and business paid only for the precise amounts of energy it used. The new company could light five times as many incandescent bulbs as the old, in addition to an eight-fold increase in power-generating capacities. Although the bonded debt of the reincorporated venture stood at $750,000, its efficient delivery of services to more and more consumers produced enough income to cover these liabilities. In 1903, for example, the company grossed $180,000, which left over $86,000 in net receipts to redeem $37,500 worth of bond coupons.[37]

The direct involvement of the manufacturing giant in the modernization of

Houston's electrical services epitomizes the superior economic power of the utilities industry to respond to the general urban crisis of the 1890s. The muscular infusion of funds by General Electric to save one of its local operating companies originated in the national integration of the private sector during the past decade. To be sure, the interstate holding company and other national instruments forged in the private sector were subject to gross abuse in the twentieth century. In fact, the absence of federal regulation encouraged harmful financial practices.[38] Yet the national structure of the private sector undoubtedly facilitated the rapid diffusion of modern technologies during the critical stages of the revolution in urban services.

In comparison, the fiscal powers of the municipal corporation were still constrained in a constitutional straitjacket at the turn of the century. The fragmented structure of the federal system virtually precluded an analogous national attack on the urban crisis. On the contrary, local units of government were left alone to struggle uphill against the Gilded Age legacy of the legal reformers. Major institutional adjustments in municipal charters and general "home rule" amendments in state constitutions became prerequisites to restoring the fiscal vitality of the city government. Only then could it begin to finance a vast expansion of public services and facilities to meet the demands of social justice.

The struggle over a public light plant set the stage for the 1900 elections. During the preceding two years, of course, the rapid strides of the General Electric Company to build a modern facility were fast eliminating a pressing need for a city owned alternative. However, public support for the Brashear-Potter plan remained strong. In November 1899, Houstonians reconfirmed the 1897 referendum on public ownership after a recently enacted state law restricted the suffrage in municipal bond elections from "taxpayers" to "property taxpayers."[39] Only the light commissioners, who were Rice appointees, kept the council from signing a contract with Westinghouse for a municipal plant. By January, a frustrated Brashear demanded council action against the board to remove its intransigent members. The aldermen unanimously passed an ordinance that terminated the positions of all the commissioners and permitted the mayor to select a more agreeable board.[40]

The timing of the commissioners' removal reflected an astute political sensitivity to the central importance that the city electric plant had assumed by 1900. The administration's actions coincided with the start of the campaign for local offices. Brashear followers were organizing municipal ownership clubs in each ward to promote candidates who professed the proper viewpoint. To be sure, other issues such as public improvement priorities, tax collection policies, and labor legislation continued to play a prominent role in the campaign. But after the recent referendum, no office seeker denied support for the principles of public ownership. Post-election events, however, would reveal that some candidates were secretly opposed to this policy option.[41]

In spite of the Brashear faction's control of the party machinery, an organized coalition of Democrats were well prepared to contest the mayor's bid for a second term. In mid-January, John T. Browne, former mayor (1892–96) and a self-made businessman, announced his candidacy. Endorsed by Johnson's *Daily Post*, Browne expressed the complaints of the utility companies, big taxpayers, and business elite against the incumbent. Giving recognition to the broad base of support for municipal ownership, the challenger's platform advocated a city light plant and waterworks. However, the former mayor qualified his stand by demanding prior elimination of the "spoils or factional system" of patronage that was an intrinsic feature of a ward-centered structure of politics. A better reflection of Browne's true position was his charge that the administration was pursuing a destructive course of harassment against the city's business corporations. Browne pledged to replace the mayor's "nagging" posture towards corporations with a policy of encouraging capital investment in Houston. He promised to give fair and equal treatment to all business enterprises, a clear reference to the franchise tax imposed on the utility and the railroad companies. Browne also called for tax reform; but unlike the incumbent, the challenger favored relief from city hall's unrelenting prosecution of corporate tax dodgers and delinquent property owners.[42]

In contrast, Brashear proudly displayed his record of achievement in shifting the balance of power in government–business relations towards the public welfare. An unequivocal faith in municipal ownership was the hallmark of his platform. Listing the social advances made during his brief administration, the mayor promised further progress in the improvement of neighborhood schools and parks as well as streets and sanitation. In addition to defending his record, Brashear assumed the offensive by labelling Browne a tool of the streetcar company, a "mossback," and an enemy of organized labor. By March, local observers were characterizing the campaign as a bitter duel. Indeed, the assassination of a Brashear spokesman at a rally and the mysterious theft of the city books were indicative of a heated political contest.[43]

More importantly, the intensity of the battle shattered the recently forged unity of the Democrats, throwing the decisive vote from the primary to the general election. Less than ten days before the March 30 poll of the party, the Browne faction bolted. It rejected an executive committee ruling that allowed Brashear to appoint two of the three election judges in four wards, leaving Browne to enjoy the same advantage in only two districts. The belated rejection of the party primary made two significant differences in the structure of the election. First, the aldermanic contests were changed from ward-by-ward races to at-large polls. Second, black Houstonians again became a potent political force to be reckoned with, since they comprised about one fifth of the electorate. Triggering a last minute flurry of voter registrations, the walkout by the Browne faction helped encourage a record 10,500 citizens to become eligible to participate in the general election.[44]

With an 80 percent turnout, the results of the balloting on April 3, 1900, were

TABLE 7.1   Municipal Election Results, 1900

Ward	Brashear Ticket	Total Vote	Home Ward	Brashear Loyalist	Browne Ticket	Total Vote	Home Ward
1	Robinson*	4,223	X		Miller	3,863	X
	Sonnen	4,268			Puls	3,496	
2	Rosenthal	3,843	X		Miller	4,524	X
	Levy	3,381			Thompson	3,888	
3	Woolford	4,511	X	X	Wolkarte	3,502	
	Thomas	4,841	X	X	Edwards	3,142	
4	Tuffly	4,297		X	Bollfras	3,652	X
	O'Leary	3,970			Staples	3,685	X
5	Bennett	4,487	X	X	McAughan	3,615	X
	Aubertin	4,268			Carter	3,440	
6	Halverton	4,175	X		Anderson	3,107	
	Mueller	4,063	X	X	Hartman	3,341	

SOURCE: Council Minutes, Book K: 199–201, 321.
*Italicized name indicates a winner.

extremely close. Brashear edged Browne by a mere 241 votes, while the contests for council seats were equally tight. On the one hand, the change to an at-large tally was crucial in almost half of the aldermanic races. Five contestants carried their home wards but lost in the city-wide totals, with Brashear's slate winning a net gain of three seats. On the other hand, the fact that Brashear's ticket captured ten of the twelve positions was a Pyrrhic victory at best. Five winners on the mayor's side soon deserted the administration and joined the two opposition aldermen to form an unbreakable majority in the council. Further analysis of the election returns confirms the ward-centered locus of political power in Houston. No consistent patterns of correlation can be drawn among Brashear loyalists, deserters, and opponents, or between winners and losers (see Table 7.1). Although the mayor's reelection marked a personal triumph as well as a mandate for municipal ownership, the nearly equal strength of his detractors suggested that the urban crisis was far from reaching a peaceful settlement.[45]

The National Matrix

Brashear's victory at the ballot box was short-lived because the opposition refused to accept the majority mandate. Rather than mute the shrill voices of discord dividing the community, the mayor's reelection amplified all the sources of social, political, economic, and racial polarization. By 1900, a municipal light plant had become the ideological symbol of Brashear's dynamic efforts to shift government-business relations towards the primacy of the public welfare. But the growth of governmental responsibility for the well-being of society entailed the painful extraction of tax and regulatory concessions from the utility corporations and other powerful elements of the urban economy. These anti-administration forces were joined by city boosters who objected to the mayor's neighborhood-centered brand of progressive reform. They believed that no city in the New South could afford even the appearance of attacking business enterprise or investment capital from the North. Torn by self-doubt and uncertainty, the commercial-civic elite tended to link distasteful policy alternatives to the city's democratic structure of ward-centered politics.

In the midst of this deepening crisis of confidence, two fortuitous events of tremendous importance tipped the delicate balance of political power against the parochial interests of Brashear's followers. The conjunction of the Galveston catastrophe in September 1900 and the Spindletop gusher four months later completely altered Houston's place in the national matrix of interdependent regions and urban centers. Galveston's loss was Houston's gain. After fifty years of tandem growth, the island city's destruction catapulted its inland rival into a position that could lead to a permanent ascendency. If its power brokers could cement solid bonds with the national centers of capital and influence, Houston could become the international entrepôt of the Southwest and North Central sections of the country. The incredibly large pools of liquid gold discovered at nearby Beaumont also promised to boost Houston's role in the national economy to major proportions. The city's business leaders fully realized that they had to seize these rich opportunities quickly before Galveston recovered or another upstart challenger like Beaumont captured the virtually unlimited potential of the oil industry.[46]

The national repercussions set off by the shock waves on the Texas Gulf Coast added all the more urgency within Houston to reestablish conditions of political stability and social order. Throughout 1900–1901, however, the deadlock of public policy remained unbroken. Intractable conflict became endemic inside the council chambers as well as between city hall and the franchise holders. The struggle over government-business relations intensified as each side pressed for victory in the courts and on the political battlefield. Moreover, the business elite was becoming convinced that extreme measures alone could restore a consensus on city planning. Open calls for Jim Crow and mass disfranchisement signalled the emergence of significant support for a politics of exclusion.

At first Brashear's reelection appeared to spell a quick settlement of the controversy over city planning, not its deterioration into an interminable impass. Although his margin of victory was slim, it was sufficient to assure friend and foe alike that the mayor would continue pursuing his version of progressivism for at least two more years. In addition, Brashear's platform on urban reform seemed politically fortified by the recent referendum on the light plant and the selection of ten out of twelve aldermen on his public ownership ticket. The return of economic prosperity to the city also buttressed the administration's fiscal position while undercutting the will of the franchise holders to resist at an ever-mounting price of lost profits and opportunities for business expansion. Yet the mayor soon found himself locked in a losing battle over municipal ownership. The stalemate in the council spread from one issue to the next until policy formation on government-business relations was brought to a complete standstill.

The presence of an anti-Brashear majority in the council did not surface until the administration unveiled detailed plans for the construction of a municipal electric station. Before August 1900, in contrast, the aldermen generally worked in harmony to improve the public welfare by imposing new regulations and taxes on the utility companies. For example, the council approved motions to require the telephone companies to place their wires in underground conduits, to "instruct" the waterworks to extend mains, and to order the street railway to restore services on the Louisiana Street line or remove its tracks. But when the Board of Public Works submitted several contract bids of about $100,000 each to build a light plant, five administration aldermen surprised everyone by joining the two members of the opposition in an effort to kill the proposal. A timely veto by the mayor kept it alive, while the *Post* noted ominously that "the council divided seven to five on all important propositions." [47]

At the next "stormy session," the conflict over municipal ownership ended in a general stalemate. An administration bill to institute an eight-hour day for city workers went down to a 7–5 defeat. A narrow albeit resolute majority of seven began to stymie every measure put forth by the administration. At the same time, the mayor's veto was equally effective in blocking any alternative steps, since a two-thirds majority of eight was needed to override his opposition. By mid-August, Brashear and his supporters throughout the community were fully alarmed at the possibility that their entire reform program was facing utter rejection in spite of its popular mandate. [48]

Over the next few weeks, the debate over municipal ownership reached a climax. On the one hand, a variety of ad hoc and organized groups from the community crowded into the council chambers to confront the aldermen with compelling arguments in favor of the light plant. Led by J. J. Pastoriza, a citizens' coalition presented the politicians a petition with 800 to 1,000 names. The Houston Labor Council submitted a similar appeal from its membership. Accusing the anti-administration seven of "repudiating" the people's will, both groups protested any further delay in the erection of the public facility. Edward J. O'Beirne, an experienced engineer and leading contender for the contract, reminded the aldermen that electrical technologies were no longer uncertain experiments but rather well-established systems. Defending his plans, the expert from Birmingham, Alabama, promised that the proposed plant would provide adequate capacity to power the city's 286 street lights. As Houston grew larger, he and other speakers reasoned, extra equipment could be added organically to the municipal system to keep pace with public needs.

The anti-administration aldermen severely criticized O'Beirne's specifications. At the same time, four of the five deserters reaffirmed their fidelity to the principles of municipal ownership. Instead, they centered their attack on the inadequacies of the plan, which was limited to street lighting. Labelling it a fake and a fraud, the aldermen claimed that Houston needed a much larger and more expensive facility. Louis Sonnen of the first ward, for example, pledged his adherence to the ideals of municipal ownership. However, he vowed to withhold his support until the mayor presented a scheme with a minimum expenditure of $250,000 for the initial construction of the system. Only representative Henry Halverton of the sixth ward announced an ideological opposition to the public ownership option. The present reign of patronage politics, the grocery store owner continued, precluded an "efficiently, satisfactorily and successfully" run government operation. Standing steadfast against the citizens' appeals, the seven-man majority rejected every motion to take positive action on the city light plant.[49]

Although the personal motives for their turnabout remain hidden, some of the reasons why the five aldermen deserted the administration can be gleaned from contemporary comments. In a letter to the *Post*, Pastoriza observed that the utility companies were exerting tremendous pressure on the politicians. It was not necessary to charge them with bribery, the reformer stated, to reach the logical conclusion that the companies were influencing them nonetheless.[50] Other foes of the administration were also applying whatever political leverage they could muster to defeat Brashear's reform program. In any case, the desertion of the aldermen illustrates the ward-centered structure of urban politics in Houston. Local elections promoted the formation of temporary coalitions of ward leaders who lined up behind a promising mayoral candidate. But their bases of popular support remained independently rooted in their home districts. The intractable conflict over the light plant highlighted the decentralized nature of the city's political and governmental institutions. The mayor had few weapons at his disposal with which to force the aldermen to follow his leadership.

From our vantage point, the council majorities' principal criticism that the proposed system grossly underestimated the city's needs cannot withstand careful scrutiny. The plan clearly met the current demands of the public sector for street lighting. More importantly, the rebuttal of O'Beirne, Pastoriza, and others that the electric plant could be expanded organically to parallel urban growth in the future reflected an accurate assessment of the technological and business history of the utilities industry. Each urban public service in Houston and most other places had started with a relatively small system, adding extensions piecemeal in a race to keep up with increasing demand.

If the private Citizens' company was providing adequate capacity and services, then the objections of the anti-administration forces to a small duplicate facility might also gain a convincing degree of credibility. However, the city was receiving poor services at high rates, according to an independent investigator for the National Board of Fire Insurance Underwriters. In May 1900, the outside expert made an extensive survey of Houston's electrical services. While praising Brashear's safety legislation to regulate the use of electricity, the expert noted that Houston consumed relatively little light and power compared to other cities. Only 2,800 incandescent lamps were in service, he pointed out, in a metropolitan area with a population of over 50,000 people.[51] The insurance investigator was not the only one who doubted whether the Citizens' company could supply sufficient services to the community. The receiver of the enterprise postponed the sale of the rebuilt utility during the council debate. Instead, he announced that an additional $60,000 worth of generating equipment would be installed immediately at the central station.[52] In sum, a municipal plant would have complemented the private service, not enervated it by leaving the company with large amounts of idle generating capacity.

In 1900, of course, the municipal ownership debate was hopelessly mired in a tangled web of ideology and politics. Embittered by the defeat of his electric station plans, Brashear exercised the limits of his authority as the mayor to retaliate against the utility companies. After September, he frequently wielded the veto to prevent the council majority from forging any new agreements with the franchise holders. In October, moreover, the mayor delivered a painful sting to their pocketbooks by sharply jacking up tax assessments.

In addition to a $1,021,000 jump in franchise valuations, the administration added $50,000 to the tax rolls for the utility companies' property and $100,000 for their capital stock. The government's position also hardened in other costly areas of continuing conflict such as withholding payment from the light and the water companies and refusing to compromise on the transit firm's paving taxes. While Brashear lost the duel over municipal ownership, the franchise holders failed to reach a concert of mutuality with city hall.[53]

In contrast to the intransigent state of government-business relations, the council worked harmoniously together in the areas of public improvements and municipal finance. This complete dichotomy in policy formation reinforces the hypothesis that the polarization of reform politics in Houston hinged on ideological positions towards the proper relationship between the public and the private sectors. Throughout 1900, the aldermen found it easy to agree on departmental budgets, public works planning, and fiscal matters because ward-centered practices of logrolling ensured a fair distribution of governmental services to each district. Even after the light plant imbroglio, for example, the council quickly reached an unanimous accord on refunding $800,000 in special assessments to contractor Richard Storrie and the property owners. Since only current property holders would benefit from the tax credit scheme, an ad hoc group of real estate speculators protested the refunding plan. But the aldermen and the Mayor stood united on this controversial issue; together, they rebuffed the appeals of the big taxpayers.[54]

To Mayor Brashear, however, a council consensus on public improvements was no compensation for the deadlock on government-business relations. Without the coordination of these two crucial aspects of city building, the reformer's efforts at comprehensive urban planning could only result in failure. On January 21, 1901, Brashear submitted his resignation without explanation except for a thin disguise of poor health.[55] In large measure, the mayor himself had become the target of the anti-administration forces. He probably hoped that by stepping aside, the impasse would be broken and the process of political compromise could be resumed.

Less than a month later the continuing strength of Brashear's position on municipal reform was confirmed by a Democratic primary to select a mayoral successor. Although the number of Houstonians voting in the all-white poll matched the 4,000 who turned out for the previous party runoff, this figure represents only half of those who were permitted to participate in the general election. In a field of four candidates, loyalist John Woolford of the third ward won by a plurality. The 46-year-old cotton weigher and politician collected 1,500 votes, compared to approximately 1,100 each for an "independent" and an anti-administration challenger, in addition to 300 for a second "splinter" loyalist.[56]

The diffuse spread of the election returns suggests that political alignments were becoming blurred by confusing crosscurrents of conflicting ideologies, changing community values, and shifting perspectives on urban progressivism. An endemic crisis of confidence was supplanting earlier struggles over alternative approaches to city building in the New South. A dizzy feeling of vertigo, of self-doubt about the goals of urban planning, infected officials and citizens alike. At city hall, calls for retrenchment and restoration of aldermanic supremacy over the executive became the hallmark of the conservative backlash against Brashear's initiatives to expand governmental duties to promote the general welfare. The stalemate in the council over government-business relations dragged on with no prospect of relief. At the same time, cries against the evils of the saloon and the gambling hall began resounding in the streets with loud echoes that penetrated the council chambers. The outbreak of a moral crusade underscores the pervasive sense of bewilderment and loss as older patterns of a small-town community gave way to a more modern configuration of urban life.[57]

In the midst of this interregnum of uncertainty, outside events and national forces intervened with such decisive impact that they largely determined the disposition of the urban crisis. During the 1890s, complex processes of interdependence were inexorably locking Houston into the national matrix. The accelerated pace of modernization in the cities of the New South was fueled by increasingly pervasive, extralocal influences such as business cycles, organizational impulses, reform currents, and technological innovations. But it was two chance events that tipped the precarious balance of political power in Houston against the parochial advocates of community welfare and in favor of the city boosters who placed greatest emphasis on promoting urban growth.

The close conjunction of two fortuitous events in 1900–1901 helped Houston emerge victorious over Galveston as the central place of the region. Galveston's misfortune and the skill of Bayou City businessmen in taking advantage of the rich new opportunities presented by the oil boom shattered the previous pattern of the sister cities' lockstep development. The island city's growth was seriously retarded, while its rival's was significantly accelerated. Incredibly large finds of petroleum in the vicinity added national urgency to the need for a safe deep water port on the Texas Gulf. The Galveston disaster convinced Congress to abandon the island port in favor of refurbishing the now-decrepit ship channel. Old lines of trade and transportation were indelibly redrawn in the coastal area. Two years later, in 1904, a second major discovery of black gold in the Humble field, just a few miles outside of Houston ended any question about the location of the oil industry headquarters in Texas, if not the entire country. By the end of the decade, these two traumatic events and the responses to them had combined to create new patterns of urban-rural relationships throughout the Southwest.

The Galveston hurricane of September 1900 washed away 6,000 people and $30,000,000 in property. The storm and tidal wave hit the exposed city of 38,000 residents squarely, cutting a wide path of death and destruction right through the middle of the community. Although Houston suffered considerable property damage, the fifty-mile buffer of land diminished the fury of the storm to below lethal levels. The inland town was fully prepared to react with dispatch when that most famous of all oil gushers came in at Spindletop four months later.[58]

Houston's success in capturing the oil boom rested on the abilities of its business leaders to recognize the far-reaching implications of Spindletop for the cities of the region. Local businessmen could occupy key positions as the managers of major national and international ventures. Houstonians could also organize competition as independent producers. In fact, civic leaders had been debating vigorously for over a year about the best way to make a "Greater Houston." On the eve of the energy revolution in the Southwest, former mayor H. Baldwin Rice, timberland baron John H. Kirby, and other members of the influential Houston Business League agreed that there were three essential ingredients in the prescription for achieving metropolitan status. Speaker after speaker called for the need for greater unity within the business community, the modernization of the ship channel, and the attraction of more foreign investment in local manufacturing enterprises.[59] Giving top priority to growth, a typical booster argument stated that, "[t]he answer is cooperation among the businessmen and property owners, more thought, more getting together. . . . Industrial development is the important factor in city building. . . . The world is now a neighborhood, made so by rapid transit and competition in the carrying trade by rail and water."[60] The booster advocated the establishment of more factories to exploit the countryside's diverse bounty of cotton, grains, rice, and lumber. The golden opportunities opened by the hurricane and the oil boom galvanized Houston's businessmen into a powerful united front behind this perceptive, if traditional, vision of progress.

The immediate reactions of Houstonians to Spindletop revealed a keen appreciation of the intimate relationship between the natural resources of the region and the man-made environment of its urban nodes. Within two weeks of the Lucas gusher at Spindletop, the Business League was organizing a pipeline consortium to bring the fuel to the city. The inauguration of the project coincided with Mayor Brashear's resignation, but the timing of the two announcements was probably not directly related to each other. Houston's major consumers of energy realized that dramatic reductions in material and labor bills would result if they converted their furnaces from expensive imported coals to less costly fuel oils. Local railroad and shipping executives were reaching similar conclusions, which were to lower transportation costs significantly throughout the Southwest. Kirby, B. F. Bonner, and other incorporators of the Consumers' Gas and Fuel [pipeline]

Company drew even broader connections between cheap energy, industrial development, and urban growth. In March, with the satisfactory conversion of the city's largest energy user, the American Brewing Association, the *Houston Daily Post* announced triumphantly that "[t]he fuel problem for manufacturing in Houston has been solved. . . . Houston has now reached a point where expansion will be made a business." [61]

While imaginative Houstonians were laying industrial foundations for the city's growth, they were also undertaking shrewd political maneuvers aimed at absorbing their rival's share of the regional economy. As in the past, this meant the construction of a deep water canal that would neutralize Galveston's superior location. Throughout the 1890s, Houston's congressional representative, Thomas Ball, had spearheaded a concerted lobbying campaign by serving on the strategic Rivers and Harbors Committee. Nevertheless, its all-powerful chairman, Theodore Burton, had frustrated every effort of the Texans because the Army Corps of Engineers had already chosen Galveston as the best transshipment point in the Southwest. What years of intense lobbying failed to achieve, one terrible storm accomplished. In 1902, Burton relented and Congress dutifully appropriated one million dollars to begin dredging a modern shipping lane to the safer inland port. [62]

The importance of this crucial decision in Washington cannot be overestimated. If Galveston had become the site of the port, Houston might have been bypassed in the twentieth century. However, the destruction of Galveston diverted the flow of trade at least temporarily to Houston. Perhaps the innovative responses of the island city's commercial-civic elite might have produced a recovery analogous to Chicago's rise from the ashes in the 1870s or San Francisco's revival after the earthquake of 1906. The creation of America's first commission form of government and the erection of a sea wall clearly demonstrated the abilities of the island's leaders to adapt to change. Galveston did not lack local supporters, but outside backers. [63]

The knowledge that protected shipping facilities were becoming available in Houston offered Galveston's traditional customers an attractive alternative to returning to the dangerously exposed island. With its vunerability still fresh in everyone's mind, moreover, the managers of the region's newly emerging industries such as oil, lumber, and rice rejected Galveston in favor of the more secure inland site. [64] In short, the ship channel project prevented the island city from ever regaining its commercial momentum (see Charts 4.1–3). Instead, Galveston went into permanent eclipse behind the steady ascendancy of its long-time rival.

Houston's rapid growth in size and wealth created opportunity for those in positions of power to shape the course of change. From 1898 to 1901, Mayor Brashear took the initiative in forging a new balance between private and public interests. Under his leadership, the city government assumed an augmented level of responsibility for the community's welfare. The functions and scope of the public sector were expanded over the environment and the private enterprises that supplied essential services. Brashear's defeat in the municipal ownership dispute was a minor loss compared to the much larger body of durable achievements effected during his administration. The mayor occupied a strategic position in setting the community's future course as Houston moved through a metamorphosis in its growth from a small city to a sprawling metropolis. This significant transition in the process of city building resulted partially from Brashear's comprehensive planning, his systematic handling of problems that had been accumulating without solution under the uncoordinated policies of his predecessors.

The mayor's style of progressive leadership was representative of the age of urban reform. In smaller and medium-sized cities like Houston, the modernization of politics often produced localistic reformers like Brashear. Young native sons from elite families continued booster traditions, but they also adopted new ideals of social justice. Brashear's youth and roots in the community combined to focus his reform perspectives on the neighborhoods. His success in politics was built on an ability to formulate comprehensive plans that enhanced the quality of life throughout the metropolitan area. For three years, the mayor created council majorities by logrolling and building temporary coalitions of individual ward chieftains. Without rejecting older notions of the promotional state, Brashear attempted to turn city government into an instrument of social reform.[65]

By 1901, however, the mayor's dynamic uses of power and expenditures of money brought the urban crisis to a second critical watershed. Retrenchment and restoration of aldermanic supremacy became the goals of the anti-Brashear faction. But the momentum built into the enlarged administrative machinery effectively defied any sharp curtailment in public commitment to enhance the social welfare. The frustration of the council majority in achieving substantial cutbacks in departmental operations indicated that officials still had not found efficient mechanisms to control the bureaucracy. In addition, Mayor Woolford and the loyalist aldermen successfully resisted the efforts of the utility companies to gain major concessions on contracts, taxes, and regulations. The political deadlock over franchise relationships was pushing more and more of these intractable conflicts into the courts. The promise of comprehensive planning in helping to overcome the environmental impact and the social dislocations of rapid urban growth intensified the struggle to shape the course of progressive reform.

In large part, the influence of national forces on local politics accounts for Brashear's failure to resolve the urban crisis in favor of parochial neighborhood interests. Although such outside forces as the judicial system, utility manufacturers, and money markets could not create a coherent vision of the coming city, they did limit the alternatives available to local planners. In the Houston example, a federal court receivership shielded the electric company from political attack, while General Electric rebuilt the utility up to modern standards. In contrast, other judicial rulings sharply restricted the fiscal powers of the municipal government at the very time when rapid growth demanded commensurate increases in public spending. This powerful extralocal configuration of law and economics effectively closed the option of public ownership in spite of its broad popular support among Houston voters. In the area of franchise relations, the national matrix narrowed the range of policy options open to Brashear and other city leaders to those choices conforming to an emerging political economy of regulated capitalism.

Another major factor in Brashear's defeat was the tightening nexus of government-business relations in late nineteenth century cities. Bound together through the instrumentality of the right-of-way franchise, each side struggled to enhance its legal, political, and financial position at the expense of the other. Brashear's politics of confrontation over minimum standards and maximum rates did not solve problems; instead, the disputes often landed in the courts for arbitration. The judiciary broadened the scope of the police power but it brought this area of urban policy under its own expanding jurisdiction. The state and national courts helped to shift the balance of power between the two sectors towards social justice, while reserving to themselves the critical task of defining its practical meaning. In effect, the Supreme Court's "rule of reason" gave the bench wide latitude to exercise its own discretion in the determination of urban public policy.[66]

The courts' assumption of final authority over utility rates and service standards intensified local reform battles and forestalled compromise on other aspects of the economics of public improvements. The struggle to shift the balance of regulatory power toward the public sector became entangled in related contests over utility taxation, franchise policy, and government contracts. In both the regulatory and the financial areas of government-business relations, the judiciary gave emphasis to a pressing need for structural reform. But the constitutional legacy of the Gilded Age locked the city's fiscal options into a rigid mold. Court decisions and state constitutional amendments placed severe limitations on the power of the cities to create long-term bonded debts. This heritage of structural reform tied the growth of public revenues to the expansion of real estate values. After the onset of a national depression in 1893, however, the gap between the mounting demands for better urban services and the shrunken ability of government and business to meet these expectations opened into a broad gulf. In Houston and in other places, changes in the scale of operations needed to supply essential services throughout sprawling metropolitan areas eclipsed increments in ad valorem property assessments. Looking for the economic roots of the urban crisis, the *Daily Post* pointed out that

> [q]uestions arise in a city like Houston that vitally affect the health, comfort, and prosperity of all the citizens that in less densely populated communities would be of but minor importance. What to some would be luxuries to us becomes necessities and must be had at any cost. Solid streets, drainage, sewerage, lights, water works, police and fire protection must be had because they cannot be dispensed with, and the aims and comforts of urban life be met.[67]

After 1900, the settlement of the perplexing controversy over city politics and planning became an urgent necessity to Houston's commercial-civic elite. United by the rich opportunities suddenly opened by the Galveston catastrophe and the Spindletop gusher, Houston's business community turned to its elite leadership to act as interregional brokers with national sources of capital and influence. But a chronic state of political instability and social unrest at home contradicted the prescription of the New South creed for attracting Northern investment and industry. During the pivotal year of 1901, this endemic conflict appeared to be seriously undermining and perhaps wrecking the city's prospects for regional preeminence. Anxious to resolve the crisis, the Houston Business League intervened to decide the outcome of the 1902 elections. The elite's handpicked ticket would pose a potent challenge to the ward-centered politicians.

8 "The Metropolis of a Great State," 1902–1910

The crisis of the 1890s was real enough in Houston. Urban Texans, like most Americans, had found it painfully difficult to answer Henry Adams' query about where the nation was headed as it entered the machine age. But after more than a decade of social tension, economic dislocation, and political upheaval, reformers were generating novel solutions for almost every problem of modern life.¹ By the early 1900s, grassroots struggles for the reins of power were percolating from county conventions and ward meetings to the federal capital, especially after Teddy Roosevelt's elevation to the presidency. The national thrust of progressivism was moving towards a compromise. Regulated capitalism represented a middle path between conflicting ideologies of individual liberty and social justice, between capitalism and socialism. At the same time, national influences were sweeping the resolution of local crises into this mainstream approach to the political economy.² The final battle for municipal reform in Houston proved to be no exception.

Between 1902 and 1906, the city's commercial-civic elite boldly redirected the course of public policy to conform with national pathways of progressivism. The rich opportunity suddenly opened by the Spindletop gusher and the Galveston disaster acted as a catalyst that brought a metropolitan vision of the city into sharp relief among a much wider spectrum of business and professional groups. Broader concepts of urban planning among the business elite were already coming into focus as a result of a ten-year process of rapid growth and geographical sprawl. The dramatic events on the Texas Gulf Coast simply accelerated the crystallization of a holistic definition of the city among the middle class. More and more members of the prestigious Business League placed the problems of city building within a context of Houston's regional hegemony and national interdependence. A holistic perspective of the city and a national outlook guided the metropolitans who now looked upon the ward-centered system of politics as the root cause of an intolerable stalemate at city hall. In 1902, the Business League mobilized an overwhelming political movement to defeat the parochial interests that gave greater priority to the immediate improvement of the neighborhoods than to the future expansion of the metropolis.

Led by Mayor Oran T. Holt, the metropolitans strove to enact a far-reaching program of reform that closely emulated the national enthusiasm for a "politics of efficiency" in public administration. Progressives everywhere attempted to apply new techniques of "scientific management" to the business of government, by replacing corruptible politicians with professional experts. To divorce

181

politics from administration required extensive changes in institutional structures.[3] Houston's reformers freely incorporated the model plans of the National Municipal League in a completely new municipal charter. The metropolitans, moreover, called in a nationally renowned accounting firm to impose centralized budgetary practices on the bureaucracy. By the end of the mayor's two-year term, an impressive catalog of institutional adjustments and franchise settlements defined a public program that fit comfortably within the broad outlines of municipal reform in the United States.

The Holt administration also adopted the New South strategy of cooperation in government-business relations. Repudiating Brashear's policy of confrontation, the metropolitans followed regional approaches to achieve the full integration of their city into the national mainstream of urban-industrial development. In Houston, the city council vigorously pursued a course of accommodation with the Northern-owned utility corporations. To the metropolitans, the resolution of the city's long-standing disputes with the franchise holders was an essential step in securing a steady flow of Northern capital to underwrite Houston's oil industry, shipping facilities, and other public works projects. Without appearing to violate platform planks for municipal ownership, city officials reached compromises with every established firm owned by outside investors.

However, enduring traditions of localism were as characteristic of the Progressive Era as more recent trends toward national conformity. Each place and its surrounding hinterland was different; again, Houston proved to be no exception.[4] Seemingly unresolvable aspects of the crisis drove the metropolitans to improvise indigenous solutions to the dilemmas of urban planning. The inability of managerial reforms to balance the budget spurred the reformers to search for structural mechanisms that could restore their control of city hall. In 1902, the incoming councilmen had a well-defined list of allocation priorities, but the bureaucracy seemed to undermine their efforts to reorient public policy to promote economic growth. As the anti-Brashear aldermen had already discovered, the momentum built into the administrative machinery resisted any sharp curtailment in public commitment to advancing the general welfare of the entire community.[5] Although a unified budget promised to bring the bureaucracy under the control of elected officials, well-organized groups in the community still opposed any cutbacks in services to the neighborhoods. The Labor Council, for example, strongly objected to the shift from a neighborhood to a metropolitan vision of urban planning.

To defeat these parochial interests, the metropolitans initially adopted a regional approach, a politics of exclusion. They blamed the ward politicians and their patronage workers and labor union allies for unchecked budgetary deficits. With the expulsion of black Houstonians from the Democratic primary serving as a precedent, the disfranchisement of poor people generally fit well within the regional pattern of progressive reform. Throughout the New South, the disfranchisement of blacks went hand-in-hand with the enactment of Jim Crow laws excluding this group from the benefits of public services. As one student of

Southern politics, J. Morgan Kousser, notes, "[d]iscrimination in voting, in other words, paralleled discrimination in government services, a condition unlikely to have been coincidental."[6] In 1903, a state poll tax act drastically reduced the number of voters eligible to participate in subsequent municipal elections. To be sure, Houston's metropolitans were not solely responsible for the passage of the measure. However, they soon took advantage of its intended purpose, which helped them suppress the organized labor movement in the foremost center of union activity in Texas.

When a politics of exclusion failed to produce a balanced budget, the metropolitans advocated an even more drastic solution to the problems of municipal administration—a commission form of government. A few precedents existed for the fusion of executive and legislative functions, but only in cities in which unusual or emergency situations prevailed. In 1901, the utter destruction of Galveston seemed to call for just this kind of radical departure from American constitutional theory, which held the separation of powers to be an essential bulwark of democracy.[7] In Houston, the mounting frustrations of competent, businesslike officials to bring unaccountable expansions of the public sector under control generated pressures to take additional reform steps. After the metropolitans easily won the 1904 elections, they began maneuvering in Austin to gain approval of a new city charter. The following year, Houston became the first city in the United States to institute a commission form of government in the absence of extraordinary exigencies.

The installation of the new structure of government marked the final climax of the battle for municipal reform in Houston. This original creation epitomized urban progressivism: indigenous diversity within a national framework. Houston's commission form of government represented the achievement of a politics of efficiency by means of a politics of exclusion. The at-large election of a few prominent citizens perfectly complemented the administration of local government by a small board of experts. They would manage the municipal corporation like the directors of a modern business corporation. With the triumph of the metropolitan slate of commissioners in 1905, the civic crisis came to an end. The commission fully translated a metropolitan vision of urban planning into public policy over the next eight years of uninterrupted leadership under former mayor H. Baldwin Rice. A growth-oriented strategy of city building ensured Houston the coveted crown as the hub of the Southwest. Yet the suppression of urban democracy and its ward-centered system of politics was a high price to pay for the modernization of the Texas city's society and environment.

Metropolitan Perspectives

In 1902, Houston's prospects for regional ascendency were anything but secure. After years of divisive infighting over urban planning, an endemic state of civic crisis threatened to relegate the coastal city to a subordinate role behind such fast-rising rivals as San Antonio, Dallas, and Fort Worth. And despite radical changes on the Gulf Coast, which worked in the inland entrepôt's favor during 1900–1901, the deadlock of government threw Houston's future into serious doubt. Moreover, the stark contrast between the policy stalemate in the public sector and the fast expanding opportunities in the private sector created unbearable anxieties among powerful segments of the business community. These mounting tensions turned the approaching municipal elections into a second critical watershed in the struggle for the reins of power at city hall. Unlike the closely matched contest between the Brashear and the Rice factions four years earlier, however, the intervention of outside forces triggered a decisive realignment of the urban polity. The formation of a metropolitan party permanently tipped the balance of power into the hands of the commercial-civic elite.

In large part, a metropolitan vision of Houston was a logical outgrowth of the urban crisis and the ensuing struggle to resolve the problems of rapid growth over a sprawling area. According to one scholar, urbanization inherently involves a "dynamics of conceptual change," which is fueled by social, economic, and political processes as well as by spatial transformations.[8] During the pivotal decade of the 1890s, the redefinition of the Texas community in metropolitan terms accurately reflected its metamorphosis from a compact city to a fragmented patchwork of urban neighborhoods and suburban districts. At the same time, the spread of a national matrix helped to place these local patterns of urbanization within a broad context of interdependence. Internal growth and external influences combined to evoke new ways of looking at the city. Newspaper editor Rene Johnson succinctly described this holistic viewpoint: "Houston is no longer a town to be operated along lines that prevailed ten or twenty years ago. It is a city now, the metropolis of a great state."[9] Of course, perceptions of change often lag behind reality. What was obvious to such cosmopolitan leaders as Johnson and timber baron John Kirby in the late nineties remained obscure to the more provincial Houstonians until much later. But in this case, the dramatic events of 1900–1901 sharply accelerated the dynamics of conceptual change. They acted as catalysts to consolidate the new metropolitan imagery of the city among the business and professional classes, who became infected with the same sense of pressing urgency to end the crisis as the commercial-civic elite had held since Mayor Brashear's reelection. To Houston's most cosmopolitan leaders, political disorder—Brashear's aggressive assault on outside corporations in particular—represented the main stumbling block on a golden highway to regional preeminence and national standing. In 1902, the middle classes rallied in overwhelming numbers behind the elite's handpicked candidates. Endorsed by the Business League, the Holt ticket promised to replace civic turmoil with private prosperity and social stability, besides municipal progress.

In the New South, a metropolitan concept of city building became a double-edged instrument of administrative reform and political repression. On the one hand, broadening the institutional frameworks of reform could cure many of the root problems of the crisis of public services with economy and efficiency. Whether building a sanitary sewer network, a professional fire department, or a recreational parks system, urban planners needed a centralized structure of administration to improve social services and environmental conditions throughout the sprawling area. On the other hand, the emergence of a metropolitan viewpoint would accentuate existing class and racial lines of discord. As holistic principles of municipal reform spread among the middle class, its alienation from those with narrower neighborhood perspectives increased, making a reversal from political polarization to social reconciliation much more difficult. On the contrary, the commercial-civic elite would exploit this growing divergence in the community's self-image to drive an ideological wedge between labor and capital. After breaking the strength of the Labor Council in 1904, the metropolitans would use the rhetoric of structural reform to justify the complete elimination of minority and parochial interests from the democratic process.[10]

Even before fortuitous events radically boosted Houston's prospects in 1900–1901, metropolitan dimensions of urban planning were evolving out of the intramural controversy over municipal reform. During the mid-1890s, the chronic failure of piecemeal approaches to the problems of modernizing public services pointed reformers towards the necessity of drawing more comprehensive blueprints for city building. In turn, the arduous task of detailing allocation priorities led officials to realize that the coordination of public and private efforts to upgrade utility services was essential to success. Outside experts such as the state insurance underwriters and the sanitary engineer Alexander Potter also helped local leaders expand their horizons beyond municipal borderlines to encompass the whole sprawling complex of built-up areas. Years of intense civic debate familiarized Houstonians with large-scale models of planning like the electric fire alarm network and the unified sewerage system. By 1900, the growth of metropolitan perspectives corresponded closely to the burgeoning spatial configurations of the city.

The sudden leap in Houston's commercial and industrial fortunes highlighted the entrepôt's favorable position in the national matrix. Before the hurricane and the oil gusher, in contrast, this extralocal focus on urban development was a perspective restricted largely to members of the commercial-civic elite who had extensive contacts outside of the community. But during 1901, the regional and national contexts of urban life became obvious to the casual observer as well as the ardent city booster. A trail of refugees from devastated Galveston was quickly superceded by a flood of oil speculators and wildcatters. By May, land values (and rents) were "skyrocketing" throughout the area. Five months later, the city was noticeably "crowded with strangers." They quickly became a normal part of the rail hub's daily routines, in spite of outbursts of moral indignation against the invasion of gamblers, guntoters, and rowdies. The influx of newcomers and capital provided convincing evidence to contemporaries that Houston was indeed swelling to "metropolitan proportions."[11]

The spreading acceptance of holistic images of the city encouraged the commercial-civic elite to intervene openly in local politics to break the council deadlock. Until the watershed in Houston's economic prospects, recurring appeals for businessmen to organize a reform party went unheeded. In 1898, for

example, Rene Johnson campaigned for an "Improvement League" to complement his three-year-old inspiration, the Houston Business League. The new association, the *Daily Post* editor argued, "would devote its chief time, not to obtaining new factories or trade displays, but to secure clean streets, paved streets,
extended sewer systems, good drainage, good water, parks and a score of things
to make the city more attractive and life within it more comfortable." Unless the
businessmen united to take these "domestic" matters out of the hands of the
ward-centered politicians, Houston could expect to "drop out of the procession
of progress and prosperity entirely and see public spirited rivals distance [it]."[12]
Two years later, the elite's leading spokesmen, such as Kirby, and Rice, joined in
the call for concerted political action by the business community in order to
create a "Greater Houston." Before mid-1901, however, the traditional vehicle of
civic involvement, the Democratic party, faced no serious challenges. But the
unseemly drama of political disorder at city hall increasingly appeared to present
the single most glaring threat to Houston's ascendancy. In December, the *Daily
Post* renewed its editorial plea for a "Progressive Club" of businessmen to
spearhead the election of the next city administration.[13]

Although a separate party was not forthcoming, the Business League served
as a made-to-order substitute. The composition of this association deserves careful analysis because for the next three years its leaders directed the course of
urban reform to a final resolution of the crisis. The ability of a businessmen's
group to manage city politics with such decisive results stemmed from the broad
base of its membership. In comparison to its nearby counterpart, the Galveston
Deep-Water Committee, the League was a relatively open organization. By 1902
it was coordinating business activity throughout the metropolitan area by em-
bracing all specialized groups, such as the Cotton Exchange, the Bankers' Clear-
ing House, and the Manufacturers' Association. Within three years, the League's
membership list would double, to comprise a virtual Who's Who of business and
professional leaders, including approximately 150 firms and 400 individuals.[14]

Within this broadly based association of business leaders, an inner elite
wielded tremendous power that extended into the community as well as outside
of it. While never a closed circle, a web of kin, corporate, and political relationships knit Houston's top families into an interlocking directorate of the urban
economy and its expanding hinterland. Typically, former mayor Rice became a
director of the Boston-owned streetcar company and a vice-president of the
Planters' National Bank, a Kirby-owned timberland and oil venture, a national
brewery's regional affiliate, and a major cotton-processing firm. Other family
names, such as House, Brashear, Baker, Dillingham, Dunn, and Wilson, were
equally familiar fixtures in Houston's commercial and civic life. Yet the elite always took a pragmatic attitude toward admitting new members into its inner circle. For example, a vice president of the League and Holt's campaign manager,
B. F. Bonner, moved from Lufkin to the center of the lumber industry in the late
nineties to oversee John Kirby's extensive operations. As his chief lieutenant,
Bonner was soon a director of the Planters' bank, a second lumber concern, and
a local milling firm, besides organizing his own oil company.[15]

The Business League supplied a solid foundation of support for the inner elite to launch a radical departure from recent electoral practices. The city's key power brokers believed that bold political tactics would repair the weak links in their grand strategy for economic hegemony over the Southwest. For the first time, Houston had the opportunity to cement its hold on the region's industrial development and trade flows if enough outside capital could be secured. But during this pivotal period, the Brashear faction of narrow neighborhood interests posed a potentially fatal threat to the consummation of these bonds with Northern investors. To defeat the challenge from below the business leaders completely ignored ward caucus procedures in naming a full slate of candidates. It is ironic that the ticket's standard-bearer, Oran Holt, could trace his political career back to the origins of the ward-centered system in 1886, when he joined Dan Smith's insurgency against elite rule. Now Holt lent his support to ending the disorders of urban democracy by reestablishing the locus of power at the top.

Kirby and his lieutenants managed the campaign of the metropolitan party from inside the Business League. They picked Holt to head the ticket because the lawyer was prominent in the Texas Democracy and was well respected as the retired counsel of such national firms as the Southern Pacific railroad and the Union Compress Company. By amassing control of over one million acres of timber and oil lands in East Texas, Kirby was a key figure in cementing Houston's economic hold over the region.[16] His success, however, was heavily dependent upon the continuing confidence of East Coast money men in his risky, over-extended ventures. Although the power broker declined to fill Mayor Brashear's vacant seat in 1901, he now entered the political arena to restore stability in government-business relations and municipal administration.[17]

A second unique feature of the 1902 contest helped him to accomplish these goals. Kirby and Holt ran Houston's first centrally orchestrated political campaign. Eschewing grassroots canvassing, they personally selected an aldermanic ticket composed of a typical group of skilled workers and small proprietors, but with only one incumbent. Kirby's lieutenants also organized ward-level committees out of a "Holt Central Municipal Ownership Club." In concert with both principal newspapers, the metropolitans cast the contest in the fashionable rhetoric of the muckrakers—the People versus the Interests.

The weakness of the opposition further amplified the strength of the metropolitans. In late February, a month after Holt entered the race, former city attorney James S. Stewart agreed to lead a ticket including the other eight councilmen who were seeking reelection. The metropolitans immediately cast Stewart into the role of the lackey of the Interests, who gave away utility franchises and shielded fat cats from prosecution for tax delinquency. The ringleaders Rice and Brashear were also portrayed in the worst light, but they barely mustered a rebuttal, let alone a telling attack on the metropolitan party. In addition, maverick newspaper editor William Bailey's retirement a year earlier silenced a worthy nemesis of the commercial-civic elite. Without a major daily to counter the constant barrage of charges, the Stewart ticket fought a losing uphill battle.[18]

By April, the well-orchestrated Holt campaign had steamrolled two out of every three voters into repudiating the men who had been governing the city. In this primary contest of a record 6800 votes, most citizens apparently agreed with the metropolitans that good men would restore economy and efficiency in municipal administration. In the third ward, for example, the largest residential preserve of the middle class, the mayor-elect accumulated over 80 percent of the 2000 votes cast. In contrast, the regulars retained their council seats only in the smallest ward, the second. In this downtown district, a ten-way race helped the incumbents narrowly overcome their challengers.[19]

In effect, the metropolitans were restructuring urban politics into a new form that followed the emerging national pattern of a politics of efficiency. From the outset of the campaign, for example, they adroitly exploited the municipal ownership issue to defuse the Brashear faction's most potent cause. Under his leadership, public ownership stood for the dual ideals of a nostalgic restoration of local self-rule and a progressive movement towards social justice. During the mayor's aborted second term, however, the issue of a public electric plant became absorbed in extralocal questions about government-business relations in the New South. In 1902, the metropolitans skillfully stripped municipal ownership of its ideological symbolism and re-dressed it as a simple expedient in the economical delivery of essential services. Striking a responsive chord among Houston's middle class, the business elite decisively broke the grasp of the ward-centered politicians on the reins of power.

As the election returns demonstrate, the 1902 contest marked a successful revolt of the business elite against the ward-centered politicians who represented the parochial interests of their neighborhood constituencies. Holt's managers reversed the growth of an indigenous type of grassroots democracy by prepackaging and selling an entire election campaign from a central office. In proclaiming the "end of the ring," editor Johnson exposed some of the deep-seated anxieties that motivated the metropolitans to intervene in the local election. "Capital shuns the city," the reformer carped, because of Brashear's stand against non-Southern utility corporations. The pressing necessity of reorienting government-business relations took on the aspect of a religious crusade to purge society of a moral sickness. "With maladministration in the municipal department, private enterprise catches the contagion; slack business and business methods prevail in poorly governed cities," Johnson sermonized.[20] To the metropolitans, the interrelated issues of franchise relationships and municipal administration demanded immediate attention by the incoming administration.

National Trends

Mayor Holt's program of administrative reforms closely paralleled his reorientation of government-business relations. The creation of a "businesslike" administration at city hall constituted a logical complement to the forging of a partnership with the franchise holders. Both acts represented a commitment to supply Houston with urban services on a par with modern standards. And both reform impulses drew upon a blend of national and regional responses to the crisis of the 1890s. In the area of municipal administration, however, fundamental flaws in the American model of efficiency left the inherently political questions involved in planning allocation priorities unanswered. Gradually, the metropolitans followed regional patterns of progressive reform. A politics of exclusion provided a simple, if draconian, remedy for the dilemmas of urban planning in the New South.

At first, the metropolitans believed that the national guidelines for efficiency and economy in municipal government would serve to eliminate Houston's chronic budgetary deficits. For over forty years, the modernization of the American city's accounting methods had been a major goal of middle-class reformers. The creation of municipal budgets marked the epitome of the politics of efficiency. In 1889, Houston initiated annual budget practices that were updated in 1895 and placed under the direction of an auditor three years later. In the 1902 elections, however, the metropolitans complained that "the financial department has been shrouded in mystery . . . beyond even the faintest knowledge of those who pay taxes." [21]

Rapid urbanization frequently provoked this kind of alienation and feeling of impotence among local leaders. By the early 1900s, Houston's municipal corporation had grown into a big business. With annual budgetary appropriations of about $700,000, in addition to contracts for costly public works projects, the problems of corporate management were substantial (see Table 8-1). Far more important to most citizens was the level and quality of services provided to their neighborhoods and places of work. The city dweller's well-being and property values were dependent on public services such as schools, police and fire protection, street lighting, sewer connections, and garbage disposal.

One of Brashear's major accomplishments had been to extend these urban amenities, which were now regarded as individual and communal necessities, more widely throughout all sections of the city. Each alderman, moreover, carefully guarded the interests of his ward in the distribution of funds and personnel. [22] However, the abilities of elected officials to expand the government's involvement in the welfare of the community were greater than their commensurate skills in retarding these trends. As the bureaucratic machinery grew larger, the location and workings of its control mechanisms seemed to become more and more elusive. Once a particular level of service had been established, subsequent cutbacks to achieve fiscal savings were either unacceptable to all concerned or inequitable to the affected wards and their representatives. Consequently, retrenchment goals usually failed, even though the council made earnest efforts. During 1900–1901, the resulting frustrations were directed against the chief executive. [23] And in the 1902 elections, the metropolitans subjected every incumbent to angry denunciation for incompetence and corruption.

One of the new administration's first objectives was to impose centralized levers of fiscal control over the bureaucracy. Mayor Holt looked to outside experts

TABLE 8.1   Allocation of Public Revenues, 1897–1912

Year	1897	1901	1905	1912
Population	40,000	46,000	56,000	90,000
Interest				
Amount	$88,000	$170,000	$320,100	$493,300
Percentage of total	23.8	29.4	33.5	24.2
Per capita expenditure	$2.20	$3.70	$5.72	$5.50
General Expenses				
Amount	$33,500	$58,600	$86,900	$197,300
Percentage of total	9.5	10.1	9.5	9.7
Per capita expenditure	$.84	$1.28	$1.55	$2.19
Public Safety*				
Amount	$82,000	$108,600	$150,730	$351,900
Percentage of total	22.2	18.7	15.7	17.2
Per capita expenditure	$2.05	$2.36	$2.70	$3.91
Health				
Amount	$22,700	$32,800	$12,390	$39,100
Percentage of total	6.1	3.9	1.3	1.9
Per capita expenditure	$.57	$.50	$.22	$.43
Roads and Bridges†				
Amount	$52,000	$60,800	$97,710	$273,900
Percentage of total	14.0	10.5	10.2	13.4
Per capita expenditure	$1.30	$1.32	$1.75	$3.04
Utility Services				
Amount	$43,000	$45,800	$81,670	$321,600
Percentage of total	11.6	7.9	8.5	15.8
Per capita expenditure	$1.07	$1.00	$1.46	$3.56
Education				
Amount	$51,000	$81,000	$123,230	$222,200
Percentage of total	13.8	14.0	12.8	10.9
Per capita expenditure	$1.27	$1.76	$2.20	$2.47
Sanitation†				
Amount	‡	$15,900	$55,320	$84,900
Percentage of total		2.7	5.8	4.2
Per capita expenditure		$.35	$.99	$.94
Recreation				
Amount	‡	$15,900	$9,530	$53,400
Percentage of total		2.7	1.0	2.6
Per capita expenditure		$.35	$.17	$.59
Totals				
Amount	$370,000	$580,000	$957,800	$2,041,000
Percentage of total	101.0	99.9	98.3	100.9
Per capita expenditure	$9.25	$12.60	$17.10	$22.70

SOURCES: Council Minutes, Books: J–P: passim; U. S. Bureau of Census statistics, as listed in *Texas Almanac* (Dallas: Dallas Morning News, 1972), p. 63.
*Includes expenditures for police and fire services.
†Includes only current budgetary appropriations.
‡None.

for assistance in the reform of the city's budgetary practices. With Kirby's help, the mayor convinced the aldermen to employ the nationally respected firm of Haskins and Sells instead of cheaper local talent. Kirby promised to pay the New Yorkers' fees if even greater savings were not gained from the accountants' installation of modern business methods of corporate management. By February 1903, a unified system of fiscal checkreins was tied securely to the burgeoning bureaucracy.[24] The advances wrought by the national experts in the management of the city encouraged the metropolitans to take bolder steps in the same direction.

National theories of municipal efficiency guided the charter reformers as they reshaped the structure of Houston's government. In October 1902, Alderman Edgar Watkins of the third ward presented the council with a draft of a new charter. Watkins was an attorney and a heavyweight in the Business League. His report anticipated that the proposed reforms would provoke divisive opposition from several organized groups. To allay their fears, the aldermen disclaimed originality and innovation by citing his indebtedness to the civic principles of Cleveland's Tom "Golden Rule" Johnson and the model charter of the National Municipal League. Perhaps these reform ideas were common currency among Houston's metropolitan elite; but in a local setting, the *Post*'s judgment that the proposal represented a "radical departure" from the past was a more accurate characterization of the charter.[25]

The new charter embodied the theories of the national efficiency movement in a series of amendments aimed at divorcing democratic politics from the administration of municipal services. One set of structural reforms simply appeared to strengthen the public sector's capacity to improve the metropolitan environment and the social welfare. In addition to an annexation proposal, the charter authorized the local government to operate charitable and educational institutions, set utility rate schedules for private consumers, create pension funds for city employees, protect travellers from ticket scalpers, and compel property owners to construct sidewalks. At the same time, Watkins concentrated administrative power in the mayor's office by drawing clear lines of institutional responsibility between the executive and the legislature. The centralization of power was pursued further by reducing many elective offices to appointive positions.

Another set of charter amendments, however, attempted to undermine the foundations of Houston's ward-centered structure of politics. These reforms more fully exposed the political implications of the proposed administrative adjustments. The annexation proviso, for example, was coupled with a scheme for redistricting the city from six to as many as nine wards. Under Watkins' plan, the power of the inner city districts would be diluted by subdividing the suburban areas of middle-class homeowners. Moreover, the charter drafter hoped to extend the central authority of city hall over primary election procedures. Although ostensibly aimed at safeguarding the ballot box, this measure would sap the democratic vitality out of the grassroots process of nominating candidates at the ward level. Taken together, the two sets of structural reforms illustrate the inextricable overlap of politics and administration.[26]

Their intimate connections were not hidden from the charter's detractors, especially the suburbanites who opposed annexation. Sending a delegation to Austin in February 1903, they found themselves in the strange company of the waterworks lobby and the ward politicians. The suburbanites, however, presented their own compelling arguments that dwelt less on the centralization of political power than on the questionabale ability of city hall to extend services to outlying areas. They pointed to the lack of such urban amenities and utilities in Houston's peripheral neighborhoods as proof of their contentions. The suburbs, they concluded, would be taxed for the exclusive benefit of the central city.[27]

To neutralize the anti-charter forces, the Holt administration marshalled a parade of organizational supporters before the legislature. Not surprisingly, the Business League and the Manufacturers' Association were in the forefront of the metropolitan lobby. When the legislature seemed nevertheless determined to scale the annexation scheme and to drop the appointive proviso, the *Post*'s editor retorted, "[d]on't hold Houston back. Let it grow." Johnson admitted that the election of key administrative officers was based on sound democratic principles, but asserted that the appointive proviso was, "the best of [them] all. [T]he elimination of so many elected officials reduces to the minimum the pernicious influence of the striker and the heeler, the peanut politician and the boss who are the bane of municipal life."[28] While the lawmakers allowed these two concessions to the opposition stand, the new charter emerged from the legislature essentially intact.[29]

Despite the nearly complete victory of the charter reformers, the "pernicious influence" of ward politics continued to subvert efficient public administration. Restructuring the machinery of government "to put municipal affairs on a business basis," in Mayor Holt's words, failed to resolve the endemic conflict over budgetary appropriations and planning priorities.[30] Throughout 1903, it became increasingly obvious in the council that the metropolitan elite still faced formidable challenges to its leadership as well as to its New South approach to city building. Led by the inner-city aldermen, the champions of neighborhood improvements tenaciously fought with the administration to have each departmental appropriation and every public works project distributed on a ward-by-ward basis. Although the Holt faction usually defeated these parochial interests, the commercial-civic elite started giving serious consideration to more stringent remedies for the suppression of political dissent.

To the metropolitans, the persistence of political discord in the council posed the last major obstacle thwarting the inauguration of efficiency and economy in the administration of government services. After reaching an accommodation with the electric company in February 1903, for example, the administration decided to reexamine the placement of the city's 365 street lights. Two months later, the Light Committee recommended that the lamps be redistributed in proportion to the number of voters in each ward. The Holt faction settled the ensuing controversy only after agreeing to add 100 new lamps to equalize services among the wards (see Table 8-2). Adding $8500 annually to the budget, the compromise cost the administration most of the savings promised by the new contract with the utility company. In a similar manner, setting public works priorities also became enmeshed in divisive debate between the metropolitans and the ward politicians.[31]

The national reform ideal of segregating the city's administrative functions from its political foundations proved to be an illusion. The management of muni-

TABLE 8.2   Redistribution of Street Lamps, 1903

Ward	Current Distribution	Proposed Redistribution (by voter strength)	Final Redistribution (100 additional lamps)
1	34	30	38
2	45	38	49
3	81	115	146
4	76	74	94
5	94	74	95
6	35	34	43
Totals	365	365	465

SOURCE: Council Minutes, Book M:466–67.

cipal services was inextricably linked to questions of social policy, as the controversy over the street lights showed. Since community needs for city services and facilities constantly exceeded public revenues, the problems of allocating scarce resources remained, irrespective of the machinery of government. Budgetary tools and structural reforms could help to clarify the lines of responsibility for decision making; however, they could not by themselves decide issues of urban planning and social justice. Melvin Holli, an historian of urban progressivism, confirms that

> [b]y concentrating on the mechanistic and bureaucratic aspects of city government and by throwing the weight of their influence behind the election of businessmen, the [national] theorists grossly oversimplified the problems of the city. Wiping out lower-class and foreign-born corruption unfortunately took precedence in their minds over the social needs of the city. The theorists confined themselves to dealing with the plumbing and hardware of city government and finally became narrow administrative reformers.[32]

Regional Solutions

The Holt administration's second major reform program applied regional approaches to bring Houston into conformity with a national political economy of regulated capitalism. The New South strategy of urban growth dictated a posture of accommodation in government-business relations. But efforts to reach compromises with Houston's franchise holders stopped at the color line, where white Southerners refused to budge from their racist positions. The stark contrast between the councilmen's easy flexibility in settling disputes with the transit company and their unyielding stand on segregating its streetcars highlights the Janus-faced nature of the New South creed. For the metropolitans, the black minority comprised a convenient scapegoat. Public officials vented their mounting frustrations in bringing city hall and its budget deficits under their complete control by attacking a politically disarmed group. The council's imposition of Jim Crow rules also suggested that a broader application of a politics of exclusion could supply a simple solution to the problems of politics and planning. The disfranchisement of most poor Texans in 1903 set the stage for the metropolitan elite to consolidate its power in a commission form of government.

During the pivotal year of 1902, Mayor Holt believed that settlement of the tangled disputes with the foreign-owned rapid transit and electric power companies would demonstrate a businesslike spirit of compromise to Wall Street and Capitol Hill. In addition, corporate managers like Holt and his aldermanic leaders reversed Brashear's policy of confrontation because they accepted natural monopoly theories. These metropolitans recognized that a combination of the municipal government's fiscal limitations and the established firms' entrenched positions virtually eliminated every policy option except regulated monopoly. The removal of public utility issues from politics became the first step towards the scientific management of urban services. Power struggles over tax and regulatory concessions had to give way to a process of administrative supervision. Only then, the metropolitans believed, could the experts achieve economy and efficiency in the delivery of essential services to the community.

The Holt administration's policy of accommodation reflected not only regional strategies but also shifting patterns of leadership that were occurring throughout the national matrix. In the merging urban-industrial society, the scientific manager was replacing the entrepreneur as the preferred director of public policy. Typically, corporate lawyers took over the negotiations between the city council and the franchise holders in Houston. New talents were required to cope with the problems of government-business relations as the regulated monopoly alternative gained irreversible ascendancy. Promotional and financial difficulties faded while needs for organizational and legal adjustments loomed. Each side's growing dependence on the other for success promoted renewed efforts to reach mutually beneficial agreements.[33]

Two examples serve to illustrate the new dimensions of government-business relations under the supervision of the corporate experts. In the case of the street railway, hard bargaining between like-minded negotiators produced a comprehensive settlement within a year. With neither private competition nor public ownership posing a viable alternative, the resolution of existing conflicts immediately brought about several major improvements in transit services. In the second example, repeated failures to strike an accommodation with the Houston Water Company resulted in a protracted duel in the political and judicial arenas. Unwilling to compromise, the local owners of the waterworks employed a variety of legal and corrupt tactics to block municipal ownership. Moreover, they sought the protection of the federal courts to forestall the state bench from ruling in countersuits for a forfeiture of their franchise. Although the appeal to the courts by both sides represented a businesslike approach to the stalemate, the judicial process was slow, expensive, and ultimately unpredictable. In the meantime, services and extensions continued to fall behind the needs of the sprawling city for this crucial public utility.

When the neophyte public officials entered their offices, numerous suits were pending between the city government and its franchised corporations. One of Mayor Holt's first objectives was to break the deadlock in government-business relations involving the street railway, the electric company, the waterworks, and the steam railroads. For example, Brashear's aggressive approach had generated three cases in the state district court between the city and the transit firm. In September 1899, Mayor Brashear initiated the first suit to force the electric railway to pay its special assessment taxes. Four months later, the transit concern retaliated by securing a temporary injunction against the enforcement of a free transfer ordinance. Just before the mayor's resignation in January 1901, the company began another court action to obtain a writ of mandamus that would compel the city to include the firm in any paving assessment refund.[34] These legal disputes prevented the settlement of other outstanding issues of equal importance. On the one hand, the railway managers ignored subsequent regulations that required the installation of car vestibules to protect motormen from the elements and that specified the use of grooved rails to prevent the rapid deterioration of street pavement. On the other hand, the company wanted relief from the city's street repair duties and franchise tax payments, besides refusing to grant extension privileges to expanding suburban districts.[35]

In 1901–1902, the almost complete turnover of elected officials and transit company officers created opportunities for both sides to reappraise the situation with a fresh perspective. The new owners of the Houston Electric Railway Company anxiously desired to renovate and expand their profitable venture. To forward these goals, they placed managerial responsibility in the hands of the innovative firm of Stone and Webster. By specializing in street railway administration, engineering, and finance, the Boston consultants brought a new level of professional expertise to the industry. The railway's investors also employed Houston's most respected corporation law office of Baker, Botts, Baker and Lovett to bargain with the city council.[36] This dual team of managers and negotiators accurately mirrored the new configurations of leadership that were emerging on the local as well as the national level.

The company was prepared to make several major concessions or at least to bring the company in compliance with existing regulations. The rapid transit's officers seemed to acknowledge that a cooperative spirit was essential for establishing certainty and stability in public utility relationships with local government. They also recognized that pending litigation effectively precluded additional route extensions and might result in a franchise forfeiture. Financing the utility would remain relatively expensive until the company reached an accord with the city.[37]

Mayor Holt also was committed to a policy of compromise. Fulfillment of his campaign pledges depended on achieving out-of-court settlements with the franchise holders. Holt's platform promised to secure substantial compensation from all utility corporations if municipal ownership proved impractical. Holt, moreover, pledged to inaugurate a cross-town system of free transfers. Since the city lacked specific authority in the charter to enforce such a regulation, neither Brashear nor Holt dared contest the injunction against the transfer ordinance. The administration sought to correct this and other deficiencies in the municipal corporation's police powers, but direct negotiations offered a shorter route to success.[38]

In May 1902, alderman Louis E. Miller of the second ward introduced an omnibus compromise proposal for the transit company. Actually, Robert S. Lovett of the railway company authored the comprehensive deal. The company agreed to pay some of its $120,000 in outstanding paving taxes, issue free transfers, install vestibules, and construct additional routes. In exchange, the railway expected the city to extend its franchise by ten years to 1933 and to submit the question of special assessment liability (except for the space between the tracks) to the courts. In effect, the company offered to conform to existing law if the city granted it a longer franchise. After two months of deliberation, a special committee of the council reported an amended version of the compromise that added new provisions in the public's favor. The council wanted a 1 percent income tax, extra paving commitments to reinforce railway foundations, and a stiff forfeiture clause for any breach of the ordinance-contract.

Both sides found serious flaws in the other's opening positions. City Attorney Thomas H. Stone presented the most cogent criticisms of the settlement plan from the public's point of view. In a reasoned report, Stone warned the aldermen that the proposal was "pregnant with future disputes." The city attorney pointed out, for instance, that the income tax proviso failed to include any mechanism for inspecting the company's books. The agreement also seemed to foreclose any rate adjustments or new taxes in the future. In contrast, railway negotiator Lovett strongly objected to the sweeping forfeiture clause except as a condition during the ten-year extension of privileges. After hearing Lovett reject the proposal, the council decided in a close 6–5 vote to follow the city attorney's advice to renew the court battle on the company's paving liability.[39]

Nevertheless, both parties continued the search for a satisfactory compromise formula. In August, however, the intervention of groups ranging from the Labor Council to the Manufacturers' Association delayed a settlement. The negotiators found themselves caught in a citizens' crusade for one of the progressive era's most popular reforms, the referendum. The organizational lobby opposed a settlement without the prior approval of the voters. Alderman Watkins of the third ward, an administration stalwart, supported the appeal for the institution of a referendum. But most of his colleagues refused to add new complications to an already complex process of negotiations. After a two-month respite to quiet the reformers, the company again initiated discussions by conceding special tax liability for six inches on each side of the tracks, a pre-Brashear rule. In December, the two sides finally reached an agreement that paid the municipal treasury over $80,000 worth of delinquent assessments and ensured quick action on a free transfer policy and other reform measures.[40]

The compromise marked a major victory for the public welfare. The terms of the settlement led to services that were neither innovative nor extraordinary compared with those of mass transit franchises elsewhere. Yet large groups of Houstonians—the commuters and the taxpayers—received substantial benefits. Consider that during each month of 1902, about 175,000 passengers (or 25 percent of the total ridership) enjoyed free transfer privileges instead of paying multiple fares. The reforms ended the threat to the company's franchise and credit status while permitting the railway to extend services to promising areas at the fringes of the metropolis. The city's major concession, adding ten years to the franchise, proved of questionable value to the company in the postwar period. In the short run, both the public and the utility gained from the termination of the controversy.[41]

The cooperative spirit displayed between the Holt administration and the transit firm helped to establish a new pattern of government-business relations with the other utilities. In January, 1903, the gas company voluntarily lowered consumer rates after the council sent it informal requests. A month later, the aldermen accepted a proposal from the electric company to scale the city's $85,000 worth of unpaid bills. In the new spirit of accommodation, the utility reduced the debt by one third and agreed to reduce rates by an equal proportion. Within a year, the Holt administration put government-business relations on an entirely new course with all of Houston's out-of-state utility corporations.[42]

The detente effected between the public authority and these private enterprises reflected a general acceptance of the regulated monopoly option. The metropolitans believed that the established firms would remain Houston's exclusive suppliers of their respective services. Except for the municipal ownership alternative, competition against the existing utility companies was highly improbable. By the early 1900s, entrepreneurial and investor opportunities had shifted to exploiting undeveloped markets and to purchasing going concerns. From 1900 to 1906, the council received petitions for franchises only from promoters of the new services of interurban electric railways and oil pipelines. During the same period, the ownership of urban utilities also continued to gravitate from local businessmen to interstate holding companies. In Houston, outside capitalists bought two of the three utility ventures still under local control, the gasworks and the independent telephone company.[43]

The single exception to these evolving patterns of managerial organization and national ownership, the Houston Water Company, also maintained a unique posture of antagonism towards the city government. Increasingly out of step with utility industry trends, this local enterprise had changed little in terms of technology or leadership since its origins in the late 1870s. The waterworks remained under the tight-fisted control of Timothy Scanlan, who had amassed a fortune in urban real estate after serving as mayor during Reconstruction.[44] Scanlan's stubborn refusal to install meters epitomized the outmoded management of the utility. The absence of these devices prevented the systematic repair of leaks, which, in turn, precluded the maintenance of minimum pressure levels. Without meters, moreover, private customers had to pay flat rates of charge regardless of how much water they consumed. The entrepreneur's approach to franchise relationships embodied a similar brazen attitude towards the community.

The involvement of extralocal agencies in the bitter duel between the utility and the city illustrates the enlarging role of the state and national governments in urban policy formation. By the 1890s, the legal reformers of the Gilded Age had effectively shifted the locus of regulatory power over public utilities to the state legislature at the expense of both the municipal government and the business corporation. In the process, the bench had also expanded its own jurisdiction over local disputes between public and private interests. In the case of the Houston waterworks, political deadlock at home sent both sides up the federal hierarchy in search of a favorable form of arbitration. Mayor Holt initially sought to bolster the city's fiscal structure in order to fulfill campaign promises of municipal ownership. But Scanlan wielded enough clout in the legislature to checkmate the charter reformers. The aging entrepreneur's intransigence left the administration little choice except to proceed in the state courts for a forfeiture of the franchise. The water company countered by appealing to the federal bench, which took over the management of the city's water supply until the franchise issue could be decided by the state judiciary.

In April 1902 the Holt administration immediately opened discussions with Scanlan in hopes of setting a sale price for the utility. A special committee of the council was created to study the 1878 franchise, which included a provision for municipal ownership at the expiration of the grant in 1903. Rather than enter negotiations, however, the company president initiated a suit in the state district court. The utility asked for a writ of mandamus to order the city to pay $56,000 in overdue payments for fire hydrant service. The company's hard line toward the city convinced the council to buy the facility. To build a separate system, the study committee reported, would entail a long and troublesome legal controversy. In the meantime, the established firm would probably allow its services to deteriorate below acceptable levels to maintain the public health and a vigorous growth rate. In September, the council sent the company an official notice of the city's intention to exercise its purchase option.[45]

Although the city had countersued the enterprise for a breach of contract, it had not contested the firm's exclusive franchise rights. The council had purposely limited the court action in order to weaken the company's position without foreclosing opportunities for negotiators to settle on the purchase price. After hearing testimony on this question, the appraisement board placed a $1.1 million price tag on the waterworks. The figure was $400,000 less than the company's, but a large portion of the difference resulted from the board's refusal to include a "going concern" or "goodwill" factor. To the aldermen, on the other hand, the conclusions of the June 1903 report still overestimated the utility's true worth by a substantial amount. Instead the council offered $750,000 to Scanlan, who promptly declined the proposition.[46]

Faced with no more room for compromise, the city prepared for a final showdown in the courts. Between August and November 1903, the aldermen repealed the company's privileges in the streets and prohibited its use of the bayou's polluted waters. The administration also filed suit for a judicial forfeiture of the franchise, initiated public hearings on rate overcharges, and solicited bids from outside investors who would assume the costly task of constructing another facility. Significantly, all of the interested investors shied away from the unsettled dispute, which would throw any new water franchise into legal limbo.[47] But to the aldermen, the refusal of these outside capitalists to compete against the established firm only reinforced belief in natural monopoly theories.

Before the state bench ruled on the waterworks cases, a federal marshal delivered a sweeping injunction to the city from a national district court. The company's attorney, Joseph C. Hutchison, had seized the opening presented by the anti-pollution ordinances to obtain national jurisdiction on an obligation of contract issue. City Attorney Stone admitted the error. The 1878 franchise specifically empowered the utility to use bayou water. The attorney for the water company confessed delight at the city council's blunder, which permitted the removal of the whole controversy from the state arena to a more favorable judicial forum.[48]

Yet, District Judge Walter T. Burns placed the public health of the city above the contestants' economic and political interests. In December 1903, his rulings on the preliminary court order gave neither side a predominant victory. He continued the injunction to prevent municipal officials from enforcing the franchise repeal ordinance. In addition, the judge ordered the city to stop pollutants from entering the bayou from its incomplete sewerage system. Two months later, Burns denied the company's contention that the franchise forfeiture dispute belonged in a national court. The jurist remanded this suit back to state jurisdiction. Although the basic stalemate continued for another three years, the court arranged an interim settlement that protected both parties' rights and promoted the community welfare. Finally, in 1906, the city purchased the utility.[49]

Except for the waterworks, Mayor Holt put franchise relationships on an entirely new footing by the end of his two-year term. A spirit of compromise brought Houston into conformity with the regional strategy for attracting investment capital to the urban centers of the New South. The metropolitans replaced confrontation and stalemate with cooperation and accommodation. By December 1903, the decision by the administration to set consumer rates for every utility service provoked little controversy. On the contrary, the predictable order and stability long desired by utility industry spokesmen in their dealings with local government now prevailed in the Texas city. Moreover, the process of institutionalizing these close bonds of interdependence advanced the immediate interest of the community in obtaining better services.

The examples of the street railway and the waterworks shed light on emerging patterns of government-business relations in the United States. During the nineties, the triumph of natural monopoly concepts in theory and practice virtually eliminated competition as a policy tool in upgrading essential services and reducing their costs. Whether by regulated monopoly or municipal ownership, government supervision would play an intimate role in managing almost every aspect of supplying the cities with public utilities. In good measure, this outcome of progressivism represented a translation of the jurisprudence of Gilded Age reformers into public policy. Jurists and legislators largely completed earlier efforts to clarify the broad grey areas between the public and private sectors. The progressives, however, shifted the balance of power towards social justice and away from the individual liberty side of the spectrum. The political economy retained great flexibility, while the scope and range of governmental regulation embraced a widening field of public interests.[50]

In the case of Houston, Texas, regional traditions of local autonomy presented no serious challenges to the national thrust of government-business relations. The franchise policy of accommodation wrought by the metropolitans obviated any pressing need for the utilities to escape from the jurisdiction of local authorities to the safer and more distant shelter of a state utility commission. The new partnership between the city government and the out-of-state corporations symbolized Houston's success in becoming an integral part of the national matrix. Other New South cities in Texas also reshaped the structure of their utility franchises to fit within the mold of the American compromise of regulated capitalism.

At the same time, unwarranted interference from outside corporations in the area of race relations met with stiff and unrelenting opposition from Houston and other cities in the region. On the contrary, the coming of Jim Crow to Houston suggested a grand answer to the dilemmas of politics and administration. In a Southern setting, a policy of exclusion offered an acceptable resolution of the interminable crisis of urban planning. Throughout the region, disfranchisement was becoming the precursor to discrimination in public services and facilities. The U.S. Supreme Court's ruling in *Plessy* v. *Ferguson* stamped this sectional policy with an official seal of national legitimacy. In Texas, the Terrill Election Law of 1903 not only conformed to these patterns of discrimination but also encouraged local leaders to emulate them. Once Houston's metropolitans wielded a club of exclusion against the black minority, it was easily turned against the ward politicians and their labor union supporters. As Professor Kousser contends, "[i]f Progressivism had a general theme in the South it was hardly 'democratic' . . . . , but the stabilization of society, especially the economy, in the interests of the local established powers, at the expense of the lower strata of society." [51]

The timing of Houston's first Jim Crow proposal, July 1903, was directly linked to the revival of ward politics in the council and the passage of the poll tax law in the state capital. The Holt administration was wholly responsible for the proposal; neither citizen nor traction company petitions initiated the move towards segregated streetcars. The metropolitans probably hoped the new issue would restore a sense of unity among the fractious aldermen. Many blacks were workers who depended on public transportation for commuter services and most of their leaders promised to boycott the transit company unless it provided entirely separate cars with Negro conductors. The Labor Council and a few aldermen supported this Booker T. Washington type of approach.

However, the council was determined to enact a local regulation modeled after New Orleans' year-old act. The ordinance empowered and required motormen to enforce the segregation of black and white riders into separate compartments on each car. Only the railway company's strong opposition to any form of racial discrimination delayed final passage of the act until October. For the rest of that hot summer, violent incidents increased as Negroes refused to vacate their seats for whites. By the end of August, racial tension in the city threatened to erupt into riot.[52]

In October, the promised boycott of the mass transit system quickly developed into an effective protest. The railway lost 15 percent of its patrons to a makeshift hackney service that was organized by Negro churches and fraternal associations. Nonparticipating members faced expulsion, while violence confronted those seen riding the cars. In November, Stone and Webster's local manager, H. K. Payne, complained about the company's loss of revenue. Payne hinted that the company's posture of cooperation with the local government might change drastically. But the council refused even to consider Payne's proposal for a different system of segregation. To local observers, the administration's visceral reactions amounted to "a remarkable display of the intensity of race prejudice in this matter." [53]

The Holt administration's intransigent position highlights the regional complexion of urban progressivism. The metropolitans adhered doggedly to the New South creed, which drew the limit of deference to North capital at the color line. In the area of race control, there was no room for compromise with Houston's non-Southern corporations. On the contrary, the controversy seemed to draw the metropolitans closer together and to fortify their resolve to prevail in the struggle for the reins of power at city hall. Emboldened by their tough stand against the Boston company, they laid plans for a final showdown with the ward politicians in the upcoming elections. A politics of exclusion easily carried over from the black minority to the parochial interests who put the improvement of their neighborhoods ahead of the growth of the city.

The Holt administration could impudently deny civil rights and municipal services to one third of the community because blacks were disfranchised. The local white primary rule of 1898 had been the preliminary step towards excluding Negroes from political power; the 1903 Terrill act completed the process. The Texas poll tax eliminated a substantial portion of white voters as well. Between 1900 and 1904, the city's registration rolls shrank drastically from 76 percent to 32 percent of the eligible voters.[54] The metropolitans no longer needed to weigh the concerns of blacks and poorer whites in deciding public policy. A solid victory in the March 1904 primaries would clear the way for the commercial-civic elite to consolidate its grip on the reins of power.

The metropolitans carefully plotted a campaign strategy that isolated and fragmented the political opposition. To prearrange victory at the polls, the Holt forces reconciled their differences with the city's two "bosses," Brashear and Rice. Taking many local pundits by surprise, the defection of these elite leaders denied the ward politicians a unifying figurehead. At a well-planned kickoff rally at the Opera House, the metropolitans announced their candidate for mayor, Andrew L. Jackson. Although an unknown newcomer to politics, the railroad attorney was a logical successor to Holt, who had chosen earlier to seek national office. Jackson promised to continue the policies of the present administration, including its emphasis on sewerage and drainage improvements.[55]

An opposing coalition formed around the mayoral bid of Alderman Louis Miller. The *Houston Chronicle* and organized labor joined ranks behind the ward politicians. However, only tenuous bonds were forged among these parochial interests. During the week before the March 5 primary, moreover, the Miller-Jackson contest turned into a naked duel between labor and capital. Narrowing the number of organized interests represented by the electorate exacerbated existing conflicts among the remaining groups. Most labor unions worked diligently on Miller's behalf because they feared that Brashear's unexpected move into the camp of his former enemies signalled a conspiracy to curtail their political power.[56]

The primary returns indicated that the metropolitans retained a solid, albeit non-exclusive, leadership of the party and the government. Even though Miller carried four wards, Jackson accumulated a 9 percent lead in the final tallies by racking up big majorities in the third and fourth districts. In addition, five out of the eight aldermanic incumbents were reelected. On the other hand, Jackson's margin of victory, 400 out of 4400 votes, was distressingly narrow, despite a severe cut in the registration rolls. Moreover, four ward politicians who had been defeated two years earlier were returned to office.[57] Jackson, like his predecessor, would have to compromise with these representatives of parochial interests to get his program through the council.

The real losers of the contest were the workers. Union leaders' fears that Brashear's defection would combine with an electoral defeat to isolate the workers soon proved to be prophetic. The political leverage of organized labor among elected officials diminished as power continued to gravitate towards the metropolitan elite.

But to Houston's best men, Jackson's victory was less of a vindication of a policy of efficiency than an incentive to pursue a course of exclusion. The failure of national programs of managerial and structural reform to divorce politics from administration pointed the metropolitans towards regional models of progressivism. Although fiscal facts played a negligible role in the campaign, the results of Mayor Holt's management of the budget were not encouraging. Departmental expenditures still outpaced tax revenues, while new bond issues kept the city at the upper limit of indebtedness.[58] Honest businessmen in charge of the most modern machinery of government appeared incapable of harnessing the growth of the public sector. More draconian measures seemed to be called for to curb the insatiable demands of both neighborhood and metropolitan interests for better municipal services. Success in excluding blacks from the polity suggested that, in the future, the commercial-civic elite rely more heavily on Southern models of discrimination to resolve the urban crisis.

Indigenous Contributions

With the last political hurdles removed, the commercial-civic elite moved decisively to consolidate power in a commission form of government. The Houston commission was an original creation, an indigenous response to progressivism. Local variations within national and regional contexts characterized the age of urban reform. In Houston, the reign of the corporate experts epitomized the national cult of efficiency. The commission form, *McClure's Magazine* proclaimed, meant "a revolution in local government in America; for it is organized on entirely new lines—the lines of a business corporation." [59] At the same time, this structural reform embodied a Southern penchant for social stability through a politics of exclusion. The repression of ward-centered politics did not halt the modernization of urban services, but restricted their benefits to the white middle and upper classes. In the twentieth century, city building in the New South became a double-edged process of enhancing the general welfare of some while segregating others in unimproved neighborhoods. [60]

In Houston, the elections of March 1904 triggered two repressive plans into motion for the restoration of political order and social control. Even before the inauguration of Jackson, the street railroad company started conspiring to break the transit workers' union. Forced to defend its members, the Houston Labor Council was drawn into the ensuing strike and was crushed under the superior strength of Stone and Webster's national organization. Amidst a climate of fear and resentment against the disruption of daily routines, the metropolitans began manipulating the politics of structural reform for anti-democratic ends. Left without an organizational base of support in the community, the ward politicians were practically helpless to block the charter reformers.

Although a private company triggered the final confrontation with Houston's Labor Council, public policy was closely tied to the transit firm's course of action. The stubborn refusal of the Holt administration to amend its Jim Crow regulations left the utility confronting a sharp decline in revenues. These serious losses resulted not only from the boycott of black riders but also from free transfers and half-fares for children, as well as from costly new standards for construction. With no possibility of a policy change after Jackson's victory on March 5, 1904, transit managers decided to cut its payrolls by breaking the workers' union. During April and May, the company secretly imported an army of trained strikebreakers. On June 1, the company completed its preparations for a final battle with the union, whose local president was provocatively discharged. [61]

The Labor Council endorsed the strike, but other segments of the community no longer supported the union cause. At first, commuters were afraid to ride the heavily guarded streetcars. During this initial phase of the disruptive conflict, the Labor Council collected funds for the creation of an alternative omnibus service, helped prevent violence, and attempted to mediate the dispute. However, the effectiveness of the boycott quickly eroded because suburbanites were dependent on commuter services. In addition, the community reacted negatively to several dynamitings of company property. Unlike a similar confrontation in 1898, rapid urbanization had broken the close identity of interest between skilled workers and other occupational groups. Moreover, popular antipathy towards the out-of-state corporation had largely dissipated. By the end of August, even the Labor Council began searching for an honorable way to terminate its costly and increasingly divisive position on the transit strike. [62]

After another month of declining support for the boycott, the Labor Council had to admit defeat. Assuming the railway union's debts, the Council officially withdrew its strike endorsement and ended the bitter duel between labor and capital. Consequently, according to a recent scholarly assessment, Houston's skilled workers struggled for four to six years just to recover from the burdens of the failure.[63] "The labor question has been eliminated," a city booster explained, "[t]he only point insisted on is that the laborer shall understand that the City of Houston comes first and his [union] organization second."[64] The economic and political eclipse of organized labor during 1904 allowed the Business League to enjoy a growing reputation as the representative voice of the community.

League members on the city council and in the popular press soon began to assert that Houston needed a commission form of government. The commission idea had been circulating in Houston and other Texas cities for a long period. As early as 1887, some opponents of Mayor Dan Smith's plan to settle the bond controversy had urged the adoption of an appointive board modeled after the 1880 fiscal reorganization of Memphis.[65] Houston's financial recovery quenched enthusiasm for radical experiments for over a decade, but new patterns of progressive reform in neighboring cities revived interest in structural innovations. In 1899, Dallas inaugurated a hybrid system of municipal government. The rival urban center created a supervisory board with extensive administrative duties and final authority over council actions on finance and franchises. In addition to an elective mayor, the board was composed of a fire commissioner and a police commissioner appointed by the governor.

Two years later, Galveston businessmen installed a full-fledged commission government in their hurricane-stricken city. A local observer recalled that previous institutional reforms had failed because of the ward-centered nature of local politics. "The city's greatest trouble," the reformer argued, "[was the] boards of aldermen, their political juggling, their caucuses and speechmaking."[66] In the weeks following the destructive storm, the problems of financing a recovery stimulated proposals for placing the municipal corporation in a receivership similar to the Memphis example. The members of the elite Deepwater Committee translated this attractive idea into a city charter. In March, it easily gained the approval of the legislature. Perhaps the most radical feature of the structural reform consisted of the complete merger of the legislative and executive functions of government. Moreover, the governor was to appoint three members of the five-person board; the others were to be chosen by at-large elections.[67]

Among Houston's metropolitans, the Dallas and Galveston experiments became models of the municipal ideal against which to contrast perceived failures at home. To city boosters like Rene Johnson, the commission's appointive feature seemed to solve the most pressing problem of removing politics from the business of the municipal corporation. Although the journalist supported Mayor Holt's administration during 1902–1903, he continued to call for an end to local democracy. Increasingly, the editor became discouraged about the "decent people," whose civic apathy was blamed for governmental corruption and extravagance. Only the selection of respected businessmen by the governor, he came to believe, could supply a "veto power in some form removed from immediate responsibility to corrupt voters and yet responsive to decent public opinion." [68] In a most revealing editorial, Johnson confessed his loss of faith in the democratic process

> [f]or the sake of economy and efficiency, [I] will be quite willing to waive some privileges now enjoyed, for between a privilege which brings abuse and a limited liberty which brings universal success and comfort, the wiseman will not hesitate to choose that which makes for his prosperity and comfort. [69]

In March 1903, however, the highest appellate court for criminal cases disagreed. The judicial analogue to the state supreme court for civil matters voided the appointive provisions of the Galveston charter. The criminal court ruling meant that the election of municipal officials was fully restored in Galveston. It would also have to become a part of any other city commission plan in Texas. [70]

Houston's metropolitan elite easily absorbed and incorporated the impact of the judicial decision into its arguments. In March 1904, for instance, the *Post* reasoned that the election of "preeminent men" would promote the attainment of an "ideal system" of commission government. Voting would simply buttress the confidence of the community in its public officials. Even though Mayor Jackson filled the reformers' description of the "capable businessman" in government, sentiment for radical change continued to grow. [71]

On the eve of the transit strike in May, the mayor published a report on the city's financial condition that set the stage for the manipulation of structural reform by the metropolitan elite. The statement revealed that the Holt administration had not reduced the approximately $300,000 floating debt it had inherited from the Brashear "ring." Even worse, Mayor Jackson predicted an additional deficit of $150,000 for the current year. The council responded to the report by ordering City Attorney Stone to prosecute delinquent taxpayers who collectively owed a sum equal to the total projected deficit. Moreover, the aldermen set up an ad hoc charter committee to take advantage of recent court rulings that upheld the creation of special assessment districts. [72]

But neither the charter committee nor the city attorney followed the council's directives. Instead, Business League member and alderman of the sixth ward John Z. Gaston called for a joint citizen-council group to investigate the feasibility of adopting a commission form of government. During the peak of the labor clash in July, the ward politicians had defeated Gaston's proposal by a 7 to 5 vote. Nevertheless, the champion of the commission form pledged to renew the question because he believed that Houston's financial problems stemmed from structural defects in the system, not the individuals in charge of it. If politics within government were eliminated, the alderman asserted, then a business administration would quickly liquidate the municipal debt. Near the end of the month, League member Stone admitted that he had not filed a single tax suit during the present administration. The council rebuked the city attorney and again ordered him to take immediate action. Demanding more "horse sense" and less abstract theory, the finance committee charged that only rich Houstonians were avoiding payment of their municipal dues by hiding behind legal technicalities.[73]

The close interconnection between this tax revolt and the budgetary deficit caused no alterations in the metropolitans' drive for a commission form of government. Confident that most voters supported their position, they pressed for a referendum on the issue. In October, the daily newspapers and many prominent civic leaders tried to persuade a council majority that existing institutional arrangements encouraged political corruption and financial ruin. In contrast, Gaston promised that, "a commission, freed from the local political environment, directly chargeable with the conduct of the city's affairs, would in a very short time be able to discharge the indebtedness, inaugurate needed improvements and give employment to double the number of labourers now utilized." [74]

Still unconvinced, the council rejected Gaston's resolution for a referendum. Aldermanic leader Henry M. Halverton, also from the sixth ward, explained the reasons for the majority's opposition to the commission idea. The ward politician and small proprietor feared that a municipal structure with only five officials elected at-large would squeeze out the little man and result in government by the rich. He emphasized that the city's administrators set spending levels and allocation priorities, not the institutional framework they worked within. Gaston's accusations that the council had lost control of the public purse strings, Halverton pointed out, was contradicted by the reformer's voting record in favor of bond issues and other expenditures. Moreover, the majority leader disputed the validity of the invidious comparisons drawn between Galveston's efficiency and Houston's extravagance. On the contrary, the alderman asserted, the quality of services provided to the community was more important than a strict economy.[75]

The metropolitans were outraged at the council's defeat of their referendum proposal. Editor Johnson and Business League President Henry Dickinson immediately announced plans for the organization of a citizens' committee to take the issue directly to the state capital. On November 2, the heads of all of the city's central economic associations, except the Labor Council, responded to the call for independent action. Without any countervailing base of community support, the ward politicians could not stand firm against this kind of organizational pressure. Halverton also attended the meeting and surrendered to the metropolitans' demand for a referendum. A week later, the council voted on whether or not Houston should be governed by a mayor and four commissioners elected at-large and approved Gaston's resolution 9 to 2.

The urban polity greeted the reformers' success with little, if any, enthusiasm. As the December poll drew near, Johnson admitted that "so far as the *Post* can judge from appearance, the apathy of the people is almost impenetrable." Similar predictions of disinterest in the question were fulfilled when only 2100 voters, or about one third of the number registered, participated in the referendum. They approved the measure by a sizeable margin. However, the small turnout seems to reflect community sentiment that the reform goals of the metropolitans were a foregone conclusion.[77]

Over the next few months, two very different city commission charters emerged. Both versions incorporated large sections of the 1903 reform charter without amendment. The significant differences between the draft proposals centered on the organization of political power and administrative responsibility. As much as the metropolitans concentrated authority in a single board of corporate experts, the ward politicians dispersed it among several institutions of government. In addition, Gaston's plan disregarded the common assumption that the commission system would begin after the current officials' terms expired in April 1906. Instead, the structural reformer specified that the new charter would become effective immediately upon ratification by the legislature.

The contrasting features of the two charter plans embodied opposing faiths in the democratic process. On the one hand, the metropolitans' commission proposal attempted to maximize the centralization of power at the expense of grassroots participation at the ward level. Gaston drafted this blueprint of municipal government with the help of twelve citizens, including six members of the Business League. The reformer's most important original contribution was the grafting of the strong mayor provisions of the National Municipal League's model charter on top of Galveston's corporate board structure of government. Unlike the island city's government by committee, Gaston gave the chief executive a veto over board actions besides exclusive authority over all municipal employees. In many respects, this indigenous innovation was a precursor to another contemporary creation, the city manager.[78]

On the other hand, the ward politicians crafted a more balanced configuration of power among the mayor, the board, and the community. In February 1905, the aldermen unveiled their plan, which restricted and amended many of the provisions of the Gaston proposal. The necessity of gaining the commissioners' consent curbed the mayor's authority to hire and fire city workers, although his veto power was retained. The council also added sections that dispersed power in order to protect the public from governmental abuses. For example, the commission lost control over school finances and primary elections. Moreover, 20 percent of the voters could subject the commissioners to a recall.[79]

Unwilling to accept any modifications, the supporters of the metropolitans' charter shifted the battle to the state capital. The recent defeats of the Labor Council and other parochial interests left the metropolitan elite virtually unopposed in the charter contest in Austin. Jackson, Kirby, Johnson, and Rice led the lobby for the strong mayor plan with reinforcements from a parade of fellow members of the Business League and representatives of other organizational groups such as the Cotton and Lumber Exchanges. Against this formidable phalanx of local luminaries, the seven aldermen who lobbied for their alternative proposal appeared to represent no one but themselves. Only the metropolitans' charter was reported out of committee to the legislature where final passage was quickly secured.[80]

By the middle of March 1905, the triumph of the Business League was complete, except for the election of the appropriate men to inaugurate the new system of urban government. Initial speculation on the best choice for mayor soon narrowed to Rice. Since his retirement from public office in 1898, the former mayor had become an important member of the business community and one of Houston's major intermediators with national corporations. Rice's "commission ticket for a Greater Houston" swept the at-large elections. This victory marked the final step in the fulfillment of the metropolitans' search for control over local politics and public policy.[81]

The battle for municipal reform in Houston was over. Under a guise of administrative efficiency, the metropolitan elite manipulated the politics of structural reform for anti-democratic ends. The new framework of government and politics brought the crisis of public services to a close. The commission government insulated city officials from the demands of parochial interests for neighborhood improvements. Shielded from the conflicting pressures of a diverse urban polity, Mayor Rice was free to order public priorities in stricter conformity with New South prescriptions for the promotion of economic growth. In effect, the commission government removed politics from administration by suppressing democracy at the ward level.

Houstonians paid a high price for this indigenous solution to their urban crisis. In a Southern context, the triumph of a metropolitan viewpoint meant the exclusion of a large portion of the community from the benefits of modern public services as well as from the political process. There was no turning back of the historical expansion in the number of urban services that were regarded as indispensable "public utilities." But whether or not the commissioners would extend them into the neighborhoods of black and poor white city dwellers became an entirely different question. In the twentieth century, government policy hardened traditional patterns of racial and class discrimination into rigid lines of geographical segregation.

9 Conclusion: The Reign of the Corporate Expert

By 1910, Houston's metropolitan elite could have provided Henry Adams with at least a crude road map of where the Texas city was headed in the twentieth century. Under the reign of the corporate experts, the coastal entrepôt was well on its way to becoming the urban center of the Southwest and the national headquarters of the oil industry. If many parts of Houston's growth-oriented plan of city building remained to be filled in, the administrative machinery was now in place to generate bureaucratic solutions to the problems of environmental engineering and social management. "In other words," Mayor Rice proudly explained, "the [commission] system makes it possible to administer the affairs of the city in a prompt and businesslike way." In contrast, he argued that "under the old system the conduct of public business was continually obstructed by a system of petty log-rolling going on among and between the representatives of the numerous subdivisions of the city."[1] To Rice and other progressives, the commission's close structural parallel to the board of directors of a modern business corporation comprised the essence of the "Texas Idea" of municipal reform.[2]

Houston's reliance on business models of efficiency for the resolution of its civic crisis was emblematic of American progressivism. The metropolitan elite blended national impulses together with regional and local currents of reform into an original creation, a strong mayor form of commission government. Houston's resort to a board of administrators elected at large also fits into Robert Wiebe's characterization of the period as a "search for order." Spearheaded by a new middle class of corporate managers, the American gospel of efficiency was translated into just this type of institutional innovation. To these municipal reformers, the elimination of the inherently divisive, albeit democratic, structure of ward-centered politics was a primary goal. "Now laws established an outline for management," the historian concludes, "a flexible authority to meet and follow the major issues of urban living. In fact, the fewer laws the better if those few properly empowered the experts, for administration was expected to replace the tedious, haphazard process of legislative compromise."[3]

In the New South, unfortunately, the national search for greater efficiency in the administration of governmental services was often perverted into a politics of exclusion. To be sure, municipal reformers elsewhere pursued similar discriminatory goals in the distribution of both public services and political power. But success in achieving these anti-democratic ends by the manipulation of structural reform was restricted largely to the South. The coming of Jim Crow in the wake of the Populist revolt could not have occurred at a worse time for the working classes of the section's urban centers. In the 1890s, long-stalled drives for mass disfranchisement gained new momentum when metropolitan elites began supporting their rural counterparts in the state legislatures. After the turn of the century, the stark contrast of an up-to-date neighborhood bordering a neglected ghetto became an all too common sight in the segregated cities of the South.[4]

The paradoxes of Southern progressivism were not lost on contemporaries. "It seems strange to say in one breath that Houston has the best and most dangerous form of government that can be conceived," one city booster admitted.[5] After the momentous events of 1900–1901, the commercial-civic elite reversed its previous acceptance of an expanding diversity of organized interests in the political process. Yet these same leaders maintained a commitment to improving the quality of urban life, at least for the white middle-class members of the community. The modernization of the metropolitan environment proceeded side by side with exclusionary trends in politics and society.

During 1905–1906, the policies of the Rice administration illustrated the double-edged nature of municipal reform in the New South. On the one hand, the labor movement lost its recently won support at city hall. Among the commissioners' first acts was the repeal of ordinances that provided economic protection for unskilled municipal workers and employees of public contractors. Equivalent union-scale regulations for skilled mechanics were also repealed. On the other hand, workingmen and most other Houstonians benefited from the mayor's settlement of the water supply controversy. With taxpayer approval, the administration purchased the established firm for approximately one million dollars. Over the next five years, the commissioners spent large amounts of money to improve the distributive network and to install a meter system.[6]

The structure of the commission government helps to account for the Janus-like quality of urban planning during Rice's eight years in office. The municipal charter of 1905 gave the mayor virtually unlimited discretion in the formation and the execution of public policy. To the metropolitans, "[t]his so-called 'one-man' feature of the commission embodies its whole aim and intention." Rice agreed that the wholesale scrapping of the legislative process was one of the system's cardinal virtues.[7] Direct appeals to the mayor's office replaced petitions to the open forum of council debate. If the workers or other interest groups failed to win him over to their cause, they had little further recourse. Indeed, a correspondent for *Outlook*, a national magazine of progressive thought, confirmed that, "the Houston charter . . . is more remarkable for the things it omits than for those it contains. You will search in vain . . . for the scheme of government that is in actual operation."[8]

The restoration of political order and social stability allowed Mayor Rice and the metropolitan elite to implement a growth-oriented strategy of city building without serious opposition from parochial interests. Neighborhood improvements took second place in urban planning behind public works projects to boost Houston's ascendancy over the Southwest. The financing of the Port of Houston was indicative of the new bonds of cooperation forged between city hall and downtown. After 1905, the commercial-civic elite put government policy in harness with the oil and trade industries to upgrade the Texas city to metropolitan proportions. In 1909, for example, the city's bankers purchased an entire issue of navigation bonds to advance construction of the inland waterway. The bankers could afford to finance these debts at home because the oil boom was rapidly raising their deposits to levels far above the national average. A commission government under Rice's leadership gave local money men the confidence to underwrite public sector projects.[9]

By the time Rice retired from office in 1913, Houston was well on its way towards consolidating its preeminence in the region. Although the Port of Houston initially paid few dividends after it opened the following year, it brought the city accumulating rewards during the postwar period. Like the financing of the shipping facility, the new partnership between government and business turned the expansion of the urban economy into a self-sustaining process in the 1920s. The city's advantages in petroleum production and refining brought its commercial promise to realization and fulfilled its industrial potential. By 1930, oil exports made Houston the third largest port in the nation, topped only by New York and Los Angeles. With 292,000 people, moreover, the coastal metropolis became the biggest city in Texas by finally overcoming its last serious competitor, Dallas. Since then, Houston has continued to maintain its hold on the urban crown of the Southwest (see Table 9.1).[10]

Houston's rise to this coveted position rested on the foundations of urban planning laid by the metropolitan reformers in the decade after Spindletop. Their triumph over more parochial interests put the coastal entrepôt on a path of city building that followed a regional strategy of economic growth. The Houston experience of administrative reform and political repression was typical of urban progressivism in the New South, where the outcome of municipal reform was cast into a peculiar mold. The needs and aspirations of the section included a dependency on Northern capital, a primacy of commercial agriculture, a tradition of race supremacy, and a pattern of elite leadership. This regional configuration gave progressivism a distinctive thrust towards expanding governmental responsibilities for the social welfare while constricting political participation in the formation of public policy. During the twentieth century, the social geography of most Southern urban centers graphically reflected the resulting exclusionary plans of city building. Two segregated communities—one modern and one unimproved—grew up alongside of one another.

In contrast, the cities of the North pursued a separate course in resolving their crises of public services. Of course, any regional comparisons are difficult because reform in each city produced a unique result. Nevertheless, sharp differences between the sections make some basic generalizations possible, at least for the larger, better studied cities. In these centers of the North, parochial and metropolitan factions engaged in similar struggles for the reins of power at city hall. But the greater diversity of the North's ethnic populations and economic interests supplied a more effective counterweight to the exclusionary impulses of

TABLE 9.1   Population of Southern Cities, 1930*

Southern Rank	National Rank	City	Population
1	7	Baltimore	805,800
2	15	New Orleans	455,800
3	25	Louisville	307,800
4	28	Houston	289,600
5	33	Atlanta	266,600
6	34	Dallas	260,400
7	35	Birmingham	257,700
8	36	San Antonio	254,600
9	39	Memphis	252,000
10	46	Richmond	182,900
11	48	Fort Worth	160,900
12	51	Nashville	153,200
13	62	Jacksonville	129,800
14	63	Norfolk	128,900
15	66	Chattanooga	119,600
16	77	Miami	110,500
17	82	Knoxville	105,800
18	89	El Paso	102,000
19	91	Tampa	101,300

SOURCE: U.S., Department of Commerce, Bureau of the Census, *Statistical Abstract of the United States, 1930*, p. 4.
*Cities with more than 100,000 residents.

elite groups. Immigrant politicians entrenched at the ward level usually defeated legislative efforts to restrict the political rights of the newcomer, whether European or Afro-American. Instead, the middle and upper classes began a mass exodus to suburban enclaves, which resisted annexation to the central cities. Although black ghettos also emerged in the early twentieth century, their origins stem less from an exclusionary plan of city building than from a pervasive culture of race and class discrimination.[11]

Irrespective of their political responses to the crisis of the nineties, the cities of the North and the South were both drawn inexorably into a national matrix of urban centers and interdependent regions. Twenty years of municipal reform helped to steer the United States between full-fledged socialism and unbridled competition onto a middle route of regulated capitalism. The detente effected between Houston's metropolitans and the out-of-state corporations brought the Southern city into conformity with the national framework of the political economy. Texas, however, stayed on the sidelines of a stampede of the states to create public utility commissions. The accommodational posture of its cities towards the utility companies combined with tenacious traditions of local autonomy to forestall this administrative approach to government-business relations. Yet in Texas as elsewhere, the utility industries secured the key objectives they had outlined long before.

In the battle over public utility franchises, the progressive compromise meant the defeat of municipal ownership and an acceptance of privately owned "natural" monopolies. In the early 1900s, several factors combined to neutralize the once highly charged ideological issue of municipal ownership. At base, the rapid modernization of the city's transit, gas, communications, and electrical services under private management defused discontent with and parochial resentments against the utility corporation. The social scientist's advocacy of "natural" monopoly theories in the public utility sector also helped to reduce pressures against the established firms. By placing this industry in a special category, the experts created expectations that nonmarket, administrative approaches would solve the problems of upgrading urban services.[12] In contrast, an expanding array of governmental responsibilities for the public health, safety, and welfare left little surplus in municipal treasuries to match the vast amounts of private capital invested in utility enterprises.

Yet, monopolies in urban utilities were not natural; their ultimate causes lay in the failures of federalism. Until state and national laws regulated corporate consolidations and financial manipulations, the maintenance of franchise competition was beyond governmental control at the local level. The federal structure of government was fatally fragmented compared to the high degree of integration that the utilities industry had achieved during the Gilded Age. Speculators easily outmaneuvered municipal officials, who attempted to prohibit mergers by the structural reform of franchise contracts and city charters. The sophisticated weapons of the private sector—the intrastate trust and the interstate holding company—were tailor-made to defeat the crude defenses of city governments against utility mergers and monopolies. Unfortunately, American city dwellers had to wait until the Great Depression of the 1930s before the national government began responding to widespread financial abuse in the utilities industry.[13] In the meantime, theories of "natural" monopoly encouraged a premature abandonment of the regulated competition alternative, perhaps the public sector's most powerful tool with which to advance the public welfare.

American federalism often pointed municipal reformers beyond city hall to state and national arenas for solutions to the urban crisis of the nineties. The Gilded Age legacy of the legal reformers stripped the city of any inherent right to self-government while simultaneously expanding the state's police power over its citizens and corporations. Increasingly, the progressives resorted to their state lawmakers not only to surmount constitutional limitations but also to circumvent political hurdles at the local level. In Texas, Hogg Democrats reinforced these centralizing trends. State statutes embodying urban policy statements became increasingly common at the turn of the century. In 1900, for example, the legislature spearheaded a major overhaul of city school systems. Other laws dictated the issuance of free streetcar transfers and half-fare tickets for children, prescribed the work conditions of rapid transit motormen, and authorized city governments to set utility rates for private customers.[14] In short, a national matrix of intergovernmental relations now paralleled the earlier development of the private sector into an integrated complex of business and finance.

In the area of urban services, the uneven pace of national integration between government and business tipped the balance of power in favor of the utility corporation. Soon after the National Civic Federation released its benchmark report on public utilities in 1907, Wisconsin enacted a Utility Commission Act. Drafted by economist-committeeman John R. Commons, it became a model that shaped similar legislation in over thirty states within a decade. The exhaustive investigation by a blue-ribbon committee of national experts had failed to settle the controversy over who supplied city services at the lowest cost, business or government. Signalling the end of the middle class's hopes that the science of statistics could conclusively solve this riddle, important reform groups abandoned the cause of municipal ownership.[15]

Utility expert Delos Wilcox observed bitterly that "the public service companies themselves appear to furnish the chief motive power behind the commission movement in those communities where state regulation has not been fully established."[16] The inauguration of state commissions raised additional barriers in the path of municipal ownership and utility competition by formalizing and protecting existing franchise relations. Local governments now had to prove the impossible: that a dire public necessity existed for expropriating or upsetting the established firms. Businessmen not only escaped from interfirm competition but also benefited from the interposition of administrative buffers between their companies and consumer-voters.[17]

But no conspiracy is needed to account for the quick passage of the utility commission laws. The endorsement of famous progressive leaders, state-oriented governors like Robert LaFollette of Wisconsin, Charles Evans Hughes of New York, and Woodrow Wilson of New Jersey, represented independent and persuasive voices for reform action. Many municipal reformers joined in their call for state commissions because of the difficulties of reversing the constitutional restrictions of the Gilded Age. The failure of the 1907 report to prove the economic superiority of municipal ownership presented a sharp contrast to the rapid pace of investment in urban services by private companies and the rich promise of gaining new tax revenues from them. Local leaders united with state-oriented politicians, utility companies, and efficiency advocates to press for the creation of administrative agencies.[18]

The outcome of public utility reform during the progressive period followed a largely predetermined path towards private monopoly under state control. The general reassessment of urban public services that began in the late 1880s prematurely abandoned franchise competition and revived municipal ownership as the only promising alternative to regulated monopoly. But until major structural reforms could first reinvigorate the city's fiscal powers and federal relationships, public ownership champions remained disarmed. The democratic implications of these structural reforms gradually fractured broadly based coalitions for municipal ownership into conflicting ideological camps. The divided forces of reform were fatally weak compared with the financial and structural strengths nurtured by the utility industry since the 1870s. Its strategies to solidify these advantages into permanent and legitimized vested rights coincided with the efforts of elite groups to establish centralized state utility commissions.

Utility industry leaders found state-level agencies to be the most advantageous structural arrangement for the unfettered pursuit of their own interests. The utility commissions were poorly equipped to cope with the industry's continuing transformation into large-scale, increasingly interstate holding companies. Most operating companies also began crossing city jurisdictional lines and many would span state boundary limits. Businessmen so successfully eluded effective economic regulation by cracks in federalism's rigid structure that Felix Frankfurter believed that the utility industry was "practically immune" to the law.[19]

The removal of franchise authority from locally elected officials eliminated the consumer's most powerful lever to keep companies responsive. The commission laws severed the consumer-voter's direct and continuous ties to franchise policy makers at city hall. More remote interconnections between consumers and utility companies pleased industry managers, but worried home rule critics who suspected that industry would "capture" the distant regulators. Law professor Frank Parsons, the president of the Public Ownership League, cautioned that, "So thoro [sic] is control of the big monopolies over the machinery of regulation that even in the states where this method has been most fully tried the giant companies regard the system as a protection and not as a menace."[20] Whether or not the utility commissions maintained their independence, the Great Crash of 1929 would demonstrate that they had added little to a viable regulatory solution for privately owned public utilities. The ruinous collapse of holding company pyramids highlighted the gaps in the federal system that had long given the private sector a preponderant influence in shaping the course of government-business relations.[21]

The fractured structure of American federalism also ensured that urban progressivism was marked by indigenous diversity within a national context. In the absence of central or regional plans for the modernization of the cities' essential services, each place wrought a unique solution to the crisis of the nineties. The disposition of the battle for municipal reform in Houston fit within these patchwork patterns. The city's strong mayor type of commission forged the national cult of efficiency and the New South penchant for a politics of exclusion into a novel form of municipal government. The rapid spread of this structural innovation throughout the South and the Midwest reflected the tightening bonds of national interdependence as well as the representative character of reform in Houston. In the twentieth century, America turned urban planning over to the corporate experts. Under their supervision, a nation of fragmented and segregated metropolitan areas was erected, setting the stage for the present crisis of the inner cities.

Abbreviations

1. *City Directory for [year]*   W. A. Leonard, comp., *General Directory of the City of Houston* (Houston: Gray, 1866–1878); Morrison and Fourmy, comps., *General Directory of the City of Houston* (Galveston and Houston: Morrison and Fourmy, 1879–1920)

2. CM Book:(no.)   Houston, City Council Minutes (Houston: City Secretary's Office)

3. *DHT*   *Daily Houston Telegraph*

4. *GDP*   *Galveston Daily Post*

5. *HC*   *Houston Chronicle*

6. *HDP*   *Houston Daily Post*

7. no. _____ 11th DC (filing date)   suit no. _____ Eleventh Judicial District Court of Texas (Houston: Harris County Court House)

8. 11th DIM Book:(no.)   Eleventh Judicial District Index and Minute Book (no.) (Houston: Harris County Court House)

9. no. _____USCC (filing date)   U.S. Circuit Court, East District of Texas at Galveston (Fort Worth: Federal Records Depository)

10. USIM Book:(no.)   U.S. Circuit Court, East District of Texas at Galveston, Index and Minute Book (no.) (Galveston: U.S. Customs House)

Notes

Chapter 1

1. Richard C. Wade, *The Urban Frontier: The Rise of Western Cities, 1790–1830* (Cambridge: Harvard University Press, 1959); Allan R. Pred, *The Spatial Dynamics of U.S. Urban-Industrial Growth, 1800–1914: Interpretive and Theoretical Essays* (Cambridge: M.I.T. Press, 1966).

2. There are several useful general works on the antebellum history of Houston. The first has become a basic source for most later accounts: Benajah Harvey Carroll, *Standard History of Houston, Texas* (Knoxville: Crew, 1912). Cf. its modern counterpart by David G. McComb, *Houston: The Bayou City* (Austin: University of Texas Press, 1969). Also see Kenneth W. Wheeler, *To Wear a City s Crown* (Cambridge: Harvard University Press, 1968); Marilyn McAdams Sibley, *The Port of Houston: A History* (Austin: University of Texas Press, 1968); and Earl W. Fornell, *The Galveston Era: The Texas Crescent on the Eve of Secession* (Austin: University of Texas Press, 1961). Fornell's excellent description of the economic rivalry between the two coastal towns should be placed in the context offered by James P. Baughman, "The Evolution of Rail-Water Systems of Transportation in the Gulf Southwest, 1836–1890," *Journal of Southern History* 34 (August 1968): 357–81.

3. Frederic Gaillardet, *Sketches of Early Texas and Louisiana* (reprint ed.; Austin: University of Texas Press, 1966), p. 56.

4. George W. Bonnell, *Topographical Description of Texas* (reprint ed.; Austin: Texican Press, 1964), pp. 28–29; Sibley, *Port of Houston*, chaps. 1–2; Wheeler, *City's Crown*, pp. 3–19; Frank L. Owsley, "The Pattern of Migration and Settlement on the Southern Frontier," *Journal of Southern History* 11 (May 1945): 147–76.

5. Gustav Dresel, *Gustav Dresel's Houston Journal*, trans. and ed. Max Freund (Austin: University of Texas Press, 1954), p. 100. Cf. Carville Earle and Ronald Hoffman, "Urban Development in the Eighteenth Century South," *Perspectives in American History* 10 (1976): 7–78.

6. For cotton statistics, see Sibley, *Port of Houston*, pp. 72–76; *City Directory for 1866*, p. vii. A complete compilation of population statistics for Texas cities and counties from 1850 to 1970 is found in the *Texas Almanac, 1972* (Dallas: Dallas Morning News, 1972), pp. 146–65.

7. Roy Lubove, "The Urbanization Process: An Approach to Historical Research," *Journal of the American Institute of Planners* 33 (January 1967): 33–39. Cf. Michael H. Frisch, *Town into City: Springfield, Massachusetts, and the Meaning of Community, 1840–1880* (Cambridge: Harvard University Press, 1972). To be sure, many other urban functions caused social and environmental change. However, the causal connections between the two remain largely hidden behind the countless market decisions that cumulatively shaped most facets of city life. In contrast, the municipal polity, rather than the private sector, took the leading role in building the infrastructure of the urban environment.

8. Harry N. Scheiber, "Urban Rivalry and Internal Improvements in the Old Northwest, 1820–1860," *Ohio History* 71 (October 1962): 227–39; David R. Goldfield, "Urban-Rural Relations in the Old South: The Example of Virginia," *Journal of Urban History* 2 (February 1976): 146–68.

9. George Rogers Taylor, *The Transportation Revolution, 1815–1860* (New York: Rinehart, 1951).

10. Quoted in McComb, *Houston*, p. 11.

11. Sibley, *Port of Houston*, chaps. 1–2.

12. Nelson Manfred Blake, *Water for the Cities: A History of the Urban Water Supply Problem in the United States* (Syracuse: Syracuse University Press, 1956); Charles Rosenberg, *The Cholera*

Years: The United States in 1832, 1849, and 1866 (Chicago: University of Chicago Press, 1962); Roger Lane, *Policing the City: Boston, 1822–1885* (Cambridge: Harvard University Press, 1967).

13. Elting E. Morison, *From Know-How to Nowhere: The Development of American Technology* (New York: Basic Books, 1974). Robert Wiebe has stressed the localism and autonomy of American communities in two seminal studies: *The Search for Order, 1877–1920* (New York: Hill and Wang, 1967), and *The Segmented Society: An Introduction to the Meaning of America* (New York: Oxford University Press, 1975).

14. Blaine A. Brownell, *The Urban Ethos in the South, 1920–1930* (Baton Rouge: Louisiana State University Press, 1975).

15. *History of Texas, Together with a Biographical History of the Cities of Houston and Galveston* (Chicago: Lewis, 1895), pp. 313–17; Rupert Norval Richardson, *Colonel Edward M. House: The Texas Years, 1858–1912* (Abilene: Hardin-Simmons University, 1964), pp. 1–7.

16. Mary Susan Jackson, "The People of Houston in the 1850s" (Ph.D. diss., Indiana University, 1975), chap. 2.

17. Ibid., chaps. 4 and 6.

18. Ibid., chaps. 3, 6–7.

19. W. D. Farnham, "The Weakened Spring of Government: A Study in Nineteenth Century American History," *American Historical Review* 68 (June 1965): 662–80.

20. James Willard Hurst, *Law and the Conditions of Freedom in the Nineteenth Century United States* (Madison: University of Wisconsin Press, 1965); Morton J. Horwitz, *The Transformation of American Law, 1780–1860* (Cambridge: Harvard University Press, 1977), chap. 4.

21. Robert A. Lively, "The American System: A Review Article," *Business History Review* 29 (March 1955): 81–96; Jon C. Teaford, *The Municipal Revolution in America: Origins of Modern Urban Government, 1650–1825* (Chicago: University of Chicago Press, 1975).

22. Edward Berry Weisel, "City, County, State: Intergovernmental Relation in Texas, 1835–1860" (Ph.D. diss., Rice University, 1975), chaps. 2 and 5; H. P. N. Gammel, comp., *Laws of Texas, 1822–1897* (10 vols.; Austin: Gammel, 1898), passim.

23. Gammel, *Laws*, 1:1298–99, 2:95, 413, 753–54; Sibley, *Port of Houston*, pp. 47–53.

24. Jackson, "People of Houston," chap. 5.

25. Ibid.

26. Sibley, *Port of Houston*, p. 68.

27. Ibid., pp. 62–72; Carroll, *Standard History*, pp. 80–81; McComb, *Houston*, pp. 30–33; Jackson, "People of Houston," pp. 26–29; Gammel, *Laws*, 2:499–502, 1536–65, 3:360–61, 563–65.

28. Gammel, *Laws*, 1:1188–92, 2:130–34; Sibley, *Port of Houston*, pp. 72–76; Wheeler, *City's Crown*, pp. 90–113; and Fornell, *Galveston Era*, pp. 157–79.

29. Gammel, *Laws*, 2:488–91, 3:632–36; St. Clair Griffin Reed, *A History of the Texas Railroads . . . and the State* (Houston: St. Clair, 1941), pp. 57–62.

30. Gammel, *Laws*, 3:571–76; Wheeler, *City's Crown*, pp. 45–80.

31. Gammel, *Laws*, 4:72–73; Fornell, *Galveston Era*, pp. 16–20.

32. Gammel, *Laws*, 3:1145–48, 1455–59; 4:449–55; and see above, note 28.

33. For state ferry regulations, see Gammel, *Laws*, 3:505–9, 1449–50. For a general act to regulate the railroads, see ibid., 3:1339–45.

34. Ibid., 4:1422–30, 1389, 1394–95, 1400–1402; Reed, *Railroads*, pp. 117–29.

35. Weisel, "City, County, State," chaps. 3–4.

36. Andrew F. Muir, "Railroads Come to Houston, 1857–1861," *Southwestern Historical Quarterly* 64 (July 1960): 42–63; Wheeler, *City's Crown*, pp. 161–63.

37. Sibley, *Port of Houston*, pp. 72–76; Jackson, "People of Houston," p. 178.

Chapter 2

1. Henry Cushing Grover, "The Dissolution of T. W. House and Company" (M.A. thesis, University of Houston, 1962), pp. 1–16; Rupert Norval Richardson, *Colonel Edward M. House: The Texas*

Years, 1858–1912 (Abilene: Hardin-Simmons University, 1964), pp. 1–7; Marilyn McAdams Sibley, *The Port of Houston: A History* (Austin: University of Texas Press, 1968), pp. 79–88.

2. Earl W. Fornell, *The Galveston Era: The Texas Crescent on the Eve of Secession* (Austin: University of Texas Press, 1961), pp. 12–15, 61, 298; E. Merton Coulter, *The South during Reconstruction, 1865–1877* (Baton Rouge: Louisiana State University Press, 1947), pp. 1–23, 252–74; Frederick Meiners, "The Texas Border Cotton Trade, 1862–1863," *Civil War History* 23 (December 1977): 293–306; Sibley, *Port of Houston*, pp. 79–88.

3. Ibid.; James P. Baughman, "The Evolution of Rail-Water Systems of Transportation in the Gulf Southwest, 1836–1890," *Journal of Southern History* 34 (August 1968): 357–81; Alwyn Barr, *Reconstruction to Reform: Texas Politics, 1876–1906* (Austin: University of Texas Press, 1971), chaps. 1–2.

4. Mary Alice Lavender, "Social Conditions in Houston and Harris County, 1869–1872" (M.A. thesis, Rice Institute, 1950); David G. McComb, *Houston: The Bayou City* (Austin: University of Texas Press, 1969), pp. 75–77, chaps. 2–3.

5. *Houston Weekly Telegraph*, 9 April, 23 September, 4–6 October 1858.

6. H. P. N. Gammel, comp., *Laws of Texas, 1822–1897* (10 vols.; Austin: Gammel, 1898), 5:1226–29; CM Book B:97, 137–38, 143, 181–88; *DHT*, 26 January 1871.

7. Gammel, *Laws*, 5:1226–29; J. W. Watson, "Gas and Gas-Making," *Harper's New Monthly Magazine* 26 (December 1862): 16–28; James Willard Hurst, *The Legitimacy of the Business Corporation in the United States, 1780–1970* (Charlottesville: University Press of Virginia, 1970), pp. 131–39.

8. Gammel, *Laws*, 5:1226–29.

9. CM Book B:233–34.

10. Gammel, *Laws*, 4:1422–33; ibid., 5:1391–92. Cf. Galveston's first street railway charter in ibid., p. 1319.

11. Glen E. Holt, "The Changing Perception of Urban Pathology: An Essay on the Development of Mass Transit in the United States," in *Cities in American History*, ed. Kenneth T. Jackson and Stanley K. Schultz (New York: Knopf, 1972), pp. 324–43; George Rogers Taylor, "The Beginnings of Mass Transportation in Urban America," *Smithsonian Journal of History* 1 (Summer and Autumn 1966): 35–50, 31–54.

12. CM Book B:132–33, 134–146. On the primacy of "getting the job done now," see James Willard Hurst, *Law and Economic Growth: The Legal History of the Lumber Industry in Wisconsin, 1836–1915* (Cambridge: Harvard University Press,˙1964), pp. 22–40, 107–15.

13. CM Book B:232–42, 252–53, 305–15, 363–69; Gammel, *Laws*, 5:1259–61; Gammel, *Laws*, 6:34–36.

14. CM Book B:2–28, 114, 119.

15. Ibid.

16. Ibid., pp. 138–44, 160–70.

17. Ibid., pp. 166, 160–70.

18. Baughman, "Rail-Water Systems," pp. 357–81; Sibley, *Port of Houston*, pp. 88–97.

19. CM Book B:329–30, 398–99, 467–68; CM Book C:81; Gammel, *Laws*, 4:116, 557–62.

20. *GDN*, 21–22 July 1868; Marion Merseburger, "A Political History of Houston, Texas, during the Reconstruction Period as Recorded by the Press, 1868–1873" (M.A. thesis, Rice Institute, 1950), pp. 1–31.

21. *DHT*, 22, 26 August 1868.

22. Cf. ibid., and U.S., Department of Interior, Census Office, Ninth Census of the United States, 1870: Population MS, Harris County, Texas, passim.

23. *DHT*, 30 August 1868. On Goldwaithe, see James D. Lynch, *The Bench and Bar of Texas* (St. Louis: Nixon-Jones, 1885), pp. 503–5; and *HDP*, 24 April 1897.

24. *DHT*, 30 August, 1 September 1868.

25. Ibid., 17 May 1868.

26. Ibid., 19 July, 11 June 1868.

27. See Sam Bass Warner, *Streetcar Suburbs: The Progress of Growth in Boston, 1870–1900*

222 CITY BUILDING IN THE NEW SOUTH

(Cambridge: Harvard University Press, 1962); Carl W. Condit, *The Railroad and the City: A Technological and Urbanistic History of Cincinnati* (Columbus: Ohio State University Press, 1977); Homer Hoyt, *One Hundred Years of Land Values in Chicago* (Chicago: University of Chicago Press, 1933).

28. Map, Houston, Texas (1873; lithograph, Houston Public Library); *City Directory for 1884*, p. 60; Houston Cotton Exchange et al., *Description of Harris County, Texas* (Houston: Coyle, 1886); *The Industries of Houston* (Houston: Elstner, 1887).

29. For the street railway, see CM Book B:237–38; *DHT*, 24 May, 4 June, 1 July 1868. For the gas company, see *DHT*, 26 January 1871; *City Directory for 1873*, p. 7.

30. Cf. note 29 above, and CM Book B:187, 283–88, 309, 390; *DHT*, 27 June, 3 July 1868.

31. *DHT*, 4 June, 1 July 1868; ibid., 10 February 1869; ibid., 1 July 1870; *Houston Daily Times*, 22 September 1868.

32. *City Directory for 1877*, p. 18.

33. *DHT*, 30 April, 5 May, 15 August 1874; *Houston Daily Age*, 30 April, 9, 31 May 1874.

34. *DHT*, 20, 24 August 1875.

35. Ibid., 2 August, 22 September 1868.

36. *City Directory for 1873*, p. 7; cf. Watson, "Gas-Making," pp. 16–28.

37. *City Directory for 1873*, p. 7. Securing high-grade coal became a chronic problem on the Texas Gulf Coast. First transportation barriers and then corporate railroad policy kept the price of coal at a premium. See *American Gas Light Journal* 52 (March 1890): 314; *American Gas Light Journal* 54 (April 1891): 558–67.

38. *City Directory for 1873*, p. 7; *DHT*, 26 January 1871.

39. *City Directory for 1884*, p. 52; William S. Speer and John Henry Brown, eds., *The Encyclopedia of the New West* (Marshall, Texas: U.S. Biographical, 1881), p. 492.

40. Ibid. Gas prices dropped from $8.00 (mcf) in 1868 to $4.00 (mcf) in 1878. See *DHT*, 19 January 1870; *DHT*, 12 December 1878. Cf. with the national average rate of $2.00–$2.40 (mcf) in 1880. See William Wallace Goodwin, comp., *Directory of Gas Light Companies* (Philadelphia: Goodwin, 1882), pp. 187–90. On the novelty of mass consumption economics, see Charles F. Adams, Jr., and Henry Adams, *Chapters of Erie, and Other Essays* (Boston: Osgood, 1871), pp. 355–80.

41. *City Directory for 1873*, p. 7.

42. U.S., Department of Interior, Census Office, Ninth Census of the United States, 1870: Products of Industry MS, Harris County, Texas, Schedule no. 4, p. 4; *Houston Daily Age*, 29 March 1874; *DHT*, 1 June 1875.

43. CM Book B:151–52, 235, 256, 329–30, 398–99, 467–71; Gammel, *Laws*, 4:116–19, 557–62; Sibley, *Port of Houston*, pp. 88–97; Baughman, "Rail-Water Systems," pp. 357–81.

44. Charles Fairman, *Reconstruction and Reunion, 1864–1888, Part One* (New York: Macmillan, 1971), chaps. 17–18; John F. Dillon, *The Law of Municipal Bonds* (St. Louis: Jones, 1876); A. M. Hillhouse, *Municipal Bonds: A Century of Experience* (New York: Prentice-Hall, 1936), pp. 31–46, 95–96; A. M. Hillhouse, *Defaulted Municipal Bonds* (Chicago: Municipal Finance Officers' Association, 1935), pp. 67–70.

45. James L. High, *A Treatise on the Law of Receivers* (3rd ed.; Chicago: Callaghan, 1894); Hurst, *Business Corporation*, passim.

46. J. A. Burhans, *The Law of Municipal Bonds* (Chicago: Kean, 1889), p. 3; Frank W. Hackett, "The Supreme Court and Municipal Bonds: Another Step," *Harvard Law Review* 6 (1892): 73–84.

47. CM Book B:411–12; Merseburger, "Political History," pp. 78–88, 101–8.

48. Merseburger, "Political History," pp. 78–88, 101–8. McComb, *Houston*, pp. 78–81.

49. *DHT*, 10 September 1871.

50. Ibid.

51. Cf. ibid., and Paul M. Gaston, *New South Creed: A Study in Myth Making* (New York: Knopf, 1970), pp. 92–116.

52. Cf. *DHT*, 10 September 1871, and John Brinckerhoff Jackson, *American Space: The Centennial Years, 1865–1876* (New York: Norton, 1972), pp. 13–28.

53. For an account of the debt, see CM Book C:403–20. The size of the central business district was calculated from Map, Houston, Texas (1873).

54. *DHT*, 11 October 1873; *GDN*, 4, 6 April, 26 August, 9, 19 November, 9–10 December 1873; ibid., 17 January 1874.

55. *Houston Daily Union*, 11 March 1871; ibid., 3 August 1869; *DHT*, 16 December 1870.

56. *DHT*, 24 May, 11, 27 June 1868.

57. Ibid., 10 September 1871; *GDN*, 6 April 1873; *GDN*, 6 January 1876.

58. *GDN*, 7, 14 November 1872; ibid., 2 September 1873; ibid., 6 January 1876. A similar process of erosion was set into motion by dredging the bayou. See ibid., 27 November 1873; ibid., 10 January 1874, where a reporter observed that "navigation is infinitely more precarious and uncertain than it was before the ship channel was projected."

59. *DHT*, 10 September 1871; ibid., 13 October 1875; CM Book C:403–20.

60. *GDN*, 14 May 1873. Cf. the grand civic center of Leeds, England, in Asa Briggs, *Victorian Cities* (London: Odhams, 1963), pp. 139–75.

61. CM Book C:266.

62. Ibid., pp. 403–20.

63. Samuel Bowles, "The Relations of State and Municipal Government and the Reform of the Latter," *Journal of Social Science* 9 (1878): 140–41. Also see Henry Carter Adams, "The Financial Standing of the States," *Journal of Social Science* 19 (1884): 27–46; and Charles Hale, "Municipal Indebtedness," *Atlantic Monthly* 38 (December 1876): 661–73.

Chapter 3

1. James P. Baughman, "The Evolution of Rail-Water Systems of Transportation in the Gulf Southwest, 1836–1890," *Journal of Southern History* 34 (August 1968): 370–73.

2. Robert H. Wiebe, *The Search for Order, 1877–1920* (New York: Hill and Wang, 1967); Kenneth Fox, *Better City Government: Innovation in American Urban Politics, 1850–1937* (Philadelphia: Temple University Press, 1977).

3. U.S., Department of the Interior, Census Office, *Social Statistics of the Cities, 1880*, pt. II, 2:322–26.

4. Clifton K. Yearley, *The Money Machines: The Breakdown and Reform of Governmental and Party Finance in the North, 1860–1920* (Albany: State University of New York Press, 1970); Howard N. Rabinowitz, "Continuity and Change: Southern Urban Development, 1860–1900," in *The City in Southern History: The Growth of Urban Civilization in the South*, ed. Blaine A. Brownell and David R. Goldfield (Port Washington, New York: Kennikat, 1977), pp. 92–122.

5. Unfortunately, there are no careful studies of urban blacks in Texas during the nineteenth century. They are ignored in Alwyn Barr, *Reconstruction to Reform: Texas Politics, 1876–1906* (Austin: University of Texas Press, 1971). Unfortunately, Barr does not fill in the gap in his *Black Texans: A History of Negroes in Texas, 1528–1971* (Austin: Jenkins, 1973). Cf. Howard N. Rabinowitz, *Race Relations in the Urban South, 1865–1900* (New York: Oxford University Press, 1978).

6. The elite accepted the Republicans at an early point. Several prominent Republicans, including Scanlan and Jacob Binz, were elected to the board of directors of the Texas Western Narrow Gage Railroad Company. The Democratic council and the property owners approved a municipal bond issue that subsidized the venture. See CM Book C:432–36.

7. Samuel P. Hays, *The Response to Industrialism, 1885–1914* (Chicago: University of Chicago Press, 1957).

8. Charles W. McCurdy, "Justice Field and the Jurisprudence of Government-Business Relations: Some Parameters of Laissez-Faire Constitutionalism, 1863–1897," *Journal of American History* 61 (March 1975): 971.

9. Wiebe, *The Search for Order*, p. 80. An essential introduction to the political economy of the Gilded Age is Morton Keller, *Affairs of State: Public Life in Late Nineteenth Century America* (Cambridge: Harvard University Press, 1971).

10. See A. M. Hillhouse, *Municipal Bonds: A Century of Experience* (New York: Prentice-Hall,

1936), p. 37, for a statistical evaluation of the census data on municipal finance. Also see Charles Fairman, *Reconstruction and Reunion, 1864–1888, Part One* (New York: Macmillan, 1971); Yearley, *Money Machines*.

11. *GDN*, 6 November 1873.

12. CM Book C:265, 263–65.

13. Ibid., p. 301.

14. Ibid., pp. 321, 360, 375.

15. Wilson's speech is recorded in full in ibid., pp. 403–13.

16. Ibid.

17. Ibid.

18. Ibid.; cf. Michael H. Frisch, *Town into City: Springfield, Massachusetts, and the Meaning of Community, 1840–1880* (Cambridge: Harvard University Press, 1972), pp. 157–219.

19. *GDN*, 16 September 1874.

20. CM Book C:419–22. Shifting the tax burden for street improvements from the general ad valorem tax to special assessment levies on adjoining property owners was an extremely important reform. Scanlan initiated the new system in Houston, but this particular scheme was ruled unconstitutional in Hitchcock v. Galveston, 96 US 341(1877); Houston, *Charter* (Houston: Small, 1874).

21. CM Book C:414, 432–36, 448. The first vote passed the measure, 955–153. The second voted registered 877–75. The referendum was required by the 1874 charter, which stipulated that all bond issues of $100,000 or more must be submitted to the taxpayers for a two-thirds majority.

22. CM Book C:504; *GDN*, 4, 9–10 December 1874; *GDN*, 5 January 1875.

23. *Galveston Weekly News*, 8 January 1877, provides a retrospective on the elections.

24. CM Book C:425, 455, details the quick rise and fall of the charter revision idea. See ibid., pp. 499–500, 508, 511, for details of the bond interest fund. The assessor-collector reports for the first quarter of 1875 also can be found in ibid., pp. 524, 549, 563, 578.

25. Ibid., pp. 526, 589.

26. Ibid., pp. 630–32.

27. CM Book D:32, 62–63, 87–88.

28. *DHT*, 17 September 1875. Cf. ibid., 14 September 1875.

29. Ibid., 24 September 1875.

30. For the public debate, see ibid., 8–29 October 1875.

31. Ibid., 17 November 1875.

32. CM Book D:138–39. Earlier, the council had obtained a state statute that strengthened the refunding scheme. See CM Book C:542–43; H. P. N. Gammel, comp., *Laws of Texas, 1822–1897* (10 vols.; Austin: Gammel, 1898), 8:1187–88.

33. CM Book D:138–39.

34. Ibid., pp. 243, 257, 272.

35. *DHT*, 9 July 1876; David G. McComb, *Houston: The Bayou City* (Austin: University of Texas Press, 1969), pp. 79–80; Charles D. Green, *Fire Fighters of Houston, 1836–1915* (Houston: Green, 1915), 109, 111, passim.

36. CM Book D:277, 296.

37. Mary Duer, Executor v. Mayor et al., no. 8924 11th DC (1874); CM Book C:529–30. In this instance of a breach of contract, a lien had been specifically inserted which permitted Masterson to order a direct method of recovery. In general, however, the state legislature put the city's funds and property outside of the garnishment powers of the judiciary. See Gammel, *Laws*, 8:283.

38. Duer v. Mayor, no. 9619 11th DC (1876); 11th DIM Book R:15–16, 27.

39. CM Book D:371, 381.

40. Ibid., pp. 378–81, 389–90. For an astute analysis of the election, see *Galveston Weekly News*, 7 January 1877.

41. Augustus Frank v. Mayor et al., no. 10436 11th DC (1879); George B. Fairchild v. Mayor et al., no. 10297 11th DC (1878).

42. Gelpcke v. Dubuque, 1 Wallace 175 (1864); Fairman, *Reconstruction*, chaps. 17–18.

43. Quoted in Charles Fairman, *Mr. Justice Miller and the Supreme Court, 1862–1890* (New York: Russell and Russell, 1939), pp. 231–232. Also see Thomas M. Cooley, "Evils in Local Government" (Six lectures delivered at Johns Hopkins University, May 1879), MS in Michigan Historical Collection, pp. 28–40; Thomas M. Cooley, *A Treatise on the Constitutional Limitations . . . of the States of the American Union* (4th ed.; Boston: Little Brown, 1878); and John F. Dillon, *The Law of Municipal Corporations* (2nd ed.; New York: Crockeroft, 1873).

44. Von Hoffman v. City of Quincy, 4 Wallace 535 (1866). Cf. Supervisors of Rock Island County v. The State Bank, 4 Wallace 435 (1866); and City of Galena v. Amy, 4 Wallace 705 (1866). For an introduction to the postbellum court, see Harold M. Hyman, *A More Perfect Union: The Impact of Civil War and Reconstruction on the Constitution* (New York: Knopf, 1973); and C. Peter Magrath, *Morrison R. Waite: The Triumph of Character* (New York: Macmillan, 1963).

45. A complete survey of cases was made of the state district, the state appellate and the U.S. Circuit Court levels of the judiciary. Between 1876 and 1890, 58 actions were instituted at the state district level. See 11th DIM Book R–W (1876–1890). On the federal level, 49 cases were reported in USIM Book: 2–7 (1872–1894).

46. Reynolds v. Mayor, no. 10320 11th DC (1878); 11th DIM Book R: 601–2. Also see Chapman v. Mayor, no. 10434 11th DC (1878); 11th DIM Book R: 525–26; and Fairchild v. Mayor, no. 10297 11th DC (1878); 11th DIM Book R: 430.

47. Chapman v. Mayor, no. 10434 11th DC (1878).

48. CM Book D: 542.

49. Ibid., pp. 555–58.

50. Ibid., pp. 557, 594, 608–10; *New York Commercial and Financial Chronicle* 23–30 (1876–1880), passim. Only the $250,000 worth of Market House Bonds, which were directly linked to the building's income, would be exchanged at a higher, 40 percent rate. At the same time, the council acted to liquidate another revenue bearing security, the Ship Channel Bonds. The administration successfully made an exchange at par with the shipping company. See CM Book D: 621–23.

51. The council recognized these dilemmas. See CM Book E: 165, 170–71, 178–88.

52. See the monthly reports of the assessor-collector in ibid., pp. 157–58, passim.

53. Consider the inaugural speech of Mayor Wilson in CM Book D: 555–58.

54. Ibid.; CM Book E: 391. For biographical information, see *City Directory for 1880*, passim.

55. CM Book E: 465. For the operating budget of 1880 of $58,000, see ibid., p. 375.

56. Ibid., pp. 392, 396, 402–3, 413–15.

57. Ibid., pp. 466–72, for the 1881 tax ordinance.

58. Ibid., pp. 564–66. Houstonians again sponsored a state statute to fortify the powers of the city to undertake a scaling of the debt. See Gammel, *Laws*, 8: 109–11.

59. These cases will be discussed in the following chapter.

60. The formation of national trade associations was a part of the larger organizational impulse of the urban-industrial transformation. See above, note 7; Alfred Chandler, Jr., "The Beginning of 'Big Business' in American Industry," *Business History Review* 33 (Spring 1959): 1–31; Jerry Israel, ed., *Building the Organizational Society* (New York: Free Press, 1972), pp. 1–15. A brief history of the American Gas Light Association is found in American Gas Light Association, *Proceedings* 1 (1873): 1–10. In 1881, the street railway and the waterworks industries followed. See *Street Railway Journal* 2 (1885): 7–12; and the American Water Works Association, *Proceedings* (St. Louis, 1881), p. 5, respectively.

61. Oscar G. Steele, "The Management of Gas Works," in American Gas Light Association, *Proceedings* 1 (1873): 31, 214. Over 100 representatives attended the seventh meeting in Philadelphia. By 1893, the association had 428 members. See ibid., 3 (1879): passim; ibid., 11 (1893): 261.

62. See above, note 60. The seventies also marked the beginning of trade directories of urban utility facilities. Significantly, the first was published by an equipment manufacturer (gas meters), William Wallace Goodwin, *Directory of Gas Light Companies* (Philadelphia: Goodwin, 1873). For a comparable census of waterwork facilities, see E. Prince, "List of Waterworks in the United States and Canada," *Engineering News* 8 (1881): passim. The U.S. Census Office undertook its own survey

of urban conditions in its *Social Statistics of the Cities, 1880.* Street railway statistics on a national scale grew out of the needs of security dealers. See Henry V. Poor, comp., *Poor's Manual of Railroads* (New York: Poor, 1889).

63. CM Book D:249–69; *DHT*, 5 November 1876. Two years later, a further $1.00 (mcf) reduction was effected. See *DHT*, 12 December 1878.

64. CM Book C:609–15; CM Book D:252–53, 269, 271, 340.

65. For the rejection of local bids, see CM Book D: 281–83, 327, 339–55. The Loweree negotiations and contract are found in CM Book E:89–90; J. James Croes, "The History and Statistics of American Waterworks—No. CCCLIX, Houston," *Engineering News* 9 (1882): 251.

66. J. James Croes, "The History and Statistics of American Waterworks—No. CCCLIX, Houston," *Engineering News* 9 (1882): 251. U.S., Department of Interior, Census Office, Tenth Census of the United States, 1880: Manufacturers—Products of Industry MS, Schedule no. 3, p. 1; id., *Social Statistics of the Cities, 1880,* pt. II, 2:322–26; M. N. Barker, comp., *The Manual of American Water-Works* (New York: Engineering News, 1888), p. 484.

67. William S. Speer and John Henry Brown, eds., *The Encyclopedia of the New West* (Marshall: U.S. Biographical, 1881), pp. 492–95; *City Directory for 1884*, p. 52; Tenth Census; 1880: Products of Industry MS, p. 1; Goodwin, *Directory* (1882), p. 189.

68. See above, note 66.

69. CM Book E:535–36; ibid., pp. 507–8, 514–15; *DHT*, 9 July 1881; *HDP*, 6–8 July 1881.

70. *HDP*, 28 July, 22 August 1881; ibid., 23 February 1882; *Houston Daily Sun*, 2, 15, 30 November 1882; CM Book E:523–44; CM Book F:66.

71. CM Book F:185–89; *HDP*, 14 March 1883. For a brief account of street railways in Galveston, see *Morrison and Fourmey's General Directory of the City of Galveston* (Galveston: Morrison and Fourmey, 1883), pp. 42–44.

72. Harold C. Passer, *The Electrical Manufacturers, 1875–1900* (Cambridge: Harvard University Press, 1953), pp. 1–203; W. Paul Strassman, *Risk and Technological Innovation: American Manufacturing Methods during the Nineteenth Century* (Ithaca: Cornell University Press, 1956), pp. 156–84.

73. Rabinowitz, "Continuity and Change," pp. 92–122; George Brown Tindall, *The Persistent Tradition in New South Politics* (Baton Rouge: Louisiana State University Press, 1975).

74. Hays, *Response to Industrialism*, p. 48, chap. 3.

75. J. A. Burhans, *The Law of Municipal Bonds* (Chicago: Kean, 1889), p. 3; John F. Dillon, *The Law of Municipal Bonds*, (St. Louis: Jones, 1876), passim.

76. *City Directory for 1884*, p. 60.

Chapter 4

1. Reverend John E. Green, *John E. Green and His Forty Years in Houston* (Houston: Dealy-Ody-Elgin, 1928), pp. 65–68.

2. Ibid.

3. U.S., Department of Interior, Census Office, *Compendium of the Eleventh Census, 1890*, pp. 393, 434–36.

4. See Jerry Israel, ed., *Building the Organizational Society* (New York: Free Press, 1972); Louis Galambos, "The Emerging Organizational Synthesis in Modern American History," *Business History Review* 44 (Autumn 1970): 279–90.

5. Quoted in David G. McComb, *Houston: The Bayou City* (Austin: University of Texas Press, 1969), pp. 11–12.

6. I have considered this theme in "Houston at the Crossroads: The Emergence of the Urban Center of the Southwest," *Journal of the West* 18 (July 1979): 51–61.

7. *City Directory for 1884*, p. 60.

8. Eugene C. Baker, ed., *Texas History* (Dallas: Southwest, 1924), pp. 528–31; Billy M. Jones, *The Search for Maturity* (Austin: Steck-Vaughn, 1965), pp. 108–33.

9. William Brady, *Glimpses of Texas* (Houston, 1871), as quoted in McComb, *Houston*, p. 112.

10. McComb, *Houston*, pp. 97–98; Jones, *Search for Maturity*, pp. 103–5. Cf. James Willard

Hurst, *Law and Economic Growth: The Legal History of the Lumber Industry in Wisconsin, 1836– 1915* (Cambridge: Harvard University Press, 1964).

11. Henry Cushing Grover, "The Dissolution of T. W. House and Company" (M.A. thesis, University of Houston, 1962), pp. 27–34; Rupert Norval Richardson, *Colonel Edward M. House: The Texas Years, 1858–1912* (Abilene: Harden-Simmons University, 1964), pp. 22–24. In Texas, fully one half of the farms would be in a condition of tenancy by the turn of the century. See Jones, *Search for Maturity*, p. 122; and the important work by Lawrence Goodwyn, *Democratic Promise: The Populist Movement in America* (New York: Oxford University Press, 1976).

12. See above, note 6; James P. Baughman, "The Evolution of Rail-Water Systems of Transportation in the Gulf Southwest, 1836–1890," *Journal of Southern History* 34 (August 1968): 357–81.

13. A. W. Spraight, *The Resources . . . of Texas* (Galveston: Bels, 1882), pp. 135–37; *HDP*, 12 December 1886. The growth of the cotton processing industry in Texas is the subject of Louis Tuffly Ellis, "The Texas Compress Industry: A History" (Ph.D. diss., University of Texas, 1964).

14. Ibid., pp. 94–119.

15. See Allan R. Pred, *The Spatial Dynamics of U.S. Urban-Industrial Growth, 1800–1914: Interpretive and Theoretical Essays* (Cambridge: M.I.T. Press, 1966); and Jane Jacobs, *The Economy of Cities* (New York: Random House, 1969).

16. *City Directory for 1884*, p. 60. McComb, *Houston*, pp. 109–10.

17. McComb, *Houston*, pp. 109–10. *The Industries of Houston* (Houston: Elstner, 1887), pp. 7–11.

18. *The Industries of Houston* (Houston: Elstner, 1887), pp. 7–11. Robert C. Zeigler, "The Workingman in Houston, Texas, 1865–1914" (Ph.D. diss., Texas Tech University, 1972), pp. 73–91, passim. Cf. John H. M. Laslett, *Labor and the Left* (New York: Basic Books, 1970), pp. 144–69.

19. Houston Cotton Exchange et al., *Description of Harris County, Texas* (Houston: Coyle, 1886), pp. 6–7; *HDP*, 21 December 1886.

20. Zeigler, "Workingman," pp. 55–65, considers housing conditions. On a ward-by-ward basis, census and school records show a fairly even distribution of whites and blacks. However, the pie-shaped division of the wards makes these statistics difficult to interpret. An unscientific survey of the census manuscripts for 1880 indicates that certain blocks and streets were predominantly black or white.

21. John Brinckerhoff Jackson, *American Space: The Centennial Years, 1865–1876* (New York: Norton, 1972), p. 78. For an introduction to spacial perceptions of the city, see Kevin Lynch, *The Image of the City* (Cambridge: M.I.T. Press, 1960).

22. Throughout the nineteenth century, the Texas legislature paid deference to local self-government. See Edward Berry Weisel, "City, County, State: Intergovernmental Relations in Texas, 1835–1860" (Ph.D. diss., Rice University, 1975); and review the votes on city charters in H. P. N. Gammel, comp., *Laws of Texas, 1822–1897* (10 vols.; Austin: Gammel, 1898), passim.

23. Erwin R. A. Seligman, *Essays in Taxation* (New York: MacMillan, 1895), pp. 282–304; Victor Rosewater, *Special Assessments: A Study in Municipal Finance* (2nd ed.; New York: Columbia University Press, 1898); Willard v. Presbury, 14 Wallace 676 (1871); Roundtree v. Galveston, 42 Texas 612 (1875).

24. Gammel, *Laws*, 9:19.

25. Ibid., pp. 241–42.

26. Ibid.; Leonard A. Jones, *A Treatise on the Law of Liens* (2nd ed.; Indianapolis: Bowin-Merril, 1894), p. 3, defines a lien as "an obligation or claim annexed to or attaching upon property, without satisfying such property cannot be demanded by its owner. Lien in its proper sense, is a right the laws gives. . . ; a lien at law is an implied obligation whereby property is bound for the discharge of some debt or engagement." If a lien can be "foreclosed" under statutory provision, the land can be sold at public auction with legal title transferring to the purchaser. In Houston, paving efforts reached a milestone when the two railroad depots were connected by improved streets. See *HDP*, 17 October 1882.

27. Gammel, *Laws*, 9:500–504.

28. Between 1880 and 1886, the minutes of the city council read more like the records of a road and bridge commission than those of a municipal government. An attention to the bonded debt prob-

lem proved the only general exception to this characterization. The process of reform in this area is particularly interesting during the early stages of the Baker administration. See CM Book E:463–65, 545–70; CM Book F: 13–18, 80–81, 100, 142–45.

29. For insight into the legal profession, see Arnold M. Paul, *Conservative Crisis and the Rule of Law: Attitudes of Bar and Bench, 1887–1895* (New York: Harper and Row, 1960).

30. In Texas, various substantive and procedural objections to special assessments were decided against the taxpayer in Roundtree v. Galveston, 42 Texas 612 (1875); Allen v. Galveston, 51 Texas 320 (1880); Galveston v. Heard, 54 Texas 420 (1881); Galveston v. Loonie, 54 Texas 517 (1881); Highland v. Galveston, 54 Texas 527 (1881); and the benchmark case, Lufkin v. Galveston, 58 Texas 545 (1883). The court was to insist that legislatively determined procedures be followed in Adams et al. v. Fisher, 63 Texas 651, 75 Texas 657 (1888). Justice John Stayton agreed with the principle that the assessment system rested upon special benefit. However, municipal corporations were not required to demonstrate an "actual enhancement" in the value of each piece of assessed property. For a similar ruling holding Houston authorities only to the procedures defined in their municipal charter, see Texas Transportation Company v. Boyd, 67 Texas 153 (1886). Houston's system of certificates received judicial sanction in Taylor v. Boyd, 63 Texas 533 (1885). On a national level, see Davidson v. New Orleans, 96 US 97 (1877); and Spencer v. Merchant, 125 US 345 (1888). The Supreme Court was asked to employ the federal judiciary as supervisor over state taxing practices. Lawyers argued that authority to tie these national checkreins onto the states was found in the Fourteenth Amendment's due process clause. But in *Davidson*, Justice Samuel Miller rejected their arguments and added that "there exists some strange misconception of the scope of this [due process] provision." In *Spencer*, Justice Horace Gray forcefully denied review powers for the national courts over the policy question of how state legislatures decided to levy taxes for public purposes. Due process of law only required notice of the assessment and an opportunity for a hearing at some stage of the proceedings. The Supreme Court refused to arbitrate special assessment equities.

31. *City Directory for 1884*, p. 45; *HDP*, 8 April 1886; McComb, *Houston*, p. 109.

32. New Orleans Gas Company v. Louisiana Light Company, 115 US 650 (1885). For insight into the Court's objections to government created monopolies, see Butchers' Union Company v. Crescent City Company, 111 US 746 (1884). City governments had no inherent powers to grant monopoly franchises. See Jackson County Horse Railway Company v. Interstate Rapid Transit Company, 24 Fed. 306 (1885); Saginaw Gas-Light Company v. City of Saginaw, 28 Fed. 529 (1886); and Spring Valley Water Works v. Schottler, 110 US 347 (1884). In Texas, see Galveston City Railway Company v. Gulf City Street Railway Company, 63 Texas 529 (1885), 65 Texas 502 (1886); Fort Worth Street Railway Company v. Rosedale Street Railway Company, 68 Texas 169 (1887); and the landmark case, City of Brenham v. Brenham Water Company, 67 Texas 542 (1887).

33. CM Book F:455–57. The Citizens' group suggested that an expert hydraulic engineer be employed to undertake a study of the city's water supply needs. They also proposed statutory reforms to create better regulation of hydrant pressure.

34. Ibid., pp. 461–62, 547–48; *HDP*, 15 September 1886.

35. *HDP*, 9 July 1881.

36. CM Book F:626. The ordinance also required the company to obtain the written consent of the mayor before the enterprise could replace its tracks.

37. Harold C. Passer, *The Electrical Manufacturers, 1875–1900* (Cambridge: Harvard University Press, 1953), pp. 1–3; W. Paul Strassmann, *Risk and Technological Innovation: American Manufacturing Methods during the Nineteenth Century* (Ithaca: Cornell University Press, 1956), pp. 156–84.

38. See Thomas R. Navin and Marian V. Sears, "The Rise of a Market for Industrial Securities, 1887–1902," *Business History Review* 29 (June 1955): 105–08; Charles Hoffman, "The Depression of the Nineties," *Journal of Economic History* 16 (June 1956): 141–45; Vincent P. Carosso, *Investment Banking in America* (Cambridge: Harvard University Press, 1970), pp. 29–50.

39. *HDP*, 23 February, 28 July, 22 August 1882; *Houston Daily Sun*, 30 November, 7 December 1882; CM Book E:506, 508–19, 542–45; CM Book F:66.

40. *HDP*, 18 July 1883; ibid., 14 March 1883. For a brief look at Sinclair's Galveston operation, see *General Directory of the City of Galveston, 1882* (Galveston: Morrison and Fourmy, 1883), pp. 42–44.

41. *Houston Evening Journal*, 13 September 1884.

42. Ibid., 18 September 1884.

43. Andrew Morrison, *The City of Houston* (n.p., 1891), pp. 19–20. These trends were noticed earlier. See the special edition of the *HDP*, 19 August 1886. In 1886, the company employed 60 men and 119 mules to keep 41 cars in operation. Five years later these figures stood at 100 men, 300 horses and mules, and 50 cars.

44. Harold I. Sharlin, *The Making of the Electrical Age* (New York: Abelard-Schuman, 1963), pp. 147–50; Arthur A. Bright, Jr., *The Electric Lamp Industry: Technological Change and Economic Development from 1800 to 1947* (New York: MacMillan, 1949), pp. 21–34. Arc lamps represented a transitional technology that combined electricity with a conventional means of producing light by burning carbon tips in the open air. The electricity arced across the carbon tips, which were held in close proximity.

45. CM Book E:575, 574–76.

46. Ibid.

47. CM Book F:31, 39, 42, 92; *HDP*, 7 June, 27 September, 9 December 1882; *Houston Daily Sun*, 2, 12, 26, November 1882. A feature article in the *HDP*, 1 March 1883, gives details of the equipment, besides reporting that the superintendent was Mr. John Caffrey, who was sent by the patent holder, the U.S. Electric Light Company of New York (a holding company for the Edison-General Electric patents). The newspaper also remarked that all of the hardware came from the East, except the two boilers for the steam engine, which were made in Houston shops.

48. The three quotations are contained in ibid., 15 December 1882; ibid., 1 March, 30 January 1883, respectively. For first reactions, also consider ibid., 13–16 December 1882; *Houston Daily Sun*, 12–15 December 1882.

49. *HDP*, 14 December 1882; ibid., 14 January 1883; *Houston Daily Sun*, 27 December 1882.

50. For the growth of the company, cf. *HDP*, 1 March 1883, and ibid., 19 August 1886. For the inauguration of public lighting services in June 1884, see CM Book F:115–16, 129–30, 167, 178, 183, 225–36, 265–66; *Houston Evening Journal*, 20 June 1884.

51. *HDP*, 29 September, 22 December 1883. Also see Sharlin, *Electrical Age*, pp. 150–69.

52. Houston Light and Power Company, *Origins and History of Houston Lighting and Power Company* (Houston: n.pub., 1940).

53. The growing obsolescence of the waterworks under private management will be considered in Part Two.

54. William H. White, "President's Address," American Gas Light Association, *Proceedings* 10 (1892): 33; Thomas Turner, "President's Address," American Gas Light Association, *Proceedings* 8 (1888): 201–08; Edward W. Bemis, "Municipal Ownership of Gas in the United States," *Publications of the American Economic Association* 4 (July 1891): 60. Bemis concurred with this evaluation and asserted further that this impact of electric lighting had become the "universal experience."

55. M. S. Greenough, "President's Address," American Gas Light Association, *Proceedings* 8 (1887): 20–30; Frederick H. Shelton, "Illuminating Water Gas—Past and Present," American Gas Light Association, *Proceedings* 9 (1889): 154–99. Shelton noted that over 50 percent of the gas produced and 30 percent of the American cities used the water gas technique. Also see Harold Baron, "Incandescent Gas Mantles," *Gassier's Magazine* 17 (1890): 513–17.

56. *HDP*, 22 April 1883.

57. See above, note 3.

58. *GDN*, 19–28 February 1886; Zeigler, "Workingman," pp. 73–91.

59. *GDN*, 19–28 February 1886; *History of Texas* (Chicago: Lewis, 1895), pp. 423–25, 589–90; *HDP*, 1 May 1890.

60. For an introduction see Stephan Thernstrom, *The Other Bostonians* (Cambridge: Harvard University Press, 1973).

61. Zeigler, "Workingman," pp. 73–91. For a larger context, see Herbert G. Gutman, *Work, Culture, and Society in Industrializing America* (New York: Vintage, 1977). For biographical sketches of Underwood and Riesner, consult *HDP*, 21 July 1898, and *History of Texas*, pp. 389–90, respectively.

62. *GDN*, 28 February, 1 April 1886; *The Industries of Houston*, pp. 18–19; E. W. Winkler, ed., *Platforms of Political Parties in Texas* (Austin: University of Texas Press, 1916), passim; *HDP*, 13 February 1902.

63. *GDN*, 13 March 1886; CM Book F:403–5, 580–84.

64. Benajah Harvey Carroll, *Standard History of Houston, Texas* (Knoxville: Crew, 1912), p. 12; *GDN*, 6 April 1886.

65. Cf. *GDN*, 4 April 1886, and CM Book F:233, where the official returns are noted.

66. At the state level, see E. Voorheis v. Mayor et al., no. 12085 11th DC; L. Voorheis v. Mayor et al., no. 12044 11th DC; Fazende and Seixas v. Mayor et al., Nos. 12252 and 12253 11th DC.

67. Van Nostrand v. City of Houston, no. 1408 USCC (1886). Similar rulings soon followed, such as Fazende and Seixas v. City of Houston, no. 1420 USCC (1886). For earlier patterns, see the report in CM Book F:403–5, which revealed that between 1882 and 1886 only $28,000 in judgments had been paid, while another $250,000 went unpaid.

68. *HDP*, 21 December 1886.

69. Ibid.; ibid., 11 January 1887; CM Book F:491, 516.

70. CM Book F:380, 403–5, 459–61, 472, 497–502, 546–47, 633–34; CM Book G:46–47.

71. CM Book F:580–84; Gammel, *Laws*, 9:848–51. Cf. Gammel, *Laws*, 5:1137–39, 8:1187–89.

72. CM Book F:580–84, 594, 627.

73. E. Voorheis v. Mayor et al., 70 Texas 331 (1881); and L. Voorheis v. Mayor et al., 70 Texas 356 (1888). For Smith's response, see CM Book G:17–19, 52–62, 89–95.

74. *GDN*, 1 March–4 April 1888; CM Book G:55–56.

75. For three months, Baker's allies on the council kept the mayor from gaining the approval of his choices for the city's appointive positions. See CM Book F:422–25, 437; *HDP*, 11 May 1886.

76. CM Book G:192. These trends will be considered in detail in the following chapters.

77. *HDP*, 14 December 1888.

Chapter 5

1. For contemporary views of the fair, see Hubert Howe Bancroft, *The Book of the Fair* (2 vols.; Chicago: Bancroft, 1893); and *Dream City* (St. Louis: Thompson, 1893). For assessments, consider Eugene S. Ferguson, "Expositions of Technology, 1851–1900," in *Technology in Western Civilization*, ed. Melvin Kranzberg and Carroll W. Pursell, Jr. (2 vols.; New York: Oxford University Press, 1967), 2:706–26; and Sigfried Giedion, *Mechanization Takes Command* (New York: Oxford University Press, 1948), pp. 96–114.

2. Henry Adams, *The Education of Henry Adams* (orig. pub. 1918; Boston: Houghton-Mifflin, Sentry ed., 1946), pp. 96–114.

3. Ibid., pp. 374–90.

4. Henry Steele Commager first proposed that the 1890s represented the great "watershed of American history" in *The American Mind* (New Haven: Yale University Press, 1950), chap. 2. Many historians have since followed Commager's provocative thesis. For a reappraisal, see John Higham, *Writing American History* (Bloomington: Indiana University Press, 1970), chap. 4.

5. A useful historiographical essay is provided in Michael H. Ebner and Eugene M. Tobin, eds., *The Age of Urban Reform: New Perspectives on the Progressive Age* (Port Washington, New York: Kennikat, 1977), pp. 156–72.

6. The state utility commission had its origins in the American Gas Light Association. See M. S. Greenough, "President's Address," American Gas Light Association, *Proceedings* 7 (1886): 225, where the Massachusetts gasman reported that "competition has been knocked on its head" by the establishment of a commission. For a description of the gasmen's creation, see Joseph B. Eastman, "The Public Utilities Commissions of Massachusetts," in Clyde Lyndon King, ed., *The Regulation of Municipal Utilities* (New York: Appleton, 1912), pp. 276–95. Eastman, an advocate of the commission, agreed with Greenough that the agency had kept "unwise competition" out with a "iron hand."

7. An indispensable synthesis of scholarship about institutions in the Gilded Age is Morton Keller, *Affairs of State: Public Life in Late Nineteenth Century America* (Cambridge: Harvard University Press, 1977). Keller's work is extended by William Graebner, "Federalism in the Progressive Era: A Structural Interpretation of Reform," *Journal of American History* 64 (September 1977): 331–57.

8. For insight into the common elements of municipal reform, consider Robert H. Wiebe, *The Search for Order, 1877–1920* (New York: Hill and Wang, 1967); Martin J. Schiesl, *The Politics of Efficiency* (Berkeley: University of California Press, 1977); Kenneth Fox, *Better City Government: Innovation in American Urban Politics, 1850–1937* (Philadelphia: Temple University Press, 1977); and Ebner and Tobin, *The Age of Urban Reform.*

9. For a catalog of reformers and their ideas, see Henry F. May, *The End of American Innocence: A Study of the First Years of Our Own Time, 1912–1917* (Chicago: Quadrangle, 1957).

10. James Willard Hurst, "Legal Elements in United States History," *Perspectives in American History* 5 (1971): 3. The Progressive Era debate is critically examined by William Letwin, *Law and Economic Policy in America: The Evolution of the Sherman Antitrust Act* (Edinburgh: Edinburgh University Press, 1966). Also see Thomas K. McGraw, "Regulation in America: A Review Article," *Business History Review* 49 (Summer 1975): 159–83; and Richard L. McCormick, "The Discovery That 'Business Corrupts Politics': A Reappraisal of the Origins of Progressivism," *American Historical Review* 86 (April 1981): 247–74.

11. Letwin, *Law and Economic Policy*, chap. 5.

12. A valuable bibliographic analysis of contemporary thought about competition and monopoly is supplied by Benjamin J. Klebaner, "Potential Competition and the American Anti-Trust Legislation of 1914," *Business History Review* 38 (Summer 1964): 163–85. The origins of "natural monopoly concept" can be traced in Richard T. Ely, "Report of the Organization of the American Economic Association," *Publications of the American Economic Association* 1, no. 1 (1886): 5–40; Richard T. Ely, *Taxation in American States and Cities* (New York: Crowch, 1887), pp. 270, 269–79; Richard T. Ely, "The Growth and Future of Corporations," *Harper's New Monthly Magazine* 75 (1887): 259–66; Edmund J. James, "The Relation of the Modern Municipality to the Gas Supply," *Publications of the American Economic Association* 1, no. 2 and 5 (1886): 53–122; and Edward W. Bemis, "Municipal Ownership of Gas in the United States," *Publications of the American Economic Association* 9, no. 4 (1891): 1–185. Ely and James based their arguments on a pioneer article by Henry Carter Adams, "The Relation of the State to Industrial Action," *Publications of the American Economic Association* 1, no. 6 (1886): 471–549. Other influential commentators were promoting the theory of beneficent monopolies at the same time. See, for example, Brown University President E. Benjamin Andrew, "The Economic Law of Monopoly," *Journal of Social Science* 26 (1890): 1–12; and investor and Yale economist Arthur T. Hadley, "Private Monopolies and Private Rights," *Quarterly Journal of Economics* 1 (1887): 28–44. The enormous influence of these advocates of a new economics is explored by Benjamin G. Rader, *The Academic Mind and Reform: The Influence of Richard T. Ely in American Life* (Lexington: University of Kentucky Press, 1966).

13. Lawrence Goodwyn, *Democratic Promise: The Populist Movement in America* (New York: Oxford University Press, 1976).

14. Ibid. is centered on Texas. Other general accounts include Alwyn Barr, *Reconstruction to Reform: Texas Politics, 1876–1900* (Austin: University Press, 1971); and Lawrence D. Rice, *The Negro in Texas, 1874–1900* (Baton Rouge: Louisiana State University Press, 1971). For state policy toward the city, see Robert C. Cotner, *James Stephen Hogg: A Biography* (Austin: University Press, 1959), pp. 248–353; and E. W. Winkler, ed., *Platforms of Political Parties in Texas* (Austin: University of Texas Press, 1916), pp. 310–44.

15. For Houston, see I. J. Isaacs, *The Industrial Advantages of Houston, Texas and Environs* (Houston: Alehurst, 1894); David G. McComb, *Houston: The Bayou City* (Austin: University of Texas Press, 1969), pp. 92–120; Marilyn McAdams Sibley, *The Port of Houston: A History* (Austin: University of Texas Press, 1968), pp. 120–29. For state-city relationships, see note 14 above; Samuel Aaron Suhler, "Significant Questions Relating to the History of Austin, Texas, to 1900" (Ph.D. diss., University of Texas, 1966), pp. 384–410. In general, see Paul Gaston, *New South Creed: A Study in Myth Making* (New York: Knopf, 1970), pp. 107–16, passim; C. Vann Woodward, *Origins of the New South* (Baton Rouge; Louisiana State University Press, 1951), pp. 142–54, 291–320, 371–73.

16. *HDP*, 13 December 1888.

17. Ibid.; ibid., December 1888–February 1889, passim, for a steady succession of editorials and stories on city planning.

18. Ibid., 27 June 1889.

19. Ibid., 7 June 1889; ibid., 14 December 1888; ibid., 2 January 1889. For a history of public health initiatives on the Texas Gulf Coast, see James Brooks Spears, Jr., "Contagion and the Constitution: Public Health in the Texas Coastal Region, 1836–1909" (Ph.D. diss., Rice University, 1974).

20. *HDP*, 2 June 1889; ibid., 25 January 1889.

21. Ibid., 8, 22–25 January 1889.

22. Cf. H. P. N. Gammel, comp., *Laws of Texas, 1822–1897* (10 vols.; Austin: Gammel, 1898), 9: 1324–35, 10: 305–21. On the real estate boom, see *HDP*, 16 March 1890; and the Houston Daily Herald, *Houston Illustrated* (Houston: Houston Daily Herald, 1893), pp. 75–83. The booster publication noted that the city had more than 50 miles of sewers and 30 miles of improved streets. See ibid., p. 13. For tax assessment statistics, consult CM Book H:89.

23. Gammel, *Laws*, 9:1324–35.

24. Ibid.; and ibid., 10:305–21.

25. *HDP*, 14, 16 March 1889. The earlier story reported that the "rumor" was in the air about the coming of the electric street railway. For a partial list of Holmes's partners, see ibid., 24 January 1890.

26. Ibid., 26 March, 9–10 April, 28 July 1889; CM Book G:193–203.

27. Mayor Smith had the Holmes correspondence published in *HDP*, 1 August 1889.

28. Ibid.

29. For Houston's first attempt to create a streetcar suburb, Magnolia Park, see ibid., 9 April 1889; ibid., 24 February 1891; CM Book G:241–42, 219. For the growth of the Bayou City effort, see *HDP*, 13 February, 2 March 1890.

30. *HDP*, 6 July 1889. The editorial pointed to steam dummy lines in suburban Memphis, Nashville, Atlanta, and Birmingham.

31. Ibid., 24 February 1891. Also see Chapter 6.

32. U.S., Department of Interior, Census Office, *Eleventh Census of the United States, 1890: Compendium*, p. 738–39.

33. The annual message of Mayor Scherffius is reported in CM Book H:12–15.

34. Ibid., G:338–39.

35. The phrase, "sphere of influence," comes from an analysis of government-business relations by Walter Fisher, president of Chicago's Municipal Voters' League and a leading utility expert. See his remarks in the National Civic Foundation, *Report on Municipal and Private Operation of Public Utilities* (3 vols.; New York: National Civic Foundation, 1907), pt. I, 1:38.

Chapter 6

1. *HDP*, 19 March 1889.

2. Ibid., 20 March 1889; Houston City Street Railway Company v. William Boyd et al., no. 13198 11th DC (1889); Mayor et al. v. Houston City Street Railway Company, no. 13199 11th DC (1889); Houston City Street Railway Company v. Bayou City Street Railway Company, no. 13205 11th DC (1889).

3. Henry V. Poor, comp., *Poor's Manual of Railroads* (New York: Poor, 1889), appendix, p. 59. Boyd's initial plan and later delay is reported in *Street Railway Journal* 4 (1888): 55, 88; and *HDP*, 9 March 1889. The Boyd franchise is in CM Book G:68–71.

4. *HDP*, 20 March 1889.

5. Ibid., 26 March, 9–10 April 1889; CM Book G:193–96, 200–207.

6. Quotation by Walter Fisher, in the National Civic Foundation, *Report on Municipal and Private Operation of Public Utilities* (3 vols.; New York: National Civic Foundation, 1907), pt. I, 1:38. The inability of the progressives to agree on a single approach to utility franchises is succinctly ana-

lyzed by David Nord, "The Experts versus the Experts: Conflicting Philosophies of Municipal Utility Regulation in the Progressive Era," *Wisconsin Magazine of History* 58 (Spring 1975): 219–36.

7. New frontiers of scholarship on the urban crisis of the nineties are opened by Alan D. Anderson, *The Origin and Resolution of an Urban Crisis: Baltimore, 1890–1930* (Baltimore: Johns Hopkins University Press, 1977).

8. Ibid.; U.S., Department of Interior, Census Office, *Eleventh Census of the United States, 1890: Population Compendium*, 1:738–39. Cf., David P. Thelen, *The New Citizenship: Origins of Progressivism in Wisconsin, 1885–1900* (Columbia: University of Missouri Press, 1972); Sam Bass Warner, *Streetcar Suburbs: The Progress of Growth in Boston, 1870–1900* (Cambridge: Harvard University Press, 1962).

9. The emergence of environmentalism and social intrumentalism is the subject of studies by Morton White, *Social Thought in America: The Revolt against Formalism* (Boston: Beacon, 1947); Samuel Haber, *Efficiency and Uplift: Scientific Management in the Progressive Era* (Chicago: University of Chicago Press, 1964); Dana Francis White, "The Self-Conscious City" (Ph.D. diss., George Washington University, 1969); Thomas C. Haskell, *The Emergence of Professional Social Science: The American Social Science Association and the Nineteenth-Century Crisis of Authority* (Urbana: University of Illinois Press, 1977). Bellamy's book, first published in 1889, became an instant best seller that deeply influenced an entire generation of reformers.

10. Walton Clark, "Public Ownership of Gas Properties," as quoted in American Gas Light Association, *Proceedings* 9 (1898):67; Nord, "The Experts," pp. 221–36.

11. From the earliest discussions of utility franchises in 1866, Houstonians professed an abiding faith in the coming of competition among private suppliers. See above, Chapter 2.

12. For a general survey of Houston urban services in the mid-eighties, see the special edition of the *HDP*, 19 September 1886. More detailed descriptions of the various utilities can be found in M. N. Baker, comp., *The Manual of American Water-Works* (New York: Engineering News, 1888), p. 484; E. C. Brown, comp., *Brown's Directory of American Gas Companies* (New York: Progressive Age, 1892), pp. 112–14; *Poor's Manual* (1889), appendix, pp. 58–59; *City Directory for 1884*, p. 350; *HDP*, 3 January 1889.

13. CM Book F:265–75, 304–06, 316, 334, 597, 603–30; *HDP*, 5 December 1889.

14. CM Book F:614–17; CM Book G:1–3, 8–9, 16. For a brief account of the Fort Wayne company, see Harold C. Passer, *The Electrical Manufacturers, 1875–1890* (Cambridge: Harvard University Press, 1953), pp. 53–56.

15. According to its contract, the Fort Wayne company lost $15 per day for not having an operational plant by August 1888. The company paid the city about $3850 after almost losing the contract. See CM Book G:156, 177–79, 183, 193; *HDP*, 17, 27 November, 8 December 1888; *HDP*, 10 January, 29 March 1889.

16. Houston Light and Power Company, *Origins and History of the Houston Lighting and Power Company* (Houston: n. pub., 1940), pp. 7–13. However, the Citizens' company soon experienced problems of overloaded circuits that were similar to those of its predecessor. The demand for services kept outstripping the supply. See *HDP*, 20, 24 August, 5 December 1889.

17. *HDP*, 23 January 1889; *City Directory for 1894*, pp. 3–4; *Brown's Directory* (1892), pp. 112–14; Arthur L. Hunt, "Manufactured Gas," U.S., Department of Commerce, Bureau of the Census, *Twelfth Census of the United States, 1900: Manufacturing—Special Reports on Selected Industries*, vol. 10, pt. IV, pp. 705–22.

18. Andrew Morrison, *The City of Houston* (n.p., 1891), pp. 19–20; Houston Daily Herald, *Houston Illustrated* (Houston: Houston Daily Herald, 1893), pp. 75–83.

19. Morrison, *City of Houston*, pp. 15–16; *City Directory for 1894*, pp. 3–4. The relationship between excessive waste and the absence of an efficient meter system was established in the early eighties. See John C. Kelly, "The Benefits of the Meter System as Shown by Practical Results," American Water Works Association, *Proceedings* 1 (1882): 38–43; Edwin Darling, "Water Meters," American Water Works Association, *Proceedings* 1 (1882): 166–70; "Water Meters," *Fire and Water* 1 (1887): 242–44. For an analysis of Houston's water system, see "Water Meters," *Fire and Water*, 9 (1891): 275.

20. In 1882, the gas company had 300 private customers who, together with the city, consumed about 5.5 million cubic feet of gas. The value of this gas equaled $22,000. A decade later, the utility was generating 30 million cubic feet, which produced $90,000 worth of business. In 1899, the company reported sales of the same amount of gas to 1100 customers. See U.S., Department of Interior, Census Office, Tenth Census of the United States, 1880: Manufactures—Products of Industry MS, Schedule no. 3, p. 1; William S. Speer and John Henry Brown, eds., The Encyclopedia of the New West (Marshall: U.S. Biographical, 1881), pp. 492–95; Morrison, City of Houston, p. 17; Moody's Manual (1901), p. 536.

21. Morrison, City of Houston, pp. 16–18; Houston Daily Herald, Houston Illustrated, p. 39. For statistics of the Houston City company reorganization, see Poor's Manual (1895), appendix, pp. 1128–29; and Parlin v. Houston City Street Railroad Company, no. 302 (Equity) USCC (1895). For a comparison with national developments, see Edward E. Higgins, "The Intrinsic Value of Street Railway Investments," Street Railway Journal 10 (1894): passim. The calculations presented here are confirmed by the company's own figures. Conversion to electric traction cost about $16,700–$25,000 per mile, including the cost of building a central power station. See HDP, 13 June 1891.

22. Of the seventy positions for mayor and alderman between 1874 and 1888, twenty-one were filled by men connected to a franchised corporation (including steam railroad managers). Consult the corresponding City Directory, passim; CM Book G:193–96, 200–07.

23. HDP, 9–10 April, 28 July, 1 August 1889; GDN, March 1890, provides excellent coverage of the Houston Democratic primaries. Also see HDP, 2, 26 February 1890.

24. HDP, 23 January 1890; GDN, 18, 29 March 1890. For demographic data, see U.S., Census, 1890: Population Compendium, 1:738–39.

25. GDN, 6, 19, 30 March 1890. Cf. Carl Harris, Political Power in Birmingham, 1871–1921 (Knoxville: University of Tennessee Press, 1975); and George Brown Tindall, The Persistent Tradition in the New South (Baton Rouge: Louisiana State University Press, 1975).

26. HDP, 23 January, 1 April 1890; GDN, 13, 14, 19 March, 1–5 April 1890. For biographical information, see Industries of Houston (Houston: Elstner, 1887), p. 81; and his obituary in HDP, 26 November 1894.

27. CM Book H:42; CM Book G:536–38, 452–61, 520–30. The Carter grant gave him electric traction privileges and a thirty-five year extension of the existing franchises. In exchange, Carter made a major and expensive concession by agreeing to pay the costs of street paving along a six-inch strip on either side of the railway's right of way, in addition to the space between its tracks. During the following months, the administration approved a series of right of way extensions for Carter's company. See ibid., pp. 499–501, 549, 568, 586. The Rapid Transit Company bill was passed 6–3 over the mayor's veto, but the project did not materialize. Opposition aldermen had so encumbered and restricted the franchise that the promoters chose not to develop the utility. However, the important point remains the mayor's objection to competition in any form. In contrast, a separate proposal for a noncompetitive, interurban line between Houston and Galveston easily won administration support. See ibid., pp. 493, 499–501.

28. Sister M. Agatha, The History of Houston Heights (Houston: Premier, 1956).

29. Houston City Street Railway Company v. Mayor et al., no. 13689 11th DC (1890); Houston City Street Railway Company v. Mayor et al., 83 Texas 548 (1892). For the council's efforts to get the utility to repair the streets, see CM Book G:354, 373, 416, 422.

30. GDN, 29 March 1890; Agatha, Houston Heights, pp. 15–27, 115–18.

31. For council actions between July 1890 and January 1895, see CM Book G:508, 515, 527, 586–89, 595; CM Book H:10, 18, 22, 25, 52, 57–59, 63, 67–70, 93, 100, 128, 134, 157, 182, 199, 205, 234, 256, 262, 267–68, 290, 372, 393.

32. CM Book G:354, 373, 515; CM Book H:25, 67, 70, 100, 129, 134, 234, 255, 267–68, 271, 329, 342, 354–55, 578, 688.

33. Parlan v. Houston Company; and USIM Book 8:380. More details on Carter's manipulations are contained in the Kirby Papers, University of Houston, Houston, Texas, Box 174 (Inventory List), Box 184 (New List), Carter to Parlan, 24, 29 July 1895; and Parlan to Kirby, 5, 9, 14 August 1895. Carter attempted to force Parlan to buy the six mile Houston Heights line for $60,000 by threatening

to tear up an important section of connector track. Parlan wrote to Kirby, "[m]y opinion is that Carter, notwithstanding his protestations of friendship, etc., would not hesitate to clean me out of every cent I have been foolish enough to put in his hands, if thereby he could gain any personal advantage." See also Parlan to Kirby, 9 August 1895.

34. *Poor's Manual* (1895), pp. 1125, 1129; Parlan v. Houston Company; Higgins, "Railway Investments," pp. 104–5, 165–68, 226–30; *HDP*, 25 September, 11 October 1895.

35. For a general review, see James L. High, *A Treatise on the Law of Receivers* (3rd ed.; Chicago: Callaghan, 1894); and Henry H. Swain, "Economic Aspects of Railroad Receiverships," *Economic Studies of the American Economic Association* 3 (1898): 53–101. For a list of street railway receiverships in the depression of the 1890s, see *Street Railway Journal* 8 (July 1897): 398.

36. Parlan v. Houston Company; USIM Book 9:78–81, 124–25; *Poor's Manual* (1896), p. 1232; *Poor's Manual* (1897), p. 1031; *HDP*, 11 October 1895; *HDP*, 17 January, 16 March, 4 April 1896; Kirby Papers, Box 174 (Inventory List), Parlan to Kirby, 1 January 1896.

37. Charles D. Green, *Fire Fighters of Houston, 1838–1915* (Houston: Green, 1915), pp. 115–17; CM Book H:335–38, 348. For statistics on the Houston Water Company's expansion from 28 miles of mains and 185 hydrants to over 60 miles of mains and 555 hydrants, see Baker, *Manual of Water-Works* (1888), p. 484, and Baker, *Manual of Water-Works* (1897), p. 518.

38. House v. Houston Water Company, 22 SW 277 (1893). The civil appeals decision was confirmed by the state supreme court. See House v. Houston Water Company, 88 Texas 233 (1895). Cf. Lenzen v. City of New Braunfels, 35 SW 341 (1896), where a different civil appeals court held a municipality that owned its waterworks to be liable to citizens. However, this precedent was not followed in subsequent adjudication: Butterfield v. City of Henrietta, 61 SW 975 (1901).

39. A detailed account of the proceedings was recorded in *HDP*, 6 November 1894.

40. Ibid.; CM Book H:367–68. The company worked to fulfill its pledges. See *HDP*, 26 October 1895; *City Directory for 1895*, pp. 4–5.

41. *HDP*, 6 November 1894; CM Book H:370–71, 422, 448, 466. An extra $.50 per $100 valuation was charged shortly after the investigation. For the council's reform legislation, see CM Book H:408, 422, 448, 466, 542. Normal insurance rates were restored in 1897. See *HDP*, 8 July 1897.

42. CM Book H:495, 507, 518–25, 546. None of the ventures materialized.

43. Ibid., pp. 256, 275–76, 283, 552.

44. *HDP*, 2 March–5 April 1892; *GDN*, 1 March–6 April 1892; CM Book H:55. For biographical information on Browne, see *History of Texas* (Chicago: Lewis, 1895), p. 384.

45. CM Book H:101–03, 176–77.

46. Ibid., pp. 126–29, 149–55, 160, 207; *HDP*, 23 October 1893. In 1889, the board was established to help advise the council on the specifications and the financing of public works projects. From the beginning, mayors appointed members from among the city's largest taxpayers. In 1893, the members were T. W. House, Jr., August Bering, and Eugene Pillot. See H. P. N. Gammel, comp., *Laws of Texas, 1822–1897* (10 vols.; Austin: Gammel, 1898), 9:1324–35; CM Book H:118.

47. CM Book H:438–39.

48. *HDP*, 6 March–3 April 1894; CM Book H:358–59; 367–71, 378.

49. *GDN*, 11 April 1895.

50. Higgins v. Bordages, 88 Texas 458 (1895). The overturned precedent was Lufkin v. Galveston, 58 Texas 545 (1883). A rehearing effort attracted some of the state's most prominent law firms, including Willie and Ballinger from Galveston and Ewing and Ring from Houston. The infusion of legal talent on behalf of assessment taxation reflected the vital importance of this taxing method for Texas cities. The reason for the reversal was rooted in an unusual personnel changeover on the three-member bench. Supreme court justices were elected for six-year terms, and they were customarily renominated by the Democratic party to multiple terms. However, in 1894–95, the retirement of Justice John L. Henry and the death of Chief Justice John W. Stayton allowed Governor Hogg to appoint their replacements. The governor chose two close political lieutenants: Leroy G. Denman and Thomas J. Brown. Their ruling on homesteads, as well as other areas of the law, demonstrated an intention to pursue an activist role for the state judiciary. See Robert C. Cotner, *James Stephan Hogg: A Biography* (Austin: University of Texas Press, 1959), pp. 417–18 passim; E. W.

Winkler, ed., *Platforms of Political Parties in Texas* (Austin: University of Texas Press, 1916), pp. 214, 276, 280. The homestead case fit within larger programs of the Hogg Democrats to strengthen this institution. See Cotner, *Hogg*, pp. 338–45; and Chase v. Swayne, 88 Texas 222 (1895).

51. *GDN*, 11–12 April 1895; *HDP*, 11–13 April 1895.

52. CM Book H:566–75. Houston had a bonded debt of $1,843,000, which required approximately $100,000 per year in interest maintenance. In 1894, assessed property values stood at $22,863,000; a tax of 2 percent ad valorem was levied. Paving a mile of roadway 35 feet wide cost from $30,000 for gravel to $74,000 for two layers of brick on a six-inch gravel base.

53. Ibid.; Texas, *Constitution* (1876), art. 6, sec. 3; Houston, *City Charter* (1893), sec. 59, in Gammel, *Laws*, 9:701–02.

54. *HDP*, 15 September 1895.

55. "Houston's Water Supply," *Fire and Water* 17 (June 1895): 289.

56. *GDN*, 16 July, 1–13 August 1895. On the other hand, the paper reported that the Houston Business League supported the council plan. See ibid., 31 July 1895.

57. CM Book H:602–4, 616.

58. Ibid., pp. 617, 622; *HDP*, 22 September 1895. The resolution was supported by a plurality only in the third and fourth wards. About 20 percent of the taxpayers participated. For voter registration data, see *HDP*, 26 March 1896.

59. *HDP*, 22–23 September 1895; *GDN*, 21–22 September 1895.

60. *HDP*, 24 November, 12, 17 December 1895.

61. Ibid., 17 December 1895.

62. Ibid. The combination of morality and politics was common during the Progressive Era. Cf. William D. Miller, *Memphis during the Progressive Age, 1900–1907* (Memphis: Memphis State University Press, 1957), pp. vii–x, 64–126.

63. *HDP*, 20–21 January, 21 February 1896. The Houston group became an early member of the National Municipal League, which was proposing many of the same reforms.

64. Ibid., 28, 31 January, 25 February 1896. The central importance of loyalty to the Democracy in Southern politics is examined by C. Vann Woodward, *Origins of the New South* (Baton Rouge: Louisiana State University Press, 1951), pp. 244–49; and Tindall, *Persistent Tradition*, passim.

65. *GDN*, 2, 7–10 March 1896.

66. For biographical information on the Brashear family, see *History of Texas*, pp. 470–72; and *City Directory for 1895*, p. 124. For data on the Rice family, see Dermot H. Hardy and Ingham S. Roberts, *Historical Review of Southeast Texas* (2 vols.; Chicago: Lewis, 1910), 2:491–96.

67. *GDN*, 17–20 March 1896; CM Book J:62–63. Brashear carried the fifth and the newly-created sixth ward. Both were industrialized districts.

68. Anderson, *Urban Crisis*; Martin J. Schiesl, "The Changing Role of Public Administrators in Los Angeles, 1900–1920," in *The Age of Urban Reform: New Perspectives on the Progressive Age*, ed. Michael H. Ebner and Eugene M. Tobin (Port Washington, New York: Kennikat, 1977), pp. 102–16; Dwight Waldo, *The Administrative State* (New York: Ronald 1948); Haber, *Efficiency and Uplift*.

69. Until 1887, Houston's water supply came from the bayou. The growth of the city above the waterworks, however, made the bayou an increasingly polluted source of drinking water. Fortunately, a vast pool of artesian water was discovered at relatively shallow depths. See Green, *Fire Fighters*, pp. 125–27; McComb, *Houston*, pp. 129–33. On consumption ratios and population growth, see *Fire and Water* 1 (1887): 66; and American Water Works Association, *Proceedings* (1888): 46–48.

70. CM Book H:542; Green, *Fire Fighters*, pp. 29–31 passim. In 1913, the municipal conversion to meters was completed. See Houston, *Annual Message . . . for the Year ending 28 February 1913*, (1913), pp. 18–43.

71. CM Book H:256, 275–76, 283, 552.

72. Nathan Matthews, Jr., *The City Government of Boston* (Boston: Rockwell and Churchill, 1895), p. 180; S. M. Lindsay, "Growth and Significance of Municipal Enterprises for Profit," *Journal of Social Science* 36 (1896): 154–62.

Chapter 7

1. Robert H. Peebles, "The Galveston Harbor Controversy of the Gilded Age," *Texana* 12 (1974): 74–83; Marilyn McAdams Sibley, *The Port of Houston: A History* (Austin: University of Texas Press, 1968), pp. 114, 90–125; Harold L. Platt, "Houston at the Crossroads: The Emergence of the Urban Center of the Southwest," *Journal of the West* 8 (July 1979): 51–61.

2. *HDP*, 1 December 1896. On Johnson, see A. C. Gray, "History of the Texas Press," in *History of Texas*, ed. Dudley G. Wooten (Dallas: Scarff, 1898), pp. 410–11.

3. *HDP*, 1 December 1896.

4. Daniel J. Elazar, "Urban Problems and the Federal Government: A Historical Inquiry," *Political Science Quarterly* 82 (December 1967): 505–25.

5. Essential for understanding the reactions of the judiciary in the 1890s is Arnold M. Paul, *Conservative Crisis and the Rule of Law: Attitudes of Bar and Bench, 1887–1895* (New York: Harper and Row, 1960). The best overview of government-business relations is William Letwin, *Law and Economic Policy in America: The Evolution of the Sherman Antitrust Act* (Edinburgh: Edinburgh University Press, 1966). Three contemporary primers on franchise reform are still basic reading: Lincoln Steffins, *The Shame of the Cities* (New York: Smith, 1948); Delos F. Wilcox, *Municipal Franchises* (2 vols.; New York: McGraw-Hill, 1911); and Frank Goodnow, *Municipal Problems* (New York: Columbia University Press, 1911).

6. Assessed valuations did not increase above their 1894 level of $22,860,000 until 1899, when they rose by about 10 percent to $25,740,000. In contrast, over 17,000 new residents settled within Houston over the course of the decade, bringing its population to 44,630 people at the turn of the century. Although annual demographic statistics are not available to compare against the 1894–99 fiscal figures, there is little doubt that five years without additional revenues made allocation decisions more difficult. For city finances, see CM Book H:438–39; CM Book K:155–61. For census data, consult U.S., Department of Commerce, Bureau of the Census, *Twelfth Census of the United States, 1900: Population*, vol. 1, pt. I. The geographic sprawl of Houston will be analyzed in greater detail below. For a broad interpretation of urban progressivism that gives emphasis to the depression of the nineties, see David P. Thelen, *The New Citizenship: Origins of Progressivism in Wisconsin, 1885–1900* (Columbia: University of Missouri Press, 1972).

7. C. Vann Woodward, *Origins of the New South* (Baton Rouge: Louisiana State University Press, 1951); Paul M. Gaston, *New South Creed: A Study in Myth Making* (New York: Knopf, 1970). Also useful are the historiographical essays in Blaine A. Brownell and David R. Goldfield, eds., *The City in Southern History: The Growth of Urban Civilization in the South* (Port Washington, New York: Kennikat, 1977), chaps. 4–5.

8. See above, note 1.

9. For Brashear, see *History of Texas* (Chicago: Lewis, 1895), pp. 470–72; *HDP*, 24 March 1892. For Rice, see Dermot H. Hardy and Robert S. Ingham, *Historical Review of Southeast Texas* (2 vols.; Chicago: Lewis, 1910), 2:491–96. A full examination of kinship ties among Houston's elite families lies outside the scope of this study. A brief look at Horace Baldwin Rice's relatives will illustrate these close knit patterns of power and influence. The mayor's father, Fredrick Allen, was a brother of the merchant prince, William Marsh Rice, and a partner in his commercial and railroad ventures. Fredrick married Charlotte Baldwin, whose father, Horace, also was an early pioneer, shipping magnate, and mayor. In 1883, H. B. Rice married Georgia Dumble, the daughter of yet another successful early settler. Four years later, his brother married the governor's daughter, Mary T. Ross. Of course, the two brothers also kept close ties to their uncle William's side of the family.

10. *HDP*, 7, 15 January, 11, 26 February 1898. Of the 9543 registered voters, 2026 were listed as black. For a ward-by-ward breakdown of voter statistics, see ibid., 24 March 1898. Houston's experience was a common one throughout the South during this period. See, for example, Howard N. Rabinowitz, "From Exclusion to Segregation: Southern Race Relations, 1865–1890," *Journal of American History* 63 (September 1976): 325–50; and J. Morgan Kousser, *The Shaping of Southern Politics: Suffrage Restriction and the Establishment of the One-Party South, 1880–1910* (New Haven: Yale University Press, 1974).

11. The two quotations are found in *HDP*, 9 March 1898, and CM Book J:395, respectively. For Brashear's campaign, survey *HDP*, 7 January–15 March 1898. For the aldermanic slates, see *HDP*, 13 March 1898. Cf. the budgets of 1896, 1897, and 1898 in CM Book J:20–22, 202–05, 395, respectively.

12. Efforts to organize street railway workers in Houston began a year earlier. A short strike allowed the men to join a union. See *HDP*, 4–6 July 1897. In 1898, the union demanded $.18 per hour and a nine-hour day, instead of $.16 per hour, and a twelve and a half-hour day. Besides the drive for a closed shop, the reinstatement of all strikers and their seniority became strike issues. See ibid., 10–22 March 1898; and Robert E. Zeigler, "The Workingmen of Houston, Texas, 1865–1914" (Ph.D. diss., Texas Technological University, 1972), pp. 166–88.

13. *HDP*, 20, 24 March 1898. Cf. Herbert G. Gutman, "Protestantism and the American Labor Movement: The Christian Spirit in the Gilded Age," *American Historical Review* 72 (October 1966): 74–101.

14. *HDP*, 26 March 1898. Rice carried only the third ward (900 v. 852), which contained the largest concentration of white middle-class voters.

15. Ibid., 27–31 March 1898.

16. CM Book J:620. The politics of municipal ownership will be considered below.

17. Sibley, *Port of Houston*, pp. 114, 123–27. For contemporary views, see the account of Houston's congressional representative, Thomas H. Ball, *The Port of Houston: How It Came to Pass* (Houston: n.pub., n.d. [1936]).

18. *HDP*, 12 April 1898. Also see ibid., 10 July, 4 August, 25 October 1898.

19. For biographical information on Potter, see ibid., 17 February 1899. His plans and the city council's reactions are found in the CM Book J:602–3, 625–26, 631, 685–86; *HDP*, 21 February 1899. Houston's innovative use of a garbage crematory was discussed at the League of American Municipalities, *Proceedings of the Third Annual Convention* (Syracuse, New York, 1899), p. 26. For a broader perspective on sanitary reform in the United States, see Martin V. Melosi, " 'Out of Sight, Out of Mind': The Environment and Disposal of Municipal Refuse, 1860–1920," *Historian* 35 (August 1973): 621–41. For an early progress report on the Potter plan, see *HDP*, 25 July 1900.

20. See Sibley, *Port of Houston*, pp. 123–27.

21. For the new city inspectors, see CM Book J:554, 579; Houston, Ordinance Book, (Houston: City Secretary's Office, 1910), pp. 473, 478–80. In addition, the council established a boiler inspector upon the request of Houston manufacturers. See Ordinance Book, pp. 519–28. Typically, the ordinance closely copied a national model code. For the development of the Waterworks Committee, see CM Book J:486, 592, 617–20, 646, 689.

22. CM Book J:627–28, 636, 640; Ordinance Book, pp. 492. For the resulting progress of telephone services, see *HDP*, 14, 18 March, 22 June, 15 September, 5, 29 October, 7, 23, November 1899; *HDP*, 21 March 1900. In addition, the council granted a similar franchise to the Postal Cable Telegraph Company, which also was operating by 1900. See Ordinance Book, pp. 457–59.

23. CM Book K:155–61; ibid., J:617–23.

24. *HDP*, 16–18 May, 16 June 1899.

25. CM Book J:622–23; CM Book K:66, 73–74, 155–61; Ordinance Book, p. 547.

26. CM Book J:618.

27. See for example, *HDP*, 9 May, 26 September 1899.

28. Clifton K. Yearley, *The Money Machines: The Breakdown and Reform of Governmental and Party Finance in the North, 1860–1920* (Albany: State University of New York Press, 1970), pp. 137–250, 336–64.

29. Adams Express Company v. Ohio State Auditor, 165 US 194 (1897). A year earlier, the Court drew a direct analogy between the tax power and the police power in Turnpike Company v. Sanford, 164 US 578 (1896). Also consider the reaction of a leading economist, E. R. A. Seligman, "The Taxation of Franchises," *Municipal Affairs* 6 (1903): 765–73. The *Adams Express* case was complicated by interstate commerce issues, but the Court had previously ruled on these questions in Pullman Palace Car Company v. Pennsylvania, 141 US 18 (1891).

30. Express Company v. Ohio, 165 US 194 (1897) and 166 US 185 (1897).

31. *HDP*, 9–10, 19–29 September 1899; CM Book K:55, 365. The 1876 statute was vague. See Texas, *Civil Statutes, Annotated* (Sayles, 1897), arts. 5061–62. The validity of franchise taxation was upheld in State v. Austin and Northwest Railroad Company, 94 Texas 630 (1901); and Dallas v. Dallas Consolidated Street Railway Company, 95 Texas 268 (1902).

32. *HDP*, 5 October, 30 November 1897; CM Book J:350–51, 374.

33. Massachusetts Loan and Trust Company v. Citizens' Electric Company, nos. 343 and 369 (Equity) USCC (1898); *HDP*, 8 January 1898. These utility receiverships offer a gold mine of reliable information for historians of technology, business, and economics.

34. Ibid.

35. Trust Company v. Citizens' Company, no. 343 (Equity); USIM Book 9:619–37; USIM Book 11:184–90, 425–28, 495–98. The strike by company workers can be followed in *HDP*, 13–19 June 1899. The court allowed a pay raise but refused to recognize a closed shop. For the suit against the city, see Blake Dupree, Receiver v. City of Houston, no. 1949 USCC (1900); *HDP*, 6 October 1900.

36. Trust Company v. Citizens' Company, no. 343 (Equity); James C. Bonbright and Gardiner C. Means, *The Holding Company: Its Public Significance and Its Regulation* (New York: McGraw-Hill, 1932), pp. 98–108.

37. *HDP*, 2 May 1900; 3 August 1902; 24 February, 25 October 1903. I think that the meter was the key to rapid growth for most urban utility services. As the above stories show, private users consumed very little energy until meters were installed. In 1897, for example, 15 years after the introduction of electric lighting, only 400 homes had incandescent lamps. In comparison, 6,000 Houstonians used 82,000 lights in 1908. See *City Directory for 1908*, p. 9. The importance of the meter to the gas and the water services has been noted in previous chapters.

38. David Nord, "The Experts versus the Experts: Conflicting Philosophies of Municipal Utility Regulation in the Progressive Era," *Wisconsin Magazine of History* 58 (Spring 1975): 219–36; Philip J. Funigiello, *Toward a National Power Policy: The New Deal and the Electric Utility Industry, 1933–1941* (Pittsburgh: University of Pittsburgh Press, 1973); Bonbright and Means, *The Holding Company*; Ellis W. Hawley, *The New Deal and the Problem of Monopoly* (Princeton: Princeton University Press, 1966), pp. 325–60.

39. Texas, *Civil Statutes, Supplement* (Herron, 1903), Title 25, chap. 3; CM Book K:86–87, 106–9. The result was 607–407.

40. CM Book K:141–61; *HDP*, 25 January, 7 February 1900.

41. *HDP*, 15 January–4 April 1900.

42. Ibid., 16 January, 27–28 February, 11 March 1900.

43. Ibid., 9–11 March 1900; *GDN*, 23 March, 4 April 1900.

44. *GDN*, 27, 29 March 1900; *HDP*, 22, 29–30 March 1900.

45. *HDP*, 25, 30 March, 4 April 1900; CM Book K:199–201.

46. See above, note 1; Harold F. Williamson et al., *The American Petroleum Industry*, vol. 2: *The Age of Energy, 1899–1959* (Evanston: Northwestern University Press, 1963), pp. 17–24; Seth S. Mckay and Odie B. Fauk, *Texas after Spindletop* (Austin: Steck-Vaughn, 1965), chap. 1.

47. *HDP*, 7 August 1900; CM Book K:241–43, 248–50, 256–58, 277.

48. CM Book K:321; *HDP*, 14 August 1900. The newspaper headline noted a "Stormy Session."

49. CM Book K:324, 331–32, 337–40, 350, 354; *HDP*, 25 January, 29 April, 19–21 August 1900.

50. *HDP*, 4 September 1900.

51. Ibid., 2 May 1900. The report includes a full inventory of the company's new facilities.

52. Ibid., 25 August, 27 September, 24 October 1900; Trust Company v. Citizens' Company, no. 343 (Equity).

53. CM Book K:365, 350–479 passim. By March 1901, the city had withheld almost $50,000 from the light company and $28,000 from the waterworks. At the same time, unpaid special assessments by the streetcar company accumulated to over $60,000. See ibid., p. 477; CM Book L:34.

54. For the refunding controversy, see CM Book K:380, 393–94, 406–7, 429, 435, 471–72; *HDP*, 17 November 1900. The council decision was based on the ruling in Storrie v. Houston, no. 1779 USCC (1895), which awarded the street contractor $127,000 in his suit for the balance of unpaid

assessments. For the distribution of paving assessments by ward, see CM Book L:62. For other reports on improvements and services on a ward-by-ward basis, see CM Book K:226, 242; CM Book L:42.

55. CM Book K:479; *HDP*, 26–27 January 1901. By May, Brashear was again fully occupied with his legal practice. Ironically, he was appointed the Master in Chancery in the second receivership of the street railway company. Another former mayor, H. B. Rice, served as the receiver, while a future mayor, A. L. Jackson, acted as the receiver's attorney. See *HDP*, 30 May 1901.

56. *HDP*, 26–27 January, 17–19 February 1901; CM Book L:19. For biographical information on Woolford, see *HDP*, 21 February 1901; Hardy and Ingham, *Southeast Texas*, 2:513.

57. CM Book L:30–40, 47–49, passim; *HDP*, 2–27 February, 14 May 1901.

58. See above, note 46; Herbert Mason, Jr., *Death From the Sea* (New York: Dial, 1972). Cf. E. R. Cheesborough, *Galveston's Commission Form of Government* (Galveston: Reprint for the Deepwater Committee, 1910), which provides the best contemporary account.

59. *HDP*, 4–10 January 1901.

60. Ibid., 9 January 1901.

61. Ibid., 24 March 1901; ibid., 27, 29 January 1901; James C. Simmon, "The Great Spindletop [Texas] Oil Rush," *American West* 17 (January/February 1980): 10–13, 61–62. For formation of the company, see *HDP*, 17 February, 24 March 1901.

62. Ball, *Port of Houston*; Sibley, *Port of Houston*, pp. 123–27.

63. Sibley, *Port of Houston*, p. 114.

64. See above, note 58.

65. See Michael H. Ebner and Eugene M. Tobin, eds., *The Age of Urban Reform: New Perspectives on the Progressive Age* (Port Washington, New York: Kennikat, 1977).

66. See James Willard Hurst, *Law and the Conditions of Freedom in the Nineteenth Century United States* (Madison: University of Wisconsin Press, 1956), chap. 3.

67. *HDP*, 22 May 1897. Johnson's justification of a large increase in Houston's bonded indebtedness echoed the rationale of one of the leading economists of the new school of social science experts: Henry Carter Adams, *Public Debt: An Essay in the Science of Finance* (New York: Appleton, 1895), p. 351. Carter was among the first to call for a reversal of the Gilded Age's reforms that restricted the fiscal powers of the city. Efforts to keep the cities in a fiscal straitjacket were not peculiar to the United States. See Clifton K. Yearley, "The 'Provincial Party' and the Megalopolises: London, Paris, and New York, 1850–1910," *Comparative Studies in Society and History* 15 (January 1973): 51–88.

Chapter 8

1. John Higham, *Writing American History* (Bloomington: Indiana University Press, 1970), pp. 73–102; Henry Adams, *The Education of Henry Adams* (orig. pub. 1918; Boston: Houghton Mifflin, Sentry ed., 1946), pp. 331–45; Henry F. May, *The End of American Innocence: A Study of the First Years of Our Own Time, 1912–1917* (Chicago: Quadrangle, 1959).

2. David M. Chalmers, *Neither Socialism nor Monopoly: Theodore Roosevelt and the Decision to Regulate the Railroads* (Philadelphia: Lippincott, 1976), pp. 1–44; Thomas K. McGraw, "Regulation in America: A Review Article," *Business History Review* 49 (Summer 1975): 159–83; Robert Wiebe, "The Progressive Years, 1900–1917," in *The Reinterpretation of American History and Culture*, ed. William H. Cartwright and Richard L. Watson (Washington: National Council for Social Studies, 1973), pp. 425–42.

3. Martin J. Schiesl, *The Politics of Efficiency* (Berkeley: University of California Press, 1977); Kenneth Fox, *Better City Government: Innovation in American Urban Politics, 1850–1937* (Philadelphia: Temple University Press, 1977); Samuel Haber, *Efficiency and Uplift: Scientific Management in the Progressive Era, 1890–1920* (Chicago: University of Chicago Press, 1964).

4. Blaine A. Brownell and David R. Goldfield, eds., *The City in Southern History: The Growth of Urban Civilization in the South* (Port Washington, New York: Kennikat, 1977), pp. 92–158;

Michael H. Ebner and Eugene M. Tobin, eds., *The Age of Urban Reform: New Perspectives on the Progressive Age* (Port Washington, New York: Kennikat, 1977).

5. Cf. Martin J. Schiesl, "Politicians in Disguise: The Changing Role of Public Administrators in Los Angeles, 1900–1920," in Ebner and Tobin, eds., *Age of Urban Reform*, pp. 102–16.

6. J. Morgan Kousser, *The Shaping of Southern Politics: Suffrage Restriction and the Establishment of the One-Party South, 1880–1910* (New Haven: Yale University Press, 1974), p. 229; Jack Temple Kirby, *Darkness at the Dawning: Race and Reform in the Progressive South* (Philadelphia: Lippincott, 1972); Lawrence C. Goodwyn, "Populist Dreams and Negro Rights: East Texas as a Case Study," *American Historical Review* 77 (December 1971): 1443–56.

7. Clinton Rodgers Woodruff, ed., *City Government by Commission* (New York: Appleton, 1911); Ernest S. Bradford, *Commission Government in American Cities* (New York: Macmillan, 1919). Cf. James Weinstein, "Organized Business and the City Commission and Manager Movements," *Journal of Southern History* 28 (May 1962): 166–82; and Bradley Rice, "The Galveston Plan of City Government by Commission: The Birth of a Progressive Idea," *Southwestern Historical Quarterly* 73 (April 1975): 367–408.

8. Michael H. Frisch, *Town into City: Springfield, Massachusetts, and the Meaning of Community, 1840–1880* (Cambridge: Harvard University Press, 1972), pp. 249, 244–50. Also see Jon C. Teaford, *City and Suburb: The Political Fragmentation of Metropolitan America, 1850–1970* (Baltimore: Johns Hopkins University Press, 1979).

9. *HDP*, 27 January 1904.

10. Cf. Melvin G. Holli, *Reform in Detroit: Hazen S. Pingree and Urban Politics* (New York: Oxford University Press, 1969), pp. 161–81.

11. *HDP*, 14, 17 May, 11 November 1901.

12. Ibid., 10 July, 4 August 1898.

13. Ibid., 1–10 January, 7 December 1901.

14. Cf. *City Directory for 1900*, p. 409; and *City Directory for 1905*, pp. 8–10, which contains a full list of the League's membership. An organizational history of the League is provided by Benajah Harvey Carroll, *Standard History of Houston, Texas* (Knoxville: Crew, 1912), pp. 217, 323–25.

15. For information on Rice, see *City Directory for 1905*, p. 334; on Bonner, see *HDP*, 1 May 1903.

16. See above, Chapter 6; and *HDP*, 21–24 January 1902. For Holt's political biography, see *GDN*, 1 April 1886; and E. W. Winkler, ed., *Platforms of Political Parties in Texas* (Austin: University of Texas Press, 1916), passim.

17. *HDP*, 26 January 1901; John Ozias King, "The Early History of the Houston Oil Company of Texas, 1901–1908" (M.A. thesis, University of Houston, 1958), pp. 26–37, 85–130. Besides Bonner, Kirby's men included Joe Eagle, C. A. Mitchner, and J. M. Coleman. These men ran the Holt campaign. Cf. King, "Houston Oil Company," and *HDP*, 24 January, 14 March 1902; *HC*, 7–8, 14 March, 2 April 1902. In 1904, the centerpiece of Kirby's empire, the Houston Oil Company, went into receivership.

18. Both dailies devoted extensive space to the campaign. See *HC*, 4 March–2 April 1902; and *HDP*, 14 January–2 April 1902. For a brief history of Bailey's pro-labor, pro-Brashear paper, the *Houston Herald and Evening Journal*, see A. C. Gray, "History of the Texas Press," in *Comprehensive History of Texas*, ed. Dudley Wooten (2 vols.; Dallas: Scarff, 1898), 1:410–11; and *City Directory for 1903*, pp. 54–55. The *Post*'s managing editor, Marcellus Foster, became the editor of the *Chronicle*.

19. *HDP*, 2, 5 April 1902.

20. Ibid., 1 April 1902. The *Chronicle* also drew images linking municipal reform and moral purity. See *HC*, 4, 10, 21 March 1902.

21. John M. Coleman, quoted in *HC*, 17 March 1902. Coleman was an attorney and active Holt supporter. See *City Directory for 1903*, p. 110; and *HDP*, 14 March 1902. For the development of Houston's accounting system, see CM Book G: 338–41, CM Book H: 534–36, and CM Book J: 586. Cf. Clifton K. Yearley, *The Money Machines: The Breakdown and Reform of Governmental and*

Party Finances in the North, 1860–1920 (Albany: State University of New York Press, 1970), pp. 146, 154–56.

22. See above, note 3; Alan D. Anderson, *The Origin and Resolution of an Urban Crisis: Baltimore, 1890–1930* (Baltimore: Johns Hopkins University Press, 1977). For reactions in Houston, see *HDP*, 16, 26 May, 13 June, 23 November 1900; *HDP*, 11, 13 February 1901.

23. CM Book K:492–93, CM Book L:456–57, CM Book M:50–58. City revenue between 1900 and 1903 grew from $563,000 to $759,000. The council received reports on improvements, which were divided on a ward-by-ward basis. See CM Book L:46, 62.

24. CM Book L:577–78; CM Book M:7, 318, 350–55, 374–75; *HDP*, 13, 20, 28 May 1902. Kirby was deeply impressed with Haskins and Sells from their work on his large ventures. See King, "Houston Oil Company," pp. 37–40, 85–90. The New Yorkers installed similar innovative systems in many other cities. See *National Cyclopaedia of American Biography* (54 vols.; New York: White, 1937), 19:514–15, 12:594.

25. *HDP*, 22 October 1902; CM Book M:207–8. For information on Watkins, see *HDP*, 31 March 1902.

26. These goals are outlined in CM Book M:207–08; *HDP*, 9 November 1902. The offices that would become appointive included the assessor-collector, street commissioner, chief of police, health officer, and city attorney. Cf. National Municipal League, *A Municipal Program*, a report of a Committee of the National Municipal League (New York: Macmillan, 1900).

27. *HDP*, 7, 18 February 1903. Cf. Teaford, *City and Suburb*, chaps. 2–3.

28. *HDP*, 16–18 February 1903.

29. Ibid., 27 February, 3, 7, 19, 30 March 1903; Houston, *Charter* (1904), pp. 3–63.

30. CM Book M:355.

31. Ibid., pp. 397–400, 435, 466–67; CM Book N:47–48, 56, 76–79. For reports on the deficiencies of the sewerage system, see *HDP*, 13 March, 13 May 1902.

32. Melvin G. Holli, *Reform in Detroit: Hazen S. Pingree and Urban Politics* (New York: Oxford University Press, 1969), p. 180.

33. Haber, *Efficiency and Uplift*, pp. 99–116; Robert Wiebe, *The Search for Order, 1877–1920* (New York: Hill and Wang, 1967), pp. 169–174.

34. City of Houston v. Houston City Street Railway Company, no. 24864 11th DC (1899); Houston Electric Street Railway Company v. City of Houston, no. 28686 11th DC (1900), and no. 30319 55th DC (1901). In May 1901, the company agreed to pay $20,000 in assessments if all suits were continued for one year. A few days later, the company was placed into receivership. See CM Book L:109; *HDP*, 28 May 1901, 25 October 1902.

35. CM Book L:102–03, 110, 150–51, 163, 180, 221, 276, 293, 308, 373, 392–93, 418, 446–47, 523; *HDP*, 8 October, 24 December 1901; *HDP*, 18 April, 14 May 1902; *HC*, 25–30 November 1901.

36. The new owners immediately pumped about $250,000 into capital improvements. See *HDP*, 21 August, 16 November 1902; and *City Director for 1903*, pp. 3–5. For insight into the consolidation movement, see *Street Railway Journal* 8 (1892): 94. For a history of Stone and Webster, see Russel Robb, "Early History of the Firm," *Stone and Webster Public Service Journal* 1 (1907): 4–5, 48, 233–35.

37. Throughout 1902, for example, the company's efforts to use a new city bridge were frustrated because no general compromise was effected. After a settlement was reached, the right of way grant was quickly obtained. See CM Book M:5, 80–82, 149, 166, 202, 371. By the early 1900s, even local utility men preached cooperation with municipal officials. See Southwestern Gas, Electric and Street Railroad Association, Proceedings of the Third Annual Meeting (Houston, 1901), as reported in the *Southern Industrial and Lumber Review* 7 (1901): 19–29.

38. *HDP*, 16 February, 2 November, 10 December 1902. Also see ibid., 10, 27 August 1902.

39. CM Book M:19, 40–41, 94–107; *HDP*, 5 August 1902; *HC*, 29 February, 22–29 July 1902. In October, Stone amended the city's complaint against the company to raise the city's claim from $24,000 to $230,000. See Houston v. Railway Company, no. 24864 11th DC.

40. CM Book M:127–35, 205–6, 213–16, 244, 266–67, 278–84; *HDP*, 5, 8, 13 August, 28

October, 2, 26 November, 7 December 1902. A copy of the settlement can be found in Houston, *Charter* (1904), pp. 557–62.

41. Cf. Houston, *Charter* (1904), pp. 557–62, and the franchises listed in Delos F. Wilcox, *Municipal Franchises* (2 vols.; New York: McGraw-Hill, 1911), 1:11 and passim. Cf. the financial statistics in *American Street Railway Investments* (New York: Street Railway Publishing, 1902), p. 126, and *American Street Railway Investments* (New York: Street Railway Publishing, 1906), p. 387. For the impacts of the compromise, see *HDP*, 8–9 January, 1 February, 14 March, 24 May, 17 October, 5 November 1903. In February 1903, all litigation was dropped.

42. For the change in gas rates, see CM Book M:85–86, 88, 141; *HDP*, 16 January 1903. The compromise with the electric company is found in CM Book M:397–400; *HDP*, 9 January, 24 February, 21 March 1903.

43. The competition for franchises in new types of public service enterprises was considerable. For a list of six grants to pipeline ventures, see Houston, *Charter* (1904), pp. 606–14; and Houston, Ordinance Book (Houston: City Secretary's Office, 1910), pp. 11, 158–59, 183–84, 213–15. For the interurban franchise and the Stone and Webster venture, see Houston, *Charter* (1904), pp. 565–74; and George W. Hilton and John F. Due, *The Electric Interurban Railway in America* (Stanford: Stanford University Press, 1960), pp. 378–79. For the sale of the telephone and gas companies, see *HDP*, 23 November 1902, and 2, 29 March 1905.

44. In 1903, the assessed value of Scanlan's real estate was over $200,000. The waterworks itself was worth about $1,000,000. See *HDP*, 17 April, 22 November 1903.

45. CM Book M:52–57, 207–8. In January 1903, the municipal corporation's bonded indebtedness stood at $3 million, while its assessed valuations totaled $31.3 million. See ibid., pp. 350–58. A complete text of the proposal is found in *HDP*, 9 November 1902. For the company suit, see Houston Water Company v. City of Houston, no. 32098 11th DC (1902).

46. CM Book M:262, 331–37, 346–47, 363, 544–45, 559, 569–70, 578–91; CM Book N:39–41, 47, 56, 76–79; *HDP*, 5–6, 16, 24, 27 February, 3, 19 March, 4 April–8 May, 6, 17 June 1903; Houston, Ordinance Book, 1:768–69; Houston, *Charter* (1904), pp. 3–63; City of Houston v. Houston Water Company, no. 32446 11th DC (1902).

47. City of Houston v. Houston Water Company, no. 33680 11th DC (1903); *HDP*, 3, 5 August 1903; *HC*, 31 July, 3, 5, August 1903; CM Book N:39–41, 47, 50, 56, 76–79, 104–05, 141–44, 169, 178; Houston, Ordinance Book, 2:27–28, 36–37. The tentative probes of investors never developed into serious negotiations. See *HDP*, 25 September, 15 October, 3, 7 November 1903; *HC*, 3 November 1903.

48. Houston Water Company v. City of Houston, no. 50 or 56? (Equity) USCC (Southern District of Texas, 1903). Unfortunately, the records of this case could not be located. Local newspapers, however, provided extensive coverage: see *HDP*, 3 November 1903; *HC*, 4 November 1903. For the hasty repeal of the ordinances, see CM Book N:198–99. For the removal of the city's franchise forfeiture suit to the national courts, see Houston v. Water Company, no. 33680 11th DC; and 11th DIM Book 15:405.

49. *HDP*, 1–2 December 1903; ibid., 31 January, 4–5 February, 24–31 March, 6 April, 9, 27 September, 2 October 1904; CM Book N:220, 321, 426–27. For a brief history of the city's municipal waterworks, see Houston, *Annual Report . . . for the Year ending 28 February 1913*. (1913), pp. 18–43.

50. James Willard Hurst, *Law and the Conditions of Freedom in the Nineteenth Century United States* (Madison: University of Wisconsin Press, 1965), chap. 3; Morton Keller, *Affairs of State: Public Life in Late Nineteenth Century America* (Cambridge: Harvard University Press, 1977), pt. II.

51. Kousser, *Southern Politics*, pp. 230, 196–209; see above, note 6. Cf. John Higham, *Strangers in the Land: Patterns of American Nativism, 1860–1925* (New York: Atheneum, 1963).

52. CM Book N:21, 41–42, 61–63, 70, 75, 91, 108, 122, 129–30, 157; *HDP*, 23 August 1, 9, 22 September, 13 October 1903; Houston, Ordinance Book, 2:33–34. For a look at the New Orleans model, see A. R. Holcombe, "The Separate Streetcar Law in New Orleans," *Outlook* 72 (1902): 746–47; Dale A. Somers, "Black and White in New Orleans: A Study in Urban Race Relations, 1865–1900," *Journal of Southern History* 40 (February 1974): 19–42.

53. *HDP*, 8 March 1904; ibid., 2, 5 November 1903; *HC*, 2, 5 November 1904; CM Book N:382, 412–18. Payne wanted to seat blacks from the back of the car forward and whites in an opposite manner. See Letter from H. K. Payne to the HDP (*HDP*, 15 March 1904).

54. *HDP*, 26 February, 24 March 1898; ibid., 29 March 1900; ibid., 5 April 1902; *HC*, 1 February 1904; Texas, *Revised Civil Statutes, Supplement* (Herron, 1903), Title 36, c. 9; Houston, *Charter* (1904), pp. 455–70; and U.S., Department of Commerce, Bureau of the Census, *Statistical Abstract of the United States, 1910*, p. 650. Local records and census data show that 10,500 of 13,800 eligible voters were registered in 1900, but only 5700 of 17,300 persons could vote four years later.

55. *HDP*, 16 February 1904; *HC*, 16 February 1904. For preliminary maneuvers, see *HDP*, 31 January, 3, 10–11 February 1904. After Holt lost a primary election for the U.S. Congress, he retired from active political life. See *HDP*, 1–10 August 1903.

56. *HC*, 22–23 February, 1–5 March 1904. Cf. *HDP*, 16 February–5 March 1904.

57. *HC*, 6 March 1904.

58. Cf. CM Book L:456–57; CM Book M:350–58; and *HDP*, 26 January 1904.

59. George K. Turner, "Galveston: A Business Corporation," *McClure's* 27 (1906): 610–20; H. J. Haskel, "The Texas Idea: City Government by a Board of Directors," *Outlook* 85 (1907): 839–43; George Wharton James, "Two Successful Experiments in Civic Government: Galveston and Houston," *Arena* 38 (1907): 144–49; Woodruff, *City Commission*, passim.

60. Cf. Alwyn Barr, "Occupational and Geographic Mobility in San Antonio," *Social Science Quarterly* 51 (September 1970): 396–403.

61. *HDP*, 23 March 1904; ibid., 2, 9 April, 15–30 May, 2 June 1904; Robert E. Ziegler, "The Workingman in Houston, Texas, 1865–1914" (Ph.D. diss., Texas Technological University, 1972), pp. 144–53, 203–26.

62. *HDP* , 3–7, 13 June, 7–8, 24, 31 July, 26, 30 August 1904. The community's changing attitudes towards labor were symbolized by the formation of a "Citizens' Alliance," which was pledged to preserve law and order between labor and capital. See ibid., 17, 20 July 1904; *City Directory for 1905*, p. 50.

63. *HDP*, 21 September, 12 October 1904; Zeigler, "Workingman," pp. 144–53.

64. Carroll, *Standard History*, p. 101.

65. *HDP*, 21 December 1886; ibid., 11 January 1887; CM Book F:451, 516.

66. E. R. Cheesborough, *Galveston's Commission Form of City Government* (Galveston: Reprint for the Deepwater Committee, 1910).

67. Ibid.; *GDN*, 16–29 September, 18 October, 1–2 December 1900. Also see note 59 above; and Rice, "Galveston Plan," pp. 367–408.

68. *HDP*, 11 September 1902. Also see ibid., 23 November 1900; ibid., 5 February, 31 August, 24 October 1902; ibid., 10 September 1903.

69. Ibid., 5 October 1902.

70. *Ex Parte* Lewis, 45 Texas Criminal Appeals 1, 73 SW 811 (1903). The court drew heavily on Thomas M. Cooley's reasoning in the landmark case, People v. Hurlbut, 24 Michigan 44 (1871). See editor Johnson's unhappy response in *HDP*, 27 March 1903. Cf. Brown v. City of Galveston, 97 Texas 1 (1903); and Commissioners' Court of Nolan County v. Beall, 98 Texas 104 (1909). The two historical, legal, and philosophical sides of the argument over local self-government are ably presented by Amasa M. Eaton, "The Right to Local Self-Government," *Harvard Law Review* 13–14 (1900–1901): passim; and Howard Lee McBain, "The Doctrine of an Inherent Right to Self-Government," *Columbia Law Review* 16 (1916): 190–216, 299–322.

71. *HDP*, 12 March 1904; ibid., 16 October 1903.

72. CM Book N:499, 530–33, 550; CM Book O:12–13, 21–22; *HDP*, 14–15 June 1904. The important ruling in Kettle v. City of Dallas, [80 SW 874 (1904)], established that special ad valorem tax districts were constitutional and applied to homesteads.

73. CM Book N:593–94; CM Book O:12–13, 21–22; *HDP*, 14 July, 28 August 1904. For the similar views of former alderman Watkins, who subsequently became the first vice president of the League and the president of the school board, see *HDP*, 11 September 1904. For biographical information on the two men, see *HDP*, 31 March 1902; *City Directory for 1905*, pp. 8–10 passim. The

aldermen based their accusations of tax evasion by the rich on solid fact. Consider that in September 1904, a group of four wealthy landowners attempted to persuade the council to accept 40 percent of the $29,000 assessed against their property for the previous two years. See *HDP*, 17, 20 September, 4 October 1904; CM Book O:318–21. For a list of large property owners, see *HDP*, 22 November 1903.

74. *HDP*, 24–27 October 1904; *HC*, 27–28 October 1904; CM Book O:155–56.

75. *HC*, 1–2 November 1904; *HDP*, 1 November 1904.

76. *HDP*, 1 November 1904; *HC*, 1–3 November 1904. The meeting produced a special committee composed of representatives of the Business League, Manufacturer's Association, Cotton Exchange, Commercial Bureau, Builder's Exchange, and Citizen's Alliance. The inclusion of the latter organization, which was formed in reaction to the street railway strike, suggests why the Labor Council was absent. See above, note 62.

77. *HDP*, 6 December 1904; ibid., 4, 11, 13 December 1904; *HC*, 21 November, 10 December 1904; CM Book O:214–15.

78. The mayor appointed two citizens from each ward. His choices included such fellow leaders as Kirby, J. S. Rice, State District Judge E. P. Hamblem, and former mayor John Browne. See CM Book O:238; *HDP*, 12, 25, 30 December 1904; *HDP*, 12 February 1905. A full text is found in *HDP*, 21 January 1905.

79. *HDP*, 6–12 February 1905; *HC*, 11 February 1905; CM Book O:284–91.

80. *HDP*, 16–25 February 1905, 4, 19 March 1905; *HC*, 24 February, 25 March 1905.

81. *HDP*, 19–27 March, 14–29 May 1905; *HC*, 25, 30 May 1905. The commissioners were Gaston, James A. Appleby, and James B. Marmion. For biographical data, see *HDP*, 28 May 1905.

Chapter 9

1. H. B. Rice, a speech presented to the Chicago Commercial Club on December 10, 1910, quoted in Benajah Harvey Carroll, *Standard History of Houston, Texas* (Knoxville: Crew, 1912), p. 99.

2. H. J. Haskel, "The Texas Idea: City Government by a Board of Directors," *Outlook* 85 (1907): 839–43. Also see Clinton Rodgers Woodruff, ed., *City Government by Commission* (New York: Appleton, 1911), pp. 227–42 passim.

3. Robert Wiebe, *The Search for Order, 1877–1920* (New York: Hill and Wang, 1967), p. 169; Martin J. Schiesl, *The Politics of Efficiency* (Berkeley: University of California Press, 1977).

4. J. Morgan Kousser, *The Shaping of Southern Politics: Suffrage Restriction and the Establishment of the One-Party South, 1880–1910* (New Haven: Yale University Press, 1974); Jack Temple Kirby, *Darkness at the Dawning: Race and Reform in the Progressive South* (Philadelphia: Lippincott, 1972).

5. Dr. S. O. Young, *A Thumb-Nail History of the City of Houston, Texas* (Houston: Reen, 1912), p. 22.

6. For the labor legislation, see Houston, *Charter* (1904), secs. 877–91; and Houston, Ordinance Book (Houston: City Secretary's Office, 1910), 2:221. The Houston *Annual Report . . . for the Year ending 28 February 1913.* (1913), pp. 18–43, gives a detailed account of the city waterworks and its program to install meters. For the outcome of the city's legal battle with the utility, see City of Houston v. Houston Water Company, no. 32446 11th DC; Hartford Fire Insurance Company v. City of Houston, 102 Texas 273 (1909).

7. The quotation is from Carroll, *Standard History*, p. 101; for Rice's assessment see ibid., pp. 97–99.

8. Haskell, "The Texas Idea," p. 841.

9. Marilyn McAdams Sibley, *The Port of Houston: A History* (Austin: University of Texas Press, 1968), pp. 134–38; David G. McComb, *Houston: The Bayou City* (Austin: University of Texas Press, 1969), pp. 118–19.

10. Sibley, *Port of Houston*, pp. 160–62, 168; Harold L. Platt, "Houston at the Crossroads: The Emergence of the Urban Center of the Southwest," *Journal of the West* 18 (July 1979): 51–61.

11. The bibliography of urban progressivism in the North is extensive. Start with Michael H. Ebner and Eugene M. Tobin, eds., *The Age of Urban Reform: New Perspectives on the Progressive Age* (Port Washington, New York. Kennikat, 1977), pp. 156–72.

12. David Nord, "The Experts versus the Experts: Conflicting Philosophies of Municipal Utility Regulation in the Progressive Era," *Wisconsin Magazine of History* 58 (Spring 1975): 219–36; Clyde Lyndon King, ed., *The Regulation of Municipal Utilities* (New York: Appleton, 1912).

13. Philip J. Funigiello, *Towards a National Power Policy: The New Deal and the Electric Utility Industry, 1933–1941* (Pittsburgh: University of Pittsburgh Press, 1973); Ellis W. Hawley, *The New Deal and the Problem of Monopoly* (Princeton: Princeton University Press, 1966); Irwin S. Rosenbaum, "The Common-Carrier, Public Utility Concept: A Legal-Industrial View," *Journal of Land and Public Utility Economics* 7 (1931): 155–68; Horace Gray, "The Passing of the Public Utility Concept," *Journal of Land and Public Utility Economics* 16 (1940): 8–20.

14. Texas, *Statutes* (McEachin, 1913), arts. 1018–32, 6742–45. For the impact of the independent school act in Houston, see *HDP*, 3, 19, 24 March 1901.

15. Carl D. Thompson, *Public Ownership* (New York: Crowell, 1925), 204–89; M. N. Baker, "Municipal Ownership and Operation of Water Works," *American Academy of Political and Social Sciences Annals* 57 (January 1915): 279–81; King, *Municipal Utilities*, passim.

16. Delos F. Wilcox, "The Effects of State Regulation upon the Municipal Ownership Movement," *American Academy of Political and Social Sciences Annals* 57 (January 1915): 74, 71–84.

17. See above. note 15.

18. Delos F. Wilcox, "Some Present-Day Issues of Public Utility Regulation," *American Academy of Political and Social Sciences Annals* 15 (January 1915): 62–71.

19. Felix Frankfurter, "Public Services and the Public," *Yale Review* 20 (September 1930): 17.

20. Frank Parsons, *The City for the People* (Philadelphia: Taylor, 1901), p. 107.

21. Hawley, *New Deal*, pp. 226–34, 325–43; Funigiello, *National Power Policy*; James Bonbright and Gardiner Means, *The Holding Company: Its Public Significance and Its Regulation* (New York: McGraw-Hill, 1932).

Index

house, 12, 25, 40–42, 56, 163; Mayor Smith on, 127–28; streets, bridges, and sidewalks, 31, 39–41, 61, 85–91, 126–28, 141, 143, 159, 195; wharf, 12. *See also* Environmental engineering; Ship channel

Race relations, 47–48, 71–72, 158–59, 182–83, 193, 200–201, 203, 209–12. *See also* Blacks
Railroads: in antebellum Texas, 6–7, 10–18; after Civil War, 20, 45, 78, 177; Houston facilities of, 31–33, 68, 83; and land use patterns, 30–32, 78–84. *See also* Regional development; Ship channel
Receiverships, utility: electric companies, 94–95, 164, 174; street railways, 138, 143
Reconstruction, Era of, 26, 38, 47–48, 50–51, 71–72
Regional development: in antebellum period, 6–7, 8, 17; and city growth, 77–84; national influences on, 155–56; and oil industry, 171, 175–77; and the railroads, 45, 77–84; and urban planning, 175–77, 183, 187, 210–11. *See also* Urban rivalry (Houston-Galveston)
Reichman, John, 25
Republican party, 47, 96, 100, 151
Rice, H. Baldwin, 152, 157–60, 176, 186, 201, 207–08, 210–11
Rice, William Marsh, 13, 15, 17
Riesner, Ben, 97, 101, 159
Ring, H. F., 97, 132–33
Roberts, Ingram S., 25

Sabin, Chauncy, 99
St. Joseph Infirmary, 144, 149
Sanitation. *See* Public services, health and sanitation
San Jacinto, Battle of, 5
Scanlan, Timothy, 38–39, 47; administration of, 38–43; and Houston Water Company, 67, 144–45, 197–99
Scherffius, Henry, 140, 146
Sewerage. *See* Public works, drainage and sewerage
Shaw, William, 101
Shearn, Charles, 8
Shepard, B. A., 13, 17
Ship channel: antebellum period, 12–13; early impressions, 3–5; Progressive Era, 155, 158, 161, 177, 210–11; Reconstruction period, 26–27, 31, 37
Sinclair, William, 69, 92, 135
Smith, Dan C., 97, 101, 152; administration of, 99–100, 125–30, 133, 135–40, 204;

election of, 97–98, 100
Smith, Francis J., 145
Social Reform, 120–23, 134–35, 157–60, 163, 178, 193. *See also* Progressivism, urban
Sonnen, Louis, 172, 201–02
Southern Pacific Railroad Company, 80, 83, 187. *See also* Railroads
Special assessment taxation: growth of, 86–89, 125–27; and the judiciary, 88–89, 148, 150, 155, 159, 165; origins of, 52; and the street railways, 141–43, 195–97. See also *Higgins v. Bordages*; Taxation
Spindletop, Texas, 171, 176
Sprague, Frank, 132
Stafford's Point, Texas, 14
State courts, Texas, 158; and charter reform, 87–89; and municipal bonds, 56–57, 58–60, 63; and utility regulation, 132–33, 144, 195–96, 198–99. *See also* Supreme Court, Texas.
Stevens, James H., 17
Stewart, James S., 162, 165, 187
Stone and Webster, 195, 201
Stone, Thomas H., 196, 199, 205
Storrie, Richard, 148, 174
Street railways: development of, 92–93, 128–30, 132–33; early routes of, 31–33; origins of, in Houston, 20, 22–23; and politics, 138–40; receiverships of, 138, 143; regulation of, 90–91, 141–44, 145, 172; reorganizations of, 68–69, 128–30, 135, 195; segregation of, 200–201; strikes against, 159–60, 203–04. *See also* Land use
Structural reform: in antebellum Texas, 10–12; of fiscal system, 20–23, 26–29, 50–56, 63–64, 85–91, 99, 125–28, 161, 163, 189–91, 202, 205; origins of, in Houston, 20–23; of police power, 85–91, 179; politics of 120–22, 151, 154–57. *See also* Commission form of government; Constitutional law; Managerial reform; Progressivism, urban
Suburbs, 39, 92–93, 129, 134, 137, 140, 141–43, 150, 191–92, 197, 203, 212
Supreme Court, Texas: during antebellum period, 16; and commission governemnt, 205; and municipal bonds, 99–100; and public utilities, 90, 142; and street improvements, 88–89, 142, 148, 150, 159, 165. *See also* State courts, Texas
Supreme Court, U.S.: and the cities, 48–49, 63–64, 72–73; and municipal bonds, 37–38, 48–49, 58–60, 62–63, 98–99; and